The New Feminist Criticism

The New Feminist Criticism

Essays on Women, Literature, and Theory

Edited by Elaine Showalter

PANTHEON BOOKS, NEW YORK

 Published in the United States by Pantheon Books, a division of Random House, Inc., New York, and simultaneously in Canada by Random House of Canada Limited, Toronto.

Library of Congress Cataloging in Publication Data
Main entry under title:

The new feminist criticism.

Bibliography: p.
1. Feminist literary criticism—Addresses, essays, lectures. I. Showalter, Elaine.
PN98.W64N48 1985 809'.89287 84-22625
ISBN 0-394-53913-3
ISBN 0-394-72647-2 (pbk.)

Book design by Barbara Marks

Manufactured in the United States of America

First Edition

Permissions Acknowledgments

Nina Baym, "Melodramas of Beset Manhood: How Theories of American Fiction Exclude Women Authors," *American Quarterly* 33 (1981). Copyright © 1981 by the Trustees of the University of Pennsylvania. Reprinted by permission of the author and *American Quarterly*.

Rosalind Coward, "This Novel Changes Women's Lives: Are Women's Novels Feminist Novels?" *Feminist Review* 5 (1980). Copyright © 1980 by Rosalind Coward. Reprinted by permission of the author.

Rachel Blau DuPlessis, "For the Etruscans," revised version of essay first published in *The Future of Difference*, ed. Alice Jardine and Hester Eisenstein, Boston: G. K. Hall, 1981. Copyright © 1981 by Rachel Blau DuPlessis. Reprinted by permission of the author.

Sandra M. Gilbert, "What Do Feminist Critics Want? Or a Postcard from the Volcano," *ADE Bulletin* 66 (1980). Copyright © 1980 by the Association of Departments of English. Reprinted by permission of the Modern Language Association of America.

Susan Gubar, " 'The Blank Page' and the Issues of Female Creativity," *Critical Inquiry* 8 (Winter 1981). Copyright © 1982 by The University of Chicago. Reprinted by permission of The University of Chicago Press.

Carolyn G. Heilbrun, "Feminist Criticism: Bringing the Spirit Back to English Studies," *ADE Bulletin* 62 (1979). Copyright © by the Association of Departments of English. Reprinted by permission of the Modern Language Association of America.

Ann Rosalind Jones, "Writing the Body: Toward an Understanding of *l'Écriture féminine*," *Feminist Studies* 7, no. 2 (1981). Copyright © 1981 by *Feminist Studies*. Reprinted by permission of the publisher, Feminist Studies, Inc., c/o Women's Studies Program, University of Maryland, College Park, Md. 20742.

Annette Kolodny, "A Map for Misreading: Or, Gender and the Interpretation of Literary Texts," *New Literary History* (1980). Copyright © 1980 by The Johns Hopkins University Press. Reprinted by permission of The Johns Hopkins University Press.

Annette Kolodny, "Dancing Through the Minefield: Some Observations on the Theory, Practice, and Politics of a Feminist Literary Criticism," *Feminist Studies* 6 (1980). Copyright © 1980 by Annette Kolodny. Reprinted by permission of the author.

Deborah E. McDowell, "New Directions for Black Feminist Criticism," *Black American Literature Forum* 14 (1980). Copyright © 1980 by Deborah E. McDowell and *Black American Literature Forum*. Reprinted by permission of the author and Indiana State University.

Nancy K. Miller, "Emphasis Added: Plots and Plausibilities in Women's Fiction," *PMLA* 96 (1981). Copyright © 1981 by the Modern Language Association of America. Reprinted by permission of the Modern Language Association of America.

Alicia Ostriker, "The Thieves of Language: Women Poets and Revisionist Mythmaking," *Signs* 8 (1981). Copyright © 1981 by The University of Chicago. Reprinted by permission of The University of Chicago Press.

Lillian S. Robinson, "Treason Our Text: Feminist Challenges to the Literary Canon," *Tulsa Studies in Women's Literature* 2 (1983). Copyright © 1983 by *Tulsa Studies in Women's Literature.* Reprinted by permission of *Tulsa Studies in Women's Literature.*

Elaine Showalter, "Toward a Feminist Poetics," *Women's Writing and Writing About Women*, ed. Mary Jacobus (London: Croom Helm, 1979). Copyright © 1979 by Elaine Showalter. Reprinted by permission of the author.

Elaine Showalter, "Feminist Criticism in the Wilderness," *Critical Inquiry* 8 (Winter 1981). Copyright © 1981 by The University of Chicago. Reprinted by permission of The University of Chicago Press.

Barbara Smith, "Toward a Black Feminist Criticism," *Conditions: Two* 1, no. 2 (October 1977), and available as a pamphlet from The Crossing Press, Trumansburg, New York. Copyright © 1977 by Barbara Smith. Reprinted by permission of the author.

Jane P. Tompkins, "Sentimental Power: *Uncle Tom's Cabin* and the Politics of Literary History," *Glyph* 2 (1978). Copyright © by The Johns Hopkins University Press. Reprinted by permission of The Johns Hopkins University Press.

Bonnie Zimmerman, "What Has Never Been: An Overview of Lesbian Feminist Criticism," *Feminist Studies* 7, no. 3 (1981). Copyright © 1981 by Feminist Studies. Reprinted by permission of the publisher, Feminist Studies, Inc., c/o Women's Studies Program, University of Maryland, College Park, Md. 20742.

Contents

Acknowledgments

Many people have helped in the making of this book, and I want to express my appreciation to them here. Heartfelt thanks first to Sara Bershtel at Pantheon Books for her steady encouragement, and for her outstanding editorial and critical expertise. I am grateful to Jeslyn Medoff at Rutgers and Chris Gwilt at Princeton for their efficient research assistance. Special thanks go to all the feminist critics who generously offered advice and support, especially Isobel Armstrong, Nina Auerbach, Alice Jardine, Myra Jehlen, Mary Jacobus, Joan Lidoff, Marlene Longenecker, Jane Marcus, Wendy Martin, Catherine Stimpson, Gayatri Spivak, and Cheryl Wall. My only regret about this anthology is that it could not have been three times as long.

As always, English Showalter helped at every stage, from permissions to proof. Finally, this book is dedicated to my daughter Vinca, for whose generation the feminist critical revolution has become history.

The New Feminist Criticism

Introduction

The Feminist Critical Revolution

During the last decade, our academic, literary, and cultural institutions have all felt the impact of a feminist critical revolution. Feminist criticism has flourished in combination with every other critical approach from formalism to semiotics, and in the literary study of every period and genre from the Middle Ages to the mass media. Since the late 1960s, when feminist criticism developed as part of the international women's movement, the assumptions of literary study have been profoundly altered. Whereas it had always been taken for granted that the representative reader, writer, and critic of Western literature is male, feminist criticism has shown that women readers and critics bring different perceptions and expectations to their literary experience, and has insisted that women have also told the important stories of our culture. While literary criticism and its philosophical branch, literary theory, have always been zealously guarded bastions of male intellectual endeavor, the success of feminist criticism has opened a space for the authority of the woman critic that extends beyond the study of women's writing to the reappraisal of the whole body of texts that make up our literary heritage. Whether concerned with the literary representations of sexual difference, with the ways that literary genres have been shaped by masculine or feminine values, or with the exclusion of the female voice from the institutions of literature, criticism, and theory, feminist criticism has established gender as a fundamental category of literary analysis.

While the the number of feminist studies of particular writers, genres, and works is now vast, this book, *The New Feminist Criticism,* is the first collection of essays in feminist critical theory. It brings together eighteen of the most important and controversial essays written by pioneers in the field over the past decade. Most of these essays first appeared in feminist journals like *Signs, Feminist Studies,* and *Feminist Review,* others in academic journals like *PMLA* and *Critical Inquiry.* They reflect the many voices in which contemporary feminist criticism speaks, and represent the coming of age of feminist criticism as a theoretical as well as a practical enterprise.

Although the essays apply their insights to a wide variety of poets, novelists, and essayists, including Charlotte Brontë, Harriet Beecher Stowe, Thomas Hardy, H. D., Edith Wharton, Adrienne Rich, Doris Lessing, and Toni Morrison, their primary concern is to develop theories of sexual difference in reading, writing, and literary interpretation. Furthermore, the essays in this book are not pieces of a single large critical system, but rather represent a variety of positions and strategies engaged in a vigorous internal debate. Feminist criticism differs from other contemporary schools of critical theory in not deriving its literary principles from a single authority figure or from a body of sacred texts. Unlike structuralists who hark back to the linguistic discoveries of Saussure, psychoanalytic critics loyal to Freud or Lacan, Marxists steeped in *Das Kapital*, or deconstructionists citing Derrida, feminist critics do not look to a Mother of Us All or a single system of thought to provide their fundamental ideas. Rather, these have evolved from several sources—from extensive readings in women's literature; from exchanges with feminist theorists in other disciplines, especially history, psychology, and anthropology; and from the revision and reconsideration of literary theory itself.[1] Linguistics, psychoanalysis, Marxism, and deconstruction have all provided feminist critical theory with important analytical tools. Although we are still far from agreement on a theoretical system (a prospect that many, in fact, would find horrifyingly reductive), all these essays are unified by the faith that feminist concerns can bring a new energy and vitality to literary studies, for men as well as for women.

That all the essays in this volume are by women, however, reflects a meaningful aspect of the history of feminist critical thought. Women generated feminist criticism, fought for its importance, and often suffered in their careers for being identified with a radical critical movement. It is in the writing of women, moreover, that we find the fullest expression of the problematic of a feminist criticism: how to combine the theoretical and the personal. Feminist criticism reveals in its own history and form many of the patterns of influence and rebellion that mark the female literary tradition as a whole. Here too women writers searched for a language of their own, a style, a voice, and a structure with which they could enter a discipline previously dominated by men. The raw intensity of feeling and the insistence on the relationship of literature to personal experience that accompanied these early phases often expressed itself in an autobiographical or even confessional criticism shocking to those trained in the impersonal conventions of most academic critical writing. Sometimes angry and denunciatory, sometimes lyrical and emotional, feminist criticism flaunted its politics and its feelings. While feminist criticism neither must nor should be the exclusive province of women, it is important to understand that its history and expression were determined by issues of gender and sexual difference.

In the United States, feminist criticism was created by literary and academic women—editors, writers, graduate students, university instructors and professors—who had participated in the women's liberation movement of the late 1960s and who shared its polemical force, activist commitment, social concern, and sense of communal endeavor. Kate Millett's *Sexual Politics* (1970), for example, the first major book of feminist criticism in this country, was at the same time a work of literary analysis and of impassioned political argument. It was through the women's liberation movement that we began to draw connections between our own work and our own lives, to note the disparities between the identifications and ambitions that had attracted us, along with thousands of other women, to the study and teaching of literature, and the limited and secondary roles granted to fictional heroines, women writers, or female scholars.

Feminism spoke to our lived and our literary experience with the fierce urgency of a revelation or a Great Awakening; and it was no coincidence that Kate Chopin's rediscovered novel *The Awakening* (1899) became one of the most popular feminist literary texts of the early years. (Doris Lessing's *The Golden Notebook* [1962] and Monique Wittig's *Les Guérillères* [1969] perhaps occupied similar positions in England and France.) Sandra Gilbert compared the beginnings of feminist critical awareness to a conversion experience, noting that "most feminist critics speak . . . like people who must bear witness, people who must enact and express in their own lives and words the revisionary sense of transformation that seems inevitably to attend the apparently simple discovery that the experiences of women in and with literature are different from those of men."[2] The experience of feminist critical enlightenment seemed to transform all that went before it; it was an intellectual revolution, charged with the excitement of violating existing paradigms and discovering a new field of vision.

In its earliest years, feminist criticism concentrated on exposing the misogyny of literary practice: the stereotyped images of women in literature as angels or monsters, the literary abuse or textual harassment of women in classic and popular male literature, and the exclusion of women from literary history.[3] Feminist critics reinforced the importance of their enterprise by emphasizing the connections between the literary and the social mistreatment of women, in pornography, say, or rape. Over the past fifteen years, these efforts to make readers question the innocence, insignificance, or humor of antifeminist characterizations have succeeded in changing the atmosphere of literary response. Male critics too have noted that in the atmosphere of the 1980s, with its heightened sensitivity to questions of sexism and gender, literary misogyny can no longer be overlooked or excused. For this reason, as Lawrence Lipking observes, "Something peculiar has been happening lately to the classics. Some of them now seem less heroic, and some of them less funny."[4] We may expect that the next decade will see even more vigorous feminist questioning of our criteria of aesthetic value, and even more drastic reestimations of the old masters.

The second phase of feminist criticism was the discovery that women writers had a literature of their own, whose historical and thematic coherence, as well as artistic importance, had been obscured by the patriarchal values that dominate our culture. Although critics and writers had talked for centuries about women's writing, when feminist criticism set out to map the territory of the female imagination and the structures of the female plot, it was doing something completely new. The focus on women's writing as a specific field of inquiry, moreover, led to a massive recovery and rereading of literature by women from all nations and historical periods. As hundreds of lost women writers were rediscovered, as letters and journals were brought to light, as new literary biographies explored the relationship between the individual female talent and the literary tradition, the continuities in women's writing became clear for the first time.

The books that first began to define women's writing in feminist terms were Patricia Meyer Spacks's *The Female Imagination* (1975) and the late Ellen Moers's *Literary Women* (1976). My book *A Literature of Their Own* (1977) outlined a literary history of English women writers in the nineteenth and twentieth centuries. In 1979, Sandra Gilbert and Susan Gubar's monumental study, *The Madwoman in the Attic,* offered a full theoretical account of the situation of the nineteenth-century woman writer, her anxieties about authorship as a monstrous and unwomanly activity that transgressed cultural boundaries, and her rewriting of male mythologies in her own texts. Since 1979, these insights have been tested, supplemented, and extended so that we now have a coherent, if still incomplete, narrative of female literary history, which describes the evolutionary stages of women's writing during the last 250 years from imitation through protest to self-definition, and defines and traces the connections throughout history and across national boundaries of the recurring images, themes, and plots that emerge from women's social, psychological, and aesthetic experience in male-dominated cultures.

The concept of a female aesthetic logically emerged from the recognition of such connections in women's writing. As the black aesthetic of the 1970s celebrated a black consciousness in literature, so too the female aesthetic celebrated a uniquely female literary consciousness. Supported by such feminist writers, artists, and poets as Adrienne Rich, Marge Piercy, Judy Chicago, Susan Griffin, and Alice Walker, the female aesthetic spoke of a women's culture that had been neglected and had to be revived, of a "women's language," and of literary styles and forms that came out of a specific female psychology.

The precise nature of the female aesthetic, however, has been the subject of continuing controversy. In feminist writing of the early 1970s, it was frequently identified with lesbian consciousness and with the politics of lesbian separatism. The Amazon was repeatedly invoked as the emblem of female creative autonomy, from the muse of the poetry journal *Amazon Quarterly* to Ti-Grace Atkinson's feminist manifesto, *Amazon Odyssey.* In "Toward a Feminist Aesthetic," published in 1977 in the women's-culture journal *Chrysalis,* Julia Penelope Stanley and Susan Wolfe equated the flowing, conjunctive, nonlinear style of such avant-garde lesbian writers as Gertrude Stein with "women's style" in general.[5] In a paper read at the MLA in 1976, Adrienne Rich identified lesbian identity with creative and imaginative autonomy: "It is the lesbian in every woman who is compelled by female energy, who gravitates towards strong women, who seeks a literature that will express that energy and strength. It is the lesbian in us who drives us to feel imaginatively, render in language, grasp, the full connection between woman and woman. It is the lesbian in us who is creative, for the dutiful daughter of the fathers is only a hack."[6]

Many feminist critics, however, opposed both the concept of an essential female identity that expressed itself through only one literary style, and the privileging of lesbian creative identity. By the 1980s, the lesbian aesthetic had differentiated itself from the female aesthetic. As lesbian feminist criticism became more specialized, feminist critics turned their attention to the analysis of mother-daughter relations, and the figure of the mother replaced that of the Amazon for theorists of the female aesthetic. Some critics studied metaphors of childbirth in art and creativity. Others asked whether women's writing is characterized by what Joan Lidoff calls a "female poetics of affiliation," dependent on the daughter's relation to the mother.[7] This transition to a focus on the mother coincided with important research on maternity in other fields of women's studies. Among the most influential works were the historian Carroll Smith-Rosenberg's classic essay "The Female World of Love and Ritual" (1975), which demonstrated that in nineteenth-century America a strong woman's culture had produced idyllically close mother-daughter relationships;[8] Adrienne Rich's *Of Woman Born: Motherhood as Experience and Institution* (1976); and Nancy Chodorow's psychological study *The Reproduction of Mothering* (1978), which argued that the relationship of the infant to the female parent was the key factor in the construction of gender identity.

Yet while feminist criticism was one of the daughters of the women's movement, its other parent was the old patriarchal institution of literary criticism and theory; and it has had to come to terms with the meaning of its mixed origins. Our efforts to define the difference of women's writing as the expression of a female aesthetic led us to a renewed interest in theories from psychoanalysis and aesthetics. The process of studying women's writing, furthermore, led us to challenge the fundamental theoretical assumptions of traditional literary history and criticism, from periodic divisions (such as "the American Renaissance") that were exclusively based on male literary landmarks to the underlying ideas about genre, the literary career, and the role of the critic. Finally, the project of creating a criticism of our own led us to think about the structure of other critical revolutions and our relationship to them. In its third phase, therefore, feminist criticism demanded not just the recognition of women's writing but a radical rethinking of the conceptual grounds of literary study, a revision of the accepted theoretical assumptions about reading and writing that have been based entirely on male literary experiences.

Another reason for the increased prominence of theoretical questions in feminist criticism since the mid-1970s is the influence of radical critical thought from other countries. As American feminist criticism has circulated abroad, so too work by English and French feminist critics has been made available in the United States. Several leading European theoreticians have come to speak at American conferences, or to teach in American universities. As a result, the different currents of English and French feminist criticism have influenced the direction of American critical theory.

American feminist criticism has always had its strongest institutional base in the academic community, both in departments of literature and in women's studies; and most of the American contributors to this book are connected with the university. They are concerned with the immediate impact of feminist ideas about literature on the classroom, the curriculum, and the literary canon. In Great Britain, however, where women's studies courses and programs are less established than in American universities and colleges, the institutional bases for feminist criticism have been outside the universities, in radical politics, journalism, and publishing. The English contributions to international feminist criticism have been an analysis of the connection between gender and class, an emphasis on popular culture, and a feminist critique of Marxist literary theory. There are historical and social reasons for this difference. According to Olive Banks, a sociologist who has studied the English feminist movement, "The main difference between the United States and Britain . . . is the closer link in Britain between socialism or Marxism and feminism. . . . There was never the deep rift between radical men and women that occurred, and indeed persisted, in the United States and kept the two groups not only apart but hostile to each other."[9] It is striking that the leading

English feminist critics such as Mary Jacobus, Rosalind Coward, Michèle Barrett, Juliet Mitchell, and Cora Kaplan combine Marxist theoretical interest in the production and ideology of literature with feminist concerns for women's writing.

Whereas Anglo-American feminist criticism, for all its internal differences, tries to recover women's historical experiences as readers and writers, French feminist theory looks at the ways that "the feminine" has been defined, represented, or repressed in the symbolic systems of language, metaphysics, psychoanalysis, and art. French feminist theory had its base in the institutes and seminars of the Neo-Freudian psychoanalyst Jacques Lacan, the deconstructionist philosopher Jacques Derrida, and the structuralist critic Roland Barthes. All of these theoreticians played an important role in directing feminist concern to the study of language.

Taking up questions of women's relation to language, French feminists have described *l'écriture féminine,* a practice of writing "in the feminine" which undermines the linguistic, syntactical, and metaphysical conventions of Western narrative. *L'écriture féminine* is not necessarily writing *by* women; it is an avant-garde writing style like that of Joyce, Bataille, Artaud, Mallarmé, or Lautréamont. However, the most radical French feminist theorists also believe that *écriture féminine* is connected to the rhythms of the female body and to sexual pleasure (*jouissance*), and that women have an advantage in producing this radically disruptive and subversive kind of writing. They urge the woman writer to ally herself with everything in the culture which is muted, silenced, or unrepresented, in order to subvert the existing systems that repress feminine difference. For Julia Kristeva, female discourse that breaks with tradition is a political act of dissidence, a form of feminist action. For Hélène Cixous, the best-known and most widely translated theorist of *l'écriture féminine,* women's writing has genuinely revolutionary force. As she writes in her manifesto, "The Laugh of the Medusa," "when the repressed of their culture and their society return, it is an explosive, utterly destructive, staggering return, with a force never yet unleashed."[10]

Over the past ten years, French feminist critics have themselves attempted to make criticism a mode of *écriture féminine,* emphasizing textual pleasure and making extensive use of puns, neologisms, coded allusions, typographical breaks, and other devices of surrealist and avant-garde writing. Whether these revolutionary critical styles alone can ever have revolutionary social impact is a question much debated by more empirical and activist American feminists. Nonetheless, while at first the orientation of the French theorists seems very different from the Anglo-American tradition, it also bears many similarities to considerations of the female aesthetic and women's writing. Monique Wittig, for example, has been the French champion of the

Amazon, or *guérillère,* the lesbian who eludes sexual, political, and linguistic categories. Cixous and Kristeva, among others, have been involved in the process of "rethinking the maternal" on the level of language and writing.[11] The influence of their work on Anglo-American feminist criticism is likely to be significant in the next decade; and its initial impact will be seen in many of the essays here.

All of these influences—the women's liberation movement, the development of women's studies, and the impact of European theory—have shaped the feminist criticism of the 1980s. The intellectual trajectory of feminist criticism has taken us from a concentration on women's literary subordination, mistreatment, and exclusion, to the study of women's separate literary traditions, to an analysis of the symbolic construction of gender and sexuality within literary discourse. It is now clear that what we are demanding is a new universal literary history and criticism that combines the literary experiences of both women and men, a complete revolution in the understanding of our literary heritage.

The essays in this book are organized into three sections. In Part I, "What Do Feminists Critics Want? The Academy and the Canon," the writers challenge the institutional bases of literature within universities and critical establishments, and show how our concept of "literature" has excluded, misinterpreted, and misread women's work. The first two essays were originally presented as talks to conventions of English department chairmen, and they are polemical, witty, and eloquent defenses and explanations of the feminist critical enterprise for those who might be expected to resist it. Carolyn Heilbrun's "Bringing the Spirit Back to English Studies" diagnoses resistance to feminist criticism as men's unconscious "fear of female dominance" in the profession. But in fact, she explains, the study of sexual difference in literature is not a threat, but rather "the key to new vitality" that counters the sense of exhaustion and irrelevance plaguing the field of literary studies. Sandra Gilbert paraphrases Freud's famous question about women to ask "What Do Feminist Critics Want?" The answer, she tells us, is everything: a "revisionary imperative," a complete and cataclysmic change in all our ideas of literary history and literary meaning. Although this transformation begins with the recognition that women have been alienated from the literary heritage of Western culture, she argues that feminist criticism cannot limit itself to literature by women, for every text can be seen as determined by aesthetic and political assumptions about gender that might be called "sexual poetics." Its fullest ambitions are to explore and decode all the hidden connections between "textuality and sexuality, genre and gender, psychosexual identity and cultural authority."

Annette Kolodny's "A Map for Rereading: Gender and the Interpretation of Literary Texts" shows how the critical enterprise itself is influenced by gender. Analyzing two short stories by Charlotte Perkins Gilman and Susan Glaspell, Kolodny shows how they have been underrated and misunderstood by male readers inadequately trained to decipher their specific systems of meaning or to understand their contexts in a female tradition. The interpretative strategies of criticism, she argues, are not natural and universal but rather "learned, historically determined, and thereby necessarily gender-inflected."

Nina Baym's "Melodramas of Beset Manhood" takes on the literary canon, the form that cultural authority has taken in literary study. Feminist critics do not accept the view that the canon reflects the objective value judgments of history and posterity, but see it instead as a culture-bound political construct. In practice, "posterity" has meant a group of men with the access to publishing and reviewing that enabled them to enforce their views of "literature" and to define a group of ageless "classics." It is a curious fact of literary history that canon formation has been particularly aggressive following wars, when nationalist feeling runs high and there is a strong wish to define a tradition. In the years immediately following World War II, as Baym shows, critical theories defined nineteenth-century American literature on a model so quintessentially masculine as to exclude women writers from any serious consideration. In the mythical story of confrontation between the strong individual and "the ideal of America," women appear as representatives of the society that drags the hero down. Moreover, women writers are the authors of the bad best-sellers against which serious artists like Hawthorne and Melville have had to defend themselves. In short, as Baym notes, the American woman writer has entered literary history as the enemy.

Jane Tompkins's "Sentimental Power: *Uncle Tom's Cabin* and the Politics of Literary History" deals with a dramatic example of Baym's thesis: the neglect and trivialization of Harriet Beecher Stowe. In her analysis of *Uncle Tom's Cabin,* she shows how the sentimental novel of the nineteenth century offered critiques of American society as powerful and important as those of Hawthorne or Melville. Essays like Jane Tompkins's have been crucial in helping us get past the biases of American literary history, to uncover and decipher the meanings of an American women's tradition.

Lillian Robinson takes the argument a step further. While Tompkins, like Annette Kolodny and Sandra Gilbert, has assured her audience that feminist criticism will not lead to a diminished canon, Robinson's "Treason Our Text: Feminist Challenges to the Literary Canon" argues that feminist critics should not restrict their efforts to constructing a "female counter-canon" of women's writing based on alternative evaluative standards. Instead, Robinson calls for a radical challenge to dominant aesthetic traditions and literary values. Rather than uncovering and rereading a women's literature, we ought to ask whether the "great monuments" of male literature, especially those that denigrate women, still ought to be considered masterpieces.

The essays in Part II, "Feminist Criticisms and Women's Cultures," explore the intellectual and political issues that emerged in the development of feminist literary theory. What are the relationships between gender, race, and class? How should feminist criticism account for differences between women? Do black women writers and lesbian writers have their own literary traditions which mainstream feminist criticism has neglected or suppressed? Is women's writing necessarily "feminist"? Is feminist criticism necessarily radical, or even politically linked to the goals of the women's movement? What ought to be the connections or alliances between feminist criticism and other schools of contemporary critical theory? Should feminist critics imitate, borrow, or revise Marxist, structuralist, and poststructuralist methodologies, or should we resist "scientific" critical methods that might narrow our enterprise?

My essay "Toward a Feminist Poetics," which was presented in 1978 as the opening lecture in the first series on women and literature at Oxford University, deals with the question of feminist criticism's relationship to traditional critical models. At that point, feminist criticism seemed to be at an impasse. Attacked by some male critics for its apparent lack of theoretical coherence, it could not seem to resolve the conflict between spontaneity and methodology, or to find a way of defining its subject that included all the different modes of critical and political commentary that feminism had produced. I suggest that the study of women's writing and female creativity, which I call "gynocritics," offers the most exciting prospect for a coherent feminist literary theory, and the opportunity to break away from dependency on male models in forging a criticism of our own.

Annette Kolodny's "Dancing Through the Minefield" takes up the problem of defining the "theory, practice, and politics" of a feminist literary criticism from a different perspective. Originally published in *Feminist Studies* in 1980, and winner of the Florence Howe Award of the Modern Language Association for the best essay in feminist criticism of the year, it remains one of the most controversial essays in the field. Kolodny's view is that feminist criticism should not seek a single methodology or conceptual model but should instead be pluralist in its theory and practice, making free use of all the methodologies and approaches that can serve its needs. Pluralism, she maintains, is "the only critical stance consistent with the current status of the larger women's movement" in all its ideological variety.

Kolodny's advocacy of pluralism, however, touched off sparks in some sectors of the feminist critical community. Marxist feminist critics such as Jane Marcus, Lillian Robinson, and Gayatri Spivak objected to the concept of pluralism as a liberal myth. As Spivak pointed out, "To embrace pluralism . . . is to espouse the politics of the masculinist establishment. Pluralism is the method employed by the *central* authorities to neutralize opposition by seeming to accept it. The gesture of pluralism on the part of the *marginal* can only mean capitulation to the center."[12] In "An Interchange on Feminist Criticism: On 'Dancing Through the Minefield,'" Judith Kegan Gardiner, Elly Bulkin, and Rena Grasso Patterson also took issue with the politics of feminist criticism Kolodny had defined. Gardiner suggested that rather than being essentially pluralistic, American feminist criticism was divided into liberal, radical, and socialist schools, each with its particular political alignment, methodologies, and goals. Bulkin and Patterson criticized the absence of black and lesbian feminist criticism from a discussion purporting to be comprehensive. In their responses to Kolodny, they also pointed out the heterosexism, ethnocentrism, and class bias of much feminist critical writing of the 1970s.[13]

These vital questions of differences between women in terms of race and sexual orientation were also being vigorously raised by black and lesbian feminist critics. Barbara Smith's "Toward a Black Feminist Criticism" (1977) was one of the very first efforts to define the specificity of black women's writing and to break the "massive silence" surrounding the question of black feminist criticism and black lesbian writers. It is an angry protest against the neglect of a black women's literary tradition by male critics of Afro-American literature, and by white feminist critics of women's literature. Smith presents a reading of Toni Morrison's *Sula* as a black lesbian novel to demonstrate how "both sexual and racial politics . . . are inextricable elements in Black women's writing."

Deborah McDowell's "New Directions for Black Feminist Criticism" takes up the question where Barbara Smith leaves off. Agreeing that black women's writing has been excluded by white feminist critics as well as by Afro-American male scholars, she goes on to point out the weaknesses of a polemical and rhetorical black feminist criticism. Afro-American feminist critics, she insists, must abandon slogans. Rather, they must situate the study of black women's writing in the contexts of black history and culture and explore its thematic and stylistic correspondences with the literature of black men, as well as investigate its special uses of language and imagery.

For lesbian feminist critics, the problems are again different. Bonnie

Zimmerman's "What Has Never Been: An Overview of Lesbian Feminist Criticism" begins by challenging the heterosexist assumptions of contemporary feminist writing, but concentrates on the difficulties of defining the "lesbian text" and the "lesbian aesthetic," since so many lesbian writers have concealed or disguised their sexual identity and repressed it in their writing. Yet despite the problems involved, Zimmerman makes a strong case for a tradition of lesbian writing, as well as for a lesbian feminist criticism that emphasizes powerful bonds between women as a significant aspect of all women's writing.

In "Are Women's Novels Feminist Novels?" the English Marxist-feminist critic Rosalind Coward asks whether stories about bonds between women, or about female sexuality, are automatically feminist. Originally published in the *Feminist Review* in 1979, the essay is a response to "Summer Reading," an earlier article in the same journal by Rebecca O'Rourke, which had recommended novels about women such as Marilyn French's *The Women's Room* as examples of new feminist writing. Coward takes a sterner line about what we mean when we describe a text as feminist. She insists that a genuinely feminist criticism must question the appeal to a "common experience of womankind" in popular novels, analyze the specific representations of femininity and sexuality, and even ask whether reprinting novels about women's experience is simply the way the publishing industry has cashed in on the women's movement. It is not their share in the common experiences of womankind, that makes women or texts feminist, argues Coward, but their shared commitment to certain political aims and objectives.

Part III, "Women's Writing and Feminist Critical Theories," takes up various approaches to the literature of women: its social contexts, modes, genres, themes, structures, and styles. My essay "Feminist Criticism in the Wilderness," which introduces this section, evaluates four theories of sexual difference in women's writing—biological, linguistic, psychological, and cultural—and attempts to show that women's writing has its own unique character, whether because it draws on female body images, uses a "women's language," expresses the female psyche, or, as I conclude, reflects women's complex cultural position. The essays in this section represent the various theoretical positions in this critical debate.

Rachel DuPlessis's "For the Etruscans" relates the ideology of feminism to the language, process, and style of feminist criticism, embodying theoretical issues in the form of the essay itself. Feminist criticism, she maintains, is a mode of woman's writing that should emphasize sexual, linguistic, and psychological difference. Through the juxtaposition of varied kinds of writing—quotations from Freud, Virginia Woolf, Anaïs Nin, Raymond Williams, Julia Kristeva; excerpts from her own journal; letters and notes from other participants in a workshop; passages of formal analysis—DuPlessis tries to represent and re-create the texture of the modern female aesthetic she is attempting to define: fluid, nonlinear, decentralized, nonhierarchic, and many-voiced.

The essays by Susan Gubar and Alicia Ostriker analyze the metaphors and strategies through which women writers explore their creativity, and implicitly shed light on the metaphors and strategies of the feminist critic as well. Responding to discussions of a "female language" in American and French feminist criticism, Ostriker argues, in "The Thieves of Language," that rather than *creating* a new poetic language, women poets revise the language of male myths from a woman-centered perspective, as she herself revises male critical myths about the traditions of twentieth-century poetry. In "The 'Blank Page' and the Issues of Female Creativity," Gubar shows how woman has been represented as the blank or virgin page, the passive creation of art rather than its autonomous creator. She shows that these cultural metaphors of women as spaces to be inscribed by the phallic pen have appeared even in women's writing in poems and stories that describe female creative inspiration as a form of violation, "a painful wounding, a literal influence of male authority." But as twentieth-century women writers redefined the creative act in female terms of giving birth rather than in male terms of inseminating, so modern feminist critics are redefining the critical act as a restoration of the "blank pages" of a neglected women's literature to literary history.

The last two essays apply American feminist perspectives to French theories of sexual difference and literary form. Nancy K. Miller's essay, "Emphasis Added: Plots and Plausibilities in Women's Fiction," asks why "French women's fiction has from its beginnings been *discredited*"—that is, seen as a violation of the terms of narrative and psychological plausibility. Like Kolodny, she argues that the misreading of women's texts is the result of an inappropriate set of narrative expectations based on a Freudian model of artistic motives. When we understand that women's as well as men's fiction contains dreams of ambition as well as dreams of love, the apparent anomalies of plot in such novels as *La Princesse de Clèves* and *The Mill on the Floss* will be resolved.

In "Writing the Body: Toward an Understanding of *l'Écriture féminine,*" Ann Rosalind Jones examines the linguistic and psychoanalytic theories of women's writing in the work of Julia Kristeva, Luce Irigaray, Hélène Cixous, and Monique Wittig and asks how American feminist critics can learn from the new French feminisms. Acknowledging the "theoretical depth and polemical energy" of French feminist criticism, Jones nonetheless concludes that Anglo-American feminist poetics must insist on an analysis of specific cultural contexts rather than merely relying on an idealized and abstract view of the feminine: "A historically responsive and powerful unity among women will come from our ongoing, shared practice, our experience in and against the material world."

As these essays show, the last decade of feminist criticism has been enormously ambitious and productive; and as critical movements go, we are still very young. The increased power of feminist perspectives within the university has led to innumerable changes in literary textbooks, in curriculum structure, and in the publication of articles and books. Moreover, it now appears that other schools of modern criticism are learning some lessons from our movement, and beginning to question their own origins and directions. Indeed, several leading male literary theorists have recently begun to incorporate feminist criticism into their work, and women are playing a larger role in the shaping of literary theory in every school. Feminist, black, and poststructuralist critics, both male and female, have been drawing closer together, if only because in the atmosphere of the 1980s they represent an avant-garde that shares the same enemies: namely, those who urge a return to the "basics" and the "classics"—the old canon that blames new-fangled theories and rebellious minorities for what is called "the crisis," but what may well be the renaissance, in the humanities.

Some would contend that acceptance by the critical establishment is a dangerous sign that the vitality and integrity of American feminist criticism are being compromised. They fear, moreover, that the move to theory in feminist criticism makes us lose touch with the texts and what they tell us about women's lives. Jane Marcus, for example, has complained that while feminist literary historians "have been doing literary housekeeping," the hard work of research, editing, and reinterpretation, the male theoreticians "have been gazing at the stars."[14] Yet if the women's movement has taught us anything, it is that we must all share the housework but must also get the chance to gaze at the stars. These essays show some of the ways that feminist critics are successfully managing both.

NOTES

[1]For further discussion of these ideas, see my essay "Women's Time, Women's Space: Writing the History of Feminist Criticism," *Tulsa Studies in Women's Literature* 3 (Fall–Winter 1984): 29–43.

[2]Sandra M. Gilbert, "Life Studies, or, Speech After Long Silence: Feminist Critics Today," *College English* 40 (April 1979): 850.

[3]The term "textual harassment" is from Mary Jacobus, "Is There a Women in This Text?" *New Literary History* 14 (Fall 1982): 117–41.

[4]Lawrence Lipking, "Aristotle's Sister: A Poetics of Abandonment," *Critical Inquiry* 10 (September 1983): 79.

[5]Julia Penelope Stanley and Susan J. Wolfe (Robbins), "Toward a Feminist Aesthetic," *Chrysalis*, no. 6 (1978), pp. 57–71.

[6]Adrienne Rich, *On Lies, Secrets, and Silence* (New York: W. W. Norton, 1979).

[7]Joan Lidoff, "Fluid Boundaries: The Origins of a Distinctive Women's Voice in Literature," work in progress, University of Texas at Austin.

[8]Carroll Smith-Rosenberg, "The Female World of Love and Ritual: Relations Between Women in Nineteenth-Century America," *Signs* 1 (Fall 1975): 1–29.

[9]Olive Banks, *Faces of Feminism: A Study of Feminism as a Social Movement* (New York: St. Martin's Press, 1981), p. 238.

[10]Hélène Cixous, "The Laugh of the Medusa," trans. Keith Cohen and Paula Cohen, in *New French Feminisms*, ed. Elaine Marks and Isabelle de Courtivron (Amherst: University of Massachusetts Press, 1980), p. 256.

[11]See Carolyn Burke, "Rethinking the Maternal," in *The Future of Difference*, ed. Hester Eisenstein and Alice Jardine, pp. 107–13 (Boston: G. K. Hall, 1980).

[12]Gayatri Spivak, "A Response to Annette Kolodny," unpublished paper, 1980, University of Texas at Austin, p. 2.

[13]Judith Kegan Gardiner, Elly Balkin, and Rena Grasso Patterson, "An Interchange on Feminist Criticism: On 'Dancing Through the Minefield,'" *Feminist Studies* 8 (Fall 1982): 629–75.

[14]Jane Marcus, "Storming the Toolshed," *Signs* 7 (Spring 1982): 624.

I

What Do Feminist Critics Want?

The Academy and the Canon

Bringing the Spirit Back to English Studies

Carolyn G. Heilbrun

Let us admit that English studies are in the doldrums. What I really believe is that they are in a state it would be meiotic to call parlous, but doldrums will do. As one of my colleagues put it to me, professors of English today must either choose wearily to teach "the same old stuff" or else dig their way into new theories that are concealed in a thicket of language so dense as to be virtually impenetrable. Meanwhile, students arrive unconvinced that literature holds important truths and insufficiently educated in myths and the Bible to catch even the most obvious of civilized echoes.

There is, I believe, hope in the midst of this, a hope whose name is feminist, or women's, studies; but that hope too is imperiled. Those already in the establishment turn away from this solution in horror; those who aspire to the establishment fearfully avert their eyes. Yet, as I shall attempt to argue, feminist criticism offers a vital alternative, recognizable among the old texts, waiting for exploration and enlightenment.

Let us be blunt. Today's youth, whatever the reasons, no longer go to literature and what we used to call "culture" as to the fountain of wisdom and experience. Youth today respond rather to an alternative culture, outside the English classroom, vital, challenging, relevant, and usually electronically transmitted. From this culture they receive vibrations far more intense than those literature, taught in the old way, is able to convey. Furthermore, today's youth are living out experiences only fantasized by previous generations. If students are to see literature as capable of informing them about any of the aspects of life, they must become convinced that literature is as capable of revolutionary exploration as their own lives are.

Against such obstacles, what maneuvers? I am reminded of Robert Graves, returning to Oxford after the horrors of the World War I trenches. "The Anglo-Saxon lecturer," Graves wrote, "was candid about his subject: it was, he said, a language of purely linguistic interest. . . . I thought of Beowulf lying wrapped in a blanket among his platoon of drunken thanes in the Gothland billet."[1] Edmund Blunden, his lungs gassed from the war, attended the same lectures and with Graves found *Beowulf* fascinating as they translated everything into trench-warfare terms. So it is, even more fundamentally, with the women and men who begin to perceive how great is the sexual revolution that now confronts us. The vitality that can be felt in one's pulses as one looks at literature from this new vantage point has often been described to me. The question is: How shall English departments learn not to be afraid of this new way of looking at literature, not to trivialize it, since trivialization is the main expression of that fear?

Nothing so well exemplifies the exclusion of women from the profession of English studies as the Penguin Modern Masters series, edited by Frank Kermode. Kermode proclaims his task thus: "By Modern Masters we mean the men who have changed and are changing the life and thought of our age. The authors of these volumes are themselves masters, and they have written their books in the belief that general discussion of their subjects will henceforth be more informed and more exciting than before." In each volume, on the page preceding these remarks, are listed the masters and those, "themselves masters," who have been chosen to write the books.

Need I say that all, in both lists, are male? Nor is the exclusion of women from either list immediately self-explanatory. The "Masters," beginning with Freud, Marx, Lenin, and Einstein, soon dwindle into figures like Fanon, McLuhan, Orwell, Mailer, Reich. Far be it from me to suggest that Mailer and Orwell do not have their place in the stars. But are there no women to stand beside them? Are there no women who might have written, perhaps even from a different point of view, on Laing, Beckett, Lawrence, or Jung? I, thirty years girl and woman in the field of English studies, wonder anew that among all the changes of "the life and thought of our age," only the feminist approach has been scorned, ignored, fled from, at best reluctantly embraced. Join us if you wish, male stars and drudges alike have said to young women scholars—and indeed, they allow, in their less guarded moments, that women are now a majority of the best students—but do so to study the Masters, male Masters, and learn from us, male masters, in the old way. There is no room for a feminist viewpoint here: that is a fad, an aberration. There is no male or female viewpoint; there is only the human viewpoint, which happens always to have been male. Any other conclusion is inconceivable, not to be thought of. Deconstruction, semiology, Derrida, Foucault may question the very meaning of meaning as we have learned it, but feminism may not do so. Saussure, Jonathan Culler announces (in the Modern Master on Modern Master that happens to lie before me), has taught us "that you cannot hope to attain an absolute or Godlike view of things but must choose a perspective, and that within this perspective objects are defined by their relations to one another."[2] So long, of course, as the perspective chosen is not feminist.

Let us remain calm, manly, objective. Is there not a certain wry humor to be found in the fact that while no one in the profession can agree on what is literature, or meaning, or the metalanguage, everyone can agree on the deplorable state of English studies? As Gerald Graff, in a book devoted to the phenomenon he calls "Literature Against Itself," expresses it, "The loss of belief—or loss of interest—in literature as a means of understanding weakens the educational claims of literature and leaves the literature teacher without a rationale for what he professes."[3] Graff's book makes many debatable points —that is its strength—but probably no one will debate the lack of rationale felt by teachers of literature on every side. That is where we are, and any book or article on the subject will try to explain how we got there.

Let me choose Jonathan Culler once again, this time not speaking as master on master:

> If there is a crisis in literary criticism it is no doubt because few of the many who write about literature have the desire or arguments to defend their activity. . . . The historical scholarship which was once the dominant mode of criticism could at least, whatever its faults, be defended as an attempt to bring supplementary and inaccessible information to bear on the text and thus to assist understanding. But the orthodoxy bequeathed by the "New Criticism," which focuses on "the text itself" . . . is more difficult to defend. . . . What then are we to say of criticism? What more can it do?[4]

Et cetera. Culler considers that he has a solution in structuralist poetics. Others offer other debatable, uncertain solutions. The only answer the profession has failed seriously to consider, politically to act on, is feminism. Yet feminism, able to combine structuralism, historical criticism, New Criticism, and deconstructionism, reaches into our past to offer, through fundamental reinterpretation, a new approach to literary studies. Moreover, it offers vitality to counter what threatens us: the exhaustibility of our subject.

Meanwhile, as English professors wait, like Auden, "hoping to twig from what we are not what we might be next," feminist criticism has been victimized by analogy. Either it is called a "fad," like psychoanalytic criticism, a regrettable minority imperative, like black studies, or it is considered a nonacademic dalliance, like the study of popular, nontraditional forms of art. It touches on all these, as do all literary studies, but is not comparable to them. Rather, feminist studies are justified by the centrality they offer, a centrality literary studies enjoyed in the nineteenth century, when, in Ortega y Gasset's words, art was important "on account of its subjects, which dealt with the profoundest problems of humanity, and on account of its own significance as a human pursuit from which the species derived its justification and dignity."[5]

While literary critics are losing their audience both in the classroom and without, the fear of feminism persists, even as the feminist audience grows. Why? There are, I believe, several answers, all of which stem from the belief that women's studies are not mainstream, are not central, are not where the power is. Women and men alike avoid a commitment that promises only marginality. Let me be more explicit.

Men's fears are palpable. Men have long been members of a profession whose masculinity can, particularly in our American society, be questioned. I suspect that the macho attitudes of most English professors, their notable male bonding, can be directly attributed to the fear of female dominance. Now comes the additional threat of the profession's being feminized. More students are women. The pressure for studying women authors and hiring women professors increases. Those in power in departments still safely male-dominated close their ranks. These male fears are profound, and no less so for being largely unconscious. Meanwhile, the old familiar habits of male dominance and scorn of female interests in the profession make these attitudes appear natural and right.

Women students and professors, in a tight market and cruel economic situation, are in no position to fight those who control jobs. While willing to benefit, passively if possible, from affirmative-action programs, they accept the fears induced by their professors and eschew feminism, particularly as an academic study. If to this we add the burden of anxiety borne by all women who confront the male power structure, we have a situation in which there are few inducements to either sex to undertake feminist studies. Why then not ignore the whole thing? Why not let the question gracefully disappear?

The answer, I believe, does not lie in the political rights of women, who are half the students, who earn half the doctorates (or more), and who comprise, in their sex, half the peoples of the world. The answer lies, rather, in the political situation of English studies today, in the threatened state of literature.

Our young teachers still begin eagerly and enthusiastically to teach the literature we have all taught for so long. But the most gifted of them, certainly in modern studies, emphasize far more the latest critical theories and methods than they do the literature itself. Meanwhile, their older colleagues face, whether they admit it or not, an enormous sense of loss, of lack of clarity in the purposes from which they speak; the old Arnoldian pride in literature is gone, and little has arisen to take its place. As philosophy did in the middle of this century, literary studies have begun to ask about methodology and language, have begun to question what in fact we "know" and to suggest that in fact we know little. Only the old-time textual scholars remain apparently content, with fewer and fewer students, but even they whisper, sometimes, of their sense of surviving from a vanished world.

My own experience here is offered as one individual's literary adventure. When I began, first alone and then with a colleague from another department, to teach from a feminist approach the French and English novel (by both male and female authors), a vitality entered the classroom that I had not experienced, I realized, for many years, nor had the students. We had a sense, as we used to have when I was young and the field of modern British literature was relatively unexplored, of being near the center of the life and thought of our age. Novels one was certain had been exhausted by endless analysis now declared themselves to us as full of new possibility, revealing new truths, reconstructing themselves in new ways. If they were indeed self-consuming artifacts, they at least left the students alive at the end of the class, full of hope for new, vital achievement.

One of the outstanding figures in the department in which I teach is a scholar once devoted exclusively to the new methodology. It was from his writings that I first gained some understanding of Derrida, Foucault, and others. For a long time it seemed to me that he and I were at the opposite poles of English studies. Nothing connected us. The body of humanist documents that I had known had vanished to leave behind two newly evolved professors speaking different languages, sharing nothing.

Then this scholar published a book whose subject was the Western world's view of the East, and especially of Islam. My erudite and brilliant colleague had filled the book with references to scholars unknown to me, quoted in languages also unknown. But at the heart of the book was an extraordinary vibrancy. In writing of how the Western world had seen Arabs only as it chose to see them, for its own purposes, and had even imposed that view on the Arabs themselves and on history, my colleague had suggested that we review the literary uses of orientalism to suggest ways in which they had been distorted to serve the needs of the Western culture.

All at once, this formerly incomprehensible colleague had revealed the source of life in humanist studies. I saw that if "women" were substituted for "Arabs," we would begin to understand the way in which the male world had viewed women, and equally, I saw the plea that feminist scholars now might make for a fresh start from a new perspective. I realized, in reading his book, that women had differed from Arabs in one important way: far more than Arabs internalized the Western view, women have internalized the male view of themselves, have accepted it as the "truth," as Arabs rarely accepted—or at least not for so long—the Western view of their ineptitudes and essential inhumanity. Despite this difference, I could learn much from the way my colleague had taken his profound knowledge of Derrida and Foucault, and used it to reveal how long-accepted attitudes can be reconsidered, leaving the texts that had seemed unarguable ready for new interpretations.

There remains the problem of fighting opposition on all sides. I do not know if my colleague would countenance feminist studies. Most of my male colleagues, and some female ones, still feel the most profound disinclination to reconsider texts in the light of feminism, though they may be more easily persuaded in a less threatening atmosphere. Oddly enough, feminism is above all viewed as narrow, confining. By some mysterious fiat, the study of women in literature is narrower, more peripheral, less mainstream than the study of American Indians or minor religious sects in the seventeenth century. Is it perhaps because there is no humanistic or literary study without a feminist aspect that studying such an aspect appears both superfluous and superficial? Have we not all had mothers, and known the fact for years? Who needs to study it? Everything to be said on the subject has been said, and those who say it again are too passionate and intense.

Yet feminist courses continue to attract students wherever they are offered. The National Endowment for the Humanities has found a rapidly growing demand for such courses among its summer seminars for college teachers. Department chairpersons, sometimes reluctantly, must more and more admit the evidence of the popularity, the vitality, of such undertakings. Only when they are earmarked as injurious to the reputation of the student or placed outside the requirements for departmental certification are feminist courses avoided. The blunt fact is that the feminist aspect has been so steadily ignored that almost any period or work will reveal a while new landscape to those who teach and learn from this point of view. That now rare phenomenon, excitement, reappears in the classroom.

My hope is that eventually the viewpoint of feminism will begin to permeate all courses, whether taught by men or women, as psychoanalysis has done. Even if, like a professor friend of mine, we refer to psychoanalytic studies, endearingly, as "shrink crit," we will never look at literature again as we did before Freud, whether or not we have specifically studied him and his theories. While nothing is drearier than facile psychoanalytic interpretations of literature (or facile Marxist interpretations), we cannot live as though no light had been cast on the world by Freud or Marx, or for that matter, by Einstein and Darwin. Feminism, too, will in time become such a generally enlightening discipline.

My own hopes rest also on sheer economic pressure to assure feminism new life. Scholars have edged away from feminism because it appears faddish, because the media have to some extent embraced and therefore demeaned it. But today, even the soundest of historians dealing with imperialism have allowed new attitudes toward Third World peoples to infuse their work. Teachers of literature can do no less for women.

Of course, all this is problematic. (Gerald Graff says that "the word 'problematic' is perhaps the one indispensable piece of equipment for anybody wishing to set up shop as a literary critic today."[6]) Nevertheless, the discomfort we all feel about feminism, as about other matters, is no reason to avoid the subject. The discomfort of the male establishment, or even of some female members of that establishment, seems insufficient cause.

In 1931, when Willa Cather was the first woman to be granted an honorary degree by Princeton University, Louise Bogan, writing in the *New Yorker,* rejoiced that Cather's stature was such that Princeton was willing "to forget and forgive her sex."[7] That attitude, the unspoken one of most of the male establishment, is no longer possible. Women applying to graduate schools today, and earning the most prized fellowships, are no longer willing to have their sex forgotten and forgiven. Nor are they unprepared to face down the response their request for feminist studies is bound to provoke, the response recorded for all time by Joanna Russ:

> That's not an issue.
> That's not an issue *any more.*
> Then why do you keep on bringing it up?
> You keep on bringing it up because you are crazy.
> You keep on bringing it up because you are hostile.
> You keep on bringing it up because you are intellectually irresponsible.
> You keep on bringing it up because you are shrill, strident, and self-indulgent.
> How can I possibly listen to anyone as crazy, hostile, intellectually irresponsible, shrill, strident, and self-indulgent as you are?
> Especially since what you're talking about is not an issue.
> (Any more.)[8]

Let us face the fact: the spirit has largely gone from our studies. That at least is my experience, and the experience of most of those I speak with. It is not only that the sparks strike less and less often. It is not only that we are losing our audience, while hugging to ourselves the importance of our endeavors. Deep within most of us is a sense of futility, and a desire to search for new approaches to literature to rescue it from its currently moribund state. Feminism is not the only prescription, but it is an enlivening one. And those who have examined everything from the meaning of meaning to the metatext may discover that this apparently frivolous discipline offers them, in our own time, the key to new vitality. Is there one of those Modern Masters whose problems with women and his own concept of femininity have not been as important as they have been ignored? Can Frank Kermode find nothing missing from his accounts of the modern world?

NOTES

[1]Robert Graves, *Goodbye to All That* (Garden City, N.Y.: Anchor Books, 1957), pp. 292–93.

[2]Jonathan Culler, *Ferdinand de Saussure* (New York: Penguin Books, 1977), p. xv.

[3]Gerald Graff, *Literature Against Itself: Literary Ideas in Modern Society* (Chicago: University of Chicago Press, 1979), p. 7.

[4]Jonathan Culler, *Structuralist Poetics: Structuralism, Linguistics, and the Study of Literature* (Ithaca, N.Y.: Cornell University Press, 1975), pp. vii–viii.

[5]José Ortega y Gasset, *The Dehumanization of Art,* quoted in Graff, *Literature Against Itself,* p. 8.

[6]Graff, *Literature Against Itself,* p. 8.

[7]Louise Bogan, "American-Class," *New Yorker,* August 8, 1931; reprinted in James Schroeter, ed., *Willa Cather and Her Critics* (Ithaca, N.Y.: Cornell University Press, 1967).

[8]Joanna Russ, "Reviews and Responses," *Frontiers* 4 (Fall 1979): 68.

What Do Feminist Critics Want?

A Postcard from the Volcano

Sandra M. Gilbert

At the risk of revealing something that will be bad for all feminist critics everywhere, I must confess that I have hardly been able to make up my mind what aspect of feminist criticism to discuss here. I have therefore decided to offer, not a single, unified essay, but what may well seem to be three mini-essays, complete with three different (and I think rather impressive) titles: (1) "The Revisionary Imperative: Feminist Criticism and Western Culture"; (2) "Redundant Women: The Economics of Feminist Criticism"; and (3) "Feminist Mysteries: Male Critics and Feminist Criticism."

Before I launch into the first of these "essays," however, let me take a moment to explain my odd self-division, for so bizarre a rhetorical strategy does require some justification. To begin with, I should note that when I was first asked to participate in this seminar, I felt not only honored but extraordinarily pleased and excited. I knew that as a feminist critic I was going to have an exceptional opportunity, an opportunity to tell an important audience (which would consist largely of chair*men* rather than of chair*persons*) about the work I do and the field I represent. Few feminist critics have such chances. Indeed, we seem lately to have been left to speak more and more to one another rather than to those "out there" whose minds we passionately wish to reach. Thus, flushed with comfortable anticipation, I accepted this opportunity in the most optimistic mood.

However, my mood soon darkened. For when I began thinking about what I ought to say, discussing the matter with friends, organizing priorities, considering possible titles, my confusion grew. As a representative feminist critic, I must make this occasion count and therefore—so my feminist friends told me and so I heartily agreed—I must not only outline a theory of literary criticism but also summarize a number of crucial moral and political points. Here, in brief and in no special order, are some of the suggestions that were urged on me:

Tell them what we can do for them.
Tell them what they can do for us.
Tell them to hire feminists.
Tell them not to fire feminists.
Tell them about the case of X or the fate of Y (feminists who were fired or feminists who weren't).
Tell them to come to our talks.
Tell them to read our books.
Tell them what we do.
Tell them we don't do what they think we do.
Tell them why they think we do what we don't really do.
Tell them why they think we are what we really aren't.
Tell them who we really are and what we really do.

Such a bewildering proliferation of points made three distinct essays almost inevitable. Each would deal in some sense with a pair of central questions—namely, What do feminist critics want? and, How can English departments give it to them?—or with the converse of those questions—namely, What do English departments want? and, How can feminist critics give it to them? But one of these presentations, the most important in the long run, would have to outline a theory of what feminist critics want philosophically, as a way of thinking about literary texts. A second, perhaps more immediately pressing discussion would have to analyze the politics of what feminist criticism wants from the structural realities of English departments—that is, what jobs and courses it imagines for its proponents. And a third, the most interesting to a social and literary historian like me, would try to bridge the gulf between the first two. This last little essay would have to present, in other words, a kind of sociology or psychohistory of feminist criticism as it has functioned in today's academy, explaining why and how the philosophy underlying this particular critical "ism" has so far had comparatively little effect on such political realities of English departments as hiring, promotion, and curriculum development.

Of course, all these potential discussions had even more in common than their concern with different aspects of feminist criticism. It is an axiom of the women's movement that the personal *is* the political: the very title of Kate Millett's influential analysis of feminism and masculinism today—*Sexual Poli-*

tics—insists on an inescapable connection between private relationships (bedroom or parlor politics, as it were) and public ones. For feminist critics, however, the axiom can be modified and expanded: not only is the personal the political; the aesthetic is the political, the literary is the political, the rhetorical is the political. In other words, even what appears to be the theoretical cannot easily be disengaged or abstracted from the practical, for every text can be seen as in some sense a political gesture and more specifically as a gesture determined by a complex of assumptions about male-female relations, assumptions we might call sexual poetics.

Perhaps this can most readily be seen if we look back and notice the form in which both I and my feminist colleagues conceived of the points my presentation should make: "Tell *them* what we can do for them. . . . Tell *them* what we do. . . . Tell *them* who we really are." On reflection, my constant reiteration of the word "them" seems odd. Wouldn't it have been more natural *not* to dwell so obsessively on the otherness of my audience? Couldn't my friends and I have devised a list that would read, for example, "describe what we do, explain who we are, analyze our assumptions, defend our poetics," and so forth? Yet I think that we all felt it inevitable to list things in terms of what *I*, representing *us*, should say to *them.* For women's alienation from the sources of power is profound, and I want to argue here that it is not just a personal or a political alienation but that—at least until quite recently—it has also been a philosophical alienation, an aesthetic alienation, a literary alienation.

Ultimately, in fact, it is women's ubiquitous cultural alienation that necessitates what I have called a "revisionary imperative." Thus, as both a problem and a perception, women's otherness is the intellectual center around which my first discussion revolves. For of course women—especially educated women like me, a representative feminist critic—do not seem *obviously* alienated. On the contrary, in our use of academic tools—texts, techniques, terminology—I imagine we must appear as deeply implicated in cultural intellectual styles and subjects as our male colleagues are. What, then, do I mean when I speak of the cultural alienation of women and what is this revisionary imperative that I insist on as a solution to the problem? I can best begin to answer these questions by telling one of many stories about my own feminist "conversion."

In 1970 I had a job interview with an English department chairman who quite unexpectedly confided in the middle of an otherwise ordinary conversation that he was alarmed by the demands of some female graduate students. These radical young women believed that classes ought to be devoted to the study of women—women in literature, literature by women!

"They want to throw out a thousand years of Western culture," he suddenly said. He spoke bitterly, with a soft, regretful Southern accent. "A thousand yeahs of Westuhn culchuh!"

I was shocked. "Surely not!" I exclaimed.

Looking something like the majestic procession that passes through the third act of *Die Meistersinger,* a thousand years of Western culture paraded across my mind: grave monkish scholars, impassioned poets, thought-worn philosophers, and beautiful stately ladies, all dimly glowing, all holding out faintly imploring hands to me, their heir and guardian. *Remember us,* they seemed to signal as their noble robes swept by. *Don't throw us out!*

"Surely," I added (a bit priggishly, I now realize), "we're all equally committed to the preservation of Western culture."

But of course I was wrong. For what feminist criticism and scholarship have taught me in the last twelve years is that, although we obviously can't "throw out a thousand years of Western culture," we can and must redo our history of those years. Nothing may have been thrown out of that record, but something has been left out: "merely," in Carolyn Kizer's ironic understatement, "the private lives of one-half of humanity"—the private lives of women and sometimes their public lives, too.[1] When I say we must redo our history, therefore, I mean we must review, reimagine, rethink, rewrite, revise, and reinterpret the events and documents that constitute it.

I should note here, incidentially, that words beginning with the prefix *re-* have lately become prominent in the language of feminist humanists, all of whom feel that, if feminism and humanism are not to be mutually contradictory terms, we must return to the history of what is called Western culture and reinterpret its central texts. Virginia Woolf speaks of "rewriting history"; Adrienne Rich notes that women's writing must begin with a "re-vision" of the past; Carolyn Heilbrun observes that we must "reinvent" womanhood; and Joan Kelly declares that we must "restore women to history and . . . restore our history to women."[2] All, I would argue, are articulating the revisionary imperative that has involved feminist critics in a massive attempt to reform "a thousand years of Western culture."

I myself began to experience this revisionary imperative a few years after my interview with that harassed chairman, and at first my revisionary activities seemed minor enough. My nine-year-old daughter was reading *Little Women* and loving it so much that I reread it along with her. A few months later we read/reread *Jane Eyre* and *Wuthering Heights.* Rereadings led to reinterpretations, and my revisionary impulse became so strong that I was delighted when Susan Gubar, a colleague who was also revising her ideas about these books, suggested that we team-teach a course in literature by women.

Revisionary as we felt—and we were both by now reading and rereading key feminist texts—my colleague and I were not entirely prepared for the new view of literary history that our classroom reinterpretations revealed. We had believed, I guess, that women and men participate equally in a noble republic of the spirit and that both sexes are equal inheritors of "a thousand years of Western culture." Rereading literature by both women *and* men, however, we learned that, though the pressures and oppressions of gender may be as invisible as air, they are also as inescapable as air, and, like the weight of air, they imperceptibly shape the forms and motions of our lives. Assumptions about the sexes, we saw, are entangled with some of the most fundamental assumptions Western culture makes about the very nature of culture—that "culture" is male, for example, and "nature" female—and we decided that, at least until the nineteenth century, even apparently abstract definitions of literary genres were deeply influenced by psychosocial notions about gender.[3] Again and again, as we explored such sexual poetics, we encountered definitions of cultural authority and creativity that excluded women, definitions based on the notion that (in the words of Gerard Manley Hopkins) "the male quality *is* the creative gift."[4] The treasures of Western culture, it began to seem, were the patrimony of male writers, or to put it another way, Western culture itself was a grand ancestral property that educated men had inherited from their intellectual forefathers, while their female relatives, like characters in a Jane Austen novel, were relegated to modest dower houses on the edge of the estate.

This distinction between male patrimony, on the one hand, and female penury, on the other, can be seen in countless self-defining texts by male and female writers. But perhaps quotations from two volcano poems, besides being particularly pertinent here, will begin to illustrate both my meaning and my subtitle. Wallace Stevens's "A Postcard from the Volcano" employs very much the same metaphor of the world as ancestral property that I have just used. Imagining his own and his generation's extinction by the symbolic Mount Saint Helens that annihilates every generation, Stevens prophesies also the imaginings of his heirs, "children picking up [his] bones" who will never entirely comprehend his passions. But these uncomprehending children *will* inherit a cosmic mansion that has been in some deep way transformed by his language, his literary authority, his power: "We knew for long the mansion's look," he notes. "And what we said of it became / A part of what it is . . . ," adding that when he is gone "Children . . . will say of the mansion that it seems / As if he that lived there left behind / A spirit storming in blank walls."[5]

Emily Dickinson, who wrote many more volcano poems than Stevens did, had quite a different attitude toward both the mansion of the cosmos and her own Vesuvian presence:

On my volcano grows the Grass
A meditative spot—
An acre for a Bird to choose
Would be the General thought—

How red the Fire rocks below—
How insecure the sod
Did I disclose
Would populate with awe my solitude.[6]

For Dickinson, the gulf between appearance and reality is bleaker, blacker, and more unbridgeable than the one Stevens records. Trained and defined as a lady, she is conscious that she herself seems to be a sort of decorous (and marginal) landscape, "a meditative spot" on the edge of the patriarchal estate, a quiet "acre for a Bird to choose." What is unimaginable is her volcanic (and powerful) interiority: the fierce fire, the insecure sod, and the awesomely quaking rock that not only enforce but create her "solitude." Moreover, it is that solitude, so different from Stevens's authoritative wistfulness, which in turn both determines and defines her alienation. Alone, unknown, and unimaginable, she is *other* and possibly awful to everyone, even to herself.

Reading many texts like these two volcano poems and trying to understand their implications for a sexual poetics, I began to have a different version —literally a re-vision—of "a thousand years of Western culture," that grand procession from *Die Meistersinger.* Those grave scholars, impassioned poets, and thought-worn philosophers were all male; the cosmos was their hereditary home, their ancestral mansion, as it was Stevens's, and thus they were the apprentices as well as the lords and masters who marched across Wagner's glittering stage, while the beautiful stately ladies of my vision, like Wagner's Eva, were quite conscious of being their goals, their prizes, the objects of their desire. And if, like the voice that was great within Wallace Stevens or like Wagner's master singers, the men had the power of speech, the women, like Emily Dickinson, knew that they had, or were supposed to have, the graceful obligation of silence.

But what of the women who refused to be silent or who (again like Dickinson) could not manage an enduring silence? My colleague and I realized that, more than most other participants in a thousand years of Western culture, these women had been forgotten, misunderstood, or misinterpreted. Yet it was they who inspired Virginia Woolf's remark that "towards the end of the eighteenth century a change came about which, if I were rewriting history, I should describe more fully, and think of greater importance than the Crusades or the Wars of the Roses. The middle-class woman began to write."[7]

Significantly, as my colleague and I reread the literature of these women, we saw that what they wrote may have seemed docile enough—may have seemed, indeed, "A meditative spot / An acre for a Bird to choose"—but that, like Dickinson's work, it was often covertly subversive, even volcanic, and almost always profoundly revisionary. In fact, we came to understand that the revisionary imperative we had experienced was itself both an essential part of the female literary tradition we were attempting to recover and a crucial antidote to the female cultural alienation we were trying to overcome. Thus, as we have argued elsewhere, women writers have frequently responded to sociocultural constraints by creating symbolic narratives that express their common feelings of constriction, exclusion, dispossession.[8] In these narratives madwomen like Bertha Mason Rochester function as doubles through whom sane ladies like Jane Eyre (and Charlotte Brontë) can act out fantastic dreams of escape, or volcanic landscapes serve as metaphors through which apparently decorous spinsters like Emily Dickinson can image the eruption of anger into language. But in creating such symbolic narratives these literary women were revising the world view they had inherited from a society that said women mattered less than men did, a society that thought women barely belonged in the great parade of culture, that defined women as at best marginal and silent tenants of the cosmic mansion and at worst guilty interlopers in that house.

Replacing heroes with heroines, these writers insisted, like Jane Eyre, that "women feel just as men feel . . . they suffer from too rigid a constraint . . . precisely as men would suffer." Revising the story of Western culture, they looked at an ordinary woman—a shopgirl, for instance—and declared, with Virginia Woolf, "I would as soon have her true history as the hundred and fiftieth life of Napoleon or seventieth study of Keats which old Professor Z and his like are now inditing."[9] Creating new accounts of the Creation, they asked, with the eighteenth-century poet Anne Finch, Countess of Winchilsea, "How are we fall'n? by mistaken rules? / And Education's, more than Nature's fools . . . ?"[10] In other words, over and over again these women writers asked, as we feminist critics did and do, what has caused the cultural alienation—the silence, the marginality, the secondary status—of women.

But of course, to ask and to try to give revisionary answers to such questions about literary women is also to ask and answer questions about literary men, about the dynamics of male-female relations in the world of letters, about the nexus of genre and gender, about the secret intersections of sexuality and textuality. That these questions address long-standing problems and long-established texts is undeniable, and it is equally undeniable that literary women have asked and answered them for centuries. I would also argue, though, that until quite recently such literary questions and answers have been as prudently disguised, as decorously encoded, as all the symbolic and revisionary narratives the female imagination has produced. What may most distinguish the new literary movement called feminist criticism is precisely its effort to bring to consciousness such ancient, half-conscious questions about textuality and sexuality. Indeed, if I were to try to articulate very succinctly what feminist criticism, as a way of thinking about literary texts, wants philosophically, I would say that at its most ambitious it wants to decode and demystify all the disguised questions and answers that have always shadowed the connections between textuality and sexuality, genre and gender, psychosexual identity and cultural authority.

Such an enterprise is profoundly exciting. The impulse to revise our understanding of Western literary history and culture is, after all, energizing (and here I understate the case); as a well-known (male) medievalist remarked to me not long ago, "Everything has to be done again," and at the very least our awareness of such a revisionary imperative makes us feminist critics feel *needed.* Moreover, the questions about sexuality and textuality that we have lately decoded or brought to consciousness seem equally invigorating, for all touch on issues that are almost bracingly ontological. What, for instance, could be more fundamental, more a matter of ultimate realities, than an exploration of the relationships between sexual self-definition and literary authority, or an examination of the hidden psychosexual meanings of writing itself, the quintessentially cultural activity that distinguishes us not only from animals but also from one another?

Sadly, however—and here I move into my second essay—many of our male colleagues and students (and a few of our female ones) seem indifferent to the crucial questions that concern us feminist critics; worse, some even seem rather scornful of the excitement our enterprise has generated. Of course, I don't want to generalize too drastically; like every feminist critic, I must confess that some of my best friends are men, for I have a number of male colleagues who not only support and encourage my work (like the medievalist I quoted before) but engage in what I would call feminist criticism themselves. Yet it is nevertheless true—and I imagine I hardly need to document this assertion—that even the word "feminist" often evokes masculinist snickers or worse. Even if we are not seen as wanting to "throw out a thousand yeahs of Westuhn culchuh," we are perceived as self-indulgent, trendy, frivolous, polemical, or marginal. Indeed, where Bloomians, Derrideans, Marxists, or Freudians sometimes encounter the rage with which people respond to ideas that seem genuinely threatening (because truly important), we often meet with the kind of scorn that people reserve for notions they find boring or irritating (because merely trivial).

In an essay that appeared recently in a special issue of the *A D E Bulletin,*

Carolyn G. Heilbrun puts this point so woefully well that I think I can do no better than quote her here: "I, thirty years girl and woman in the field of English studies, wonder anew that among all the changes of 'the life and thought of our age,' only the feminist approach has been scorned, ignored, fled from, at best reluctantly embraced. . . . Deconstruction, semiology, Derrida, Foucault may question the very meaning of meaning as we have learned it, but feminism may not do so."[11] And of course Heilbrun is by and large perfectly correct. Countless new journals of feminist thought have sprung up in the last decade—*Feminist Studies, Women's Studies, Signs, Frontiers, Chrysalis, Michigan Papers in Women's Studies, Women and Literature,* and so forth—most of which regularly publish interesting and useful feminist criticism of literature from classical antiquity to the present. In addition, the pages of more general literary/intellectual periodicals, ranging from *PMLA* to *Partisan Review,* from *Critical Inquiry* to *Contemporary Literature,* have begun to include essays in feminist literary criticism with fair regularity. Even the annual MLA convention has lately devoted what seems to be at least a fifth of its sessions to feminist literary issues. Yet within most English departments, as Heilbrun suggests, business goes on pretty much as usual, as if the intellectual transformation recorded in so many journals and meetings simply had not happened. Or rather, business goes on with the usual ferment over the new ideas of newly interesting men—Derrida, Foucault, Lacan, for instance—just as if no significant feminist transformations had taken place.

More specifically, I would elaborate on Heilbrun's statement by noting that what amounts to the massive rejection (or perhaps more accurately, the denial) of feminist criticism has taken three separate but related forms: simple indifference, apparently supportive tokenism, and outright hostility. The first —indifference—is by far the commonest and in some ways the most vexing form of rejection. As every feminist critic knows, many—indeed, most—of our male colleagues (and a few of our female ones) don't come to our talks, don't read our essays and books, don't in fact concede that we exist as thinkers, teachers, and writers who are part of a significant intellectual movement. Of course, a number of these nonlisteners and nonreaders are probably infamous types we would all, alas, recognize: people who rarely go anywhere except to the supermarket or the faculty club and whose most common out-of-class reading is *TV Guide.* I'm sure, too, that some apparently indifferent souls are really overworked administrators kept late at their desks by affirmative-action forms and budgetary crises, persons whose indifference is more a matter of appearance than reality. Nevertheless, of those who stay away—those who neither read nor listen, those who claim to be ignorant and those who claim to be bored—it seems to me that at least forty or fifty percent are in some sense denying or rejecting the whole enterprise of feminist criticism, and doing so for reasons that at first seem quite inexplicable.

The second form of rejection, which I have called "apparently supportive tokenism," is almost, though not quite, as vexing as simple indifference. Unlike the indifferent nonreader, the tokenist does concede the existence of feminist criticism and even, so it seems at first, the importance of this new literary approach. The tokenist occasionally reads or approvingly quotes an article by a feminist critic and quite genuinely believes that, in Lillian Robinson's words, "every good department should stock one" such creature.[12] But really—and this is why tokenists are tokenists—these apparently supportive colleagues only support feminist criticism because it is "in," it is popular, it is trendy. In fact, they cannot distinguish between one feminist and another, or even between one woman and another. An editor of a very well-known anthology, for instance, told me that, yes, he'd just added some poems by an eighteenth-century literary woman to his book; but when I asked him *which* eighteenth-century literary woman he'd used, he couldn't remember her name. She was a woman, period: a nameless token of trendiness.

In the same way, the tokenist believes that feminist courses should be offered because they bring up enrollments, like classes in sci-fi, film, ecology, and lit., or the detective novel. But he doesn't differentiate among them because they aren't, of course, serious, like courses in Great Books from Plato to Pynchon. The tokenist's point of view is best expressed in the almost liturgical academic credo that J. Hillis Miller offered not long ago at an ADE seminar:

> I believe in the established canon of English and American literature and in the validity of the concept of privileged texts. I think it is more important to read Spenser, Shakespeare, or Milton than to read Borges in translation, or even, to say the truth, to read Virginia Woolf.[13]

Note here that the Serious (indeed, the "privileged"!) Literary Canon is the traditional masculinist one—Spenser, Shakespeare, Milton, not, for example, Shakespeare, Milton, Jane Austen, or Shakespeare, Wordsworth, George Eliot —while the interesting otherness of a feminist writer like Virginia Woolf is equated with what Miller evidently perceives as the spurious brilliance of a trendy foreigner: "Borges *in translation*" (my emphasis).

The third form of rejection suffered by feminist criticism is outright hostility, and of course it is tautological even to name this. Nevertheless, it exists: if the indifferent person never heard of feminist criticism and the tokenist thinks every department should stock *one* feminist critic, the hostile man or woman is obviously the person who demands, "What need one?" Lately—and this is not a tautological point—our male colleagues are increasingly reluctant to express such hostility (though a few female colleagues seem to feel "privileged" to do so). Hostility does linger in some benighted places, however, and gets expressed in all kinds of sadly or comically misogynistic ways. In one department, the measured, elegant, and theoretical work of an accomplished young critic was dismissed as "the last war whoop of feminism." In another, members of a search committee rejected almost every feminist critic who applied for a job in Victorian literature (and three-quarters of the female applicants for the job were feminist critics) with the wonderfully ambiguous phrase "fem. dupe." Consciously, they meant that because these women defined themselves as feminists their credentials must inevitably duplicate those of the one feminist critic who already taught in that department. In other words, "What need *two*?" Unconsciously—well, I wouldn't venture to articulate what they meant unconsciously by "fem. dupe."

In any case, though this form of rejection is distressing (and sometimes costly) for feminist critics, it is certainly clearer and thus less puzzling (and therefore less irksome) than indifference or tokenism. But of course, all these modes of rejection are in some sense both bewildering and painful. Metaphorically speaking, they define those of us who do this kind of work as what the Victorians used to call "redundant women"—women, said the social critic W. R. Greg, "who in place of completing, sweetening, and embellishing the existence of others are compelled to lead an independent and incomplete existence of their own."[14] Defining us as "redundant," moreover, they devalue our work to students, discourage our admirers, dishearten our junior colleagues, and force us into destructive competition with one another for a few token jobs.

Why? To return to my quotation from Carolyn Heilbrun, why is it that "among all the changes of 'the life and thought of our age,' only the feminist approach has been scorned, ignored, fled from, at best reluctantly embraced"? I want to be very fair, so I will concede that a few feminist critics may be at least in part to blame. Some of the early work in the field, and to a lesser extent some work still being done, has been naïve. Some feminist critics, for example, have confused the political with the polemical; quite natural feelings of frustration and anger at injustice have got italicized into shrieks. Other feminist critics, confusing desire with reality, have made what psychologists call "positive role models" out of personages in literary texts or movements who were probably anything but positive. Still other feminist critics have confused fiction with reality and taxed imaginary beings with *not* being "positive role models."

But these failings are minor, and I suspect each is associated with the intellectual excitement, the revisionary passion, and the undissociated sensibility that are the unique strengths of feminist criticism. Indeed, since feminist criticism does have such strengths, it seems disproportionately hostile to reject or deny its central ideas because of the naïveté of a few of its proponents. Recently, moreover, so much good work has appeared that it seems in another sense disproportionate to blame all feminist critics for the failings of a few. On the contrary, we feminist critics know what our revisionary passion can create because we have produced overviews of women's literature like Elaine Showalter's *A Literature of Their Own* and Ellen Moers's *Literary Women,* fine biographical studies like Cynthia Wolff's *A Feast of Words* and Phyllis Rose's *Woman of Letters,* anthologies like Louise Bernikow's *The World Split Open,* and essay collections like Adrienne Rich's *Lies, Secrets and Silence.*

We know, too—and we wish more of our colleagues knew—that although lately almost everyone thinks literary studies are in the doldrums, the intellectual excitement generated by feminist criticism is especially able to regenerate literary studies. My second topic was to be "what feminist criticism wants from English departments"—in other words, what jobs and courses it imagines for its proponents. But that issue is inextricably related to yet another one of my subjects: what feminist criticism can do for English departments. Because, as Heilbrun also notes, feminist criticism does bring a unique vitality to both the classroom and the curriculum, I think we need, not token jobs and courses, not concessions to trendiness, but as many jobs and courses as the economy of literature will allow. Feminist revisions of traditional periodization and of the received literary canon, for example, suggest that there is far more to learn and to teach than we ourselves were ever taught. At the same time, feminist connections between the personal and the political, the theoretical and the practical, renew those bonds of feeling and thought that T. S. Eliot, that paradigmatic patriarchal critic, regarded as irrevocably severed. In fact, the feminist classroom, as anybody who has entered one will tell you, is the home of *un*dissociated sensibilities and thus—do I dare to say it?—a volcanically energetic place. But (of course) it is or should be productively volcanic, for the competent teacher of, say, literature by women must learn to harness or channel the powers of Vesuvius.

Finally, though all feminist approaches to literature are in some sense revisionary, our approaches to literature are also as various as those of our most scornfully masculinist colleagues: we are Marxists, Freudians, deconstructionists, Yale rhetoricians, and Harvard historians. Thus we can contribute to jobs and courses in all the ways that all such theorists can. At the same time, however, the revisionary imperative that we have in common gives us also a common interest not just in the social, rhetorical, or psychological strategies of writing but in the meaning of writing as a psychosexual act, a matter I have already called "bracingly ontological." It would seem, therefore, that only the most artificially depressed economy could define us as "redundant." Why, then—why, for the ritual third time around—why doesn't everybody think our work is as necessary as we think it is? Here, at last, I move into my third essay: I want briefly, as I conclude my exposition of what feminist critics want, to explore the associated mystery of what masculinist critics *don't* want, and why.

Putting aside the possibility that feminist criticism really is boring and trivial, a possibility I am not only unwilling to discuss but constitutionally unable to consider, I suppose I should begin my investigation of these feminist/masculinist mysteries by speculating that many of our colleagues may really find us alarming, or at least unnerving. Precisely that passionately *un*dissociated sensibility which gives volcanic energy to the feminist classroom may appear quite threatening. After all, those who have long been silent, those who have not revealed "how red the fire rocks below" their decorously meditative surfaces, would seem to be the Vesuvian creatures most likely to erupt into murderous rage. This is a point deeply understood by Emily Dickinson. In a fairly early piece, she observes that once volcanoes stop being acres for birds to choose, one discovers that

those old-phlegmatic mountains
Usually so still

Bear within—appalling Ordnance.
Fire, and smoke, and gun,
Taking villages for breakfast.
And appalling Men—[15]

In another poem she elaborates on this vision, noting in particular what we might only half-frivolously define as the deadly critical vocabulary of the volcano: she speaks of the

Solemn—Torrid—Symbol—
The lips that never lie—
Whose hissing corals part and shut—
And Cities ooze away—[16]

Yet, though some of our colleagues may flatter us feminist critics by seeing us as solemn symbols, we are surely not very torrid, and though we may write about madwomen, we are rarely madwomen ourselves. As for appalling ordnance and villages for breakfast, we may perhaps fantasize such possibilities but—especially in this time of lowered enrollments, a time when women have actually lost rather than gained ground in the academy—our ordnance tends to be muted and our diet abstemious.

The feminist mysteries whose rituals we enact in lecture rooms and learned journals, moreover, are certainly not death to look upon (though a classicist friend did suggest to me that some men might hesitate to come to our talks on feminist theory for fear of finding themselves in the position of Mnesilochus and Euripides in Aristophanes' *The Poet and the Women,* the play in which male interlopers at the Athenian women's festival called the Thesmophoria become the prisoners of a set of furious females, helpless hostages in the battle of the sexes). Nor does it seem likely that our feminist critical speech, powerful as I consider it, is so powerful that when we open our truthful mouths "Cities ooze away." After all, no cities of the mind seem to have oozed away lately, though some mental sidewalks may have been covered with a few inches of ash.

Or is it possible that cities, civilizations, literary styles, and subjects *have* begun to ooze away? Though I think feminist criticism is the very opposite of destructive—indeed, I think it is reconstructive rather than deconstructive —I want for a moment to meditate on the possibility that many of our colleagues ignore our work because its very existence is somehow a sign of profound changes that have recently shaken Western culture in general and English departments in particular, changes whose implications they do not want to acknowledge. Metaphorically speaking, perhaps whole intellectual villages and cities have disappeared, settlements that once seemed the strongholds of a thousand years of Western culture. In the largest sense, of course, I am referring to the democratization of society that has profoundly transformed most Western cultural institutions, including schools and universities, since the beginning of the nineteenth century. In this sense, too, I am thinking of the accelerated democratization of education that has particularly transformed English departments since the late fifties, giving us (among other phenomena) open enrollment, the sixties, enormous classes followed by tiny classes, extra sections of remedial English, generational squabbles on the faculty, and a whole new literary canon, including not just the works of Borges in translation and the novels of Virginia Woolf but also science fiction, films, women's literature, black literature, Chicano literature, Asian-American literature, native-American literature, and more, much more.

More specifically, however, I am thinking of the often disregarded but volcanic eruption of women into the public realm of literary and political culture, as opposed to the private, semiliterate domestic world that most women inhabited until the early or middle nineteenth century. As the director of the United States Census Bureau pointed out not long ago, this explosive transformation of women's lives was especially marked in the 1970s, the decade during which most feminist critics became feminist critics: "Women changed their attitudes dramatically over the decade," he remarks, and "the effects can be seen in almost every aspect of society."[17] But of course these theatrical-seeming changes had begun quite some time ago, with a feminist movement whose events and effects have been massively and I think deliberately forgotten until recently. More important, I would argue that the turn-of-the-century feminist movement was until recently forgotten for the same reason that feminist criticism has been, in Heilbrun's words, "scorned, ignored, fled from": it has been forgotten because it is central to most aspects of all our lives—central, crucial, and volcanically influential.[18]

To be quite plain, I am saying that we live the way we live now, and think the way we think now, because what was once a wholly masculinist, patriarchal culture has begun fragmentarily, haltingly, sometimes even convulsively, but, I suspect, irreversibly, to evolve into a masculinist-feminist culture, a culture whose styles and structures will no longer be patriarchal in the old way, even if they remain patrilineal. I am therefore saying as well that the way we read and write now, the way we imagine literary texts and traditions now, must inevitably and irrevocably change under the pressure of the sociocultural changes we are experiencing. And I am saying, finally, that it may be unnerving or even enervating to confront such changes, especially for those to whom they bring a diminution of authority (and of course I mean men), but also for those to whom they bring an accession of responsibility (and here of course I mean women).

Lest I seem entirely solipsistic in suggesting that changes in male-female relations must and will significantly transform our relation to literary studies, let me observe that a number of quite respectable, unimpeachably masculine (and perhaps even masculinist) literary critics have made very similar assertions. Harold Bloom, for instance, declares in *A Map of Misreading* that "the first true break with literary continuity will be brought about in generations to come, if the burgeoning religion of Liberated Woman spreads from its clusters of enthusiasts to dominate the West. Homer will cease to be the inevitable precursor, and the rhetoric and forms of our literature then may break at last from tradition."[19] Bloom, it is true, speaks prophetically, using the future tense. But what if he too is simply evading his own secret recognition that this transformation of Western literary tradition has already begun?

Certainly so astute a literary historian as Walter Ong does believe it has begun. Ong tells us, in *The Presence of the Word,* that the late-eighteenth-and early-nineteenth-century "movement to give formal schooling to girls was associated with the growing together of the academic and bourgeois worlds, and . . . helped wear down on several fronts" classical traditions that included the disputatious (and masculinist) art of the polemic, which had been central to academic life, as well as the specialized (and masculinist) use of "language teaching," specifically the teaching of Latin and Greek, "as a male initiation procedure."[20] Psychoanalytically oriented critics of *écriture* like Derrida and Irwin would perhaps influence us to observe that much of the old masculinist energy of oral culture may have been projected into sexualized fantasies about the relation of the phallic pen to "the virgin page."[21] But Ong's vision of the female invasion of history is surely supported by the Derridean perception of the very nature of writing, which, once women were taught it, allowed a detachment, an anonymity, that in the long run had to be liberating, even transformative.

To return to Virginia Woolf one last time, I should say it was no doubt her understanding of the transformative nature of writing that made her dwell so dramatically on that crucial moment in history, that moment "of greater importance than the Crusades or the Wars of the Roses [when] the middle-class woman began to write." In fact, I would argue that we feminist critics are still dwelling on and in that moment, still coming to terms with and through it. I believe that our terms, however, must eventually be everybody's, for as Ong and Bloom and others have also perceived, we are still living in that moment of cultural transformation, even if we are not dwelling on it.

In fact, what feminist critics most want from English departments is the chance to define the terms to which we are coming as we dwell with the volcanic changes we have experienced. What English departments should want from feminist critics are rigorous and responsible revisions of ourselves, our texts, our traditions. Such re-visions should function in two ways: as new visions or understandings of our literary lives and as new versions or transformations of those lives. Both approaches suggest a possibility that I think unifies all three of my essays but that few people have taken seriously since the Romantic period: the possibility that through literary study we can renew our lives.

NOTES

[1]Carolyn Kizer, "Three," from "Pro Femina," in *No More Masks! An Anthology of Poems by Women,* ed. Florence Howe and Ellen Bass (Garden City, N.Y.: Doubleday, 1973), p. 175.

[2]Virginia Woolf, *A Room of One's Own* (New York: Harcourt, Brace & World, 1928); Adrienne Rich, "When We Dead Awaken: Writing as Re-Vision," *Adrienne Rich's Poetry,* ed. Barbara Charlesworth Gelpi and Albert Gelpi (New York: W. W. Norton, 1975); Carolyn G. Heilbrun, *Reinventing Womanhood* (New York: W. W. Norton, 1979); Joan Kelly-Gadol, "The Social Relations of the Sexes: Methodological Implications of Women's History," *Signs* 1 (Summer 1976): 809–23.

[3]Sandra M. Gilbert and Susan Gubar, *The Madwoman in the Attic: The Woman Writer and the Nineteenth-Century Literary Imagination* (New Haven: Yale University Press, 1979), esp. pt. 1, "Toward a Feminist Poetics." See also Sherry Ortner, "Is Female to Male as Nature Is to Culture?" in *Woman, Culture, and Society,* ed.

Michelle Zimbalist Rosaldo and Louise Lamphere (Stanford, Calif.: Stanford University Press, 1974), pp. 67–88.

[4]Hopkins, *The Correspondence of Gerard Manley Hopkins and Richard Watson Dixon,* ed. C. C. Abbott (London: Oxford University Press, 1935), p. 133.

[5]Wallace Stevens, "A Postcard from the Volcano," *The Collected Poems* (New York: Alfred A. Knopf, 1954), pp. 158–59.

[6]Emily Dickinson, *The Complete Poems,* ed. Thomas H. Johnson (Boston: Little, Brown, 1960), no. 1677.

[7]Woolf, *A Room of One's Own,* p. 64.

[8]Gilbert and Gubar, *Madwoman in the Attic,* esp. chap. 2, "Infection in the Sentence."

[9]Woolf, *A Room of One's Own,* p. 94.

[10]"The Introduction," in *The Poems of Anne Countess of Winchilsea.* ed. Myra Reynolds (Chicago: University of Chicago Press, 1903), pp. 4–5.

[11]Carolyn G. Heilbrun, "Feminist Criticism: Bringing the Spirit Back to English Studies," in this volume, pp. 21–28.

[12]Lillian S. Robinson, *Sex, Class, and Culture* (Bloomington: Indiana University Press, 1978), p. 19.

[13]J. Hillis Miller, "The Function of Rhetorical Study at the Present Time," in *State of the Discipline, 1970s–1980s,* p. 12

[14]William Rathbone Greg, "Why Are Women Redundant?" *Literary and Social Judgments* (Boston, 1873), pp. 276, 282–83.

[15]Dickinson, *Complete Poems,* no. 175.

[16]Ibid., no. 601.

[17]Vincent Barabba, quoted in the *San Francisco Chronicle,* May 20, 1980, p. F-5.

[18]For an analysis of this massive cultural "forgetting" of the first wave of feminism, see Theodore Roszak, "The Hard and the Soft: The Force of Feminism in Modern Times," in *Masculine/Feminine: Readings in Sexual Mythology and the Liberation of Women,* ed. Betty Roszak and Theodore Roszak (New York: Harper & Row, 1969), pp. 87–104.

[19]Harold Bloom, *A Map of Misreading* (New York: Oxford University Press, 1975), p. 33.

[20]Walter Ong, *The Presence of the Word: Some Prolegomena for Culture and Religious History* (New Haven, Conn.: Yale University Press, 1967), pp. 249–50.

[21]See, e.g., John Irwin, *Doubling and Incest: Repetition and Revenge* (Baltimore: Johns Hopkins University Press, 1975), p. 163. See also Susan Gubar, " 'The Blank Page' and the Issues of Female Creativity," in this volume, pp. 292–313.

A Map for Rereading

Gender and the Interpretation of Literary Texts

Annette Kolodny

To a generation still in the process of divorcing itself from the New Critics' habit of bracketing off any text as an entity in itself, as though "it could be read, understood, and criticized entirely in its own terms,"[1] Harold Bloom has proposed a dialectical theory of influence between poets and poets, as well as between poems and poems, which, in essence, does away with the static notion of a fixed or knowable text. As he argued in *A Map of Misreading* in 1975, "a poem is a response to a poem, as a poet is a response to a poet, or a person to his parent." Thus, for Bloom, "poems . . . are neither about 'subjects' nor about 'themselves.' They are necessarily about *other poems.*"[2]

To read or to know a poem, according to Bloom, engages the reader in an attempt to map the psychodynamic relations by which the poet at hand has willfully misunderstood the work of some precursor (either single or composite) in order to correct, rewrite, or appropriate the prior poetic vision as his own. As first introduced in *The Anxiety of Influence* in 1973, the resultant "wholly different practical criticism" gives up "the failed enterprise of seeking to 'understand' any single poem as an entity in itself" and pursues instead "the quest of learning to read any poem as its poet's deliberate misinterpretation, *as a poet,* of a precursor poem or of poetry in general."[3] What one deciphers in the process of reading, then, is not any discrete entity but, rather, a complex relational event, "itself a synecdoche for a larger whole including other texts."[4] "Reading a text is necessarily the reading of a whole system of texts," Bloom explains in *Kabbalah and Criticism,* "and meaning is always wandering around between texts."[5]

To help purchase assent for this "wholly different practical criticism," Bloom asserted an identity between critics and poets as coequal participants in the same "belated and all-but-impossible act" of reading (which, as he hastens to explain in *A Map of Misreading,* "if strong is always a misreading"[6]). As it is a drama of epic proportions, in Bloom's terms, when the ephebe poet attempts to appropriate and then correct a precursor's meaning, so, too, for the critic, his own inevitable misreadings, or *misprisions,* are no less heroic —nor any the less creative. "Poets' misinterpretations or poems" may be "more drastic than critics' misinterpretations or criticism," Bloom admits, but since he recognizes no such thing as "interpretations but only misinterpretations," all criticism is necessarily elevated to a species of "prose poetry."[7] The critic's performance, thereby, takes place as one more "act of misprision [which] displaces an earlier act of misprision"—presumably the poet's or perhaps that of a prior critic; and, in this sense, the critic participates in that same act of "defensive warfare" before his own critical forebears, or even before the poet himself, as the poet presumably enacted before his poetic father/precursor.[8] Their legacy, whether as poetry or as "prose poetry" criticism, consequently establishes the strong survivors of these psychic battles as figures whom others, in the future, will need to overcome in their turn: "A poet is strong because poets after him must work to evade him. A critic is strong if his readings similarly provoke other readings."[9] It is unquestionably Bloom's most brilliant rhetorical stroke, persuading not so much by virtue of the logic of his argument as by the pleasure his (intended and mostly male) readership will take in the discovery that their own activity replicates the psychic adventures of The Poet, every critic's *figura* of heroism.[10]

What is left out of account, however, is the fact that whether we speak of poets and critics "reading" texts or writers "reading" (and thereby recording for us) the world, we are calling attention to interpretative strategies that are learned, historically determined, and thereby necessarily gender-inflected. As others have elsewhere questioned the adequacy of Bloom's paradigm of poetic influence to explain the production of poetry by women,[11] so now I propose to examine analogous limitations in his model for the reading—and hence critical—process (since both, after all, derive from his revisionist rendering of the Freudian family romance). To begin with, to locate that "meaning" which "is always wandering around between texts,"[12] Bloom assumes a community of readers (and, thereby, critics) who know that same "whole system of texts" within which the specific poet at hand has enacted his "misprision." The canonical sense of a shared and coherent literary tradition is therefore essential to the utility of Bloom's paradigm of literary influence as well as to his notions of reading (and misreading). "What happens if one tries to write, or to teach, or to think or even to read without the sense of a tradition?" Bloom asks in

A Map of Misreading. "Why," as he himself well understands, "nothing at all happens, just nothing. You cannot write or teach or think or even read without imitation, and what you imitate is what another person has done, that person's writing or teaching or thinking or reading. Your relation to what informs that person *is* tradition, for tradition is influence that extends past one generation, a carrying-over of influence."[13]

So long as the poems and poets he chooses for scrutiny participate in the "continuity that began in the sixth century B.C. when Homer first became a schoolbook for the Greeks,"[14] Bloom has a great deal to tell us about the carrying over of literary influence; where he must remain silent is where carrying over takes place among readers and writers who in fact have been, or at least have experienced themselves as, cut off and alien from that dominant tradition. Virginia Woolf made the distinction vividly over a half-century ago, in *A Room of One's Own,* when she described being barred entrance, because of her sex, to a "famous library" in which was housed, among others, a Milton manuscript. Cursing the "Oxbridge" edifice, "venerable and calm, with all its treasures safe locked within its breast," she returns to her room at the inn later that night, still pondering "how unpleasant it is to be locked out; and I thought how it is worse perhaps to be locked in; and, thinking of the safety and prosperity of the one sex and of the poverty and insecurity of the other and of the effect of tradition and of the lack of tradition upon the mind of a writer."[15] And, she might have added, on the mind of a reader as well. For while my main concern here is with reading (albeit largely and perhaps imperfectly defined), I think it worth noting that there exists an intimate interaction between readers and writers in and through which each defines for the other what s/he is about. "The effect . . . of the lack of tradition upon the mind of a writer" will communicate itself, in one way or another, to her readers; and, indeed, may respond to her readers' sense of exclusion from high (or highbrow) culture.

An American instance provides perhaps the best example. Delimited by the lack of formal or classical education, and constrained by the social and aesthetic norms of their day to conceptualizing authorship "as a profession rather than a calling, as work and not art,"[16] the vastly popular women novelists of the so-called feminine fifties often enough, and somewhat defensively, made a virtue of their sad necessities by invoking an audience of readers for whom aspirations to "literature" were as inappropriate as they were for the writer. As Nina Baym remarks in her recent study *Woman's Fiction,* "often the women deliberately and even proudly disavowed membership in an artistic fraternity." " 'Mine is a story for the table and arm-chair under the reading lamp in the livingroom, and not for the library shelves,' " Baym quotes Marion Harland from the introduction to Harland's autobiography; and then, at greater length, Baym cites Fanny Fern's dedicatory pages to her novel *Rose Clark:*

> When the frost curtains the windows, when the wind whistles fiercely at the key-hole, when the bright fire glows, and the tea-tray is removed, and father in his slippered feet lolls in his arm-chair; and mother with her nimble needle "makes auld claes look amaist as weel as new," and grandmamma draws closer to the chimney-corner, and Tommy with his plate of chestnuts nestles contentedly at her feet; then let my unpretending story be read. For such an hour, for such an audience, was it written.
>
> Should any *dictionary on legs* rap inopportunely at the door for admittance, send him away to the groaning shelves of some musty library, where "literature" lies embalmed, with its stony eyes, fleshless joints, and ossified heart, in faultless preservation.[17]

If a bit overdone, prefaces like these nonetheless point up the self-consciousness with which writers like Fern and Harland perceived themselves as excluded from the dominant literary tradition and as writing for an audience of readers similarly excluded. To quote Baym again, these women "were expected to write specifically for their own sex and within the tradition of their woman's culture rather than within the Great Tradition. They never presented themselves as followers in the footsteps of Milton or Spenser."[18]

On the one hand, of course, increased literacy (if not substantially improved conditions of education) marked the generation of American women at midcentury, opening a vast market for a literature which would treat the contexts of their lives—the sewing circle rather than the whaling ship, the nursery instead of the lawyer's office—as functional symbols of the human condition.[19] On the other hand, while this vast new audience must certainly be credited with shaping the features of what then became popular women's fiction, it is also the case that the writers in their turn both responded to and helped to formulate their readers' tastes and habits. And both together, I would suggest, found this a means of accepting (or at least coping with) the barred entryway that was to distress Virginia Woolf so in the next century. But these facts of our literary history also suggest that from the 1850s on, in America at least, the meanings "wandering around between texts" were wandering around somewhat different groups of texts where male and female readers were concerned.[20] So that with the advent of women "who wished to be regarded as artists rather than careerists,"[21] toward the end of the nineteenth century, there arose the critical problem with which we are still plagued and which Bloom so determinedly ignores: the problem of reading any text as "a synecdoche for a larger whole including other texts" when that necessarily assumed "whole system of texts" in which it is embedded is foreign to one's reading knowledge.

The appearance of Kate Chopin's novel *The Awakening* in 1899, for example, perplexed readers familiar with her earlier (and intentionally "regional") short stories not so much because it turned away from themes or subject matter implicit in her earlier work, nor even less because it dealt with female sensuality and extramarital sexuality, but because her elaboration of those materials deviated radically from the accepted norms of women's fiction out of which her audience so largely derived its expectations. The nuances and consequences of passion and individual temperament, after all, fairly define the focus of most of her preceding fictions. "That the book is strong and that Miss Chopin has a keen knowledge of certain phases of feminine character will not be denied," wrote the anonymous reviewer for the *Chicago Times-Herald.* What marked an unacceptable "new departure" for this critic, then, was the impropriety of Chopin's focus on material previously edited out of the popular genteel novels by and about women which, somewhat inarticulately, s/he translated into the accusation that Chopin had entered "the overworked field of sex fiction."[22]

Charlotte Perkins Gilman's initial difficulty in seeing "The Yellow Wallpaper" into print repeated the problem, albeit in a somewhat different context: for her story located itself not as any deviation from a previous tradition of women's fiction but, instead, as a continuation of a genre popularized by Poe. And insofar as Americans had earlier learned to follow the fictive processes of aberrant perception and mental breakdown in *his* work, they should have provided Gilman, one would imagine, with a ready-made audience for *her* protagonist's progressively debilitating fantasies of entrapment and liberation. As they had entered popular fiction by the end of the nineteenth century, however, the linguistic markers for those processes were at once heavily male-gendered and highly idiosyncratic, having more to do with individual temperament than with social or cultural situations per se. As a result, it would appear that the reading strategies by which cracks in ancestral walls and suggestions of unchecked masculine willfulness were immediately noted as both symbolically and semantically relevant did not, for some reason, necessarily *carry over* to "the nursery at the top of the house" with its windows barred, nor even less to the forced submission of the woman who must "take great pains to control myself" before her physician husband.[23]

A reader today seeking meaning in the way Harold Bloom outlines that process might note, of course, a fleeting resemblance between the upstairs chamber in Gilman—with its bed nailed to the floor, its windows barred, and metal rings fixed to the walls—and Poe's evocation of the dungeon chambers of Toledo; in fact, a credible argument might be made for reading "The Yellow Wallpaper" as Gilman's willful and purposeful misprision of "The Pit and the Pendulum." Both stories, after all, involve a sane mind entrapped in an insanity-inducing situation. Gilman's "message" might then be that the equivalent revolution by which the speaking voice of the Poe tale is released to both sanity and freedom is unavailable to her heroine. No *deus ex machina,* no General Lasalle triumphantly entering the city, no "outstretched arm" to prevent Gilman's protagonist from falling into her own internal "abyss" is conceivable, given the rules of the social context in which Gilman's narrative is embedded. When gender is taken into account, then, so this interpretation would run, Gilman is saying that the nature of the trap envisioned must be understood as qualitatively different, and so too the possible escape routes.

Contemporary readers of "The Yellow Wallpaper," however, were apparently unprepared to make such connections. Those fond of Poe could not easily transfer their sense of mental derangement to the mind of a comfortable middle-class wife and mother; and those for whom the woman in the home was a familiar literary character were hard pressed to comprehend so extreme an anatomy of the psychic price she paid. Horace Scudder, the editor of the *Atlantic Monthly* who first rejected the story, wrote only that "I could not forgive myself if I made others as miserable as I have made myself!" (Hedges, p. 40). And even William Dean Howells, who found the story "chilling" and admired it sufficiently to reprint it in 1920, some twenty-eight years after its first publication (in the *New England Magazine* of May 1892), like most readers either failed to notice or neglected to report "the connection between the insanity and the sex, or sexual role, of the victim" (Hedges, p. 41). For readers at the turn of the century, then, that "meaning" which "is always wandering around between texts" had as yet failed to find connective pathways linking the fanciers of Poe to the devotees of popular women's fiction, or the shortcut between Gilman's short story and the myriad published feminist analyses of the ills of society (some of them written by Gilman herself). Without such connective contexts, Poe continued as a well-traveled road, while Gilman's story, lacking the possibility of further influence, became a literary dead end.

In one sense, by hinting at an audience of male readers as ill-equipped to follow the symbolic significance of the narrator's progressive breakdown as was her doctor-husband to diagnose properly the significance of his wife's fascination with the wallpaper's patternings; and by predicating a female readership as yet unprepared for texts which mirrored back, with symbolic exemplariness, certain patterns underlying their empirical reality, "The Yellow Wallpaper" anticipated its own reception. For insofar as writing and reading represent linguistically based interpretative strategies—the first for the recording of a reality (that has obviously, in a sense, already been "read") and the second for the deciphering of that recording (and thus also the further decoding of a prior imputed reality)—the wife's progressive descent into madness provides a kind of commentary upon, indeed is revealed in terms of, the sexual politics inherent in the manipulation of those strategies. We are presented at the outset with a protagonist who, ostensibly for her own good, is denied both activities and who, in the course of accommodating herself to that deprivation, comes more and more to experience her self as a text which can neither get read nor recorded.

In his doubly authoritative role as both husband and doctor, John not only appropriates the interpretative processes of reading—diagnosing his wife's illness and thereby selecting what may be understood of her "meaning"; reading to her rather than allowing her to read for herself—but, as well, he determines what may get written and hence communicated. For her part, the protagonist avers, she does not agree with her husband's ideas: "Personally, I believe that congenial work, with excitement and change, would do me good." But given the fact of her marriage to "a physician of high standing" who "assures friends and relatives that there is really nothing the matter with one but temporary nervous depression—a slight hysterical tendency—what is one to do?" she asks. Since her husband (and by extension the rest of the world) will not heed what she says of herself, she attempts instead to communicate it to "this . . . dead paper . . . a great relief to my mind." But John's insistent opposition gradually erodes even this outlet for her since, as she admits, "it *does* exhaust me a good deal—having to be so sly about it, or else meet with heavy opposition" (p. 10). At the sound of his approach, following upon her first attempt to describe "those sprawling flamboyant patterns" in the wallpaper, she declares, "There comes John, and I must put this away,—he hates to have me write a word" (p. 13).

Successively isolated from conversational exchanges, prohibited free access to pen and paper, and thus increasingly denied what Jean Ricardou has called "the local exercise of syntax and vocabulary,"[24] the protagonist of "The Yellow Wallpaper" experiences the extreme extrapolation of those linguistic tools to the processes of perception and response. In fact, it follows directly upon a sequence in which (1) she acknowledges that John's opposition to her writing has begun to make "the effort . . . greater than the relief"; (2) John refuses to let her "go and make a visit to Cousin Henry and Julia"; and (3) as a kind of punctuation mark to that denial, John carries her upstairs, "and laid me on the bed, and sat by me and read to me till it tired my head." It is after these events, I repeat, that the narrator first makes out the dim shape lurking "behind the outside pattern" in the wallpaper: "it is like a woman stooping down and creeping" (pp. 21–22).

From that point on, the narrator progressively gives up the attempt to *record* her reality and instead begins to *read* it—as symbolically adumbrated in her compulsion to discover a consistent and coherent pattern amid "the sprawling outlines" of the wallpaper's apparently "pointless pattern" (pp. 20, 19). Selectively emphasizing one section of the pattern while repressing others, reorganizing and regrouping past impressions into newer, more fully realized configurations—as one might with any complex formal text—the speaking voice becomes obsessed with her quest for meaning, jealous even of her husband's or his sister's momentary interest in the paper. Having caught her sister-in-law "with her hand on it once," the narrator declares, "I know she was studying that pattern, and I am determined that nobody shall find it out but myself!" (p. 27). As the pattern changes with the changing light in the room, so too do her interpretations of it. And what is not quite so apparent by daylight becomes glaringly so at night: "At night in any kind of light, in twilight, candle light, lamplight, and worst of all by moonlight, it becomes bars! The outside pattern I mean, and the woman behind it is as plain as can be." "By daylight," in contrast (like the protagonist herself), "she is subdued, quiet" (p. 26).

As she becomes wholly taken up with the exercise of these interpretative strategies, so too, she claims, her life "is very much more exciting now than it used to be. You see I have something more to expect, to look forward to, to watch" (p. 27). What she is watching, of course, is her own psyche writ large; and the closer she comes to "reading" in the wallpaper the underlying if unacknowledged patterns of her real-life experience, the less frequent becomes that delicate oscillation between surrender to or involvement in and the more distanced observation of developing meaning. Slowly but surely the narrative voice ceases to distinguish itself from the woman in the wallpaper pattern, finally asserting that "I don't want anybody to get that woman out at night but myself" (p. 31), and concluding with a confusion of pronouns that merges into a grammatical statement of identity:

> As soon as it was moonlight and that poor thing began to crawl and shake the pattern, I got up and ran to help her.
>
> I pulled and *she* shook, and *I* shook and *she* pulled, and before morning *we* had peeled off yards of that paper. (P. 32; my italics)

She is, in a sense, now totally surrendered to what is quite literally her own text—or rather, her self as text. But in decoding its (or her) meaning, what she has succeeded in doing is discovering the symbolization of her own untenable and unacceptable reality. To escape that reality she attempts the destruction of the paper which seemingly encodes it: the pattern of bars entrapping the creeping woman. " 'I've got out at last,' said I, 'in spite of you and Jane. I've pulled off most of the paper, so you can't put me back!' " (p. 36). Their paper pages may be torn and moldy (as is, in fact, the smelly wallpaper), but the meaning of texts is not so easily destroyed. Liberation here is liberation only into madness: for in decoding her own projections onto the paper, the protagonist has managed merely to reencode them once more, and now more firmly than ever, within.

With the last paragraphs of the story, John faints away—presumably in shock at his wife's now totally delusional state. He has repeatedly misdiagnosed, or misread, the heavily edited behavior with which his wife has presented herself to him; and never once has he divined what his wife sees in the wallpaper. But given his freedom to read (or, in this case, misread) books, people, and the world as he chooses, he is hardly forced to discover for himself so extreme a text. To exploit Bloom's often useful terminology once again, then, Gilman's story represents not so much an object for the recurrent misreadings, or misprisions, of readers and critics (though this, or course, continues to occur) as an exploration, within itself, of the gender-inflected interpretative strategies responsible for our mutual misreadings, and even horrific misprisions, across sex lines. If neither male nor female reading audiences were prepared to decode properly "The Yellow Wallpaper," even less, Gilman understood, were they prepared to comprehend one another.

It is unfortunate that Gilman's story was so quickly relegated to the backwaters of our literary landscape because, coming as it did at the end of the nineteenth century, it spoke to a growing concern among American women who would be serious writers: it spoke, that is, to their strong sense of writing out of nondominant or subcultural traditions (both literary and nonliterary), coupled with an acute sensitivity to the fact that since women and men learn to read different worlds, different groups of texts are available to their reading and writing strategies. Had "The Yellow Wallpaper" been able to stand as a potential precursor for the generation of subsequent corrections and revisions, then, as in Bloom's paradigm, it might have made possible a form of fiction by women capable not only of commenting upon but even of overcoming that impasse. That it did not—nor did any other woman's fiction become canonical in the United States[25]—meant that, again and again, each woman who took up the pen had to confront anew her bleak premonition that, both as writers and as readers, women too easily became isolated islands of symbolic significance, available only to, and decipherable only by, one another.[26] If any Bloomian "meaning" wanders around between women's texts, therefore, it must be precisely this shared apprehension.

On the face of it such statements should appear nothing less than commonsensical, especially to those most recent theorists of reading who combine an increased attentiveness to the meaning-making role of the reader in the deciphering of texts with a recognition of the links between our "reading" of texts and our "reading" of the world and one another. Among them, Bloom himself seems quite clearly to understand this when, in *Kabbalah and Criticism,* he declares: "That which you are, that only can you read."[27] Extrapolating from his description of the processes involved in the reading of literary texts to a larger comment on our ability to take in or decipher those around us, Wolfgang Iser has lately theorized that "we can only make someone else's thought into an absorbing theme for ourselves, provided the virtual background of our own personality can adapt to it."[28] Anticipating such pronouncements in almost everything they have been composing for over a hundred years now, the women who wrote fiction, most especially, translated these observations into the structures of their stories by invoking that single feature which critics like Iser and Bloom still manage so resolutely to ignore: and that is, the crucial importance of the *sex* of the "interpreter" in that process which Nelly Furman has called "the active attribution of significance to formal signifiers."[29] Antedating both Bloom and Iser by over fifty years, for example, Susan Keating Glaspell's 1917 short story "A Jury of Her Peers" explores the necessary (but generally ignored) gender marking which *must* constitute any definition of "peers" in the complex process of unraveling truth or meaning.[30]

The opening paragraph of Glaspell's story serves, essentially, to alert the reader to the significations to follow: Martha Hale, interrupted at her kitchen chores, must drop "everything right where it was" in order to hurry off with her husband and the others. As she does so, her eye makes "a scandalized sweep of her kitchen," noting with distress that "in no shape for leaving: her bread all ready for mixing, half the flour sifted and half unsifted." The point, of course, is that highly unusual circumstances demand this of her; "it was no ordinary thing that called her away." When she seats herself "in the big two-seated buggy" alongside her impatient farmer husband, the sheriff and his wife, and the county attorney, the story proper begins.

All five drive to a neighboring farm where a murder has been committed —the farmer strangled, his wife already arrested. The men intend to seek clues to the motive for the crime, while the women are, ostensibly, simply to gather together the few necessities required by the wife incarcerated in the town jail. Immediately upon approaching the place, however, the very act of perception becomes sex-coded: the men look at the house only to talk "about what had happened," while the women note the geographical topography which makes it, repeatedly in the narrative, "a lonesome-looking place." Once inside, the men "go upstairs first—then out to the barn and around there" in their search for clues (even though the actual crime took place in the upstairs master bedroom), while the women are left to the kitchen and parlor. Convinced as they are of "the insignificance of kitchen things," the men cannot properly attend to what these might reveal and, instead, seek elsewhere for "a clue to the motive," so necessary if the county attorney is to make his case. Indeed, it is the peculiar irony of the story that although the men never question their attribution of guilt to Minnie Foster, they nonetheless cannot meaningfully interpret this farm wife's world—her kitchen and parlor. And, arrogantly certain that the women would not even "know a clue if they did come upon it," they thereby leave the discovery of the clues, and the consequent unraveling of the motive, to those who do, in fact, command the proper interpretative strategies.

Exploiting the information sketched into the opening, Glaspell has the neighbor, Mrs. Hale, and the sheriff's wife, Mrs. Peters, note, among the supposedly insignificant kitchen things, the unusual, and on a farm unlikely, remnants of kitchen chores left "half done," denoting an interruption of some serious nature. Additionally, where the men could discern no signs of "anger—or sudden feeling" to substantiate a motive, the women comprehend the implications of some "fine, even sewing" gone suddenly awry, "as if she didn't know what she was about!" Finally, of course, the very drabness of the house, the miserliness of the husband to which it attests, the old and broken stove, the patchwork that has become Minnie Foster's wardrobe—all these make the women uncomfortably aware that to acknowledge fully the meaning of what they are seeing is "to get her own house to turn against her!" Discovery by discovery, they destroy the mounting evidence—evidence which the men, at any rate, cannot recognize as such; and, sealing the bond between them as conspirators in saving Minnie Foster, they hide from the men the canary with its neck broken, the penultimate clue to the strangling of a husband who had so systematically destroyed all life, beauty, and music in his wife's environment.

Opposing against one another male and female realms of meaning and activity—the barn and the kitchen—Glaspell's narrative not only invites a semiotic analysis but, indeed, performs that analysis for us. If the absent Minnie Foster is the "transmitter" or "sender" in this schema, then only the women are competent "receivers" or "readers" of her "message," since they alone share not only her context (the supposed insignificance of kitchen things) but, as a result, the conceptual patterns which make up her world. To those outside the shared systems of quilting and knotting, roller towels and bad stoves, with all their symbolic significations, these may appear trivial, even irrelevant to meaning; but to those within the system, they comprise the totality of the message: in this case, a reordering of who in fact has been murdered and, with that, what has constituted the real crime in the story.

For while the two women who visit Minnie Foster's house slowly but surely decipher the symbolic significance of her action—causing her husband's neck to be broken because he had earlier broken her canary's neck—the narrative itself functions, for the reader, as a further decoding of what that symbolic action says about itself. The essential crime in the story, we come to realize, has been the husband's inexorable strangulation, over the years, of Minnie Foster's spirit and personality; and the culpable criminality is the complicity of the women who had permitted the isolation and the loneliness to dominate Minnie Foster's existence: " 'I wish I had come over to see Minnie Foster sometimes,' " declares her neighbor guiltily. " 'I can see now—' She did not put it into words."

> "I wish you'd seen Minnie Foster [says Mrs. Hale to the sheriff's wife] when she wore a white dress with blue ribbons, and stood up there in the choir and sang."
>
> The picture of that girl, the fact that she had lived neighbor to that girl for twenty years, and had let her die for lack of life, was suddenly more than she could bear.
>
> "Oh, I *wish* I'd come over here once in a while!" she cried. "That was a crime! That was a crime! Who's going to punish that?"

The recognition is itself, of course, a kind of punishment. With it comes, as well, another recognition, as Mrs. Peters reveals experiences in her own life of analogous isolation, desperate loneliness, and brutality at the hands of a male. Finally they conclude: "We all go through the same things—it's all just a different kind of the same thing! If it weren't—why do you and I *understand?* Why do we *know*—what we know this minute?" By this point the narrative emphasis has shifted: to understand why it is that they know what they now know is for these women to recognize the profoundly sex-linked world of meaning which they inhabit; to discover how specialized is their ability to read that world is to discover anew their own shared isolation within it.

While neither the Gilman nor the Glaspell story necessarily excludes the male as reader—indeed, both in a way are directed specifically at educating him to become a better reader—they do nonetheless insist that, however inadvertently, he is a *different kind* of reader and that, where women are concerned, he is often an inadequate reader. In the first instance, because the husband cannot properly diagnose his wife or attend to her reality, the result is horrific: the wife descends into madness. In the second, because the men cannot even recognize as such the very clues for which they search, the ending is a happy one: Minnie Foster is to be set free, no motive having been discovered by which to prosecute her. In both, however, the same point is being made: lacking familiarity with the women's imaginative universe, that universe within which their acts are signs,[31] the men in these stories can neither read nor comprehend the meanings of the women closest to them—and this in spite of the apparent sharing of a common language. It is, in short, a fictive rendering of the dilemma of the woman writer. For while we may all agree that in our daily conversational exchanges men and women speak more or less meaningfully and effectively with one another, thus fostering the illusion of a wholly shared common language, it is also the case that where figurative usage is invoked—that usage which often enough marks the highly specialized language of literature—it "can be inaccessible to all but those who share information about one another's knowledge, beliefs, intentions, and attitudes."[32] Symbolic representations, in other words, depend on a fund of shared recognitions and potential inference. For their intended impact to take hold in the reader's imagination, the author simply must, like Minnie Foster, be able to call upon a shared context with her audience; where she cannot, or dare not, she may revert to silence, to the imitation of male forms, or, like the narrator in "The Yellow Wallpaper," to total withdrawal and isolation into madness.

It may be objected, of course, that I have somewhat stretched my argument so as to conflate (or perhaps confuse?) *all* interpretative strategies with language processes, specifically reading. But in each instance, it is the survival of the *woman as text*—Gilman's narrator and Glaspell's Minnie Foster—that is at stake; and the competence of her reading audience alone determines the outcome. Thus, in my view, both stories intentionally function as highly specialized language acts (called "literature") which examine the difficulty inherent in deciphering other highly specialized realms of meaning—in this case, women's conceptual and symbolic worlds. And further, the intended emphasis in each is the inaccessibility of female meaning to male interpretation.[33] The fact that in recent years each story has increasingly found its way into easily available textbooks, and hence into the women's-studies and American literature classrooms, to be read and enjoyed by teachers and students of both sexes, happily suggests that their fictive premises are attributable not so much to necessity as to contingency.[34] Men can, after all, learn to apprehend the meanings encoded in texts by and about women—just as women have learned to become sensitive readers of Shakespeare and Milton, Hemingway and Mailer.[35] Both stories function, in effect, as a prod to that very process by alerting the reader to the fundamental problem of "reading" correctly within cohabiting but differently structured conceptual worlds.

Sandra M. Gilbert and Susan Gubar have tried to correct the omission of women writers from Bloom's male-centered literary history in *The Madwoman in the Attic: The Woman Writer and the Nineteenth-Century Literary Imagination* (New Haven, Conn.: Yale University Press, 1979).

[12]Bloom, *Kabbalah and Criticism,* pp. 107–8.

[13]Bloom, *Map of Misreading,* p. 32.

[14]Ibid., pp. 33–34.

[15]Virginia Woolf, *A Room of One's Own* (1928; reprint ed., Baltimore: Penguin Books, 1972), pp. 9–10, 25–26.

[16]Nina Baym, *Woman's Fiction: A Guide to Novels By and About Women in America, 1820–1870* (Ithaca, N.Y.: Cornell University Press, 1978), p. 32.

[17]See ibid., pp. 32–33.

[18]Ibid., p. 178.

[19]I paraphrase rather freely here from some of Baym's acutely perceptive and highly suggestive remarks, ibid., p. 14.

[20]The problem of audience is complicated by the fact that in nineteenth-century America distinct classes of so-called highbrow and lowbrow readers were emerging, cutting across sex and class lines; and, for each sex, distinctly separate "serious" and "popular" reading materials were also being marketed. Full discussion, however, is beyond the scope of this essay. In its stead, I direct the reader to Henry Nash Smith's clear and concise summation in the introductory chapter to his *Democracy and the Novel: Popular Resistance to Classic American Writers* (New York: Oxford University Press, 1978), pp. 1–15.

[21]Baym, *Woman's Fiction,* p. 178.

[22]From "Books of the Day," *Chicago Times-Herald,* June 1, 1899, p. 9; excerpted in Kate Chopin, *The Awakening,* ed. Margaret Culley (New York: W. W. Norton, 1976), p. 149.

[23]Charlotte Perkins Gilman, *The Yellow Wallpaper,* Afterword by Elaine R. Hedges (Old Westbury, N.Y.: Feminist Press 1973), pp. 12, 11. Page references to this edition will henceforth be cited parenthetically in the text, with references to Hedges's excellent Afterword preceded by her name.

[24]Jean Ricardou, "Composition Discomposed," trans. Erica Freiberg, *Critical Inquiry* 3 (Fall 1976): 90.

[25]The possible exception here is Harriet Beecher Stowe's *Uncle Tom's Cabin; or, Life Among the Lowly* (1852).

[26]If, to some of the separatist advocates in our current wave of New Feminism, this sounds like a wholly acceptable, even happy circumstance, we must nonetheless understand that, for earlier generations of women artists, acceptance within male precincts conferred the mutually understood marks of success and, in some quarters, vitally needed access to publishing houses, serious critical attention, and even financial independence. That this was *not* the case for the writers of domestic fictions around the middle of the nineteenth century was a fortunate but anomalous circumstance. Insofar as our artist-mothers were separatist, therefore, it was the result of impinging cultural contexts and not (often) of their own choosing.

[27]Bloom, *Kabbalah and Criticism,* p. 96.

[28]Wolfgang Iser, *The Implied Reader: Patterns of Communication in Prose Fiction from Bunyan to Beckett* (Baltimore: Johns Hopkins University Press, 1974), p. 293.

[29]Nelly Furman, "The Study of Women and Language: Comment on Vol. 3, No. 3," *Signs* 4 (Fall 1978): 184.

[30]First published in *Every Week,* March 15, 1917, the story was then collected in *Best Short Stories of 1917,* ed. Edward O'Brien (London, 1917). My source for the text is Mary Anne Ferguson's *Images of Women in Literature* (Boston: Houghton Mifflin, 1973), pp. 370–85.

[31]I here paraphrase Clifford Geertz, *The Interpretation of Cultures* (New York: Basic Books, 1973), p. 13, and specifically direct the reader to the parable from Wittgenstein quoted on that same page.

[32]Ted Cohen, "Metaphor and the Cultivation of Intimacy," *Critical Inquiry* 5 (Fall 1978): 78.

[33]It is significant, I think, that the stories do not suggest any difficulty for the women in apprehending the men's meanings. On the one hand this simply is not relevant to either plot; and on the other, since in each narrative the men clearly control the public realms of discourse, it would of course have been incumbent upon the women to learn to understand them. Though masters need not learn the language of their slaves, the reverse is never the case: for survival's sake, oppressed or subdominant groups always study the nuances of meaning and gesture in those who control them.

[34]For example, Gilman's "The Yellow Wallpaper" may be found, in addition to the Feminist Press reprinting previously cited, in *The Oven Birds: American Women on Womanhood, 1820–1920,* ed. Gail Parker (Garden City, N.Y.: Doubleday, 1972), pp. 317–34; and Glaspell's "A Jury of Her Peers" is reprinted in *American Voices, American Women,* ed. Lee R. Edwards and Arlyn Diamond (New York: Avon Books, 1973), pp. 359–81.

[35]That women may have paid a high psychological and emotional price for their ability to read men's texts is beyond the scope of this essay, but I enthusiastically direct the reader to Judith Fetterley's provocative study of the problem in *The Resisting Reader: A Feminist Approach to American Fiction* (Bloomington: University of Indiana Press, 1978).

[36]Bloom, *Kabbalah and Criticism,* p. 96.

[37]Ibid., p. 100.

[38]Bloom, *Map of Misreading,* pp. 33–34.

[39]Ibid., p. 4.

[40]Adrienne Rich, "When We Dead Awaken: Writing as Re-Vision," *College English* 34 (October 1972): 18; reprinted in *Adrienne Rich's Poetry,* ed. Barbara Charlesworth Gelpi and Albert Gelpi (New York: W. W. Norton, 1975), p. 90.

[41]Bloom, *Map of Misreading,* p. 36.

[42]Norman Mailer, "Evaluations—Quick and Expensive Comments on the Talent in the Room," collected in his *Advertisements for Myself* (New York: Berkley, 1966), pp. 434–35.

[43]Bloom, *Map of Misreading,* p. 36. What precisely Bloom intends by the phrase is nowhere made clear; for the purposes of this essay, I have assumed that he is referring to the recently increased publication of new titles by women writers.

Melodramas of Beset Manhood

How Theories of American Fiction Exclude Women Authors

Nina Baym

This paper is about American literary criticism rather than American literature. It proceeds from the assumption that we never read American literature directly or freely, but always through the perspective allowed by theories. Theories account for the inclusion and exclusion of texts in anthologies, and theories account for the way we read them. My concern is with the fact that the theories controlling our reading of American literature have led to the exclusion of women authors from the canon.

Let me use my own practice as a case in point. In 1977 there was published a collection of essays on images of women in major British and American literature, to which I contributed.[1] The American field was divided chronologically among six critics, with four essays covering literature written prior to World War II. Taking seriously the charge that we were to focus only on the major figures, the four of us—working quite independently of each other—selected altogether only four women writers. Three of these were from the earliest period, a period which predates the novel: the poet Anne Bradstreet and the two diarists Mary Rowlandson and Sarah Kemble Knight. The fourth was Emily Dickinson. For the period between 1865 and 1940 no women were cited at all. The message that we—who were taking women as our subject—conveyed was clear: there have been almost no major women writers in America; the major novelists have all been men.

Now, when we wrote our essays we were not undertaking to reread all American literature and make our own decisions as to who the major authors were. That is the point: we accepted the going canon of major authors. As late as 1977, that canon did not include any women novelists. Yet, the critic who goes beyond what is accepted and tries to look at the totality of literary production in America quickly discovers that women authors have been active since the earliest days of settlement. Commercially and numerically they have probably dominated American literature since the middle of the nineteenth century. As long ago as 1854, Nathaniel Hawthorne complained to his publisher about the "damned mob of scribbling women" whose writings—he fondly imagined—were diverting the public from his own.

Names and figures help make this dominance clear. In the years between 1774 and 1799—from the calling of the First Continental Congress to the close of the eighteenth century—a total of thirty-eight original works of fiction were published in this country.[2] Nine of these, appearing pseudonymously or anonymously, have not yet been attributed to any author. The remaining twenty-nine are the work of eighteen individuals, of whom four are women. One of these women, Susannah Rowson, wrote six of them, or more than a fifth of the total. Her most popular work, *Charlotte* (also known as *Charlotte Temple*), was printed three times in the decade it was published, nineteen times between 1800 and 1810, and eighty times by the middle of the nineteenth century. A novel by a second of the four women, Hannah Foster, was called *The Coquette* and had thirty editions by mid-nineteenth century. *Uncle Tom's Cabin,* by a woman, is probably the all-time biggest seller in American history. A woman, Mrs. E.D.E.N. Southworth, was probably the most widely read novelist in the nineteenth century. How is it possible for a critic or historian of American literature to leave these books, and these authors, out of the picture?

I see three partial explanations for the critical invisibility of the many active women authors in America. The first is simple bias. The critic does not like the idea of women as writers, does not believe that women can be writers, and hence does not see them even when they are right before his eyes. His theory or his standards may well be nonsexist but his practice is not. Certainly, an *a priori* resistance to recognizing women authors as serious writers has functioned powerfully in the mind-set of a number of influential critics. One can amusingly demonstrate the inconsistencies between standard and practice in such critics, show how their minds slip out of gear when they are confronted with a woman author. But this is only a partial explanation.

A second possibility is that, in fact, women have not written the kind of work that we call "excellent," for reasons that are connected with their gender although separable from it. This is a serious possibility. For example, suppose we required a dense texture of classical allusion in all works that we called excellent. Then, the restriction of a formal classical education to men would have the effect of restricting authorship of excellent literature to men. Women would not have written excellent literature because social conditions hindered them. The reason, though gender-connected, would not be gender per se.

The point here is that the notion of the artist, or of excellence, has efficacy in a given time and reflects social realities. The idea of "good" literature is not only a personal preference, it is also a cultural preference. We can all think of species of women's literature that do not aim in any way to achieve literary excellence as society defines it: for example, the "Harlequin Romances." Until recently, only a tiny proportion of literary women aspired to artistry and literary excellence in the terms defined by their own culture. There tended to be a sort of immediacy in the ambitions of literary women leading them to professionalism rather than artistry, by choice as well as by social pressure and opportunity. The gender-related restrictions were really operative, and the responsible critic cannot ignore them. But again, these restrictions are only partly explanatory.

There are, finally, I believe, gender-related restrictions that do not arise out of cultural realities contemporary with the writing woman, but out of later critical theories. These theories may follow naturally from cultural realities pertinent to their own time, but they impose their concerns anachronistically, after the fact, on an earlier period. If one accepts current theories of American literature, one accepts as a consequence—perhaps not deliberately but nevertheless inevitably—a literature that is essentially male. This is the partial explanation that I shall now develop.

Let us begin where the earliest theories of American literature begin, with the hypothesis that American literature is to be judged less by its form than by its content. Traditionally, one ascertains literary excellence by comparing a writer's work with standards of performance that have been established by earlier authors, where formal mastery and innovation are paramount. But from its historical beginnings, American literary criticism has assumed that literature produced in this nation would have to be groundbreaking, equal to the challenge of the new nation, and completely original. Therefore, it could not be judged by referring it back to earlier achievements. The earliest American literary critics began to talk about the "most American" work rather than the "best" work because they knew no way to find out the best other than by comparing American with British writing. Such a criticism struck them as both unfair and unpatriotic. We had thrown off the political shackles of England; it would not do for us to be servile in our literature. Until a tradition of American literature developed its own inherent forms, the early critic looked for a standard of Americanness rather than a standard of excellence. Inevitably, perhaps, it came to seem that the quality of "Americanness," whatever it might be, *constituted* literary excellence for American authors.

Beginning as a nationalistic enterprise, American literary criticism and theory has retained a nationalist orientation to this day.

Of course, the idea of Americanness is even more vulnerable to subjectivity than the idea of the best. When they speak of "most American," critics seldom mean the statistically most representative or most typical, the most read or the most sold. They have some qualitative essence in mind, and frequently their work develops as an explanation of this idea of "American" rather than a description and evaluation of selected authors. The predictable recurrence of the term "America" or "American" in works of literary criticism treating a dozen or fewer authors indicates that the critic has chosen his authors on the basis of their conformity to his idea of what is truly American. For examples: *American Renaissance, The Romance in America, Symbolism and American Literature, Form and Fable in American Fiction, The American Adam, The American Novel and Its Tradition, The Place of Style in American Literature* (a subtitle), *The Poetics of American Fiction* (another subtitle). But an idea of what is American is no more than an idea, needing demonstration. The critic all too frequently ends up using his chosen authors as demonstrations of Americanness, arguing through them to his definition.

So Marius Bewley explains in *The Eccentric Design* that "for the American artist there was no social surface responsive to his touch. The scene was crude, even beyond successful satire," but later, in a concluding chapter titled "The Americanness of the American Novel," he agrees that "this 'tradition' as I have set it up here has no room for the so-called realists and naturalists."[3] F. O. Matthiessen, whose *American Renaissance* enshrines five authors, explains that "the one common denominator of my five writers, uniting even Hawthorne and Whitman, was their devotion to the possibilities of democracy."[4] The jointly written *Literary History of the United States* proclaims in its "address to the reader" that American literary history "will be a history of the books of the great and the near-great writers in a literature which is most revealing when studied as a by-product of American experience."[5] And Joel Porte announces confidently in *The Romance in America* that "students of American literature . . . have provided a solid theoretical basis for establishing that the rise and growth of fiction in this country is dominated by our authors' conscious adherence to a tradition of non-realistic romance sharply at variance with the broadly novelistic mainstream of English writing. When there has been disagreement among recent critics as to the contours of American fiction, it has usually disputed, not the existence per se of a romance tradition, but rather the question of which authors, themes, and stylistic strategies *deserve* to be placed with certainty at the heart of that tradition" (emphasis added).[6]

Before he is through, the critic has had to insist that some works in America are much more American than others, and he is as busy excluding certain writers as "un-American" as he is including others. Such a proceeding in the political arena would be extremely suspect, but in criticism it has been the method of choice. Its final result goes far beyond the conclusion that only a handful of American works are very good. *That* statement is one we could agree with, since very good work is rare in any field. But it is odd indeed to argue that only a handful of American works are really American.[7]

Despite the theoretical room for an infinite number of definitions of Americanness, critics have generally agreed on it—although the shifting canon suggests that agreement may be a matter of fad rather than fixed objective qualities.[8] First, America as a nation must be the ultimate subject of the work. The author must be writing about aspects of experience and character that are American only, setting Americans off from other people and the country from other nations. The author must be writing his story specifically to display these aspects, to meditate on them, and to derive from them some generalizations and conclusions about "the" American experience. To Matthiessen the topic is the possibilities of democracy; Sacvan Bercovitch (in *The Puritan Origins of the American Self)* finds it in American identity. Such content excludes, at one extreme, stories about universals, aspects of experience common to people in a variety of times and places—mutability, mortality, love, childhood, family, betrayal, loss. Innocence versus experience is an admissable theme *only* if innocence is the essence of the American character, for example.

But at the other extreme, the call for an overview of America means that detailed, circumstantial portrayals of some aspect of American life are also, peculiarly, inappropriate: stories of wealthy New Yorkers, Yugoslavian immigrants, Southern rustics. Jay B. Hubbell rather ingratiatingly admits as much when he writes, "in both my teaching and my research I had a special interest in literature as a reflection of American life and thought. This circumstance may explain in part why I found it difficult to appreciate the merits of the expatriates and why I was slow in doing justice to some of the New Critics. I was repelled by the sordid subject matter found in some of the novels written by Dreiser, Dos Passos, Faulkner, and some others."[9] Richard Poirier writes that "the books which in my view constitute a distinctive American tradition . . . resist within their pages forces of environment that otherwise dominate the world," and he distinguishes this kind from "the fiction of Mrs. Wharton, Dreiser, or Howells."[10] The *Literary History of the United States* explains that "historically, [Edith Wharton] is likely to survive as the memorialist of a dying aristocracy."[11] And so on. These exclusions abound in all the works which form the stable core of American literary criticism at this time.

Along with Matthiessen, the most influential exponent of this exclusive Americanness is Lionel Trilling, and his work has particular applicability because it concentrates on the novel form. Here is a famous passage from his

1940 essay, "Reality in America," in which Trilling is criticizing Vernon Parrington's selection of authors in *Main Currents in American Thought:*

> A culture is not a flow, nor even a confluence: the form of its existence is struggle—or at least debate—it is nothing if not a dialectic. And in any culture there are likely to be certain artists who contain a large part of the dialectic within themselves, their meaning and power lying in their contradictions: they contain within themselves, it may be said, the very essence of the culture. To throw out Poe because he cannot be conveniently fitted into a theory of American culture . . . to find his gloom to be merely personal and eccentric . . . as Hawthorne's was . . . to judge Melville's response to American life to be less noble than that of Bryant or of Greeley, to speak of Henry James as an escapist . . . this is not merely to be mistaken in aesthetic judgment. Rather it is to examine without attention and from the point of view of a limited and essentially arrogant conception of reality the documents which are in some respects the most suggestive testimony to what America was and is, and of course to get no answer from them.[12]

Trilling's immediate purpose is to exclude Greeley and Bryant from the list of major authors and to include Poe, Melville, Hawthorne, and James. We probably share Trilling's aesthetic judgment. But note that he does not base his judgment on aesthetic grounds; indeed, he dismisses aesthetic judgment with the word "merely." He argues that Parrington has picked the wrong artists because he doesn't understand the culture. Culture is his real concern.

But what makes Trilling's notion of culture more valid than Parrington's? Trilling really has no argument; he resorts to such value-laden rhetoric as "a limited and essentially arrogant conception of reality" precisely because he cannot objectively establish his version of culture over Parrington's. For the moment, there are two significant conclusions to draw from this quotation. First, the disagreement is over the nature of our culture. Second, there is no disagreement over the value of literature—it is valued as a set of "documents" which provide "suggestive testimony to what America was and is."

One might think that an approach like this which is subjective, circular, and in some sense nonliterary or even antiliterary would not have had much effect. But clearly Trilling was simply carrying on a longstanding tradition of searching for cultural essence, and his essays gave the search a decided and influential direction toward the notion of cultural essence as some sort of tension. Trilling succeeded in getting rid of Bryant and Greeley, and his choice of authors is still dominant. They all turn out—and not by accident—to be white, middle-class, male, of Anglo-Saxon derivation or at least from an ancestry which had settled in this country before the big waves of immigration which began around the middle of the nineteenth century. In every case, however, the decision made by these men to become professional authors pushed them slightly to one side of the group to which they belonged. This slight alienation permitted them to belong, and yet not to belong, to the so-called "mainstream." These two aspects of their situation—their membership in the dominant middle-class white Anglo-Saxon group, and their modest alienation from it—defined their boundaries, enabling them to "contain within themselves" the "contradictions" that, in Trilling's view, constitute the "very essence of the culture." I will call the literature they produced, which Trilling assesses so highly, a "consensus criticism of the consensus."

This idea plainly excludes many groups but it might not seem necessarily to exclude women. In fact, nineteenth-century women authors were overwhelmingly white, middle-class, and Anglo-Saxon in origin. Something more than what is overtly stated by Trilling (and others cited below) is added to exclude them. What critics have done is to assume, for reasons shortly to be expounded, that the women writers invariably represented the consensus, rather than the criticism of it; to assume that their gender made them part of the consensus in a way that prevented them from partaking in the criticism. The presence of these women and their works is acknowledged in literary theory and history as an impediment and obstacle, that which the essential American literature had to criticize as its chief task.

So, in his lively and influential book of 1960, *Love and Death in the American Novel,* Leslie Fiedler describes women authors as creators of the "flagrantly bad best-seller" against which "our best fictionists"—all male—have had to struggle for "their integrity and their livelihoods."[13] And, in a 1978 reader's introduction to an edition of Charles Brockden Brown's *Wieland,* Sydney J. Krause and S. W. Reid write as follows:

> What it meant for Brown personally, and belles lettres in America historically, that he should have decided to write professionally is a story unto itself. Americans simply had no great appetite for serious literature in the early decades of the Republic—certainly nothing of the sort with which they devoured . . . the ubiquitous melodramas of beset womanhood, "tales of truth," like Susanna Rowson's *Charlotte Temple* and Hannah Foster's *The Coquette.*[14]

There you see what has happened to the woman writer. She has entered literary history as the enemy. The phrase "tales of truth" is put in quotes by the critics, as though to cast doubt on the very notion that a "melodrama of beset womanhood" could be either true or important. At the same time, ironically, they are proposing for our serious consideration, as a candidate for intellectually engaging literature, a highly melodramatic novel with an improbable plot, inconsistent characterizations, and excesses of style that have posed tremendous problems for all students of Charles Brockden Brown. But by this strategy it becomes possible to begin major American fiction historically with male rather than female authors. The certainty here that stories about women could not contain the essence of American culture means that the matter of American experience is inherently male. And this makes it highly unlikely that American women would write fiction encompassing such experience. I would suggest that the theoretical model of a story which may become the vehicle of cultural essence is: "a melodrama of beset manhood." This melodrama is presented in a fiction which, as we will later see, can be taken as representative of the author's literary experience, his struggle for integrity and livelihood against flagrantly bad best-sellers written by women. Personally beset in a way that epitomizes the tensions of our culture, the male author produces his melodramatic testimony to our culture's essence—so the theory goes.

Remember that the search for cultural essence demands a relatively uncircumstantial kind of fiction, one which concentrates on national universals (if I may be pardoned the paradox). This search has identified a sort of nonrealistic narrative, a romance, a story free to catch an essential, idealized American character, to intensify his essence and convey his experience in a way that ignores details of an actual social milieu. This nonrealistic or antisocial aspect of American fiction is noted—as a fault—by Trilling in a 1947 essay, "Manners, Morals, and the Novel." Curiously, Trilling here attacks the same group of writers he had rescued from Parrington in "Reality in America." But, never doubting that his selection represents "the" American authors, he goes ahead with the task that really interests him—criticizing the culture through its representative authors:

> The novel in America diverges from its classic [i.e., British] intention which . . . is the investigation of the problem of reality beginning in the social field. The fact is that American writers of genius have not turned their minds to society. Poe and Melville were quite apart from it; the reality they sought was only tangential to society. Hawthorne was acute when he insisted that he did not write novels but romances—he thus expressed his awareness of the lack of social texture in his work. . . . In America in the nineteenth century, Henry James was alone in knowing that to scale the moral

> and aesthetic heights in the novel one had to use the ladder of social observation.[15]

Within a few years after publication of Trilling's essay, a group of Americanists took its rather disapproving description of American novelists and found in this nonrealism or romanticism the essentially American quality they had been seeking. The idea of essential Americanness then developed in such influential works of criticism as *Virgin Land* by Henry Nash Smith (1950), *Symbolism and American Literature* by Charles Feidelson (1953), *The American Adam* by R. W. B. Lewis (1955), *The American Novel and its Tradition* by Richard Chase (1957), and *Form and Fable in American Fiction* by Daniel G. Hoffman (1961). These works, and others like them, were of sufficiently high critical quality, and sufficiently like each other, to compel assent to the picture of American literature that they presented. They used sophisticated New Critical close-reading techniques to identify a myth of America which had nothing to do with the classical fictionist's task of chronicling probable people in recognizable social situations.

The myth narrates a confrontation of the American individual, the pure American self divorced from specific social circumstances, with the promise offered by the idea of America. This promise is the deeply romantic one that in this new land, untrammeled by history and social accident, a person will be able to achieve complete self-definition. Behind this promise is the assurance that individuals come before society, that they exist in some meaningful sense prior to, and apart from, societies in which they happen to find themselves. The myth also holds that, as something artificial and secondary to human nature, society exerts an unmitigatedly destructive pressure on individuality. To depict it at any length would be a waste of artistic time; and there is only one way to relate it to the individual—as an adversary.

One may believe all this and yet look in vain for a way to tell a believable story that could free the protagonist from society or offer the promise of such freedom, because nowhere on earth do individuals live apart from social groups. But in America, given the original reality of large tracts of wilderness, the idea seems less a fantasy, more possible in reality or at least more believable in literary treatment. Thus it is that the essential quality of America comes to reside in its unsettled wilderness and the opportunities that such a wilderness offers to the individual as the medium on which he may inscribe, unhindered, his own destiny and his own nature.

As the nineteenth century wore on, and settlements spread across the wilderness, the struggle of the individual against society became more and more central to the myth; where, let's say, Thoreau could leave in chapter 1 of *Walden,* Huckleberry Finn has still not made his break by the end of chapter 42 (the conclusion) of the book that bears his name. Yet one finds a struggle against society as early as the earliest Leatherstocking tale (*The Pioneers,* 1823). In a sense, this supposed promise of America has always been known to be delusory. Certainly by the twentieth century the myth has been transmuted into an avowedly hopeless quest for unencumbered space *(On the Road),* or the evocation of flight for its own sake *(Rabbit, Run* and *Henderson the Rain King),* or as pathetic acknowledgment of loss—for example, the close of *The Great Gatsby* where the narrator Nick Carraway summons up "the old island here that flowered once for Dutch sailors' eyes—a fresh, green breast of the new world . . . the last and greatest of all human dreams" where man is "face to face for the last time in history with something commensurate to his capacity for wonder."

We are all very familiar with this myth of America in its various fashionings, and owing to the selective vision that has presented this myth to us as the whole story, many of us are unaware of how much besides it has been created by literary Americans. Keeping our eyes on this myth, we need to ask whether anything about it puts it outside women's reach. In one sense, and on one level, the answer is no. The subject of this myth is supposed to stand for human nature, and if men and women share a common human nature, then all can respond to its values, its promises, and its frustrations. And in fact, as a teacher I find women students responsive to the myth insofar as its protagonist is concerned. It is true, of course, that in order to represent some kind of believable flight into the wilderness, one must select a protagonist with a certain believable mobility, and mobility has until recently been a male prerogative in our society. Nevertheless, relatively few men are actually mobile to the extent demanded by the story, and hence the story is really not much more vicarious, in this regard, for women than for men. The problem is thus not to be located in the protagonist or his gender per se; the problem is with the other participants in his story—the entrammeling society and the promising landscape. For both of these are depicted in unmistakably feminine terms, and this gives a sexual character to the protagonist's story which does, indeed, limit its applicability to women. And this sexual definition has melodramatic, misogynist implications.

In these stories, the encroaching, constricting, destroying society is represented with particular urgency in the figure of one or more women. There are several possible reasons why this might be so. It seems to be a fact of life that we all—women and men alike—experience social conventions and responsibilities and obligations first in the persons of women, since women are entrusted by society with the task of rearing young children. Not until he reaches mid-adolescence does the male connect up with other males whose primary task is socialization; but at about this time—if he is heterosexual—

his lovers and spouses become the agents of a permanent socialization and domestication. Thus, although women are not the source of social power, they are experienced as such. And although not all women are engaged in socializing the young, the young do not encounter women who are not. So from the point of view of the young man, the only kind of women who exist are entrappers and domesticators.

For heterosexual man, these socializing women are also the locus of powerful attraction. First, because everybody has social and conventional instincts: second, because his deepest emotional attachments are to women. This attraction gives urgency and depth to the protagonist's rejection of society. To do it, he must project onto the woman those attractions that he feels, and cast her in the melodramatic role of temptress, antagonist, obstacle —a character whose mission in life seems to be to ensnare him and deflect him from life's important purposes of self-discovery and self-assertion. (A Puritan would have said: from communion with Divinity.) As Richard Chase writes in *The American Novel and Its Tradition,* "The myth requires celibacy." It is partly against his own sexual urges that the male must struggle, and so he perceives the socializing and domesticating woman as a doubly powerful threat; for this reason, Chase goes on to state, neither Cooper nor "any other American novelist until the age of James and Edith Wharton" could imagine "a fully developed woman of sexual age."[16] Yet in making this statement, Chase is talking about his myth rather than Cooper's. (One should add that, for a homosexual male, the demands of society that he link himself for life to a woman make for a particularly misogynist version of this aspect of the American myth, for the hero is propelled not by a rejected attraction but by true revulsion.) Both heterosexual and homosexual versions of the myth cooperate with the hero's perceptions and validate the notion of woman as threat.

Such a portrayal of women is likely to be uncongenial, if not basically incomprehensible, to a woman. It is not likely that women will write books in which women play this part; and it is by no means the case that most novels by American men reproduce such a scheme. Even major male authors prominent in the canon have other ways of depicting women: for example, Cooper's *Pathfinder* and *The Pioneers,* Hemingway's *For Whom the Bell Tolls,* Fitzgerald's *The Beautiful and The Damned.* The novels of Henry James and William Dean Howells pose a continual challenge to the masculinist bias of American critical theory. And in one work—*The Scarlet Letter*—a "fully developed woman of sexual age" who is the novel's protagonist has been admitted into the canon, but only by virtue of strenuous critical revisions of the text that remove Hester Prynne from the center of the novel and make her subordinate to Arthur Dimmesdale.

So Leslie Fiedler, in *Love and Death in the American Novel,* writes this of *The Scarlet Letter:*

> It is certainly true, in terms of the plot, that Chillingworth drives the minister toward confession and penance, while Hester would have lured him to evasion and flight. But this means, for all of Hawthorne's equivocations, that the eternal feminine does not draw us on toward grace, rather that the woman promises only madness and damnation. . . . [Hester] is the female temptress of Puritan mythology, but also, though sullied, the secular madonna of sentimental Protestantism.[17]

In the rhetorical "us" Fiedler presumes that all readers are men, that the novel is an act of communication among and about males. His characterization of Hester as one or another myth or image makes it impossible for the novel to be in any way about Hester as a human being. Giving the novel so highly specific a gender reference, Fiedler makes it inaccessible to women and limits its reference to men in comparison to the issues that Hawthorne was treating in the story. Not the least of these issues was, precisely, the human reference of a woman's tale.

Amusingly, then, since he has produced this warped reading, Fiedler goes on to condemn the novel for its sexual immaturity. *The Scarlet Letter* is integrated into Fiedler's general exposure of the inadequacies of the American male—inadequacies which, as his treatment of Hester shows, he holds women responsible for. The melodrama here is not Hawthorne's but Fiedler's—the American critic's melodrama of beset manhood. Of course, women authors as major writers are notably and inevitably absent from Fiedler's chronicle.

In fact, many books by women—including such major authors as Edith Wharton, Ellen Glasgow, and Willa Cather—project a version of the particular myth we are speaking of but cast the main character as a woman. When a woman takes the central role, it follows naturally that the socializer and domesticator will be a man. This is the situation in *The Scarlet Letter.* Hester is beset by the male reigning oligarchy and by Dimmesdale, who passively tempts her and is responsible for fathering her child. Thereafter, Hester (as the myth requires) elects celibacy, as do many heroines in versions of this myth by women: Thea in Cather's *The Song of the Lark,* Dorinda in Glasgow's *Barren Ground,* Anna Leath in Wharton's *The Reef.* But what is written in the criticism about these celibate women? They are said to be untrue to the imperatives of their gender, which require marriage, childbearing, domesticity. Instead of being read as a woman's version of the myth, such novels are read as stories of the frustration of female nature. Stories of female frustration are not perceived as commenting on, or containing, the essence of our culture, and so we do not find them in the canon.

So the role of entrapper and impediment in the melodrama of beset manhood is reserved for women. Also, the role of the beckoning wilderness, the attractive landscape, is given a deeply feminine quality. Landscape is deeply imbued with female qualities, as society is; but where society is menacing and destructive, landscape is compliant and supportive. It has the attributes simultaneously of a virginal bride and a nonthreatening mother; its female qualities are articulated with respect to a male angle of vision: what can nature do for me, asks the hero, what can it give me?

Of course, nature has been feminine and maternal from time immemorial, and Henry Nash Smith's *Virgin Land* picks up a timeless archetype in its title. The basic nature of the image leads one to forget about its potential for imbuing with sexual meanings any story in which it is used, and the gender implications of a female landscape have only recently begun to be studied. Recently, Annette Kolodny has studied the traditional canon from this approach.[18] She theorizes that the hero, fleeing a society that has been imagined as feminine, then imposes on nature some ideas of women which, no longer subject to the correcting influence of real-life experience, become more and more fantastic. The fantasies are infantile, concerned with power, mastery, and total gratification: the all-nurturing mother, the all-passive bride. Whether one accepts all the Freudian or Jungian implications of her argument, one cannot deny the way in which heroes of American myth turn to nature as sweetheart and nurture, anticipating the satisfaction of all desires through her and including among these the desires for mastery and power. A familiar passage that captures these ideas is one already quoted: Carraway's evocation of the "fresh green breast" of the New World. The fresh greenness is the virginity that offers itself to the sailors, but the breast promises maternal solace and delight. *The Great Gatsby* contains our two images of women: while Carraway evokes the impossible dream of a maternal landscape, he blames a nonmaternal woman, the socialite Daisy, for her failure to satisfy Gatsby's desires. The true adversary, of course, is Tom Buchanan, but he is hidden, as it were, behind Daisy's skirts.

I have said that women are not likely to cast themselves as antagonists in a man's story; they are even less likely, I suggest, to cast themselves as virgin land. The lack of fit between their own experience and the fictional role assigned to them is even greater in the second instance than in the first. If women portray themselves as brides or mothers it will not be in terms of the mythic landscape. If a woman puts a female construction on nature—as she certainly must from time to time, given the archetypal female resonance of the image—she is likely to write of it as more active, or to stress its destruction or violation. On the other hand, she might adjust the heroic myth to her own psyche by making nature out to be male—as, for example, Willa Cather seems to do in *O Pioneers!* But a violated landscape or a male nature does not fit the essential American pattern as critics have defined it, and hence these literary images occur in an obscurity that criticism cannot see. Thus, one has an almost classic example of the double bind. When the woman writer creates a story that conforms to the expected myth, it is not recognized for what it is because of a superfluous sexual specialization in the myth as it is entertained in the critics' minds. (Needless to say, many male novelists also entertain this version of the myth, and do not find the masculinist bias with which they imbue it to be superfluous. It is possible that some of these novelists, especially those who write in an era in which literary criticism is a powerful influence, have formed their ideas from their reading in criticism.) But if she does not conform to the myth, she is understood to be writing minor or trivial literature.

Two remaining points can be treated much more briefly. The description of the artist and of the act of writing which emerges when the critic uses the basic American story as his starting point contains many attributes of the basic story itself. This description raises the exclusion of women to a more abstract, theoretical—and perhaps more pernicious—level. Fundamentally, the idea is that the artist writing a story of this essential American kind is engaging in a task very much like the one performed by his mythic hero. In effect, the artist writing his narrative is imitating the mythic encounter of hero and possibility in the safe confines of his study; or, reversing the temporal order, one might see that mythic encounter of hero and possibility as a projection of the artist's situation.

Although this idea is greatly in vogue at the moment, it has a history. Here, for example, is Richard Chase representing the activity of writing in metaphors of discovery and exploration, as though the writer were a hero in the landscape: "The American novel has usually seemed content to explore . . . the remarkable and in some ways unexampled territories of life in the New World and to reflect its anomalies and dilemmas. It has . . . wanted . . . to discover a new place and a new state of mind."[19] Richard Poirier takes the idea further:

> The most interesting American books are an image of the creation of America itself. . . . They carry the metaphoric burden of a great dream of freedom—of the expansion of national consciousness into the vast spaces of a continent and the absorption of those spaces into ourselves. . . . The classic American writers try through style temporarily to free the hero (and the reader) from systems, to free them from

> the pressures of time, biology, economics, and from the social forces which are ultimately the undoing of American heroes and quite often of their creators. . . . The strangeness of American fiction has . . . to do . . . with the environment [the novelist] tries to create for his hero, usually his surrogate.[20]

The implicit union of creator and protagonist is made specific and overt at the end of Poirier's passage here. The ideas of Poirier and Chase, and others like them, are summed up in an anthology called *Theories of American Literature,* edited by Donald M. Kartiganer and Malcolm A. Griffith. The editors write, "It is as if with each new work our writers feel they must invent again the complete world of a literary form." (Yet, the true subject is not what the writers feel, but what the critics think they feel.) "Such a condition of nearly absolute freedom to create has appeared to our authors both as possibility and liability, an utter openness suggesting limitless opportunity for the imagination, or an enormous vacancy in which they create from nothing. For some it has meant an opportunity to play Adam, to assume the role of an original namer of experience.[21] One can see in this passage the transference of the American myth from the Adamic hero *in* the story to the Adamic creator *of* the story, and the reinterpretation of the American myth as a metaphor for the American artist's situation.

This myth of artistic creation, assimilating the act of writing novels to the Adamic myth, imposes on artistic creation all the gender-based restrictions that we have already examined in that myth. The key to identifying an "Adamic writer" is the formal appearance, or, more precisely, the *informal* appearance, of his novel. The unconventionality is interpreted as a direct representation of the open-ended experience of exploring and taming the wilderness, as well as a rejection of "society" as it is incorporated in conventional literary forms. There is no place for a woman author in this scheme. Her roles in the drama of creation are those allotted to her in a male melodrama: either she is to be silent, like nature, or she is the creator of conventional works, the spokesperson of society. What she might do as an innovator in her own right is not to be perceived.

In recent years, some refinements of critical theory coming from the Yale and Johns Hopkins and Columbia schools have added a new variant to the idea of creation as a male province. I quote from a 1979 book entitled *Home as Found* by Eric Sundquist. The author takes the idea that in writing a novel the artist is really writing a narrative about himself and proposes this addition:

> Writing a narrative about oneself may represent an extremity of Oedipal usurpation or identification, a bizarre act of

> self fathering. . . . American authors have been particularly obsessed with *fathering* a tradition of their own, with becoming their "own sires." . . . The struggle . . . is central to the crisis of representation, and hence of style, that allows American authors to find in their own fantasies those of a nation and to make of those fantasies a compelling and instructive literature.[22]

These remarks derive clearly from the work of such critics as Harold Bloom, as any reader of recent critical theory will note. The point for our purpose is the facile translation of the verb "to author" into the verb "to father," with the profound gender restrictions of that translation unacknowledged. According to this formulation, insofar as the author writes about a character who is his surrogate—which, apparently, he always does—he is trying to become his own father.

We can scarcely deny that men think a good deal about, and are profoundly affected by, relations with their fathers. The theme of fathers and sons is perennial in world literature. Somewhat more spaciously, we recognize that intergenerational conflict, usually perceived from the point of view of the young, is a recurrent literary theme, especially in egalitarian cultures. Certainly, this idea involves the question of authority, and "authority" is a notion related to that of "the author." And there is some gender-specific significance involved since authority in most cultures that we know tends to be invested in adult males. But the theory has built from these useful and true observations to a restriction of literary creation to a sort of therapeutic act that can only be performed by men. If literature is the attempt to *father* oneself by the author, then every act of writing by a woman is both perverse and absurd. And, of course, it is bound to fail.

Since this particular theory of the act of writing is drawn from psychological assumptions that are not specific to American literature, it may be argued that there is no need to confine it to American authors. In fact, Harold Bloom's *Anxiety of Influence,* defining literature as a struggle between fathers and sons, or the struggle of sons to escape from their fathers, is about British literature. And so is Edward Said's book *Beginnings,* which chronicles the history of the nineteenth-century British novel as exemplification of what he calls "filiation." His discussion omits Jane Austen, George Eliot, all three Brontë sisters, Mrs. Gaskell, Mrs. Humphrey Ward—not a sign of a woman author is found in his treatment of Victorian fiction. The result is a revisionist approach to British fiction that recasts it in the accepted image of the American myth. Ironically, just at the time that feminist critics are discovering more and more important women, the critical theorists have seized upon a theory that allows the women less and less presence. This observation points up just how significantly the critic is engaged in the act of *creating* literature.

Ironically, then, one concludes that in pushing the theory of American fiction to this extreme, critics have "deconstructed" it by creating a tool with no particular American reference. In pursuit of the uniquely American, they have arrived at a place where Americanness has vanished into the depths of what is alleged to be the universal male psyche. The theory of American fiction has boiled down to the phrase in my title: a melodrama of beset manhood. What a reduction this is of the enormous variety of fiction written in this country, by both women and men! And, ironically, nothing could be further removed from Trilling's idea of the artist as embodiment of a culture. As in the working out of all theories, its weakest link has found it out and broken the chain.

NOTES

[1]Marlene Springer, ed., *What Manner of Woman: Essays on English and American Life and Literature* (New York: New York University Press, 1977).

[2]See Lyle H. Wright, *American Fiction: A Contribution Towards a Bibliography*, vol. 1, *1774–1850*, 2nd ed. (San Marino, Calif.: Huntington Library Press, 1969).

[3]Marius Bewley, *The Eccentric Design: Form in the Classic American Novel* (New York: Columbia University Press, 1963), pp. 15, 291.

[4]F. O. Matthiessen, *American Renaissance* (New York: Oxford University Press, 1941), p. ix.

[5]Robert E. Spiller et al., eds., *Literary History of the United States* (New York: Macmillan, 1959), p. xix.

[6]Joel Porte, *The Romance in America: Studies in Cooper, Poe, Hawthorne, Melville, and James* (Middletown, Conn.: Wesleyan University Press, 1969), p. ix.

[7]A good essay on this topic is William C. Spengemann's "What Is American Literature?" 22 *Centennial Review* (Spring 1978): 119–38.

[8]See Jay B. Hubbell, *Who Are the Major American Authors?* (Durham, N.C.: Duke University Press, 1972).

[9]Ibid., pp. 335–36.

[10]Richard Poirier, *A World Elsewhere: The Place of Style in American Literature* (New York: Oxford University Press, 1966), p. 5.

[11]Spiller et al., *Literary History of the United States*, p. 1211.

[12]Lionel Trilling, *The Liberal Imagination* (Garden City, N.Y.: Anchor Books, 1950), pp. 7–9.

[13]Leslie Fiedler, *Love and Death in the American Novel* (New York: Criterion Books, 1960), p. 93.

[14]Charles Brockden Brown, *Wieland*, ed. Sydney J. Krause and S. W. Reid (Kent, Ohio: Kent State University Press, 1978), p. xii.

[15]Trilling, *The Liberal Imagination*, p. 206.

[16]Richard Chase, *The American Novel and Its Tradition* (Garden City, N.Y.: Anchor Books, 1957), pp. 55, 64.

[17]Fiedler, *Love and Death in the American Novel*, p. 236.

[18]Annette Kolodny, *The Lay of the Land: Metaphor As Experience and History in American Life and Letters* (Chapel Hill: University of North Carolina Press, 1975).

[19]Chase, *American Novel,* p. 5.

[20]Poirier, *A World Elsewhere,* pp. 3, 5, 9.

[21]Donald M. Kartiganer and Malcolm A. Griffith, eds., *Theories of American Literature: The Critical Perspective* (New York: Macmillan, 1962), pp. 4–5.

[22]Eric J. Sundquist, *Home as Found: Authority and Genealogy in Nineteenth-Century American Literature* (Baltimore: Johns Hopkins University Press, 1979), pp. xviii–xix.

Sentimental Power

Uncle Tom's Cabin and the Politics of Literary History

Jane P. Tompkins

Once, during a difficult period of my life, I lived in the basement of a house on Forest Street in Hartford, Connecticut, which had belonged to Isabella Beecher Hooker—Harriet Beecher Stowe's half-sister. This woman at one time in her life had believed that the millennium was at hand and that she was destined to be the leader of a new matriarchy.[1] When I lived in that basement, however, I knew nothing of Stowe, or of the Beechers, or of the utopian visions of nineteenth-century American women. I made a reverential visit to the Mark Twain house a few blocks away, took photographs of his study, and completely ignored Stowe's own house—also open to the public—which stood across the lawn. Why should I go? Neither I nor anyone I knew regarded Stowe as a serious writer. At the time I was giving my first lecture course in the American Renaissance—concentrated exclusively on Hawthorne, Melville, Poe, Emerson, Thoreau, and Whitman—and although *Uncle Tom's Cabin* was written in exactly the same period, and although it is probably the most influential book ever written by an American, I would never have dreamed of including it on my reading list. To begin with, its very popularity would have militated against it; as everybody knew, the classics of American fiction were, with a few exceptions, all *succès d'estime.*

In 1969, when I lived on Forest Street, the women's movement was just getting under way. It was several years before Kate Chopin's *The Awakening* and Charlotte Perkins Gilman's "The Yellow Wallpaper" would make it onto college reading lists, sandwiched in between Theodore Dreiser and Frank Norris. These women, like some of their male counterparts, had been unpopular in their own time and owed their reputations to the discernment of latter-day critics. Because of their work, it is now respectable to read these writers, who, unlike Nathaniel Hawthorne, had to wait several generations for their champions to appear in the literary establishment. But despite the influence of the women's movement, and despite the explosion of work in nineteenth-century American social history, and despite the new historicism that is infiltrating literary studies, the women, like Harriet Beecher Stowe, whose names were household words in the nineteenth century—women such as Susan Warner, Sarah J. Hale, Augusta Evans, Elizabeth Stuart Phelps, her daughter Mary, who took the same name, and Frances Hodgson Burnett—these women remain excluded from the literary canon. And while it has recently become fashionable to study their works as examples of cultural deformation, even critics who have invested their professional careers in that study and who declare themselves feminists still refer to their novels as trash.[2]

My principal target of concern, however, is not feminists who have written on popular women novelists of the nineteenth century but the male-dominated scholarly tradition that controls both the canon of American literature (from which these novelists are excluded) and the critical perspective that interprets the canon for society. For the tradition of Perry Miller, F. O. Matthiessen, Harry Levin, Richard Chase, R. W. B. Lewis, Yvor Winters, and Henry Nash Smith has prevented even committed feminists from recognizing and asserting the *value* of a powerful and specifically female novelistic tradition. The very grounds on which sentimental fiction has been dismissed by its detractors, grounds that have come to seem universal standards of aesthetic judgment, were established in a struggle to supplant the tradition of evangelical piety and moral commitment these novelists represent. In reaction against their world view, and perhaps even more against their success, twentieth-century critics have taught generations of students to equate popularity with debasement, emotionality with ineffectiveness, religiosity with fakery, domesticity with triviality, and all of these, implicitly, with womanly inferiority.

In this view, sentimental novels written by women in the nineteenth century were responsible for a series of cultural evils whose effects still plague us: the degeneration of American religion from theological rigor to anti-intellectual consumerism, the rationalization of an unjust economic order, the propagation of the debased images of modern mass culture, and the encouragement of self-indulgence and narcissism in literature's most avid readers—women.[3] To the extent that they protested the evils of society, their protest is seen as duplicitous, the product and expression of the very values they pretended to condemn. Unwittingly or not, so the story goes, they were apologists for an oppressive social order. In contrast to male authors like Thoreau, Whitman, and Melville, who are celebrated as models of intellectual daring and honesty, these women are generally thought to have traded in false stereotypes, dishing out weak-minded pap to nourish the prejudices of an ill-educated and underemployed female readership. Self-deluded and unable to face the harsh facts of a competitive society, they are portrayed as manipulators of a gullible public who kept their readers imprisoned in a dream world of self-justifying clichés. Their fight against the evils of their society was a fixed match from the start.[4]

The thesis I will argue in this essay is diametrically opposed to these. It holds that the popular domestic novel of the nineteenth century represents a monumental effort to reorganize culture from the woman's point of view; that this body of work is remarkable for its intellectual complexity, ambition, and resourcefulness; and that, in certain cases, it offers a critique of American society far more devastating than any delivered by better-known critics such as Hawthorne and Melville. Finally, it suggests that the enormous popularity of these novels, which has been cause for suspicion bordering on disgust, is a reason for paying close attention to them. *Uncle Tom's Cabin* was, in almost any terms one can think of, the most important book of the century. It was the first American novel ever to sell over a million copies, and its impact is generally thought to have been incalculable. Expressive of and responsible for the values of its time, it also belongs to a genre, the sentimental novel, whose chief characteristic is that it is written by, for, and about women. In this respect, *Uncle Tom's Cabin* is not exceptional but representative. It is the *summa theologica* of nineteenth-century America's religion of domesticity, a brilliant redaction of the culture's favorite story about itself: the story of salvation through motherly love. Out of the ideological materials they had at their disposal, the sentimental novelists elaborated a myth that gave women the central position of power and authority in the culture; and of these efforts *Uncle Tom's Cabin* is the most dazzling exemplar.

I have used words like "monumental" and "dazzling" to describe Stowe's novel and the tradition of which it is a part because they have for too long been the casualties of a set of critical attitudes that equate intellectual merit with certain kinds of argumentative discourse and certain kinds of subject matter. A long tradition of academic parochialism has enforced this sort of discourse through a series of cultural contrasts: light "feminine" novels versus tough-minded intellectual treatises; domestic "chattiness" versus serious thinking; and summarily, the "damned mob of scribbling women" versus a few giant intellects, unappreciated and misunderstood in their time, struggling manfully against a flood of sentimental rubbish.[5]

The inability of twentieth-century critics either to appreciate the complexity and scope of a novel like Stowe's or to account for its enormous popular success stems from their assumptions about the nature and function of literature. In modernist thinking, literature is by definition a form of discourse that has no designs on the world. It does not attempt to change things, but merely to represent them, and it does so in a specifically literary language whose claim to value lies in its uniqueness. Consequently, works whose stated purpose is to influence the course of history, and which therefore employ a language that is not only not unique but common and accessible to everyone, do not qualify as works of art. Literary texts such as the sentimental novel, which make continual and obvious appeals to the reader's emotions and use technical devices that are distinguished by their utter conventionality, epitomize the opposite of everything that good literature is supposed to be. "For the literary critic," writes J. W. Ward, summing up the dilemma posed by *Uncle Tom's Cabin,* "the problem is how a book so seemingly artless, so lacking in apparent literary talent, was not only an immediate success but has endured."[6]

How deep the problem goes is illustrated dramatically by George F. Whicher's discussion of Stowe's novel in *The Literary History of the United States.* Reflecting the consensus view on what good novels are made of, Whicher writes: "Nothing attributable to Mrs. Stowe or her handiwork can account for the novel's enormous vogue; its author's resources as a purveyor of Sunday-school fiction were not remarkable. She had at most a ready command of broadly conceived melodrama, humor, and pathos, and of these popular elements she compounded her book."[7] At a loss to understand how a book so compounded was able to "convulse a mighty nation," Whicher concludes—incredibly—that Stowe's own explanation, that "God wrote it," "solved the paradox." Rather than give up his bias against "melodrama," "pathos," and "Sunday-school fiction," Whicher takes refuge in a solution which, even according to his lights, is patently absurd.[8] And no wonder. The modernist literary aesthetic cannot account for the unprecedented and persistent popularity of a book like *Uncle Tom's Cabin,* for this novel operates according to principles quite other than those which have been responsible for determining the currently sanctified American literary classics.

It is not my purpose, however, to drag Hawthorne and Melville from their pedestals, nor to claim that the novels of Harriet Beecher Stowe, Fanny Fern, and Elizabeth Stuart Phelps are good in the same way that *Moby Dick* and *The Scarlet Letter* are; rather, I will argue that the work of the sentimental writers is complex and significant in ways *other than* those which characterize the established masterpieces. I will ask the reader to set aside some familiar categories for evaluating fiction—stylistic intricacy, psychological subtlety, epistemological complexity—and to see the sentimental novel, not as an artifice of eternity answerable to certain formal criteria and to certain psychological and philosophical concerns, but as a political enterprise, halfway between sermon and social theory, that both codifies and attempts to mold the values of its time.

The power of a sentimental novel to move its audience depends upon the audience's being in possession of the conceptual categories that constitute character and event. That storehouse of assumptions includes attitudes towards the family and towards social institutions, a definition of power and its relation to individual human feeling, notions of political and social equality, and above all, a set of religious beliefs that organize and sustain the rest. Once in possession of the system of beliefs that undergirds the patterns of sentimental fiction, it is possible for modern readers to see how its tearful episodes and frequent violations of probability were invested with a structure of meanings that fixed these works, for nineteenth-century readers, not in the realm of fairy tale or escapist fantasy, but in the very bedrock of reality. I do not say that we can read sentimental fiction exactly as Stowe's audience did—that would be impossible—but that we can and should set aside the modernist prejudices that consign this fiction to oblivion, in order to see how and why it worked for its readers, in its time, with such unexampled effect.

Let us consider the episode in *Uncle Tom's Cabin* most often cited as the epitome of Victorian sentimentalism—the death of little Eva—because it is the kind of incident most offensive to the sensibilities of twentieth-century academic critics. It is on the belief that this incident is nothing more than a sob story that the whole case against sentimentalism rests. Little Eva's death, so the argument goes, like every other sentimental tale, is awash with emotion but does nothing to remedy the evils it deplores. Essentially, it leaves the slave system and the other characters unchanged. This trivializing view of the episode is grounded in assumptions about power and reality so common that we are not even aware they have been invoked. Thus generations of critics have commented with condescending irony on little Eva's death. But in the system of belief that undergirds Stowe's enterprise, dying is the supreme form of heroism. In *Uncle Tom's Cabin,* death is the equivalent not of defeat but of victory; it brings an access of power, not a loss of it; it is not only the crowning achievement of life, it *is* life, and Stowe's entire presentation of little Eva is designed to dramatize this fact.

Stories like the death of little Eva are compelling for the same reason that the story of Christ's death is compelling: they enact a philosophy, as much political as religious, in which the pure and powerless die to save the powerful and corrupt, and thereby show themselves more powerful than those they save. They enact, in short, a *theory* of power in which the ordinary or "common-sense" view of what is efficacious and what is not (a view to which most modern critics are committed) is simply reversed, as the very possibility of social action is made dependent on the action taking place in individual hearts. Little Eva's death enacts the drama of which all the major episodes of the novel are transformations: the idea, central to Christian soteriology, that the highest human calling is to give one's life for another. It presents one version of the ethic of sacrifice on which the entire novel is based and contains in some form all of the motifs that, by their frequent recurrence, constitute the novel's ideological framework.

Little Eva's death, moreover, is also a transformation of stories circulating in the culture at large. It may be found, for example, in a dozen or more versions in the evangelical sermons of the Reverend Dwight Lyman Moody when he preached in Great Britain and Ireland in 1875. In one version it is called "The Child Angel," and it concerns a beautiful golden-haired girl of seven, her father's pride and joy, who dies and, by appearing to him in a dream in which she calls to him from heaven, brings him salvation.[9] The tale shows that by dying even a child can be the instrument of redemption for others, since in death she acquires over those who loved her a spiritual power beyond what she possessed in life.

The power of the dead or the dying to redeem the unregenerate is a major theme of nineteenth-century popular fiction and religious literature. Mothers and children are thought to be uniquely capable of this work. In a sketch entitled "Children," published the year after *Uncle Tom* came out, Stowe writes: "Wouldst thou know, O parent, what is that faith which unlocks heaven? Go not to wrangling polemics, or creeds and forms of theology, but draw to thy bosom thy little one, and read in that clear trusting eye the lesson of eternal life."[10] If children through their purity and innocence can lead adults to God while living, their spiritual power when they are dead is greater still. Death, Stowe argues in a pamphlet entitled *Ministration of Departed Spirits,* enables the Christian to begin his "real work." God takes people from us sometimes so that their "ministry can act upon us more powerfully from the unseen world."[11]

> The mother would fain electrify the heart of her child. She yearns and burns in vain to make her soul effective on its soul, and to inspire it with a spiritual and holy life; but all her own weaknesses, faults and mortal cares, cramp and confine her till death breaks all fetters; and then, first truly alive, risen, purified, and at rest, she may do calmly, sweetly, and certainly, what, amid the tampest and tossings of her life, she labored for painfully and fitfully.[12]

When the spiritual power of death is combined with the natural sanctity of childhood, the child becomes an angel endowed with salvific force.

Most often, it is the moment of death that saves, when the dying child, glimpsing for a moment the glory of heaven, testifies to the reality of the life to come. Uncle Tom knows that this will happen when little Eva dies, and explains it to Miss Ophelia as follows:

> "You know it says in Scripture, 'At midnight there was a great cry made. Behold the bridegroom cometh.' That's what I'm specting' now, every night, Miss Feely,—and I couldn't sleep out o' hearin' no ways."
>
> "Uncle Tom, what makes you think so?"
>
> "Miss Eva, she talks to me. The lord, he sends his messenger in the soul. I must be thar, Miss Feely; for when that ar blessed child goes into the kingdom, they'll open the door so wide, we'll all get a look in at the glory, Miss Feely."[13]

Little Eva does not disappoint them. At the moment when she passes "from death into life," she exclaims, "O, love!—joy!—peace!" And her exclamation echoes those of scores of children who die in Victorian fiction and sermon literature with heaven in their eyes. Dickens's Paul Dombey, seeing the face of his dead mother, dies with the words "The light about the head is shining on me as I go!" The fair, blue-eyed young girl in Lydia Sigourney's *Letters to Mothers,* "death's purple tinge upon her brow," when implored by her mother to utter one last word, whispers "Praise!"[14]

Of course, it could be argued by critics of sentimentalism that the prominence of stories about the deaths of children is precisely what is wrong with the literature of the period; rather than being cited as a source of strength, the presence of such stories in *Uncle Tom's Cabin* should be regarded as an unfortunate concession to the age's fondness for lachrymose scenes. But to dismiss such scenes as "all tears and flapdoodle" is to leave unexplained the popularity of the novels and sermons that are filled with them, unless we choose to believe that a generation of readers was unaccountably moved to tears by matters that are intrinsically silly and trivial. That popularity is better explained, I believe, by the relationship of these scenes to a pervasive cultural myth which invests the suffering and death of an innocent victim with just the kind of power that critics deny to Stowe's novel: the power to work in, and change, the world.

This is the kind of action that little Eva's death in fact performs. It proves its efficacy, not through the sudden collapse of the slave system, but through the conversion of Topsy, a motherless, godless black child who has up until that point successfully resisted all attempts to make her "good." Topsy will not be "good" because, never having had a mother's love, she believes that no one can love her. When Eva suggests that Miss Ophelia would love her if only she were good, Topsy cries out, "No, she can't bar me, cause I'm a nigger!—she'd as soon have a toad touch her! Ther can't nobody love niggers, and niggers can't do nothin'! *I* don't care."

> "O, Topsy, poor child, *I* love you!" said Eva with a sudden burst of feeling and laying her little thin, white hand on Topsy's shoulder; "I love you, because you haven't had any father, or mother, or friends;—because you've been a poor, abused child! I love you, and I want you to be good. I am very unwell, Topsy, and I think I shan't live a great while; and it really grieves me, to have you be so naughty. I wish you would try to be good, for my sake;—it's only a little while I shall be with you."
>
> The round, keen eyes of the black child were overcast with tears:—large, bright drops rolled heavily down one by one, and fell on the little white hand. Yes, in that moment, a ray of real belief, a ray of heavenly love, had penetrated the darkness of her heathen soul! She laid her head down between her knees, and wept and sobbed,—while the beautiful child, bending over her, looked like the picture of some bright angel stooping to reclaim a sinner. (P. 283)

The rhetoric and imagery of this passage, its little white hand, its ray from heaven, bending angel, and plentiful tears, suggest a literary version of the kind of polychrome religious picture that hangs on Sunday school walls. Words like "kitsch," "camp," and "corny" come to mind. But what is being dramatized here bears no relation to these designations. By giving Topsy her love, Eva initiates a process of redemption whose power, transmitted from heart to heart, can change the entire world. And indeed, the process has begun. From that time on, Topsy is "different from what she used to be" (eventually she will go to Africa and become a missionary to her entire race), and Miss Ophelia, who overhears the conversation, is different too. When little Eva is dead and Topsy cries out, "Ther an't *nobody* left now," Miss Ophelia answers her in Eva's place:

> "Topsy, you poor child," she said, as she led her into her room, "don't give up! *I* can love you, though I am not like that dear little child. I hope I've learnt something of the love of Christ from her. I can love you; I do, and I'll try to help you to grow up a good Christian girl."
>
> Miss Ophelia's voice was more than her words, and

> more than that were the honest tears that fell down her face. From that hour, she acquired an influence over the mind of the destitute child that she never lost. (P. 300)

The tears of Topsy and of Miss Ophelia, which we find easy to ridicule, are the sign of redemption in *Uncle Tom's Cabin;* not words but the emotions of the heart bespeak a state of grace, and these are known by the sound of a voice, the touch of a hand, but chiefly, in moments of greatest importance, by tears. When Tom lies dying on the plantation on the Red River, the disciples to whom he has preached testify to their conversion by weeping.

> Tears had fallen on that honest, insensible face,—tears of late repentance in the poor, ignorant heathen, whom his dying love and patience had awakened to repentance. . . . (P. 420)

Even the bitter and unregenerate Cassy, "moved by the sacrifice that had been made for her," breaks down; "moved by the few last words which the affectionate soul had yet strength to breathe, . . . the dark, despairing woman had wept and prayed" (p. 420). When George Shelby, the son of Tom's old master, arrives too late to free him, "tears which did honor to his manly heart fell from the young man's eyes as he bent over his poor friend." And when Tom realizes who is there, "the whole face lighted up, the hard hands clasped, and tears ran down the cheeks" (p. 420). The vocabulary of clasping hands and falling tears is one we associate with emotional exhibitionism, with the overacting that kills true feeling off through exaggeration. But the tears and gestures of Stowe's characters are not in excess of what they feel; if anything, they fall short of expressing the experiences they point to—salvation, communion, reconciliation.

If the language of tears seems maudlin and little Eva's death ineffectual, it is because both the tears and the redemption they signify belong to a conception of the world that is now generally regarded as naïve and unrealistic. Topsy's salvation and Miss Ophelia's do not alter the anti-abolitionist majority in the Senate or prevent Southern plantation owners and Northern investment bankers from doing business to their mutual advantage. Because most modern readers regard such political and economic facts as final, it is difficult for them to take seriously a novel that insists on religious conversion as the necessary precondition for sweeping social change. But in Stowe's understanding of what such change requires it is the *modern* view that is naïve. The political and economic measures that constitute effective action for us, she regards as superficial, mere extensions of the worldly policies that produced the slave system in the first place. Therefore, when Stowe asks the question that is in every reader's mind at the end of the novel, namely, "What can any individual do?" she recommends, not specific alterations in the current political and economic arrangements, but rather a change of heart.

> There is one thing that every individual can do—they can see to it that *they feel right.* An atmosphere of sympathetic influence encircles every human being; and the man or woman who *feels* strongly, healthily and justly, on the great interests of humanity, is a constant benefactor to the human race. See, then, to your sympathies in this matter! Are they in harmony with the sympathies of Christ? or are they swayed and perverted by the sophistries of worldly policy? (P. 448)

Stowe is not opposed to concrete measures such as the passage of laws or the formation of political pressure groups; it is just that by themselves, such actions would be useless. For if slavery *were* to be abolished by these means, the moral conditions that produced slavery in the first place would continue in force. The choice is not between action and inaction, programs and feelings; the choice is between actions that spring from "the sophistries of worldly policy" and those inspired by "the sympathies of Christ." Reality, in Stowe's view, cannot be changed by manipulating the physical environment; it can only be changed by conversion in the spirit because it is the spirit alone that is finally real.

The notion that historical change takes place only through religious conversion, which is a theory of power as old as Christianity itself, is dramatized and vindicated in *Uncle Tom's Cabin* by the novel's insistence that all human events are organized, clarified, and made meaningful by the existence of spiritual realities.[15] The novel is packed with references to the four last things —Heaven, Hell, Death, and Judgment—references which remind the reader constantly that historical events can only be seen for what they are in the light of eternal truths. When St. Clare stands over the grave of little Eva, unable to realize "that it was his Eva that they were hiding from his sight," Stowe interjects, "Nor was it!—not Eva, but only the frail seed of that bright immortal form in which she shall yet come forth, in the day of the Lord Jesus!" (p. 300). And when Legree expresses satisfaction that Tom is dead, she turns to him and says, "Yes, Legree; but who shall shut up that voice in thy soul? that soul, past repentance, past prayer, past hope, in whom the fire that never shall be quenched is already burning?" (p. 416). These reminders come thick and fast; they are present in Stowe's countless quotations from Scripture, introduced at every possible opportunity—in the narrative, in dialogue, in epigraphs, in quotations from other authors; they are present in the Protestant hymns that thread their way through scene after scene, in asides to the reader, in apostrophes to the characters, in quotations from religious poetry, sermons, and prayers, and in long stretches of dialogue and narrative devoted to the discussion of religious matters. Stowe's narrative stipulates a world in which the facts of Christ's death and resurrection and coming day of judgment are never far from our minds because it is only within this frame of reference that she can legitimately have Tom claim, as he dies, "I've got the victory."

The eschatological vision, by putting all individual events in relation to an order that is unchanging, collapses the distinctions between them so that they become interchangeable representations of a single timeless reality. Groups of characters blend into the same character, while the plot abounds in incidents that mirror one another. These features are the features, not of classical nineteenth-century fiction, but of typological narrative. It is this tradition rather than that of the English novel which *Uncle Tom's Cabin* reproduces and extends; for this novel does not simply quote the Bible, it rewrites the Bible as the story of a Negro slave. Formally and philosophically, it stands opposed to works like *Middlemarch* and *The Portrait of a Lady* in which everything depends on human action and decision unfolding in a temporal sequence that withholds revelation until the final moment. The truths that Stowe's narrative conveys can only be reembodied, never discovered, because they are already revealed from the beginning. Therefore, what seem from a modernist point of view to be gross stereotypes in characterization and a needless proliferation of incident are essential properties of a narrative aimed at demonstrating that human history is a continual reenactment of the sacred drama of redemption. It is the novel's reenactment of this drama that made it irresistible in its day.

Uncle Tom's Cabin retells the culture's central religious myth, the story of the crucifixion, in terms of the nation's greatest political conflict—slavery—and of its most cherished social beliefs—the sanctity of motherhood and the family. It is because Stowe is able to combine so many of the culture's central concerns in a narrative that is immediately accessible to the general population that she is able to move so many people so deeply. The novel's typological organization allows her to present political and social situations both as themselves and as transformations of a religious paradigm which interprets them in a way that readers can both understand and respond to emotionally. For the novel functions both as a means of describing the social world and as a means of changing it. It not only offers an interpretative framework for understanding the culture and, through the reinforcement of a particular code of values, recommends a strategy for dealing with cultural conflict, but it is itself an agent of that strategy, putting into practice the measures it prescribes. As the religious stereotypes of "Sunday school fiction" define and organize the elements of social and political life, so the "melodrama" and "pathos" associated with the underlying myth of crucifixion put the reader's heart in the right place with respect to the problems the narrative defines. Hence, rather than making the enduring success of *Uncle Tom's Cabin* inexplicable, these popular elements that puzzled Whicher and have puzzled so many modern scholars—melodrama, pathos, Sunday school fiction—are the *only* terms in which the book's success can be explained.

The nature of these popular elements also dictates the terms in which any full-scale analysis of *Uncle Tom's Cabin* must be carried out. As I have suggested, its distinguishing features, generically speaking, are not those of the realistic novel but of typological narrative. Its characters, like the figures in an allegory, do not change or develop but reveal themselves in response to the demands of a situation. They are not defined primarily by their mental and emotional characteristics—that is to say, psychologically—but soteriologically, according to whether they are saved or damned. The plot, likewise, does not unfold according to Aristotelian standards of probability but in keeping with the logic of a preordained design, a design that every incident is intended, in one way or another, to enforce.[16] The setting does not so much describe the features of a particular time and place as point to positions on a spiritual map. In *Uncle Tom's Cabin* the presence of realistic detail tends to obscure its highly programmatic nature and to lull readers into thinking that they are in an everyday world of material cause and effect. But what pass for realistic details—the use of dialect, the minute descriptions of domestic activity—are in fact performing a rhetorical function dictated by the novel's ruling paradigm; once that paradigm is perceived, even the homeliest details show up not as the empirically observed facts of human existence but as the expressions of a highly schematic intent.[17]

This schematization has what one might call a totalizing effect on the particulars of the narrative, so that every character in the novel, every scene, and every incident comes to be apprehended in terms of every *other* character, scene, and incident: all are caught up in a system of endless cross-reference in which it is impossible to refer to one without referring to all the rest. To demonstrate what I mean by this kind of narrative organization—a demonstration that will have to stand in lieu of a full-scale reading of the novel—let me show how it works in relation to a single scene. Eva and Tom are seated in the garden of St. Clare's house on the shores of Lake Pontchartrain.

> It was Sunday evening, and Eva's Bible lay open on her knee. She read,—"And I saw a sea of glass, mingled with fire."
>
> "Tom," said Eva, suddenly stopping, and pointing to the lake, "there 't is."

"What, Miss Eva?"

"Don't you see,—there?" said the child, pointing to the glassy water, which, as it rose and fell, reflected the golden glow of the sky. "There's a 'sea of glass, mingled with fire.' "

"True enough, Miss Eva," said Tom: and Tom sang—

"O, had I the wings of the morning,
I'd fly away to Canaan's shore;
Bright angels should convey me home,
To the new Jerusalem."

"Where do you suppose new Jerusalem is, Uncle Tom?" said Eva.

"O, up in the clouds, Miss Eva."

"Then I think I see it," said Eva. "Look in those clouds! —they look like great gates of pearl; and you can see beyond them—far, far off—it's all gold. Tom, sing about 'spirits bright.' "

Tom sang the words of a well-known Methodist hymn,

"I see a band of spirits bright,
That taste the glories there;
They are all robed in spotless white,
And conquering palms they bear."

"Uncle Tom, I've seen them." said Eva. . . . "They come to me sometimes in my sleep, those spirits;" and Eva's eyes grew dreamy, and she hummed, in a low voice,

"They are all robed in spotless white,
And conquering palms they bear."

"Uncle Tom," said Eva, "I'm going there."

"Where, Miss Eva?"

The child rose, and pointed her little hand to the sky; the glow of evening lit her golden hair and flushed cheek with a kind of unearthly radiance, and her eyes were bent earnestly on the skies.

"I'm going *there,*" she said, "to the spirits bright, Tom; *I'm going, before long.*" (Pp. 261–62)

The iterative nature of this scene presents in minature the structure of the whole novel. Eva reads from her Bible about a "sea of glass, mingled with fire," then looks up to find one before her. She reads the words aloud a second time. They remind Tom of a hymn that describes the same vision in a slightly different form (Lake Pontchartrain and the sea of glass become "Canaan's shore" and the "new Jerusalem"), and Eva sees what he has sung, this time in the clouds, and offers her own description. Eva asks Tom to sing again, and his hymn presents yet another form of the same vision, which Eva again says she has seen: the spirits bright come to her in her sleep. Finally, Eva repeats the last two lines of the hymn and declares that she is going "there"—to the place that has now been referred to a dozen times in this passage. Stowe follows with another description of the golden skies and then with a description of Eva as a spirit bright, and closes the passage with Eva's double reiteration that she is going "there."

The entire scene itself is a re-presentation of others that come before and after. When Eva looks out over Lake Pontchartrain, she sees the "Canaan of liberty" which Eliza saw on the other side of the Ohio River, and the "eternal shores" Eliza and George Harris will reach when they cross Lake Erie in the end. Bodies of water mediate between worlds: the Ohio runs between the slave states and the free; Lake Erie divides the United States from Canada, where runaway slaves cannot be returned to their masters; the Atlantic Ocean divides the North American continent from Africa, where Negroes will have a nation of their own; Lake Pontchartrain shows Eva the heavenly home to which she is going soon; the Mississippi River carries slaves from the relative ease of the Middle States to the grinding toil of the Southern plantations; the Red River carries Tom to the infernal regions ruled over by Simon Legree. The correspondences between the episodes I have mentioned are themselves based on correspondences between earth and heaven (or hell). Ohio, Canada, and Liberia are related to one another by virtue of their relationship to the one "bright Canaan" for which they stand; the Mississippi River and the Ohio are linked by the Jordan. (Ultimately, there are only three places to be in this story: heaven, hell, or Kentucky, which represents the earthly middle ground in Stowe's geography.)

Characters in the novel are linked to each other in exactly the same way that places are: with reference to a third term that is the source of their identity. The figure of Christ is the common term that unites all of the novel's good characters, who are good precisely in proportion as they are imitations of him. Eva and Tom head the list (she reenacts the Last Supper and he the crucifixion) but they are also linked to most of the slaves, women, and children in the novel by the characteristics they all share: piety, impressionability, spontaneous affection—and victimization.[18] In this scene, Eva is linked with the "spirits bright" (she later becomes a "bright immortal form") both because she can see them and is soon to join them and because she, too, always wears white and is elsewhere several times referred to as an "angel." When Eva dies, she will join her father's mother, who was also named Evangeline and who herself always wore white, and who, like Eva, is said to be "the direct and living embodiment of the New Testament." And this identification, in its turn, refers back to Uncle Tom, who is "all the moral and Christian virtues bound in black morocco complete." The circularity of this train of association is typical of the way the narrative doubles back on itself: later on, Cassy, impersonating the ghost of Legree's saintly mother, will wrap herself in a white sheet.[19]

The scene I have been describing is a node with a network of allusion in which every character and event in the novel has a place. The narrative's rhetorical strength derives in part from the impression it gives of taking every kind of detail in the world into account, from the preparation of breakfast to the orders of the angels, and investing those details with a purpose and a meaning that are both immediately apprehensible and finally significant. The novel reaches out into the reader's world and colonizes it for its own eschatology: that is, it not only incorporates the homely particulars of "Life Among the Lowly" into its universal scheme, but it gives them a power and a centrality in that scheme which turns the sociopolitical order upside down. The totalizing effect of the novel's iterative organization and its doctrine of spiritual redemption are inseparably bound to its political purpose, which is to bring in the day when the meek—that is to say, women—will inherit the earth.

The specifically political intent of the novel is apparent in its forms of address. Stowe addresses her readers not simply as individuals but as citizens of the United States: "to you, generous, noble-minded men and women of the South," "farmers of Massachusetts, of New Hampshire, of Vermont," "brave and generous men of New York," "and you, mothers of America." She speaks to her audience directly in the way the Old Testament prophets spoke to Israel, exhorting, praising, blaming, warning of the wrath to come. "This is an age of the world when nations are trembling and convulsed. Almighty influence is abroad, surging and heaving the world, as with an earthquake. And is America safe? . . . O, Church of Christ, read the signs of the times!" (p. 451). Passages like these, descended from the revivalist rhetoric of *Sinners in the Hands of an Angry God,* are intended, in the words of a noted scholar, "to direct an imperiled people toward the fulfillment of their destiny, to guide them individually towards salvation, and collectively toward the American city of God."[20]

These sentences are from Sacvan Bercovitch's *The American Jeremiad,* an influential work of modern scholarship which, although it completely ignores Stowe's novel, makes us aware that *Uncle Tom's Cabin* is a jeremiad in the fullest and truest sense. A jeremiad, in Bercovitch's definition, is "a mode of public exhortation . . . designed to join social criticism to spiritual renewal, public to private identity, the shifting 'signs of the times' to certain traditional metaphors, themes, and symbols."[21] Stowe's novel provides the most obvious and compelling instance of the jeremiad since the Great Awakening, and its exclusion from Bercovitch's book is a striking instance of how totally academic criticism has foreclosed on sentimental fiction; for, because *Uncle Tom's Cabin* is absent from the canon, it is not "there" to be referred to even when it fulfills a man's theory to perfection; hence its exclusion from critical discourse is perpetuated automatically, and absence begets itself in a self-confirming cycle of neglect. Nonetheless, Bercovitch's characterization of the jeremiad provides an excellent account of how *Uncle Tom's Cabin* actually worked: among its characters, settings, situations, symbols, and doctrines, the novel establishes a set of correspondences that unite the disparate realms of experience Bercovitch names—social and spiritual, public and private, theological and political—and, through the vigor of its representations, attempts to move the nation as a whole toward the vision it proclaims.

The tradition of the jeremiad throws light on *Uncle Tom's Cabin* because Stowe's novel was political in exactly the same way the jeremiad was: both were forms of discourse in which "theology was wedded to politics and politics to the progress of the kingdom of God."[22] The jeremiad strives to persuade its listeners to a providential view of human history which serves, among other things, to maintain the Puritan theocracy in power. Its fusion of theology and politics is not only doctrinal, in that it ties the salvation of the individual to the community's historical enterprise; it is practical as well, for it reflects the interests of Puritan ministers in their bid to retain spiritual and secular authority. The sentimental novel, too, is an act of persuasion aimed at defining social reality; the difference is that the jeremiad represents the interests of Puritan ministers, while the sentimental novel represents the interests of middle-class women. But the relationship between rhetoric and history in both cases is the same. In both cases it is not as if rhetoric and history stand opposed, with rhetoric made up of wish fulfillment and history made up of recalcitrant facts that resist rhetoric's onslaught. Rhetoric *makes* history by shaping reality to the dictates of its political design; it makes history by convincing the people of the world that its description of the world is the true one. The sentimental novelists make their bid for power by positing the kingdom of heaven on earth as a world over which women exercise ultimate control. If history did not take the course these writers recommended, it is not because they were not political, but because they were insufficiently persuasive.

Uncle Tom's Cabin, however, unlike its counterparts in the sentimental tradition, was spectacularly persuasive in conventional political terms: it induced a nation to go to war and to free its slaves. But in terms of its own conception of power, a conception it shares with other sentimental fiction, the novel was a political failure. Stowe conceived her book as an instrument for bringing about the day when the world would be ruled not by force but by

Christian love. The novel's deepest political aspirations are expressed only secondarily in its devastating attack on the slave system; the true goal of Stowe's rhetorical undertaking is nothing less than the institution of the kingdom of heaven on earth. Embedded in the world of *Uncle Tom's Cabin,* which is the fallen world of slavery, there appears an idyllic picture, both utopian and Arcadian, of the form human life would assume if Stowe's readers were to heed her moral lesson. In this vision, described in the chapter entitled "The Quaker Settlement," Christian love fulfills itself not in war but in daily living, and the principle of sacrifice is revealed not in crucifixion but in motherhood. The form that society takes bears no resemblance to the current social order. Man-made institutions—the church, the courts of law, the legislatures, the economic system—are nowhere in sight. The home is the center of all meaningful activity, women perform the most important tasks, work is carried on in a spirit of mutual cooperation, and the whole is guided by a Christian woman who, through the influence of her "loving words," "gentle moralities," and "motherly loving kindness," rules the world.

> For why? for twenty years or more, nothing but loving words and gentle moralities, and motherly loving kindness, had come from that chair;—head-aches and heart-aches innumerable had been cured there,—difficulties spiritual and temporal solved there,—all by one good, loving woman, God bless her! (P. 136)

The woman in question *is* God in human form. Seated in her kitchen at the head of her table, passing out coffee and cake for breakfast, Rachel Halliday, the millenarian counterpart of little Eva, enacts the redeemed form of the Last Supper. This is Holy Communion as it will be under the new dispensation: instead of the breaking of bones, the breaking of bread. The preparation of breakfast exemplifies the way people will work in the ideal society; there will be no competition, no exploitation, no commands. Motivated by self-sacrificing love, and joined to one another by its cohesive power, people will perform their duties willingly and with pleasure: moral suasion will take the place of force.

> All moved obediently to Rachel's gentle "Thee had better," or more gentle "Hadn't thee better?" in the work of getting breakfast. . . . Everything went on sociably, so quietly, so harmoniously, in the great kitchen,—it seemed so pleasant to everyone to do just what they were doing, there was an atmosphere of mutual confidence and good fellowship everywhere. (Pp. 141–42)

The new matriarchy that Isabella Beecher Hooker had dreamed of leading, pictured here in the Indiana kitchen ("for a breakfast in the luxurious valleys of Indiana is . . . like picking up the rose-leaves and trimming the bushes in Paradise"), constitutes the most politically subversive dimension of Stowe's novel, more disruptive and far-reaching in its potential consequences than even the starting of a war or the freeing of slaves. Nor is the ideal of matriarchy simply a daydream; Catharine Beecher, Stowe's elder sister, had offered a ground plan for the realization of such a vision in her *Treatise on Domestic Economy* (1841), which the two sisters republished in 1869 in an enlarged version entitled *The American Woman's Home.*[23] Dedicated "To the Women of America, in whose hands rest the real destinies of the republic," this is an instructional book on homemaking in which a wealth of scientific information and practical advice is pointed toward a millenarian goal. Centering on the home, for these women, is not a way of indulging in narcissistic fantasy, as critics have argued, or a turning away from the world into self-absorption and idle reverie; it is the prerequisite of world conquest, defined as the reformation of the human race through proper care and nurturing of its young. Like *Uncle Tom's Cabin, The American Woman's Home* situates the minutiae of domestic life in relation to their soteriological function: "What, then, is the end designed by the family state which Jesus Christ came into this world to secure? It is to provide for the training of our race . . . by means of the self-sacrificing labors of the wise and good . . . with chief reference to a future imortal existence."[24] "The family state," the authors announce at the beginning, "is the aptest earthly illustration of the heavenly kingdom, and . . . woman is its chief minister."[25] In the body of the text the authors provide women with everything they need to know for the proper establishment and maintenance of home and family, from the construction of furniture ("The bed frame is to be fourteen inches wide, and three inches in thickness. At the head, and at the foot, is to be screwed a notched two-inch board, three inches wide, as in Fig. 8"), to architectural plans, to chapters of instruction on heating, ventilation, lighting, healthful diet and preparation of food, cleanliness, the making and mending of clothes, the care of the sick, the organization of routines, financial management, psychological health, the care of infants, the managing of young children, home amusement, the care of furniture, the planting of gardens, the care of domestic animals, the disposal of waste, the cultivation of fruit, and providing for "the helpless, the homeless, and the vicious." After each of these activities has been treated in detail, they conclude by describing the ultimate aim of the domestic enterprise: the founding of a "truly 'Christian family' " will lead to the gathering of a "Christian neighborhood." This "cheering example," they continue,

> would soon spread, and ere long colonies from these prosperous and Christian communities would go forth to shine as "lights of the world" in all the now darkened nations. Thus the "Christian family" and "Christian neighborhood" would become the grand ministry, as they were designed to be, in training our whole race for heaven.[26]

The imperialistic drive behind the encyclopedism and determined practicality of this household manual flatly contradicts the traditional derogations of the American cult of domesticity as a "mirror-phenomenon," "self-immersed" and "self-congratulatory."[27]

The American Woman's Home is a blueprint for colonizing the world in the name of the "family state" under the leadership of Christian women. What is more, people like Stowe and Catharine Beecher were speaking not simply for a set of moral and religious values. In speaking for the home, they spoke for an economy—household economy—which had supported New England life since its inception. The home, rather than representing a retreat or a refuge from a crass industrial-commercial world, offers an economic *alternative* to that world, one which calls into question the whole structure of American society that was growing up in response to the increase in trade and manufacturing.[28] Stowe's image of a utopian community as presented in Rachel Halliday's kitchen is not simply a Christian dream of communitarian cooperation and harmony; it is a reflection of the real communitarian practices of village life, practices that had depended upon cooperation, trust, and a spirit of mutual supportiveness such as characterize the Quaker community of Stowe's novel.

One could argue, then, that for all its revolutionary fervor *Uncle Tom's Cabin* is a conservative book, because it advocates a return to an older way of life—household economy—in the name of the nation's most cherished social and religious beliefs. Even the woman's centrality might be seen as harking back to the "age of homespun" when the essential goods were manufactured in the home and their production was carried out and guided by women. But Stowe's very conservatism—her reliance on established patterns of living and traditional beliefs—is precisely what gives her novel its revolutionary potential. By pushing those beliefs to an extreme and by insisting that they be applied universally, not just to one segregated corner of civil life but to the conduct of all human affairs, Stowe means to effect a radical transformation of her society. The brilliance of the strategy is that it puts the central affirmations of a culture into the service of a vision that would destroy the present economic and social institutions; by resting her case, absolutely, on the saving power of Christian love and on the sanctity of motherhood and the family, Stowe relocates the center of power in American life, placing it not in the government, nor in the courts of law, nor in the factories, nor in the marketplace, but in the kitchen. And that means that the new society will not be controlled by men but by women. The image of the home created by Stowe and Catharine Beecher in their treatise on domestic science is in no sense a shelter from the stormy blast of economic and political life, a haven from reality divorced from fact which allows the machinery of industrial capitalism to grind on; it is conceived as a dynamic center of activity, physical and spiritual, economic and moral, whose influence spreads out in ever-widening circles. To this activity—and this is the crucial innovation—men are incidental. Although the Beecher sisters pay lip service on occasion to male supremacy, women's roles occupy virtually the whole of their attention and dominate the scene. Male provender is deemphasized in favor of female processing. Men provide the seed, but women bear and raise the children. Men provide the flour, but women bake the bread and get the breakfast. The removal of the male from the center to the periphery of the human sphere is the most radical component of this millenarian scheme, which is rooted so solidly in the most traditional values: religion, motherhood, home, and family. Exactly what position men will occupy in the millennium is specified by a detail inserted casually into Stowe's description of the Indiana kitchen. While the women and children are busy preparing breakfast, Simeon Halliday, the husband and father, stands "in his shirt-sleeves before a little looking-glass in the corner, engaged in the anti-patriarchal activity of shaving" (pp. 141–42).

With this detail, so innocently placed, Stowe reconceives the role of men in human history: while Negroes, children, mothers, and grandmothers do the world's primary work, men groom themselves contentedly in a corner. The scene, as critics have noted is often the case in sentimental fiction, is "intimate," the backdrop is "domestic," the tone at times is even "chatty"; but the import, as critics have failed to recognize, is world-shaking. The enterprise of sentimental fiction, as Stowe's novel attests, is anything but domestic, in the sense of being limited to purely personal concerns; its mission, on the contrary, is global and its interests identical with the interests of the race. If the fiction written in the nineteenth century by women whose works sold in the hundreds of thousands has seemed narrow and parochial to the critics of the twentieth century, that narrowness and parochialism belong not to these works nor to the women who wrote them; they are the beholders' share.[29]

NOTES

[1]Johanna Johnston, *Runaway to Heaven* (Garden City, N.Y.: Doubleday, 1963).

[2]Edward Halsey Foster, for example, prefaces his book-length study of the work of Susan and Anna Warner by saying: "If one searches nineteenth century popular

fiction for something that has literary value, one searches, by and large, in vain" *(Susan and Anna Warner* [Boston: G. K. Hall, 1978]). At the other end of the spectrum stands a critic like Sally Mitchell, whose excellent studies of Victorian women's fiction contain statements that, intentionally or not, condescend to the subject matter: e.g., "Thus, we should see popular novels as emotional analyses, rather than intellectual analyses, of a particular society" ("Sentiment and Suffering: Women's Recreational Reading in the 1960's," *Victorian Studies* 21 [Fall 1977]: 34). The most typical move, however, is to apologize for the poor literary quality of the novels in a concessive clause—"melodramatic and simplistic though the plots may be, wooden and stereotyped as the characters may appear"—and then to assert that these texts are valuable on historical grounds.

[3]Ann Douglas is the foremost of the feminist critics who have accepted this characterization of the sentimental writers, and it is to her formulation of the antisentimentalist position that my arguments throughout are principally addressed *(The Feminization of American Culture* [New York: Alfred A. Knopf, 1977]). Although her attitude toward the vast quantity of literature written by women between 1820 and 1870 is the one that the male-dominated tradition has always expressed—contempt—Douglas's book is nevertheless extremely important because of its powerful and sustained consideration of this long-neglected body of work. Because Douglas successfully focused critical attention on the cultural centrality of sentimental fiction, forcing the realization that it can no longer be ignored, it is now possible for other critics to put forward a new characterization of these novels and not be dismissed. For these reasons, it seems to me, her work is invaluable.

[4]These attitudes are forcefully articulated by Douglas, ibid., p. 9.

[5]The phrase "a damned mob of scribbling women," coined by Nathaniel Hawthorne in a letter he wrote to his publisher in 1855 and clearly the product of Hawthorne's own feelings of frustration and envy, comes embedded in a much-quoted passage that has set the tone for criticism of sentimental fiction ever since: "America is now wholly given over to a d****d mob of scribbling women, and I should have no chance of success while the public taste is occupied with their trash—and should be ashamed of myself if I did succeed. What is the mystery of these innumerable editions of *The Lamplighter,* and other books neither better nor worse? Worse they could not be, and better they need not be, when they sell by the hundred thousand." As quoted by Fred Lewis Pattee, *The Feminine Fifties* (New York: D. Appleton-Century, 1940), p. 110.

[6]J. W. Ward, *Red, White, and Blue: Men, Books, and Ideas in American Culture* (New York: Oxford University Press, 1961), p. 75.

[7]George F. Whicher, "Literature and Conflict," in *The Literary History of the United States,* ed. Robert E. Spiller et al., 3rd ed., rev. (New York: Macmillan, 1963), p. 583.

[8]Ibid., p. 586. Edmund Wilson, despite his somewhat sympathetic treatment of Stowe in *Patriotic Gore,* seems to concur in this opinion, reflecting a characteristic tendency of commentators on the most popular works of sentimental fiction to regard the success of these women as some sort of mysterious eruption, inexplicable by natural causes *(Patriotic Gore: Studies in the Literature of the American Civil War* [New York: Oxford University Press, 1966], pp. 5, 32). Henry James gives this attitude its most articulate, though perhaps least defensible, expression in a remarkable passage from *A Small Boy and Others* (New York: Charles Scribner's Sons, 1913) where he describes Stowe's book as really not a book at all but "a fish, a wonderful 'leaping' fish"—the point being to deny Stowe any role in the process that produced such a wonder:

> Appreciation and judgment, the whole impression, were thus an effect for which there had been no process—any process so related having in other cases *had* to be at some point or other critical; nothing in the guise of a written book, therefore, a book printed, published, sold, bought and "noticed," probably ever reached its mark, the mark of exciting interest, without having at least groped for that goal *as* a book or by the exposure of some literary side. Letters, here, languished unconscious, and Uncle Tom, instead of making even one of the cheap short cuts through the medium in which books breathe, even as fishes in water, went gaily roundabout it altogether, as if a fish, a wonderful "leaping" fish, had simply flown in through the air. (Pp. 159–60)

[9]Reverend Dwight Lyman Moody, *Sermons and Addresses,* in *Narrative of Messrs. Moody and Sankey's Labors in Great Britain and Ireland with Eleven Addresses and Lectures in Full* (New York: Anson D. F. Randolph, 1875).

[10]Harriet Beecher Stowe, "Children," in *Uncle Sam's Emancipation; Earthly Care, a Heavenly Discipline; and other sketches* (Philadelphia: W. P. Hazard, 1853), p. 83.

[11]Harriet Beecher Stowe, *Ministration of Departed Spirits* (Boston: American Tract Society, n.d.), pp. 4, 3.

[12]Ibid., p. 3.

[13]Harriet Beecher Stowe, *Uncle Tom's Cabin; or, Life Among the Lowly* (New York: Harper & Row, 1965), pp. 295–96. This Harper Classic gives the text of the first edition originally published by John P. Jewett & Company of Boston and Cleveland in 1852. All future references to *Uncle Tom's Cabin* will be to this edition; page numbers are given in parentheses in the text.

[14]Charles Dickens, *Dombey and Son* (Boston: Estes & Lauriat, 1882), p. 278; Lydia H. Sigourney, *Letters to Mothers* (Hartford, Conn.: Hudson & Skinner, 1838).

[15]Religious conversion as the basis for a new social order was the mainspring of the Christian evangelical movement of the mid-nineteenth century. The emphasis on "feeling," which seems to modern readers to provide no basis whatever for the organization of society, was the key factor in the evangelical theory of reform. See Sandra Sizer's discussions of this phenomenon in *Gospel Hymns and Social Religion: The Rhetoric of Nineteenth-Century Revivalism* (Philadelphia: Temple University Press, 1979): "It is clear from the available literature that prayer, testimony, and exhortation were employed to create a *community* of intense *feeling,* in which individuals underwent similar experiences (centering on conversion) and would thenceforth unite with others in matters of moral decision and social behavior" (p. 52). "People in similar states of feeling, in short, would 'walk together,' would be agreed" (p. 59). "Conversion established individuals in a particular kind of relationship with God, by virtue of which they were automatically members of a social company, alike in interests and feelings" (pp. 70–71). Good order would be preserved by "relying on the spiritual and moral discipline provided by conversion, and on the company of fellow Christians, operating without the coercive force of government" (p. 72).

[16]Angus Fletcher's *Allegory: The Theory of a Symbolic Mode* (Ithaca, N.Y.: Cornell University Press, 1964) discusses the characteristic features of allegory in such a way as to make clear the family resemblance between sentimental fiction and the allegorical mode. See, particularly, his analysis of character (pp. 35, 60), symbolic action (pp. 150 ff., 178, 180, 182), and imagery (p. 171).

[17]Fletcher's comment on the presence of naturalistic detail in allegory is pertinent here:

> The apparent surface realism of an allegorical agent will recede in importance, as soon as he is felt to take part in a magical plot, as soon as his causal relations to others in that plot are seen to be magically based. This is an important point because there has often been confusion as to the function of the naturalist detail of so much allegory. In terms I have been outlining, this detail now appears not to have a journalistic function; it is more than a mere record of observed facts. It serves instead the purposes of magical containment, since the more the allegorist can circumscribe the attributes, metonymic and synecdochic, of his personae, the better he can shape their fictional destiny. Naturalist detail is "cosmic," universalizing, not accidental as it would be in straight journalism. (Pp. 198–99)

[18]The associations that link slaves, women, and children are ubiquitous and operate on several levels. Besides being described in the same set of terms, these characters occupy parallel structural positions in the plot. They function chiefly as mediators between God and the unredeemed, so that, e.g., Mrs. Shelby intercedes for Mr. Shelby, Mrs. Bird for Senator Bird, Simon Legree's mother (unsuccessfully) for Simon Legree, little Eva and St. Clare's mother for St. Clare, Tom Loker's mother for Tom Loker, Eliza for George Harris (spiritually, she is the agent of his conversion) and for Harry Harris (physically, she saves him from being sold down the river), and Tom for all the slaves on the Legree plantation (spiritually, he converts them) and for all the slaves of the Shelby plantation (physically, he is the cause of their being set free).

[19]For a parallel example, see Alice Crozier's analysis of the way the lock of hair that little Eva gives Tom becomes transformed into the lock of hair that Simon Legree's mother sent to Simon Legree. *The Novels of Harriet Beecher Stowe* (New York: Oxford University Press, 1969), pp. 29–31.

[20]Sacvan Bercovitch, *The American Jeremiad* (Madison: University of Wisconsin Press, 1978), p. 9.

[21]Ibid., p. xi.

[22]Ibid., p. xiv.

[23]For an excellent discussion of Beecher's *Treatise* and of the entire cult of domesticity, see Kathryn Kish Sklar, *Catharine Beecher: A Study in American Domesticity* (New York: W. W. Norton, 1976; Copyright © 1973 by Yale University). For other helpful discussions of the topic, see Barbara G. Berg, *The Remembered Gate: Origins of American Feminism, The Woman and the City, 1800–1860* (New York: Oxford University Press, 1978; Sizer, *Gospel Hymns and Social Religion;* Ronald G. Walters, *The Antislavery Appeal: American Abolitionism after 1830* (Baltimore: Johns Hopkins University Press, 1976); and Barbara Welter, "The Cult of True Womanhood, 1820–1860," *American Quarterly* 18 (Summer 1966): 151–74.

[24]Catharine Beecher and Harriet Beecher Stowe, *The American Woman's Home: or Principles of Domestic Science; Being a Guide to the Formation and Maintenance of Economical, Healthful, Beautiful, and Christian Homes* (New York: J. B. Ford, 1869), p. 18.

[25]Ibid., p. 19.

[26]Ibid., pp. 458–59.

[27]These are Douglas's epithets; see *Feminization of American Culture,* p. 307.

[28]For a detailed discussion of the changes referred to here, see Christopher Clark, "Household Economy, Market Exchange, and the Rise of Capitalism in the Connecticut Valley, 1800–1860," *Journal of Social History* 13 (Winter 1979): 169–89, and Nancy F. Cott, *The Bonds of Womanhood: "Woman's Sphere" in New England, 1780–1835* (New Haven, Conn.: Yale University Press, 1977).

[29]In a recent article in *Signs,* Mary Kelley characterizes the main positions in the debate over the significance of sentimental fiction as follows: (1) the Cowie-Welter thesis, which holds that women's fiction expresses an "ethics of conformity" and accepts the stereotype of the woman as pious, pure, submissive, and dedicated to the home, and (2) the Papashvily-Garrison thesis, which sees sentimental fiction as profoundly subversive of traditional ideas of male authority and female subservience. Kelley locates herself somewhere in between, holding that sentimental novels convey a "contradictory message": "they tried to project an Edenic image," but their own tales "subverted their intentions" by showing how often women were frustrated and defeated in the performance of their heroic roles. My own position is that the sentimental novelists are both conformist and subversive, but not, as Kelley believes, in a self-contradictory way. They used the central myth of their culture, the story of Christ's death for the sins of mankind, as the basis for a new myth that reflected their own interests. They regarded their vision of the Christian home as God's kingdom on earth as the fulfillment of the Gospel, "the end . . . which Jesus Christ came into this world to secure," in exactly the same way that the Puritans believed their mission was to found the "American city of God," and that Christians believe the New Testament to be a fulfillment of the old. Revolutionary ideologies typically announce themselves as the fulfillment of old promises or as a return to a golden age. What I am suggesting here, in short, is that the argument over whether the sentimental novelists were radical or conservative is a false issue. The real problem is how we, in the light of everything that has happened since they wrote, can understand and appreciate their work. Mary Kelley, "The Sentimentalists: Promise and Betrayal in the Home," *Signs* 4 (Spring 1979): 434–46; Alexander Cowie, "The Vogue of the Domestic Novel, 1850–1870," *South Atlantic Quarterly* 41 (October 1942): 420; Welter, "Cult of True Womanhood," pp. 151–74; Helen Waite Papashvily, *All the Happy Endings: A Study of the Domestic Novel in America, the Women Who Wrote It, the Women Who Read It, in the Nineteenth Century* (New York: Harper & Bros., 1956); Dee Garrison, "Immoral Fiction in the Late Victorian Library," *American Quarterly* 28 (Spring 1976): 71–80.

Treason Our Text

Feminist Challenges to the Literary Canon

Lillian S. Robinson

> *Successful plots have often had gunpowder in them. Feminist critics have gone so far as to take treason to the canon as our text.* [1]
>
> JANE MARCUS

The lofty seat of canonized bards (Pollok, 1827).

As with many other restrictive institutions, we are hardly aware of it until we come into conflict with it; the elements of the literary canon are simply absorbed by the apprentice scholar and critic in the normal course of graduate education, without anyone's ever seeming to inculcate or defend them. Appeal, were any necessary, would be to the other meaning of "canon," that is, to established standards of judgment and of taste. Not that either definition is presented as rigid and immutable—far from it, for lectures in literary history are full of wry references to a benighted though hardly distant past when, say, the metaphysical poets were insufficiently appreciated or Vachel Lindsay was the most modern poet recognized in American literature. Whence the acknowledgment of a subjective dimension, sometimes generalized as "sensibility," to the category of taste. Sweeping modifications in the canon are said to occur because of changes in collective sensibility, but individual admissions and elevations from "minor" to "major" status tend to be achieved by successful critical promotion, which is to say, demonstration that a particular author does meet generally accepted criteria of excellence.

The results, moreover, are nowhere codified: they are neither set down in a single place, nor are they absolutely uniform. In the visual arts and in music, the cold realities of patronage, purchase, presentation in private and public collections, or performance on concert programs create the conditions for a work's canonical status or lack of it. No equivalent set of institutional arrangements exists for literature, however. The fact of publication and even the feat of remaining in print for generations, which are at least analogous to the ways in which pictures and music are displayed, are not the same sort of indicators; they represent less of an investment and hence less general acceptance of their canonicity. In the circumstances, it may seem somewhat of an exaggeration to speak of "the" literary canon, almost paranoid to call it an institution, downright hysterical to characterize that institution as restrictive. The whole business is so much more informal, after all, than any of these terms implies, the concomitant processes so much more gentlemanly. Surely, it is more like a gentlemen's agreement than a repressive instrument —isn't it?

But a gentleman is inescapably—that is, by definition—a member of a privileged class and of the male sex. From this perspective, it is probably quite accurate to think of the canon as an entirely gentlemanly artifact, considering how few works by nonmembers of that class and sex make it into the informal agglomeration of course syllabi, anthologies, and widely commented-upon "standard authors" that constitutes the canon as it is generally understood. For, beyond their availability on bookshelves, it is through the teaching and study—one might even say the habitual teaching and study—of certain works that they become institutionalized as canonical literature. Within that broad canon, moreover, those admitted but read only in advanced courses, commented upon only by more or less narrow specialists, are subjected to the further tyranny of "major" versus "minor."

For more than a decade now, feminist scholars have been protesting the apparently systematic neglect of women's experience in the literary canon, neglect that takes the form of distorting and misreading the few recognized female writers and excluding the others. Moreover, the argument runs, the predominantly male authors in the canon show us the female character and relations between the sexes in a way that both reflects and contributes to sexist ideology—an aspect of these classic works about which the critical tradition remained silent for generations. The feminist challenge, although intrinsically (and, to my mind, refreshingly) polemical, has not been simply a reiterated attack, but a series of suggested alternatives to the male-dominated membership and attitudes of the accepted canon. In this essay, I propose to examine these feminist alternatives, assess their impact on the standard canon, and propose some directions for further work. Although my emphasis in each section is on the substance of the challenge, the underlying polemic is, I believe, abundantly clear.

The presence of canonized forefathers (Burke, 1790).

Start with the Great Books, the traditional desert-island ones, the foundation of courses in the Western humanistic tradition. No women authors, of course, at all, but within the works thus canonized, certain monumental female images: Helen, Penelope, and Clytemnestra, Beatrice and the Dark Lady of the Sonnets, Bérénice, Cunégonde, and Margarete. The list of interesting female characters is enlarged if we shift to the Survey of English Literature and its classic texts; here, moreover, there is the possible inclusion of a female author or even several, at least as the course's implicit "historical background" ticks through and past the Industrial Revolution. It is a possibility that is not always honored in the observance. "*Beowulf* to Virginia Woolf" is a pleasant enough joke, but though lots of surveys begin with the Anglo-Saxon epic, not all that many conclude with *Mrs. Dalloway.* Even in the nineteenth century, the pace and the necessity of mass omissions may mean leaving out Austen, one of the Brontës, or Eliot. The analogous overview of American literary masterpieces, despite the relative brevity and modernity of the period considered, is likely to yield a similarly all-male pantheon; Emily Dickinson may be admitted—but not necessarily—and no one else even comes close.[2] Here again, the male-authored canon contributes to the body of information, stereotype, inference, and surmise about the female sex that is generally in the culture.

Once this state of affairs has been exposed, there are two possible approaches for feminist criticism. It can emphasize alternative readings of the tradition, readings that reinterpret women's character, motivations, and actions and that identify and challenge sexist ideology. Or it can concentrate on gaining admission to the canon for literature by women writers. Both sorts of work are being pursued, although, to the extent that feminist criticism has defined itself as a subfield of literary studies—as distinguished from an approach or method—it has tended to concentrate on writing by women.

In fact, however, the current wave of feminist theory began as criticism of certain key texts, both literary and paraliterary, in the dominant culture. Kate Millett, Eva Figes, Elizabeth Janeway, Germaine Greer, and Carolyn Heilbrun all use the techniques of essentially literary analysis on the social forms and forces surrounding those texts.[3] The texts themselves may be regarded as "canonical" in the sense that all have had significant impact on the culture as a whole, although the target being addressed is not literature or its canon.

In criticism that is more strictly literary in its scope, much attention has been concentrated on male writers in the American tradition. Books like Annette Kolodny's *The Lay of the Land* and Judith Fetterley's *The Resisting*

Reader have no systematic, comprehensive equivalent in the criticism of British or European literature.[4] Both of these studies identify masculine values and imagery in a wide range of writings, as well as the alienation that is their consequence for women, men, and society as a whole. In a similar vein, Mary Ellmann's *Thinking About Women* examines ramifications of the tradition of "phallic criticism" as applied to writers of both sexes.[5] These books have in common with one another and with overarching theoretical manifestos like *Sexual Politics* a sense of having been betrayed by a culture that was supposed to be elevating, liberating, and one's own.

By contrast, feminist work devoted to that part of the Western tradition which is neither American nor contemporary is likelier to be more even-handed. "Feminist critics," declare Lenz, Greene, and Neely in introducing their collection of essays on Shakespeare, "recognize that the greatest artists do not necessarily duplicate in their art the orthodoxies of their culture; they may exploit them to create character or intensify conflict, they may struggle with, criticize, or transcend them."[6] From this perspective, Milton may come in for some censure, Shakespeare and Chaucer for both praise and blame, but the clear intention of a feminist approach to these classic authors is to enrich our understanding of what is going on in the texts, as well as how—for better, for worse, or for both—they have shaped our own literary and social ideas.[7] At its angriest, none of this reinterpretation offers a fundamental challenge to the canon *as canon;* although it posits new values, it never suggests that, in the light of those values, we ought to reconsider whether the great monuments are really so great, after all.

Such is all the worlde hathe confirmed and agreed upon, that it is authentique and canonical (T. Wilson, 1553).

In an evolutionary model of feminist studies in literature, work on male authors is often characterized as "early," implicitly primitive, whereas scholarship on female authors is the later development, enabling us to see women—the writers themselves and the women they write about—as active agents rather than passive images or victims. This implicit characterization of studies addressed to male writers is as inaccurate as the notion of an inexorable evolution. In fact, as the very definition of feminist criticism has come increasingly to mean scholarship and criticism devoted to women writers, work on the male tradition has continued. By this point, there has been a study of the female characters or the views on the woman question of every major—perhaps every known—author in Anglo-American, French, Russian, Spanish, Italian, German, and Scandinavian literature.[8]

Nonetheless, it is an undeniable fact that most feminist criticism focuses on women writers, so that the feminist efforts to humanize the canon have usually meant bringing a woman's point of view to bear by incorporating works by women into the established canon. The least threatening way to do so is to follow the accustomed pattern of making the case for individual writers one by one. The case here consists in showing that an already recognized woman author has been denied her rightful place, presumably because of the general devaluation of female efforts and subjects. More often than not, such work involves showing that a woman already securely established in the canon belongs in the first rather than the second rank. The biographical and critical efforts of R.W.B. Lewis and Cynthia Griffin Wolff, for example, have attempted to enhance Edith Wharton's reputation in this way.[9] Obviously, no challenge is presented to the particular notions of literary quality, timelessness, universality, and other qualities that constitute the rationale for canonicity. The underlying argument, rather, is that consistency, fidelity to those values, requires recognition of at least the few best and best-known women writers. Equally obviously, this approach does not call the notion of the canon itself into question.

We acknowledge it Canonlike, but not Canonicall
(Bishop Barlow, 1601).

Many feminist critics reject the method of case-by-case demonstration. The wholesale consignment of women's concerns and productions to a grim area bounded by triviality and obscurity cannot be compensated for by tokenism. True equity can be attained, they argue, only by opening up the canon to a much larger number of female voices. This is an endeavor that eventually brings basic aesthetic questions to the fore.

Initially, however, the demand for wider representation of female authors is substantiated by an extraordinary effort of intellectual reappropriation. The emergence of feminist literary study has been characterized, at the base, by scholarship devoted to the discovery, republication, and reappraisal of "lost" or undervalued writers and their work. From Rebecca Harding Davis and Kate Chopin through Zora Neale Hurston and Mina Loy to Meridel LeSueur and Rebecca West, reputations have been reborn or remade and a female counter-canon has come into being, out of components that were largely unavailable even a dozen years ago.[10]

In addition to constituting a feminist alternative to the male-dominated tradition, these authors also have a claim to representation in "the" canon. From this perspective, the work of recovery itself makes one sort of *prima facie* case, giving the lie to the assumption, where it has existed, that aside from a few names that are household words—differentially appreciated, but certainly well known—there simply has not been much serious literature by women. Before any aesthetic arguments have been advanced either for or against the admission of such works to the general canon, the new literary scholarship on women has demonstrated that the pool of potential applicants is far larger than anyone has hitherto suspected.

Would Augustine, if he held all the books to have an equal right to canonicity . . . have preferred some to others?
(W. Fitzgerald, trans. Whitaker, 1849).

But the aesthetic issues cannot be forestalled for very long. We need to understand whether the claim is being made that many of the newly recovered or validated texts by women meet existing criteria or, on the other hand, that those criteria themselves intrinsically exclude or tend to exclude women and hence should be modified or replaced. If this polarity is not, in fact, applicable to the process, what are the grounds for presenting a large number of new female candidates for (as it were) canonization?

The problem is epitomized in Nina Baym's introduction to her study of American women's fiction between 1820 and 1870:

> Reexamination of this fiction may well show it to lack the esthetic, intellectual and moral complexity and artistry that we demand of great literature. I confess frankly that, although I have found much to interest me in these books, I have not unearthed a forgotten Jane Austen or George Eliot or hit upon the one novel that I would propose to set alongside *The Scarlet Letter.* Yet I cannot avoid the belief that "purely" literary criteria, as they have been employed to identify the best American works, have inevitably had a bias in favor of things male—in favor of, say, a whaling ship, rather than a sewing circle as a symbol of the human community. . . . While not claiming any literary greatness for any of the novels . . . in this study, I would like at least to begin to correct such a bias by taking their content seriously. And it is time, perhaps—though this task lies outside my scope here—to reexamine the grounds upon which certain hallowed American classics have been called great.[11]

Now, if students of literature may be allowed to confess to one Great Unreadable among the Great Books, my own *bête noire* has always been the white whale; I have always felt I was missing something in *Moby Dick* that is clearly there for many readers and that is there for me when I read, say, Aeschylus or Austen. So I find Baym's strictures congenial, at first reading. Yet the contradictory nature of the position is also evident on the face of it. Am I or am I not being invited to construct a (feminist) aesthetic rationale for my impatience with *Moby Dick*? Do Baym and the current of thought she represents accept "esthetic, intellectual and moral complexity and artistry" as the grounds of greatness, or are they challenging those values as well?

As Myra Jehlen points out most lucidly, this attractive position will not bear close analysis: "[Baym] is having it both ways, admitting the artistic limitations of the women's fiction . . . and at the same time denying the validity of the rulers that measure these limitations, disdaining any ambition to reorder the literary canon and, on second thought, challenging the canon after all, or rather challenging not the canon itself but the grounds for its selection."[12] Jehlen understates the case, however, in calling the duality a paradox, which is, after all, an intentionally created and essentially rhetorical phenomenon. What is involved here is more like the *agony* of feminist criticism, for it is the champions of women's literature who are torn between defending the quality of their discoveries and radically redefining literary quality itself.

Those who are concerned with the canon as a pragmatic instrument rather than a powerful abstraction—the compilers of more equitable anthologies or course syllabi, for example—have opted for an uneasy compromise. The literature by women that they seek—as well as that by members of excluded racial and ethnic groups and by working people in general—conforms as closely as possible to the traditional canons of taste and judgment. Not that it reads like such literature as far as content and viewpoint are concerned, but the same words about artistic intent and achievement may be applied without absurdity. At the same time, the rationale for a new syllabus or anthology relies on a very different criterion: that of truth to the culture being represented, the *whole* culture and not the creation of an almost entirely male white elite. Again, no one seems to be proposing—aloud—the elimination of *Moby Dick* or *The Scarlet Letter,* just squeezing them over somewhat to make room for another literary reality, which, joined with the existing canon, will come closer to telling the (poetic) truth.

The effect is pluralist, at best, and the epistemological assumptions underlying the search for a more fully representative literature are strictly empiricist: by including the perspective of women (who are, after all, half-the-population), we will know more about the culture as it actually was.

No one suggests that there might be something in this literature itself that challenges the values and even the validity of the previously all-male tradition. There is no reason why the canon need speak with one voice or as one man on the fundamental questions of human experience. Indeed, even as an elite white male voice, it can hardly be said to do so. Yet a commentator like Baym has only to say "it is time, perhaps . . . to reexamine the grounds," *while not proceeding to do so,* for feminists to be accused of wishing to throw out the entire received culture. The argument could be more usefully joined, perhaps, if there *were* a current within feminist criticism that went beyond insistence on representation to consideration of precisely how inclusion of women's writing alters our view of the tradition. Or even one that suggested some radical surgery on the list of male authors usually represented.

After all, when we turn from the construction of pantheons, which have no *prescribed* number of places, to the construction of course syllabi, then something does have to be eliminated each time something else is added, and here ideologies, aesthetic and extra-aesthetic, do necessarily come into play. Is the canon and hence the syllabus based on it to be regarded as the compendium of excellence or as the record of cultural history? For there comes a point when the proponent of making the canon recognize the achievement of both sexes has to put up or shut up; either a given woman writer is good enough to replace some male writer on the prescribed reading list or she is not. If she is not, then either she should replace him anyway, in the name of telling the truth about the culture, or she should not, in the (unexamined) name of excellence. This is the debate that will have to be engaged and that has so far been broached only in the most "inclusionary" of terms. It is ironic that in American literature, where attacks on the male tradition have been most bitter and the reclamation of women writers so spectacular, the appeal has still been only to pluralism, generosity, and guilt. It is populism without the politics of populism.

To canonize your owne writers (Polimanteria, 1595).

Although I referred earlier to a feminist counter-canon, it is only in certain rather restricted contexts that literature by women has in fact been explicitly placed "counter" to the dominant canon. Generally speaking, feminist scholars have been more concerned with establishing the existence, power, and significance of a specifically female tradition. Such a possibility is adumbrated in the title of Patricia Meyer Spacks's *The Female Imagination;* however, this book's overview of selected themes and stages in the female life-cycle as treated by some women writers neither broaches nor (obviously) suggests an answer to the question whether there is a female imagination and what characterizes it.[13]

Somewhat earlier, in her anthology of British and American women poets, Louise Bernikow had made a more positive assertion of a continuity and connection subsisting among them.[14] She leaves it to the poems, however, to forge their own links, and, in a collection that boldly and incisively crosses boundaries between published and unpublished writing, literary and anonymous authorship, "high" art, folk art, and music, it is not easy for the reader to identify what the editor believes it is that makes women's poetry specifically "*women's.*"

Ellen Moers centers her argument for a (transhistorical) female tradition upon the concept of "heroinism," a quality shared by women writers over time with the female characters they created.[15] Moers also points out another kind of continuity, documenting the way that women writers have read, commented on, and been influenced by the writings of other women who were their predecessors or contemporaries. There is also an unacknowledged continuity between the writer and her female reader. Elaine Showalter conceives the female tradition, embodied particularly in the domestic and sensational fiction of the nineteenth century, as being carried out through a kind of subversive conspiracy between author and audience.[16] Showalter is at her best in discussing this minor "women's fiction." Indeed, without ever making a case for popular genres as serious literature, she bases her arguments about a tradition more solidly on them than on acknowledged major figures like Virginia Woolf. By contrast, Sandra Gilbert and Susan Gubar focus almost exclusively on key literary figures, bringing women writers and their subjects together through the theme of perceived female aberration—in the act of literary creation itself, as well as in the behavior of the created persons or personae.[17]

Moers's vision of a continuity based on "heroinism" finds an echo in later feminist criticism that posits a discrete, perhaps even autonomous "women's culture." The idea of such a culture has been developed by social historians studying the "homosocial" world of nineteenth-century women.[18] It is a view that underlies, for example, Nina Auerbach's study of relationships among women in selected novels, where strong, supportive ties among mothers, daughters, sisters, and female friends not only constitute the real history in which certain women are conceived as living but function as a normative element as well.[19] That is, fiction in which positive relations subsist to nourish the heroine comes off much better, from Auerbach's point of view, than fiction in which such relations do not exist.

In contrast, Judith Lowder Newton sees the heroines of women's fiction as active, rather than passive, precisely because they do live in a man's world, not an autonomous female one.[20] Defining their power as "ability" rather than "control," she perceives "both a preoccupation with power and subtle power strategies" being exercised by the women in novels by Fanny Burney, Jane Austen, Charlotte Brontë, and George Eliot. Understood in this way, the female tradition, whether or not it in fact reflects and fosters a "culture" of its own, provides an alternative complex of possibilities for women, to be set beside the pits and pedestals offered by all too much of the Great Tradition.

Canonize such a multifarious Genealogie of Comments (Nashe, 1593).

Historians like Smith-Rosenberg and Cott are careful to specify that their generalizations extend only to white middle- and upper-class women of the nineteenth century. Although literary scholars are equally scrupulous about the national and temporal boundaries of their subject, they tend to use the gender term comprehensively. In this way, conclusions about "women's fiction" or "female consciousness" have been drawn or jumped to from considering a body of work whose authors are all white and comparatively privileged. Of the critical studies I have mentioned, only Bernikow's anthology, *The World Split Open,* brings labor songs, black women's blues lyrics, and anonymous ballads into conjunction with poems that were written for publication by professional writers, both black and white. The other books, which build an extensive case for a female tradition that Bernikow only suggests, delineate their subject in such a way as to exclude not only black and working-class authors but any notion that race and class might be relevant categories in the definition and apprehension of "women's literature." Similarly, even for discussions of writers who were known to be lesbians, this aspect of the female tradition often remains unacknowledged; worse yet, some of the books that develop the idea of a female tradition are openly homophobic, employing the word "lesbian" only pejoratively.[21]

Black and lesbian scholars, however, have directed much less energy to polemics against the feminist "mainstream" than to concrete, positive work on the literature itself. Recovery and reinterpretation of a wealth of unknown or undervalued texts has suggested the existence of both a black women's tradition and a lesbian tradition. In a clear parallel with the relationship between women's literature in general and the male-dominated tradition, both are by definition part of women's literature, but they are also distinct from and independent of it.

There are important differences, however, between these two traditions and the critical effort surrounding them. Black feminist criticism has the task of demonstrating that, in the face of all the obstacles a racist and sexist society has been able to erect, there is a continuity of black women who have written and written well. It is a matter of gaining recognition for the quality of the writing itself and respect for its principal subject, the lives and consciousness of black women. Black women's literature is also an element of black literature as a whole, where the recognized voices have usually been male. A triple imperative is therefore at work: establishing a discrete and significant black female tradition, then situating it within black literature and (along with the rest of that literature) within the common American literary heritage.[22] So far, unfortunately, each step toward integration has met with continuing exclusion. A black women's tradition has been recovered and revaluated chiefly through the efforts of black feminist scholars. Only some of that work has been accepted as part of either a racially mixed women's literature or a two-sex black literature. As for the gatekeepers of American literature in general, how many of them are willing to swing open the portals even for Zora Neale Hurston or Paule Marshall? How many have heard of them?

The issue of "inclusion," moreover, brings up questions that echo those raised by opening the male-dominated canon to women. How do generalizations about women's literature "as a whole" change when the work of black women is not merely added to but fully incorporated into that tradition? How does our sense of black literary history change? And what implications do these changes have for reconsideration of the American canon?

Whereas many white literary scholars continue to behave as if there were no major black woman writers, most are prepared to admit that certain well-known white writers were lesbians for all or part of their lives. The problem is getting beyond a position that says either "so *that's* what was wrong with her!" or, alternatively, "it doesn't matter who she slept with—we're talking about literature." Much lesbian feminist criticism has addressed theoretical questions about *which* literature is actually part of the lesbian tradition, all writing by lesbians, for example, or all writing by women about women's relations with one another. Questions of class and race enter here as well, both in their own guise and in the by now familiar form of "aesthetic standards." Who speaks for the lesbian community: the highly educated experimentalist with an unearned income or the naturalistic working-class autobiographer? Or are both the *same kind* of foremother, reflecting the community's range of cultural identities and resistance?[23]

A cheaper way of Canon-making in a corner (Baxter, 1639).

It is not only members of included social groups, however, who have challenged the fundamentally elite nature of the existing canon. "Elite" is a literary as well as a social category. It is possible to argue for taking all texts seriously as texts without arguments based on social oppression or cultural exclusion, and popular genres have therefore been studied as part of the female literary tradition. Feminists are not in agreement as to whether domestic and sentimental fiction, the female Gothic, the women's sensational novel functioned as instruments of expression, repression, or subversion, but they have successfully revived interest in the question as a legitimate cultural issue.[24] It is no longer automatically assumed that literature addressed to the mass female audience is necessarily bad because it is sentimental, or for that matter, sentimental because it is addressed to that audience. Feminist criticism has examined without embarrassment an entire literature that was previously dismissed solely because it was popular with women and affirmed standards and values associated with femininity. And proponents of the "continuous tradition" and "women's culture" positions have insisted that this material be placed beside women's "high" art as part of the articulated and organic female tradition.

This point of view remains controversial within the orbit of women's studies, but the real problems start when it comes into contact with the universe of canon formation. Permission may have been given the contemporary critic to approach a wide range of texts, transcending and even ignoring the traditional canon. But in a context where the ground of struggle—highly contested, moreover—concerns Edith Wharton's advancement to somewhat more major status, fundamental assumptions have changed very little. Can Hawthorne's "d____d mob of scribbling women" *really* be invading the realms so long sanctified by Hawthorne himself and his brother geniuses? Is this what feminist criticism or even feminist cultural history means? Is it—to apply some outmoded and deceptively simple categories—a good development or a bad one? If these questions have not been raised, it is because women's literature and the female tradition tend to be evoked as an autonomous cultural experience, not impinging on the rest of literary history.

Wisdome under a ragged coate is seldome canonicall (Crosse, 1603).

Whether dealing with popular genres or high art, commentary on the female tradition usually has been based on work that was published at some time and was produced by professional writers. But feminist scholarship has also pushed back the boundaries of literature in other directions, considering a wide range of forms and styles in which women's writing—especially that of women who did not perceive themselves as writers—appears. In this way, women's letters, diaries, journals, autobiographies, oral histories, and private poetry have come under critical scrutiny as evidence of women's consciousness *and expression.*

Generally speaking, feminist criticism has been quite open to such material, recognizing that the very conditions that gave many women the impetus to write made it impossible for their culture to define them as writers. This acceptance has expanded our sense of possible forms and voices, but it has not challenged our received sense of appropriate style. What it amounts to is that if a woman writing in isolation and with no public audience in view nonetheless had "good"—that is, canonical—models, we are impressed with the strength of her text when she applies what she has assimilated about writing to her own experiences as a woman. If, however, her literary models were chosen from the same popular literature that some critics are now beginning to recognize as part of the female tradition, then she has not got hold of an expressive instrument that empowers her.

At the Modern Language Association meeting in 1976, I included in my paper the entire two-page autobiography of a participant in the Summer Schools for Women Workers held at Bryn Mawr in the first decades of the century. It is a circumstantial narrative in which events from the melancholy to the melodramatic are accumulated in a serviceable, somewhat hackneyed style. The anonymous "Seamer on Men's Underwear" had a unique sense of herself both as an individual and as a member of the working class. But was she a writer? Part of the audience was as moved as I was by the narrative, but the majority was outraged at the piece's failure to meet the criteria—particularly, the "complexity" criteria—of good art.

When I developed my remarks for publication, I wrote about the problems of dealing with an author who is trying too hard to write elegantly, and attempted to make the case that clichés or sentimentality need not be signals of meretricious prose and that ultimately it is honest writing for which criticism should be looking.[25] Nowadays, I would also address the question of the female tradition, the role of popular fiction within it, and the influence of that fiction on its audience. It seems to me that, if we accept the work of the professional "scribbling woman," we have also to accept its literary consequences, not drawing the line at the place where that literature may have been the force that enabled an otherwise inarticulate segment of the population to grasp a means of expression and communication.

Once again, the arena is the female tradition itself. If we are thinking in terms of canon formation, it is the alternative canon. Until the aesthetic arguments can be fully worked out in the feminist context, it will be impossible to argue, in the general marketplace of literary ideas, that the novels of Henry James ought to give place—a *little* place, even—to the diaries of his sister

Alice. At this point, I suspect most of our male colleagues would consider such a request, even in the name of Alice James, much less the Seamer on Men's Underwear, little more than a form of "reverse discrimination"—a concept to which some of them are already overly attached. It is up to feminist scholars, when we determine that this is indeed the right course to pursue, to demonstrate that such an inclusion would constitute a genuinely affirmative action for all of us.

The development of feminist literary criticism and scholarship has already proceeded through a number of identifiable stages. Its pace is more reminiscent of the survey course than of the slow processes of canon formation and revision, and it has been more successful in defining and sticking to its own intellectual turf, the female counter-canon, than in gaining general canonical recognition for Edith Wharton, Fanny Fern, or the female diarists of the Westward Expansion. In one sense, the more coherent our sense of the female tradition is, the stronger will be our eventual case. Yet the longer we wait, the more comfortable the women's literature ghetto—separate, apparently autonomous, and far from equal—may begin to feel.

At the same time, I believe the challenge cannot come only by means of the patent value of the work of women. We must pursue the questions certain of us have raised and retreated from as to the eternal verity of the received standards of greatness or even goodness. And, while not abandoning our newfound female tradition, we have to return to confrontation with "the" canon, examining it as a source of ideas, themes, motifs, and myths about the two sexes. The point in so doing is not to label and hence dismiss even the most sexist literary classics, but to enable all of us to apprehend them, finally, in all their human dimensions.

NOTES

[1]Jane Marcus, "Gunpowder Treason and Plot," talk delivered at the School of Criticism and Theory, Northwestern University, colloquium "The Challenge of Feminist Criticism," November 1981. Seeking authority for the sort of creature a literary canon might be, I turned, like many another, to the *Oxford English Dictionary.* The tags that head up the several sections of this essay are a by-product of that effort rather than of any more exact and laborious scholarship.

[2]In a survey of 50 introductory courses in American literature offered at 25 U.S. colleges and universities, Emily Dickinson's name appeared more often than that of any other woman writer: 20 times. This frequency puts her in a fairly respectable twelfth place. Among the 61 most frequently taught authors, only 7 others are women; Edith Wharton and Kate Chopin are each mentioned 8 times, Sarah Orne Jewett and Anne Bradstreet 6 each, Flannery O'Connor 4 times, Willa Cather and Mary Wilkins Freeman each 3 times. The same list includes 5 black authors, all of them male. Responses from other institutions received too late for compilation only confirmed these findings. See Paul Lauter, "A Small Survey of Introductory Courses in American

Literature," *Women's Studies Quarterly* 9 (Winter 1981): 12. In another study, 99 professors of English responded to a survey asking which works of American literature published since 1941 they thought should be considered classics and which books should be taught to college students. The work mentioned by the most respondents (59 citations) was Ralph Ellison's *Invisible Man.* No other work by a black appears among the top 20 that constitute the published list of results. Number 19, *The Complete Stories of Flannery O'Connor,* is the only work on this list by a woman. (*Chronicle of Higher Education,* September 29, 1982.) For British literature, the feminist claim is not that Austen, the Brontës, Eliot, and Woolf are habitually omitted, but rather that they are by no means always included in courses that, like the survey I taught at Columbia some years ago, had room for a single nineteenth-century novel. I know, however, of no systematic study of course offerings in this area more recent than Elaine Showalter's "Women in the Literary Curriculum," *College English* 32 (May 32 1971): 855–62.

[3]Kate Millett, *Sexual Politics* (Garden City, N.Y.: Doubleday, 1970); Eva Figes, *Patriarchal Attitudes* (New York: Stein & Day, 1970); Elizabeth Janeway, *Man's World, Woman's Place: A Study in Social Mythology* (New York: William Morrow, 1971); Germaine Greer, *The Female Eunuch* (New York: McGraw-Hill, 1971); Carolyn G. Heilbrun, *Toward a Recognition of Androgyny* (New York: Harper & Row, 1974). The phenomenon these studies represent is discussed at greater length in a study of which I am a co-author; see Ellen Carol DuBois, Gail Paradise Kelly, Elizabeth Lapovsky Kennedy, Carolyn W. Korsmeyer, and Lillian S. Robinson, *Feminist Scholarship: Kindling in the Groves of Academe* (Urbana: University of Illinois Press, 1985).

[4]Annette Kolodny, *The Lay of the Land: Metaphor as Experience and History in American Life and Letters* (Chapel Hill: University of North Carolina Press, 1975); Judith Fetterley, *The Resisting Reader: A Feminist Approach to American Fiction* (Bloomington: Indiana University Press, 1978).

[5]Mary Ellmann, *Thinking About Women* (New York: Harcourt, Brace & World, 1968).

[6]Carolyn Ruth Swift Lenz, Gayle Greene, and Carol Thomas Neely, eds. *The Woman's Part: Feminist Criticism of Shakespeare* (Urbana: University of Illinois Press, 1980), p. 4. In this vein, see also Juliet Dusinberre, *Shakespeare and the Nature of Woman* (London: Macmillan, 1975); Irene G. Dash, *Wooing, Wedding, and Power: Women in Shakespeare's Plays* (New York: Columbia University Press, 1981).

[7]Sandra M. Gilbert, "Patriarchal Poetics and the Woman Reader: Reflections on Milton's Bogey," *PMLA* 93 (May 1978): 368–82. The articles on Chaucer and Shakespeare in *The Authority of Experience: Essays in Feminist Criticism,* ed. Arlyn Diamond and Lee R. Edwards (Amherst: University of Massachusetts Press, 1977), reflect the complementary tendency.

[8]As I learned when surveying fifteen years' worth of *Dissertation Abstracts* and MLA programs, much of this work has taken the form of theses or conference papers rather than books and journal articles.

[9]See R.W.B. Lewis, *Edith Wharton: A Biography* (New York: Harper & Row, 1975); Cynthia Griffin Wolff, *A Feast of Words: The Triumph of Edith Wharton* (New York: Oxford University Press, 1977); see also Marlene Springer, *Edith Wharton and Kate Chopin: A Reference Guide* (Boston: G.K. Hall, 1976).

[10]See, for instance, Rebecca Harding Davis, *Life in the Iron Mills* (Old Westbury, N.Y.: Feminist Press, 1972), with a biographical and critical Afterword by Tillie Olsen; Kate Chopin, *The Complete Works,* ed. Per Seyersted (Baton Rouge: Louisiana State University Press, 1969); Alice Walker, "In Search of Zora Neale Hurston," *Ms.,* March 1975, pp. 74–75; Robert Hemenway, *Zora Neale Hurston* (Urbana: University

of Illinois Press, 1978): Zora Neale Hurston, *I Love Myself When I Am Laughing and Also When I Am Looking Mean and Impressive* (Old Westbury: Feminist Press, 1979), with introductory material by Alice Walker and Mary Helen Washington; Carolyn G. Burke, "Becoming Mina Loy," *Women's Studies* 7 (1979): 136–50; Meridel LeSueur, *Ripening* (Old Westbury: Feminist Press, 1981); on LeSueur, see also Mary McAnally, ed., *We Sing Our Struggle: A Tribute to Us All* (Tulsa, Okla.: Cardinal Press, 1982); *The Young Rebecca: Writings of Rebecca West, 1911–1917*, selected and introduced by Jane Marcus (New York: Viking Press, 1982).

The examples cited are all from the nineteenth and twentieth centuries. Valuable work has also been done on women writers before the Industrial Revolution. See Joan Goulianos, ed., *By a Woman Writt: Literature from Six Centuries by and About Women* (Indianapolis: Bobbs-Merrill, 1973); Mary R. Mahl and Helene Koon, eds., *The Female Spectator: English Women Writers before 1800* (Bloomington: Indiana University Press, 1977).

[11]Nina Baym, *Women's Fiction: A Guide to Novels By and About Women in America, 1820–70* (Ithaca: Cornell University Press, 1978), pp. 14–15.

[12]Myra Jehlen, "Archimedes and the Paradox of Feminist Criticism," *Signs* 6 (Summer 1981): 592.

[13]Patricia Meyer Spacks, *The Female Imagination* (New York: Alfred A. Knopf, 1975).

[14]*The World Split Open: Four Centuries of Women Poets In England and America, 1552–1950,* ed. and intro. Louise Bernikow (New York: Vintage Books, 1974).

[15]Ellen Moers, *Literary Women: The Great Writers* (Garden City, N.Y.: Doubleday, 1976).

[16]Elaine Showalter, *A Literature of Their Own: British Women Novelists from Brontë to Lessing* (Princeton, N.J.: Princeton University Press, 1977).

[17]Sandra M. Gilbert and Susan Gubar, *The Madwoman in the Attic: The Woman Writer and the Nineteenth-Century Literary Imagination* (New Haven, Conn.: Yale University Press, 1979).

[18]Carroll-Smith Rosenberg, "The Female World of Love and Ritual: Relations Between Women in Nineteenth-Century America," *Signs* 1 (Fall 1975): 1–30; Nancy F. Cott, *The Bonds of Womanhood: "Woman's Sphere" in New England, 1780–1830* (New Haven, Conn.: Yale University Press, 1977).

[19]Nina Auerbach, *Communities of Women: An Idea in Fiction* (Cambridge, Mass.: Harvard University Press, 1979). See also Janet M. Todd, *Women's Friendship in Literature* (New York: Columbia University Press, 1980); Louise Bernikow, *Among Women* (New York: Crown, 1980).

[20]Judith Lowder Newton, *Women, Power, and Subversion: Social Strategies in British Fiction* (Athens: University of Georgia Press, 1981).

[21]On the failings of feminist criticism with respect to black and lesbian writers, see Barbara Smith, "Toward a Black Feminist Criticism," in this volume, pp. 168–85; Mary Helen Washington, "New Lives and New Letters: Black Women Writers at the End of the Seventies," *College English* 43 (January 1981): 1–11; Bonnie Zimmerman, "What Has Never Been: An Overview of Lesbian Feminist Literary Criticism," in this volume, pp. 200–24.

[22]See, e.g., Smith, "Toward a Black Feminist Criticism"; Barbara Christian, *Black Women Novelists: The Development of a Tradition, 1892–1976* (Westport, Conn.: Greenwood Press, 1980); Erlene Stetson, ed., *Black Sister: Poetry by Black American Women, 1764–1980* (Bloomington: Indiana University Press, 1981) and its forthcoming sequel; Gloria Hull, "Black Women Poets from Wheatley to Walker," in *Sturdy Black Bridges: Visions of Black Women in Literature,* ed. Roseann P. Bell et al.

(Garden City, N.Y.: Anchor Books, 1979); Mary Helen Washington, "Introduction: In Pursuit of Our Own History," *Midnight Birds: Stories of Contemporary Black Women Writers* (Garden City, N.Y.: Anchor Books, 1980); the essays and bibliographies in *But Some of Us Are Brave: Black Women's Studies,* ed. Gloria Hull, Patricia Bell Scott, and Barbara Smith (Old Westbury: Feminist Press, 1982).

[23]See Zimmerman, "What Has Never Been"; Adrienne Rich, "Jane Eyre: Trials of a Motherless Girl," *Lies, Secrets, and Silence: Selected Prose, 1966–1978* (New York: W. W. Norton, 1979); Lillian Faderman, *Surpassing the Love of Men: Romantic Friendship and Love Between Women from the Renaissance to the Present* (New York: William Morrow, 1981); the literary essays in *Lesbian Studies,* ed. Margaret Cruikshank (Old Westbury, N.Y.: Feminist Press, 1982).

[24]Some examples on different sides of the question are: Ann Douglas, *The Feminization of American Culture* (New York: Alfred A. Knopf, 1976); Elaine Showalter, *A Literature of Their Own* and her article "Dinah Mulock Craik and the Tactics of Sentiment: A Case Study in Victorian Female Authorship," *Feminist Studies* 2 (May 1975): 5–23; Katherine Ellis, "Paradise Lost: The Limits of Domesticity in the Nineteenth-Century Novel," *Feminist Studies* 2 (May 1975): 55–65.

[25]Lillian S. Robinson, "Working/Women/Writing," *Sex, Class, and Culture* (Bloomington: Indiana University Press, 1978), p. 252.

II

Feminist Criticisms and Women's Cultures

Toward a Feminist Poetics

Elaine Showalter

In 1977, Leon Edel, the distinguished biographer of Henry James, contributed to a London symposium of essays by six male critics called *Contemporary Approaches to English Studies.* Professor Edel presented his essay as a dramatized discussion between three literary scholars who stand arguing about art on the steps of the British Museum:

> There was Criticus, a short, thick-bodied intellectual with spectacles, who clung to a pipe in his right hand. There was Poeticus, who cultivated a Yeatsian forelock, but without the eyeglasses and the ribbon. He made his living by reviewing and had come to the B.M. to look up something or other. Then there was Plutarchus, a lean and lanky biographer wearing a corduroy jacket.

As these three gentlemen are warming to their important subject, a taxi pulls up in front of them and releases "an auburn-haired young woman, obviously American, who wore ear-rings and carried an armful of folders and an attaché case." Into the museum she dashes, leaving the trio momentarily wondering why femininity requires brainwork. They are still arguing when she comes out, twenty-one pages later.[1]

I suppose we should be grateful that at least one woman—let us call her Critica—makes an appearance in this gathering, even if she is not invited to join the debate. I imagine that she is a feminist critic—in fact, if I could afford to take taxis to the British Museum, I would think they had perhaps seen me

—and it is pleasing to think that while the men stand gossiping in the sun, she is inside hard at work. But these are scant satisfactions when we realize that of all the approaches to English studies current in the 1970s, feminist criticism is the most isolated and the least understood. Members of English departments who can remember what Harold Bloom means by *clinamen,* and who know the difference between Tartu and Barthian semiotics, will remark that they are against feminist criticism and consequently have never read any. Those who have read it, often seem to have read through a glass darkly, superimposing their stereotypes on the critical texts. In his introduction to Nina Auerbach's subtle feminist analysis of *Dombey and Son* in the *Dickens Studies Annual,* for example, Robert Partlow discusses the deplorable but nonexistent essay of his own imagining:

> At first glance, Nina Auerbach's essay . . . might seem to be a case of special pleading, another piece of women's lib propaganda masquerading as literary criticism, but it is not quite that . . . such an essay could have been . . . ludicrous . . . it could have seen dark phallic significance in curving railroad tracks and upright church pews—but it does not.[2]

In contrast to Partlow's caricature (feminist criticism will naturally be obsessed with the phallus), there are the belligerent assumptions of Robert Boyers, in the Winter 1977 issue of *Partisan Review,* that it will be obsessed with destroying great male artists. In "A Case Against Feminist Criticism," Boyers used a single work, Joan Mellen's *Women and Their Sexuality in the New Film* (1973), as an example of feminist deficiency in "intellectual honesty" and "rigor." He defines feminist criticism as the "insistence on asking the same questions of every work and demanding ideologically satisfactory answers to those questions as a means of evaluating it," and concludes his diatribe thus:

> Though I do not think anyone has made a credible case for feminist criticism as a viable alternative to any other mode, no one can seriously object to feminists continuing to try. We ought to demand that such efforts be minimally distinguished by intellectual candor and some degree of precision. This I have failed to discover in most feminist criticism.[3]

Since his article makes its "case" so recklessly that Joan Mellen brought charges for libel, and the *Partisan Review* was obliged to print a retraction in the following issue, Boyers hardly seems the ideal champion to enter the critical lists under the twin banners of honesty and rigor. Indeed, his terminology is best understood as a form of intimidation, intended to force women into using a discourse more acceptable to the academy, characterized by the "rigor" which my dictionary defines as strictness, a severe or cruel act, or a "state of rigidity in living tissues or organs that prevents response to stimuli." In formulating a feminist literary theory, one ought never to expect to appease a Robert Boyers. And yet these "cases" cannot continue to be settled, one by one, out of court. The absence of a clearly articulated theory makes feminist criticism perpetually vulnerable to such attacks, and not even feminist critics seem to agree what it is that they mean to profess and defend.

A second obstacle to the articulation of a feminist critical practice is the activist's suspicion of theory, especially when the demand for clarification comes from sources as patently sexist as the egregiously named Boyerses and Mailers of the literary quarterlies. Too many literary abstractions which claim to be universal have in fact described only male perceptions, experiences, and options, and have falsified the social and personal contexts in which literature is produced and consumed. In women's fiction, the complacently precise and systematizing male has often been the target of satire, especially when his subject is Woman. George Eliot's impotent structuralist Casaubon is a classic instance, as is Mr. Ramsay, the self-pitying philosopher in Virginia Woolf's *To the Lighthouse.* More recently Doris Lessing's Professor Bloodrot in *The Golden Notebook* lectures confidently on orgasm in the female swan; as Bloodrot proceeds, the women in the audience rise one by one and leave. What women have found hard to take in such male characters is their self-deception, their pretense to objectivity, their emotion parading as reason. As Adrienne Rich comments in *Of Woman Born,* "the term 'rational' relegates to its opposite term all that it refuses to deal with, and thus ends by assuming itself to be purified of the nonrational, rather than searching to identify and assimilate its own surreal or nonlinear elements."[4] For some radical feminists, methodology itself is an intellectual instrument of patriarchy, a tyrannical methodolatry which sets implicit limits to what can be questioned and discussed. "The God Method," writes Mary Daly,

> is in fact a subordinate deity, serving higher powers. These are social and cultural institutions whose survival depends upon the classification of disruptive and disturbing information as nondata. Under patriarchy, Method has wiped out women's questions so totally that even women have not been able to hear and formulate our own questions, to meet our own experiences.[5]

From this perspective, the academic demand for theory can only be heard as a threat to the feminist need for authenticity, and the visitor looking for a formula he or she can take away without personal encounter is not welcome.

In the United States, where women's-studies programs offer degree options in nearly three hundred colleges and universities, there are fears that feminist analysis has been coopted by academia, and counterdemands that we resist the pressure to assimilate. Some believe that the activism and empiricism of feminist criticism is its greatest strength, and point to the flourishing international women's press, to new feminist publishing houses, and to writing collectives and manifestos. They are afraid that if the theory is perfected, the movement will be dead. But these defensive responses may also be rationalizations of the psychic barriers to women's participation in theoretical discourse. Traditionally women have been cast in the supporting rather than the starring roles of literary scholarship. Whereas male critics in the twentieth century have moved to center stage, openly contesting for primacy with writers, establishing coteries and schools, speaking unabashedly (to quote Geoffrey Hartman) of their "pen-envy,"[6] women are still too often translators, editors, hostesses at the conference and the Festschrift, interpreters; to congratulate ourselves for working patiently and anonymously for the coming of Shakespeare's sister, as Virginia Woolf exhorted us to do in 1928, is in a sense to make a virtue of necessity. In this essay, therefore, I would like to outline a brief taxonomy, if not a poetics, of feminist criticism, in the hope that it will serve as an introduction to a body of work which needs to be considered both as a major contribution to English studies and as part of an interdisciplinary effort to reconstruct the social, political, and cultural experience of women.

Feminist criticism can be divided into two distinct varieties. The first type is concerned with *woman as reader*—with woman as the consumer of male-produced literature, and with the way in which the hypothesis of a female reader changes our apprehension of a given text, awakening us to the significance of its sexual codes. I shall call this kind of analysis the *feminist critique,* and like other kinds of critique it is a historically grounded inquiry which probes the ideological assumptions of literary phenomena. Its subjects include the images and stereotypes of women in literature, the omissions of and misconceptions about women in criticism, and the fissures in male-constructed literary history. It is also concerned with the exploitation and manipulation of the female audience, especially in popular culture and film; and with the analysis of woman-as-sign in semiotic systems. The second type of feminist criticism is concerned with *woman as writer*—with woman as the producer of textual meaning, with the history, themes, genres, and structures of literature by women. Its subjects include the psychodynamics of female creativity; linguistics and the problem of a female language; the trajectory of the individual or collective female literary career; literary history; and, of course, studies of particular writers and works. No term exists in English for such a specialized discourse, and so I have adapted the French term *la gynocritique:* "gynocritics" (although the significance of the male pseudonym in the history of women's writing also suggested the term "georgics").

The feminist critique is essentially political and polemical, with theoretical affiliations to Marxist sociology and aesthetics; gynocritics is more self-contained and experimental, with connections to other modes of new feminist research. In a dialogue between these two positions, Carolyn Heilbrun, the writer, and Catharine Stimpson, editor of the journal *Signs: Women in Culture and Society,* compare the feminist critique to the Old Testament, "looking for the sins and errors of the past," and gynocritics to the New Testament, seeking "the grace of imagination." Both kinds are necessary, they explain, for only the Jeremiahs of the feminist critique can lead us out of the "Egypt of female servitude" to the promised land of the feminist vision. That the discussion makes use of these Biblical metaphors points to the connections between feminist consciousness and conversion narratives which often appear in women's literature; Carolyn Heilbrun comments on her own text, "When I talk about feminist criticism, I am amazed at how high a moral tone I take."[7]

The Feminist Critique: Hardy

Let us take briefly as an example of the way a feminist critique might proceed, Thomas Hardy's *The Mayor of Casterbridge,* which begins with the famous scene of the drunken Michael Henchard selling his wife and infant daughter for five guineas at a country fair. In his study of Hardy, Irving Howe has praised the brilliance and power of this opening scene:

> To shake loose from one's wife; to discard that drooping rag of a woman, with her mute complaints and maddening passivity; to escape not by a slinking abandonment but through the public sale of her body to a stranger, as horses are sold at a fair; and thus to wrest, through sheer amoral wilfulness, a second chance out of life—it is with this stroke, so insidiously attractive to male fantasy, that *The Mayor of Casterbridge* begins.[8]

It is obvious that a woman, unless she has been indoctrinated into being very deeply identified indeed with male culture, will have a different experience of this scene. I quote Howe first to indicate how the fantasies of the male critic distort the text; for Hardy tells us very little about the relationship of Michael and Susan Henchard, and what we see in the early scenes does not suggest that she is drooping, complaining, or passive. Her role, however, is a passive one; severely constrained by her womanhood, and further burdened by her child, there is no way that *she* can wrest a second chance out of life. She cannot master events, but only accommodate herself to them.

What Howe, like other male critics of Hardy, conveniently overlooks about the novel is that Henchard sells not only his wife but his child, a child who can only be female. Patriarchal societies do not readily sell their sons, but their daughters are all for sale sooner or later. Hardy wished to make the sale of the daughter emphatic and central; in early drafts of the novel Henchard has two daughters and sells only one, but Hardy revised to make it clearer that Henchard is symbolically selling his entire share in the world of women. Having severed his bonds with this female community of love and loyalty, Henchard has chosen to live in the male community, to define his human relationships by the male code of paternity, money, and legal contract. His tragedy lies in realizing the inadequacy of this system, and in his inability to repossess the loving bonds he comes desperately to need.

The emotional center of *The Mayor of Casterbridge* is neither Henchard's relationship to his wife nor his superficial romance with Lucetta Templeman, but his slow appreciation of the strength and dignity of his wife's daughter, Elizabeth-Jane. Like the other women in the book, she is governed by her own heart—man-made laws are not important to her until she is taught by Henchard himself to value legality, paternity, external definitions, and thus in the end to reject him. A self-proclaimed "woman-hater," a man who has felt at best a "supercilious pity" for womankind, Henchard is humbled and "unmanned" by the collapse of his own virile façade, the loss of his mayor's chain, his master's authority, his father's rights. But in Henchard's alleged weakness and "womanishness," breaking through in moments of tenderness, Hardy is really showing us the man at his best. Thus Hardy's female characters in *The Mayor of Casterbridge,* as in his other novels, are somewhat idealized and melancholy projections of a repressed male self.

As we see in this analysis, one of the problems of the feminist critique is that it is male-oriented. If we study stereotypes of women, the sexism of male critics, and the limited roles women play in literary history, we are not learning what women have felt and experienced, but only what men have thought women should be. In some fields of specialization, this may require a long apprenticeship to the male theoretician, whether he be Althusser, Barthes, Macherey, or Lacan; and then an application of the theory of signs or myths or the unconscious to male texts or films. The temporal and intellectual investment one makes in such a process increases resistance to questioning it, and to seeing its historical and ideological boundaries. The critique also has a tendency to naturalize women's victimization by making it the inevitable and obsessive topic of discussion. One sees, moreover, in works like Elizabeth Hardwick's *Seduction and Betrayal,* the bittersweet moral distinctions the critic makes between women merely betrayed by men, like Hetty in *Adam Bede,* and the heroines who make careers out of betrayal, like Hester Prynne in *The Scarlet Letter.* This comes dangerously close to a celebration of the opportunities of victimization, the seduction *of* betrayal.[9]

Gynocritics and Female Culture

In contrast to this angry or loving fixation on male literature, the program of gynocritics is to construct a female framework for the analysis of women's literature, to develop new models based on the study of female experience, rather than to adapt male models and theories. Gynocritics begins at the point when we free ourselves from the linear absolutes of male literary history, stop trying to fit women between the lines of the male tradition, and focus instead on the newly visible world of female culture. This is comparable to the ethnographer's effort to render the experience of the "muted" female half of a society, which is described in Shirley Ardener's collection *Perceiving Women.*[10] Gynocritics is related to feminist research in history, anthropology, psychology, and sociology, all of which have developed hypotheses of a female subculture including not only the ascribed status, and the internalized constructs of feminity, but also the occupations, interactions, and consciousness of women. Anthropologists study the female subculture in the relationships between women, as mothers, daughters, sisters, and friends; in sexuality, reproduction, and ideas about the body; and in rites of initiation and passage, purification ceremonies, myths, and taboos. Michelle Rosaldo writes in *Woman, Culture, and Society:*

> The very symbolic and social conceptions that appear to set women apart and to circumscribe their activities may be used by women as a basis for female solidarity and worth. When men live apart from women, they in fact cannot control them, and unwittingly they may provide them with the symbols and social resources on which to build a society of their own.[11]

Thus in some women's literature, feminine values penetrate and undermine the masculine systems that contain them; and women have imaginatively engaged the myths of the Amazons, and the fantasies of a separate female society, in genres from Victorian poetry to contemporary science fiction.

In recent years, pioneering work by four young American feminist scholars has given us some new ways to interpret the culture of nineteenth-century American women and the literature that was its primary expressive form. Carroll Smith-Rosenberg's essay "The Female World of Love and Ritual" examines several archives of letters between women, and outlines the homosocial emotional world of the nineteenth century. Nancy Cott's *The Bonds of Womanhood: Woman's Sphere in New England, 1780–1835* explores the paradox of a cultural bondage, a legacy of pain and submission, which nonetheless generates a sisterly solidarity, a bond of shared experience, loyalty, and compassion. Ann Douglas's ambitious book, *The Feminization of American Culture,* boldly locates the genesis of American mass culture in the sentimental literature of women and clergymen, two allied and "disestablished" postindustrial groups. These three are social historians; but Nina Auerbach's *Communities of Women: An Idea in Fiction* seeks the bonds of womanhood in women's literature, ranging from the matriarchal households of Louisa May Alcott and Mrs. Gaskell to the women's schools and colleges of Dorothy Sayers, Sylvia Plath, and Muriel Spark. Historical and literary studies like these, based on English women, are badly needed; and the manuscript and archival sources for them are both abundant and untouched.[12]

Gynocritics: Elizabeth Barrett Browning and Muriel Spark

Gynocritics must also take into account the different velocities and curves of political, social, and personal histories in determining women's literary choices and careers. "In dealing with women as writers," Virginia Woolf wrote in her 1929 essay, "Women and Fiction," "as much elasticity as possible is desirable; it is necessary to leave oneself room to deal with other things besides their work, so much has that work been influenced by conditions that have nothing whatever to do with art."[13] We might illustrate the need for this completeness by looking at Elizabeth Barrett Browning, whose verse novel *Aurora Leigh* (1856) has recently been handsomely reprinted by the Women's Press. In her excellent introduction Cora Kaplan defines Barrett Browning's feminism as romantic and bourgeois, placing its faith in the transforming powers of love, art, and Christian charity. Kaplan reviews Barrett Browning's dialogue with the artists and radicals of her time; with Tennyson and Clough, who had also written poems on the "woman question"; with the Christian Socialism of Fourier, Owen, Kingsley, and Maurice; and with such female predecessors as Madame de Staël and George Sand. But in this exploration of Barrett Browning's intellectual milieu, Kaplan omits discussion of the male poet whose influence on her work in the 1850s would have been most pervasive: Robert Browning. When we understand how susceptible women writers have always been to the aesthetic standards and values of the male tradition, and to male approval and validation, we can appreciate the complexity of a marriage between artists. Such a union has almost invariably meant internal conflicts, self-effacement, and finally obliteration for the woman, except in the rare cases

—Eliot and Lewes, the Woolfs—where the husband accepted a managerial rather than a competitive role. We can see in Barrett Browning's letters of the 1850s the painful, halting, familiar struggle between her womanly love and ambition for her husband and her conflicting commitment to her own work. There is a sense in which she *wants* him to be the better artist. At the beginning of the decade she was more famous than he; then she notes with pride a review in France which praises him more; his work on *Men and Women* goes well; her work on *Aurora Leigh* goes badly (she had a young child and was recovering from the most serious of her four miscarriages). In 1854 she writes to a woman friend:

> I am behind hand with my poem. . . . Robert swears he shall have his book ready in spite of everything for print when we shall be in London for the purpose, but, as for mine, it must wait for the next spring I begin to see clearly. Also it may be better not to bring out the two works together.

And she adds wryly, "If mine were ready I might not say so perhaps."[14]

Without an understanding of the framework of the female subculture, we can miss or misinterpret the themes and structures of women's literature, fail to make necessary connections within a tradition. In 1852, in an eloquent passage from her autobiographical essay "Cassandra," Florence Nightingale identified the pain of feminist awakening as its essence, as the guarantee of progress and free will. Protesting against the protected unconscious lives of middle-class Victorian women, Nightingale demanded the restoration of their suffering:

> Give us back our suffering, we cry to Heaven in our hearts —suffering rather than indifferentism—for out of suffering may come the cure. Better to have pain than paralysis: A hundred struggle and drown in the breakers. One discovers a new world.[15]

It is fascinating to see how Nightingale's metaphors anticipate not only her own medical career but also the fate of the heroines of women's novels in the nineteenth and twentieth centuries. To waken from the drugged, pleasant sleep of Victorian womanhood was agonizing; in fiction it is much more likely to end in drowning than in discovery. It is usually associated with what George Eliot in *Middlemarch* calls "the chill hours of a morning twilight," and the sudden appalled confrontation with the contingencies of adulthood. Eliot's Maggie Tulliver, Edith Wharton's Lily Bart, Olive Schreiner's Lyndall, Kate Chopin's Edna Pontellier wake to worlds which offer no places for the women they wish to become; and rather than struggling they die. Female suffering thus becomes a kind of literary commodity which both men and women consume. Even in these important women's novels—*The Mill on the Floss, The Story of an African Farm, The House of Mirth*—the fulfillment of the plot is a visit to the heroine's grave by a male mourner.

According to Dame Rebecca West, unhappiness is still the keynote of contemporary fiction by English women.[16] Certainly the literary landscape is strewn with dead female bodies. In Fay Weldon's *Down Among the Women* and *Female Friends,* suicide has come to be a kind of domestic accomplishment, carried out after the shopping and the washing-up. When Weldon's heroine turns on the gas, "she feels that she has been half-dead for so long that the difference in state will not be very great." In Muriel Spark's stunning short novel of 1970, *The Driver's Seat,* another half-dead and desperate heroine gathers all her force to hunt down a woman-hating psychopath and persuade him to murder her. Garishly dressed in a purposely bought outfit of clashing purple, green, and white—the colors of the suffragettes (and the colors of the school uniform in *The Prime of Miss Jean Brodie*)—Lise goes in search of her killer, lures him to a park, gives him the knife. But in Lise's careful selection of her death-dress, her patient pursuit of her assassin, Spark has given us the devastated postulates of feminine wisdom: that a woman creates her identity by choosing her clothes, that she creates her history by choosing her man. That, in the 1970s, Mr. Right turns out to be Mr. Goodbar is not the sudden product of urban violence but a latent truth fiction exposes. Spark asks whether men or women are in the driver's seat and whether the power to choose one's destroyer is women's only form of self-assertion. To label the violence or self-destructiveness of these painful novels as neurotic expressions of a personal pathology, as many reviewers have done, is to ignore, Annette Kolodny suggests,

> the possibility that the worlds they inhabit may in fact be real, or true, and for them the only worlds available, and further, to deny the possibility that their apparently "odd" or unusual responses may in fact be justifiable or even necessary.[17]

But women's literature must go beyond these scenarios of compromise, madness, and death. Although the reclamation of suffering is the beginning, its purpose is to discover the new world. Happily, some recent women's literature, especially in the United States, where novelists and poets have become vigorously involved in the women's liberation movement, has gone beyond reclaiming suffering to its reinvestment. This newer writing relates the pain of transformation to history. "If I'm lonely," writes Adrienne Rich in "Song,"

it must be the loneliness
of waking first, of breathing
dawn's first cold breath on the city
of being the one awake
in a house wrapped in sleep[18]

Rich is one of the spokeswomen for a new women's writing which explores the will to change. In her recent book, *Of Woman Born: Motherhood as Experience and Institution,* Rich challenges the alienation from and rejection of the mother that daughters have learned under patriarchy. Much women's literature in the past has dealt with "matrophobia" or the fear of becoming one's mother.[19] In Sylvia Plath's *The Bell Jar,* for example, the heroine's mother is the target for the novel's most punishing contempt. When Esther announces to her therapist that she hates her mother, she is on the road to recovery. Hating one's mother was the feminist enlightenment of the fifties and sixties; but it is only a metaphor for hating oneself. Female literature of the 1970s goes beyond matrophobia to a courageously sustained quest for the mother, in such books at Margaret Atwood's *Surfacing,* and Lisa Alther's recent *Kinflicks.* As the death of the father has always been an archetypal rite of passage for the Western hero, now the death of the mother as witnessed and transcended by the daughter has become one of the most profound occasions of female literature. In analyzing these purposeful awakenings, these reinvigorated mythologies of female culture, feminist criticism finds its most challenging, inspiriting, and appropriate task.

Women and the Novel: The "Precious Specialty"

The most consistent assumption of feminist reading has been the belief that women's special experience would assume and determine distinctive forms in art. In the nineteenth century, such a contribution was ambivalently valued. When Victorian reviewers like G. H. Lewes, Richard Hutton, and Richard Simpson began to ask what the literature of women might mean and what it might become, they focused on the educational, experiential, and biological handicaps of the woman novelist, and this was also how most women conceptualized their situation. Some reviewers, granting women's sympathy, sentiment, and powers of observation, thought that the novel would provide an appropriate, even a happy, outlet for female emotion and fantasy. In the United States, the popular novelist Fanny Fern understood that women had been granted access to the novel as a sort of repressive desublimation, a harmless channel for frustrations and drives that might otherwise threaten the family, the church, and the state. Fern recommended that women write as therapy, as a release from the stifling silence of the drawing room, and as a rebellion against the indifference and insensitivity of the men closest to them:

> Look around, and see innumerable women, to whose barren and loveless lives this would be improvement and solace, and I say to them, write! write! It will be a safe outlet for thoughts and feelings that maybe the nearest friend you have has never dreamed had place in your heart and brain. . . . It is not *safe* for the women of 1867 to shut down so much that cries out for sympathy and expression, because life is such a maelstrom of business or folly or both that those to whom they have bound themselves, body and soul, recognize only the needs of the former. . . . One of these days, when that diary is found, when the hand that penned it shall be dust, with what amazement and remorse will many a husband or father exclaim, I never knew my wife or my child until this moment.[20]

Fern's scribbling woman spoke with fierce indirectness to the male audience, to the imagined husband or father; her purpose was to shock rather than to please, but the need to provoke masculine response was the controlling factor in her writing. At the turn of the century, members of the Women Writers Suffrage League, an important organization of English novelists and journalists, began to explore the psychological bondage of women's literature and its relationships to a male-dominated publishing industry. Elizabeth Robins, the first president of the league, a novelist and actress who had starred in early English productions of Ibsen, argued in 1908 that no woman writer had ever been free to explore female consciousness:

> The realization that she had access to a rich and as yet unrifled storehouse may have crossed her mind, but there were cogent reasons for concealing her knowledge. With that wariness of ages which has come to be instinct, she contented herself with echoing the old fables, presenting to a man-governed world puppets as nearly as possible like those that had from the beginning found such favour in men's sight.
>
> Contrary to the popular impression, to say in print what she thinks is the last thing the woman-novelist or journalist is so rash as to attempt. There even more than elsewhere (unless she is reckless) she must wear the aspect that shall

> have the best chance of pleasing her brothers. Her publishers are not women.[21]

It was to combat this inhibiting commercial monopoly that nineteenth-century women began to organize their own publishing houses, beginning with Emily Faithfull's Victoria Press in the 1870s, and reaching a peak with the flourishing suffrage presses at the beginning of this century. One of the most fervent beliefs of the Women Writers Suffrage League was that the *terra incognita* of the female psyche would find unique literary expression once women had overthrown male domination. In *A Room of One's Own,* Virginia Woolf argued that economic independence was the essential precondition of an autonomous women's art. Like George Eliot before her, Woolf also believed that women's literature held the promise of a "precious speciality," a distinctly female vision.

Feminine, Feminist, Female

All of these themes have been important to feminist literary criticism in the 1960s and 1970s, but we have approached them with more historical awareness. Before we can even begin to ask how the literature of women would be different and special, we need to reconstruct its past, to rediscover the scores of women novelists, poets, and dramatists whose work has been obscured by time, and to establish the continuity of the female tradition from decade to decade, rather than from Great Woman to Great Woman. As we re-create the chain of writers in this tradition, the patterns of influence and response from one generation to the next, we can also begin to challenge the periodicity of orthodox literary history and its enshrined canons of achievement. It is because we have studied women writers in isolation that we have never grasped the connections between them. When we go beyond Austen, the Brontës, and Eliot, say, to look at a hundred and fifty or more of their sister novelists, we can see patterns and phases in the evolution of a female tradition which correspond to the developmental phases of any subcultural art. In my book on English women writers, *A Literature of Their Own,* I have called these the Feminine, Feminist, and Female stages.[22] During the Feminine phase, dating from about 1840 to 1880, women wrote in an effort to equal the intellectual achievements of the male culture, and internalized its assumptions about female nature. The distinguishing sign of this period is the male pseudonym, introduced in England in the 1840s, and a national characteristic of English women writers. In addition to the famous names we all know—George Eliot, Currer, Ellis, and Acton Bell—dozens of other women chose male pseudonyms as a way of coping with a double literary standard. This masculine disguise goes well beyond the title page; it exerts an irregular pressure on the narrative, affecting tone, diction, structure, and characterization. In contrast to the English male pseudonym, which signals such clear self-awareness of the liabilities of female authorship, American women during the same period adopted superfeminine, little-me pseudonyms (Fanny Fern, Grace Greenwood, Fanny Forester), disguising behind these nominal bouquets their boundless energy, powerful economic motives, and keen professional skills. It is pleasing to discover the occasional Englishwoman who combines both these techniques, and creates the illusion of male authorship with a name that contains the encoded domestic message of femininity—such as Harriet Parr who wrote under the pen name "Holme Lee." The feminist content of feminine art is typically oblique, displaced, ironic, and subversive; one has to read it between the lines, in the missed possibilities of the text.

In the Feminist phase, from about 1880 to 1920, or the winning of the vote, women are historically enabled to reject the accommodating postures of femininity and to use literature to dramatize the ordeals of wronged womanhood. The personal sense of injustice which feminine novelists such as Elizabeth Gaskell and Frances Trollope expressed in their novels of class struggle and factory life become increasingly and explicitly feminist in the 1880s, when a generation of New Women redefined the woman artist's role in terms of responsibility to suffering sisters. The purest examples of this phase are the Amazon utopias of the 1890s, fantasies of perfected female societies set in an England or an America of the future, which were also protests against male government, male laws, and male medicine. One author of Amazon utopias, the American Charlotte Perkins Gilman, also analyzed the preoccupations of masculine literature with sex and war, and the alternative possibilities of an emancipated feminist literature. Gilman's utopian feminism carried George Eliot's idea of the "precious speciality" to its matriarchal extremes. Comparing her view of sisterly collectivity to the beehive, she writes that

> the bee's fiction would be rich and broad, full of the complex tasks of comb-building and filling, the care and feeding of the young. . . . It would treat of the vast fecundity of motherhood, the educative and selective processes of the group-mothers, and the passion of loyalty, of social service, which holds the hives together.[23]

This is Feminist Socialist Realism with a vengeance, but women novelists of the period—even Gilman, in her short stories—could not be limited to such didactic formulas, or such maternal topics.

In the Female phase, ongoing since 1920, women reject both imitation and protest—two forms of dependency—and turn instead to female experience as the source of an autonomous art, extending the feminist analysis of culture to the forms and techniques of literature. Representatives of the formal Female Aesthetic, such as Dorothy Richardson and Virginia Woolf, begin to think in terms of male and female sentences, and divide their work into "masculine" journalism and "feminine" fictions, redefining and sexualizing external and internal experience. Their experiments were both enriching and imprisoning retreats into the celebration of consciousness; even in Woolf's famous definition of life: "a luminous halo, a semi-transparent envelope surrounding us from the beginning of consciousness to the end,"[24] there is a submerged metaphor of uterine withdrawal and containment. In this sense, the Room of One's Own becomes a kind of Amazon utopia, population 1.

Feminist Criticism, Marxism, and Structuralism

In trying to account for these complex permutations of the female tradition, feminist criticism has tried a variety of theoretical approaches. The most natural direction for feminist criticism to take has been the revision and even the subversion of related ideologies, especially Marxist aesthetics and structuralism, altering their vocabularies and methods to include the variable of gender. I believe, however, that this thrifty feminine making-do is ultimately unsatisfactory. Feminist criticism cannot go around forever in men's ill-fitting hand-me-downs, the Annie Hall of English studies; but must, as John Stuart Mill wrote about women's literature in 1869, "emancipate itself from the influence of accepted models, and guide itself by its own impulses"[25]—as, I think, gynocritics is beginning to do. This is not to deny the necessity of using the terminology and techniques of our profession. But when we consider the historical conditions in which critical ideologies are produced, we see why feminist adaptations seem to have reached an impasse.

Both Marxism and structuralism see themselves as privileged critical discourse, and preempt the claim to superior places in the hierarchy of critical approaches. A key word in each system is "science"; both claim to be sciences of literature, and repudiate the personal, fallible, interpretative reading. Marxist aesthetics offers a "science of the text," in which the author becomes not the creator but the producer of a text whose components are historically and economically determined. Structuralism presents linguistically based models of textual permutations and combinations, offering a "science of literary meaning," a grammar of genre. The assimilation of these positivist and evangelical literary criticisms by Anglo-American scholarship in the 1960s and 1970s is not, I would argue, a spontaneous or accidental cultural phenomenon. In the Cold War atmosphere of the late 1950s, when European structuralism began to develop, the morale of the Anglo-American male academic humanist was at its nadir. This was the era of Sputnik, of scientific competition with the Soviet Union, of government money flowing to the laboratories and research centers. Northrop Frye has written about the plight of the male intellectual confronting

> the dismal sexist symbology surrounding the humanities which he meets everywhere, even in the university itself, from freshman classes to the president's office. This symbology, or whatever one should call it, says that the sciences, especially the physical sciences, are rugged, aggressive, out in the world doing things, and so symbolically male, whereas the literatures are narcissistic, intuitive, fanciful, staying at home and making the home more beautiful but not doing anything serious and are therefore symbolically female.[26]

Frye's own *Anatomy of Criticism,* published in 1957, presented the first postulates of a systematic critical theory, and the "possibility of literary study's attaining the progressive, cumulative qualities of science."[27]

The new sciences of the text based on linguistics, computers, genetic structuralism, deconstructionism, neoformalism and deformalism, affective stylistics, and psychoaesthetics, have offered literary critics the opportunity to demonstrate that the work they do is as manly and aggressive as nuclear physics—not intuitive, expressive, and feminine, but strenuous, rigorous, impersonal, and virile. In a shrinking job market, these new levels of professionalization also function as discriminators between the marketable and the marginal lecturer. Literary science, in its manic generation of difficult terminology, its establishment of seminars and institutes of postgraduate study, creates an elite corps of specialists who spend more and more time mastering the theory, less and less time reading the books. We are moving towards a two-tiered system of "higher" and "lower" criticism, the higher concerned with the "scientific" problems of form and structure, the "lower" concerned with the "humanistic" problems of content and interpretation. And these levels, it seems to me, are now taking on subtle gender identities and assuming a sexual polarity—hermeneutics and hismeneutics. Ironically, the existence of a new criticism practiced by women has made it even more possible for structuralism and Marxism to strive, Henchard-like, for systems of formal obligation and determination. Feminists writing in these modes, such as Hélène Cixous and the women contributors to *Diacritics,* risk being allotted the symbolic ghettos of the special issue or the back of the book for their essays.

It is not only because the exchange between feminism, Marxism, and structuralism has hitherto been so one-sided, however, that I think attempts at syntheses have so far been unsuccessful. While scientific criticism struggles to purge itself of the subjective, feminist criticism is willing to assert (in the title of a recent anthology) *The Authority of Experience.*[28] The experience of women can easily disappear, become mute, invalid, and invisible, lost in the diagrams of the structuralist or the class conflict of the Marxists. Experience is not emotion; we must protest now as in the nineteenth century against the equation of the feminine with the irrational. But we must also recognize that the questions we most need to ask go beyond those that science can answer. We must seek the repressed messages of women in history, in anthropology, in psychology, and in ourselves, before we can locate the feminine not-said, in the manner of Pierre Macherey, by probing the fissures of the female text.

Thus the current theoretical impasse in feminist criticism, I believe, is more than a problem of finding "exacting definitions and a suitable terminology," or "theorizing in the midst of a struggle." It comes from our own divided consciousness, the split in each of us. We are both the daughters of the male tradition, of our teachers, our professors, our dissertation advisers, and our publishers—a tradition which asks us to be rational, marginal, and grateful; and sisters in a new women's movement which engenders another kind of awareness and commitment, which demands that we renounce the pseudo-success of token womanhood and the ironic masks of academic debate. How much easier, how less lonely it is, not to awaken—to continue to be critics and teachers of male literature, anthropologists of male culture, and psychologists of male literary response, claiming all the while to be universal. Yet we cannot will ourselves to go back to sleep. As women scholars in the 1970s we have been given a great opportunity, a great intellectual challenge. The anatomy, the rhetoric, the poetics, the history, await our writing.

I am sure that this divided consciousness is sometimes experienced by men, but I think it unlikely that many male academics would have had the division in themselves as succinctly and publicly labeled as they were for me in 1976 when my official title at the University of Delaware was Visiting Minority Professor. I am deeply aware of the struggle in myself between the professor, who wants to study major works by major writers and to mediate impersonally between these works and the readings of other professors, and the minority, the woman who wants connections between my life and my work and who is committed to a revolution of consciousness that would make my concerns those of the majority. There have been times when the Minority wishes to betray the Professor by isolating herself in a female ghetto; or when the Professor wishes to betray the Minority by denying the troubling voice of difference and dissent. What I hope is that neither will betray the other, because neither can exist by itself. The task of feminist critics is to find a new language, a new way of reading that can integrate our intelligence and our experience, our reason and our suffering, our skepticism and our vision. This enterprise should not be confined to women. I invite Criticus, Poeticus, and Plutarchus to share it with us. One thing is certain: feminist criticism is not visiting. It is here to stay, and we must make it a permanent home.

NOTES

I wish to thank Nina Auerbach, Kate Ellis, Mary Jacobus, Wendy Martin, Adrienne Rich, Helen Taylor, Martha Vicinus, Margaret Walters, and Ruth Yeazell for sharing with me their ideas on feminist criticism.

[1]Leon Edel, "The Poetics of Biography," in *Contemporary Approaches to English Studies,* ed. Hilda Schiff (New York: Barnes & Noble, 1977), p. 38. The other contributors to the symposium are George Steiner, Raymond Williams, Christopher Butler, Jonathan Culler, and Terry Eagleton.

[2]Robert Partlow, Introduction to *Dickens Studies Annual,* vol. 5 (Carbondale: Southern Illinois University Press, 1976), pp. xiv–xv. Nina Auerbach's essay is called "Dickens and Dombey: A Daughter After All."

[3]Robert Boyers, "A Case Against Feminist Criticism," *Partisan Review* 44 (Winter 1977): 602, 610.

[4]Adrienne Rich, *Of Woman Born: Motherhood as Experience and Institution* (New York: W. W. Norton, 1977), p. 62.

[5]Mary Daly, *Beyond God the Father: Towards a Philosophy of Women's Liberation* (Boston: Beacon Press, 1973), pp. 12–13.

[6]Geoffrey H. Hartman, *The Fate of Reading* (Chicago: University of Chicago Press, 1975), p. 3.

[7]Carolyn G. Heilbrun and Catharine R. Stimpson, "Theories of Feminist Criticism," in *Feminist Literary Criticism: Explorations in Theory,* ed. Josephine Donovan (Lexington: University Press of Kentucky, 1976), pp. 64, 68, 72.

[8]Irving Howe, *Thomas Hardy* (London: Weidenfeld & Nicolson, 1968), p. 84. For a more detailed discussion of this problem, see my essay "The Unmanning of the Mayor of Casterbridge," in *Critical Approaches to the Fiction of Hardy,* ed. Dale Kramer (New York: Barnes & Noble, 1979), pp. 99–115.

[9]Elizabeth Hardwick, *Seduction and Betrayal: Women and Literature* (New York: Random House, 1974).

[11]Michelle Z. Rosaldo, "Women, Culture, and Society: A Theoretical Overview," in *Women, Culture, and Society,* ed. Michelle Z. Rosaldo and Louise Lamphere (Stanford, Calif.: Stanford University Press, 1974), p. 39.

[10]Shirley Ardener, ed., *Perceiving Women* (New York: Halsted Press, 1975).

[12]Carroll Smith-Rosenberg, "The Female World of Love and Ritual: Relations Betwen Women in Nineteenth-Century America," *Signs* 1 (Fall 1975): 1–30; Nancy F. Cott, *The Bonds of Womanhood: "Woman's Sphere" in New England, 1780–1835* (New Haven, Conn.: Yale University Press, 1977); Ann Douglas, *The Feminization of American Culture* (New York: Alfred A. Knopf, 1977); Nina Auerbach, *Communities of Women: An Idea in Fiction* (Cambridge, Mass.: Harvard University Press, 1978).

[13]Virginia Woolf, "Women and Fiction," *Collected Essays,* vol. 2 (London: Chatto & Windus, 1967), p. 141.

[14]Peter N. Heydon and Philip Kelley, eds., *Elizabeth Barrett Browning's Letters to Mrs. David Ogilvy* (New York: Quadrangle Books, 1973), p. 115.

[15]Florence Nightingale, "Cassandra," in *The Cause: A History of the Women's Movement in Great Britain,* ed. Ray Strachey (1928; reprint ed., Port Washington, N.Y.: Kennikat Press, 1969), p. 398.

[16]Rebecca West, "And They All Lived Unhappily Ever After," *Times Literary Supplement,* July 26, 1974, p. 779.

[17]Annette Kolodny, "Some Notes on Defining a 'Feminist Literary Criticism,'" *Critical Inquiry* 2 (Fall 1975): 84. For an illuminating discussion of *The Driver's Seat,* see Auerbach, *Communities of Women,* p. 181.

[18]Adrienne Rich, *Diving into the Wreck* (New York: W. W. Norton, 1973), p. 20.

[19]The term "matrophobia" was coined by Lynn Sukenick; see Rich, *Of Woman Born,* pp. 235 ff.

[20]Quoted in Ann Douglas Wood, "The 'Scribbling Women' and Fanny Fern: Why Women Wrote," *American Quarterly* 23 (Spring 1971): 3–24.

[21]Elizabeth Robins, *Woman's Secret,* WSPU pamphlet in the collection of the Museum of London, p. 6. Jane Marcus is preparing a full-length study of Elizabeth Robins.

[22]Elaine Showalter, *A Literature of Their Own: British Women Novelists from Brontë to Lessing* (Princeton, N.J.: Princeton University Press, 1977).

[23]Charlotte Perkins Gilman, *The Man-made World: or, Our Androcentric Culture* (1911; reprint ed., New York: Johnson Reprints, 1971), pp. 101–2.

[24]Virginia Woolf, "Modern Fiction," *Collected Essays,* vol. 2, p. 106.

[25]John Stuart Mill, *The Subjection of Women* (London, 1969), p. 133.

[26]Northrop Frye, "Expanding Eyes," *Critical Inquiry* 2 (1975): 201–2.

[27]Robert Scholes, *Structuralism in Literature: An Introduction* (New Haven, Conn.: Yale University Press, 1974), p. 118.

[28]Lee R. Edwards and Arlyn Diamond, eds., *The Authority of Experience: Essays in Feminist Criticism* (Amherst: University of Massachusetts Press, 1977).

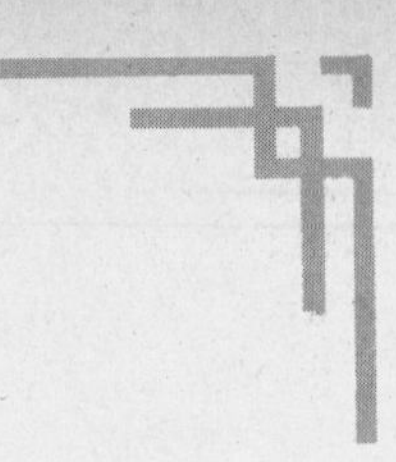

Dancing Through the Minefield

Some Observations on the Theory, Practice, and Politics of a Feminist Literary Criticism

Annette Kolodny

Had anyone had the prescience, in 1969, to pose the question of defining a "feminist" literary criticism, she might have been told, in the wake of Mary Ellmann's *Thinking About Women,*[1] that it involved exposing the sexual stereotyping of women in both our literature and our literary criticism and, as well, demonstrating the inadequacy of established critical schools and methods to deal fairly or sensitively with works written by women. In broad outline, such a prediction would have stood well the test of time, and, in fact, Ellmann's book continues to be widely read and to point us in useful directions. What could not have been anticipated in 1969, however, was the catalyzing force of an ideology that, for many of us, helped to bridge the gap between the world as we found it and the world as we wanted it to be. For those of us who studied literature, a previously unspoken sense of exclusion from authorship, and a painfully personal distress at discovering whores, bitches, muses, and heroines dead in childbirth where we had once hoped to discover ourselves, could—for the first time—begin to be understood as more than "a set of disconnected, unrealized private emotions."[2] With a renewed courage to make public our otherwise private discontents, what had once been "felt individually as personal insecurity" came at last to be "viewed collectively as structural inconsistency"[3] within the very disciplines we studied. Following unflinchingly the full implications of Ellmann's percepient observations, and emboldened by the liberating energy of feminist ideology—in all its various forms and guises—feminist criticism very quickly moved beyond merely "expos[ing] sexism in one work of literature after another,"[4] and promised instead that we might at last "begin to record new choices in a new literary history."[5] So powerful was that impulse that we experienced it, along with Adrienne Rich, as much more than "a chapter in cultural history": it became, rather, "an act of survival."[6] What was at stake was not so much literature or criticism as such, but the historical, social, and ethical consequences of women's participation in, or exclusion from, either enterprise.

The pace of inquiry in the 1970s has been fast and furious—especially after Kate Millett's 1970 analysis of the sexual politics of literature[7] added a note of urgency to what had earlier been Ellmann's sardonic anger—while the diversity of that inquiry easily outstripped all efforts to define feminist literary criticism as either a coherent system or a unified set of methodologies. Under its wide umbrella, everything has been thrown into question: our established canons, our aesthetic criteria, our interpretative strategies, our reading habits, and most of all, ourselves as critics and as teachers. To delineate its full scope would require nothing less than a book—a book that would be outdated even as it was being composed. For the sake of brevity, therefore, let me attempt only a summary outline.

Perhaps the most obvious success of this new scholarship has been the return to circulation of previously lost or otherwise ignored works by women writers. Following fast upon the initial success of the Feminist Press in reissuing gems such as Rebecca Harding Davis's 1861 novella, *Life in the Iron Mills,* and Charlotte Perkins Gilman's 1892 short story "The Yellow Wallpaper," published in 1972 and 1973, respectively,[8] commercial trade and reprint houses vied with one another in the reprinting of anthologies of lost texts and, in some cases, in the reprinting of whole series. For those of us in American literature especially, the phenomenon promised a radical reshaping of our concepts of literary history and, at the very least, a new chapter in understanding the development of women's literary traditions. So commercially successful were these reprintings, and so attuned were the reprint houses to the political attitudes of the audiences for which they were offered, that many of us found ourselves wooed to compose critical introductions, which would find in the pages of nineteenth-century domestic and sentimental fictions some signs of either muted rebellions or overt radicalism, in anticipation of the current wave of "New Feminism." In rereading with our students these previously lost works, we inevitably raised perplexing questions as to the reasons for their disappearance from the canons of "major works," and we worried over the aesthetic and critical criteria by which they had been accorded diminished status.

This increased availability of works by women writers led, of course, to an increased interest in what elements, if any, might constitute some sort of unity or connection among them. The possibility that women had developed either a unique or at least a related tradition of their own especially intrigued those of us who specialized in one national literature or another, or in historical periods. Nina Baym's recent *Woman's Fiction: A Guide to Novels by and about Women in America, 1820–1870*[9] demonstrates the Americanist's penchant for examining what were once the "best-sellers" of their day, the ranks of the popular fiction writers, among which women took a dominant place throughout the nineteenth century, while the feminist studies of British literature emphasized instead the wealth of women writers who have been regarded as worthy of canonization. Not so much building upon one another's work as clarifying, successively, the parameters of the questions to be posed, Sydney Janet Kaplan, Ellen Moers, Patricia Meyer Spacks, and Elaine Showalter, among many others, concentrated their energies on delineating an internally consistent "body of work" by women that might stand as a female countertradition. For Kaplan, in 1975, this entailed examining women writers' various attempts to portray feminine consciousness and self-consciousness, not as a psychological category, but as a stylistic or rhetorical device.[10] That same year, arguing essentially that literature publicizes the private, Spacks placed her consideration of a "female imagination" within social and historical frames, to conclude that "for readily discernible historical reasons women have characteristically concerned themselves with matters more or less peripheral to male concerns," and she attributed to this fact an inevitable difference in the literary emphases and subject matters of female and male writers.[11] The next year, Moers's *Literary Women: The Great Writers* focused on the pathways of literary influence that linked the English novel in the hands of women.[12] And finally, in 1977, Showalter took up the matter of a "female literary tradition in the English novel from the generation of the Brontës to the present day" by arguing that because women in general constitute a kind of "subculture within the framework of a larger society," the work of women writers, in particular, would thereby demonstrate a unity of "values, conventions, experiences, and behaviors impinging on each individual" as she found her sources of "self-expression relative to a dominant [and, by implication, male] society."[13]

At the same time that women writers were being reconsidered and reread, male writers were similarly subjected to a new feminist scrutiny. The continuing result—to put years of difficulty analysis into a single sentence—has been nothing less than an acute attentiveness to the ways in which certain power relations, usually those in which males wield various forms of influence over females, are inscribed in the texts (both literary and critical) that we have inherited, not merely as subject matter, but as the unquestioned, often unacknowledged *given* of the culture. Even more important than the new interpretations of individual texts are the probings into the consequences (for women) of the conventions that inform those texts. For example, in surveying selected nineteenth- and early-twentieth-century British novels which employ what she calls "the two-suitors convention," Jean E. Kennard sought to understand why and how the structural demands of the convention, even in the hands of women writers, inevitably work to imply "the inferiority and necessary subordination of women." Her 1978 study, *Victims of Convention,* points out that the symbolic nature of the marriage which conventionally concludes such novels "indicates the adjustment of the protagonist to society's values, a condition which is equated with her maturity." Kennard's concern, however, is with the fact that the structural demands of the form too often sacrifice precisely those "virtues of independence and individuality," or, in other words, the very "qualities we have been invited to admire in" the heroines.[14] Kennard appropriately cautions us against drawing from her work any simplistically reductive thesis about the mimetic relations between art and life. Yet her approach nonetheless suggests that what is important about a fiction is not whether it ends in a death or a marriage, but what the symbolic demands of that particular conventional ending imply about the values and beliefs of the world that engendered it.

Her work thus participates in a growing emphasis in feminist literary study on the fact of literature as a social institution, embedded not only within its own literary traditions but also within the particular physical and mental artifacts of the society from which it comes. Adumbrating Millett's 1970 decision to anchor her "literary reflections" to a preceding analysis of the historical, social, and economic contexts of sexual politics,[15] more recent work —most notably Lillian Robinson's—begins with the premise that the process of artistic creation "consists not of ghostly happenings in the head but of a matching of the states and processes of symbolic models against the states and processes of the wider world."[16] The power relations inscribed in the form of conventions within our literary inheritance, these critics argue, reify the encodings of those same power relations in the culture at large. And the critical examination of rhetorical codes becomes, in their hands, the pursuit of ideological codes, because both embody either value systems or the dialectic of competition between value systems. More often than not, these critics also insist upon examining not only the mirroring of life in art but also the normative impact of art on life. Addressing herself to the popular art available to working women, for example, Robinson is interested in understanding not only "the forms it uses" but, more important, "the myths it creates, the influence it exerts." "The way art helps people to order, interpret, mythologize, or dispose of their own experience," she declares, may be "complex and often ambiguous, but it is not impossible to define."[17]

Whether its focus be upon the material or the imaginative contexts of literary invention; single texts or entire canons; the relations between authors, genres, or historical circumstances; lost authors or well-known names, the variety and diversity of all feminist literary criticism finally coheres in its stance of almost defensive rereading. What Adrienne Rich had earlier called "re-vision," that is, "the act of looking back, of seeing with fresh eyes, of entering an old text from a new critical direction,"[18] took on a more actively self-protective coloration in 1978, when Judith Fetterley called upon the woman reader to learn to "resist" the sexist designs a text might make upon her—asking her to identify against herself, so to speak, by manipulating her sympathies on behalf of male heroes but against female shrew or bitch characters.[19] Underpinning a great deal of this critical rereading has been the not-unexpected alliance between feminist literary study and feminist studies in linguistics and language acquisition. Tillie Olsen's commonsense observation of the danger of "perpetuating—by continued usage—entrenched, centuries-old oppressive power realities, early-on incorporated into language,"[20] has been given substantive analysis in the writings of feminists who study "language as a symbolic system closely tied to a patriarchal social structure." Taken together, their work demonstrates "the importance of language in establishing, reflecting, and maintaining an asymmetrical relationship between women and men."[21]

To consider what this implies for the fate of women who essay the craft of language is to ascertain, perhaps for the first time, the real dilemma of the poet who finds her most cherished private experience "hedged by taboos, mined with false-namings."[22] It also explains the dilemma of the male reader who, in opening the pages of a woman's book, finds himself entering a strange and unfamiliar world of symbolic significance. For if, as Nelly Furman insists, neither language use nor language acquisition is "gender-neutral," but, is, instead, "imbued with our sex-inflected cultural values;"[23] and if, additionally, reading is a process of "sorting out the structures of signification"[24] in any text, then male readers who find themselves outside of and unfamiliar with the symbolic systems that constitute female experience in women's writings will necessarily dismiss those systems as undecipherable, meaningless, or trivial. And male professors will find no reason to include such works in the canons of "major authors." At the same time, women writers, coming into a tradition of literary language and conventional forms already appropriated, for centuries, to the purposes of male expression, will be forced virtually to "wrestle" with that language in an effort "to remake it as a language adequate to our conceptual processes."[25] To all of this, feminists concerned with the politics of language and style have been acutely attentive. "Language conceals an invincible adversary," observes French critic Hélène Cixous, "because it's the language of men and their grammar."[26] But equally insistent, as in the work of Sandra Gilbert and Susan Gubar, has been the understanding of the need for *all* readers, male and female alike, to learn to penetrate the otherwise unfamiliar universes of symbolic action that comprise women's writings, past and present.[27]

To have attempted so many difficult questions and to have accomplished so much—even acknowledging the inevitable false starts, overlapping, and repetition—in so short a time, should certainly have secured feminist literary criticism an honored berth on that ongoing intellectual journey which we loosely term in academia "critical analysis." Instead of being welcomed onto the train, however, we have been forced to negotiate a minefield. The very energy and diversity of our enterprise have rendered us vulnerable to attack on the grounds that we lack both definition and coherence; while our particular attentiveness to the ways in which literature encodes and disseminates cultural value systems calls down upon us imprecations echoing those heaped upon the Marxist critics of an earlier generation. If we are scholars dedicated to rediscovering a lost body of writings by women, then our finds are questioned on aesthetic grounds. And if we are critics determined to practice revisionist readings, it is claimed that our focus is too narrow and our results are only distortions or, worse still, polemical misreadings.

The very vehemence of the outcry, coupled with our total dismissal in some quarters,[28] suggests not our deficiencies, however, but the potential magnitude of our challenge. For what we are asking be scrutinized are nothing less than shared cultural assumptions so deeply rooted and so long ingrained that, for the most part, our critical colleagues have ceased to recognize them as such. In other words, what is really being bewailed in the claims that we distort texts or threaten the disappearance of the great Western literary tradition itself[29] is not so much the disappearance of either text or tradition but, instead, the eclipse of that particular *form* of the text and that particular *shape* of the canon which previously reified male readers' sense of power and significance in the world. Analogously, by asking whether, as readers, we ought to be "really satisfied by the marriage of Dorothea Brooke to Will Ladislaw? of Shirley Keeldar to Louis Moore?" or whether, as Kennard suggests, we must reckon with the ways in which "the qualities we have been invited to admire in these heroines [have] been sacrificed to structural neatness,"[30] is to raise difficult and profoundly perplexing questions about the ethical implications of our otherwise unquestioned aesthetic pleasures. It is, after all, an imposition of high order to ask the viewer to attend to Ophelia's sufferings in a scene where, before, he had always so comfortably kept his eye fixed firmly on Hamlet. To understand all this, then, as the real nature of the challenge we have offered and, in consequence, as the motivation for the often overt hostility we have aroused, should help us learn to negotiate the minefield, if not with grace, then with at least a clearer comprehension of its underlying patterns.

The ways in which objections to our work are usually posed, of course, serve to obscure their deeper motivations. But this may, in part, be due to our own reticence at taking full responsibility for the truly radicalizing premises that lie at the theoretical core of all we have so far accomplished. It may be time, therefore, to redirect discussion, forcing our adversaries to deal with the substantive issues and pushing ourselves into a clearer articulation of what, in fact, we are about. Up until now, I fear, we have dealt only piecemeal with the difficulties inherent in challenging the authority of established canons and then justifying the excellence of women's traditions, sometimes in accord with standards to which they have no intrinsic relation.

At the very point at which we must perforce enter the discourse—that is, claiming excellence or importance for our "finds"—all discussion has already, we discover, long ago been closed. "If Kate Chopin were *really* worth reading," an Oxford-trained colleague once assured me, "she'd have lasted—like Shakespeare"; and he then proceeded to vote against the English department's crediting a women's studies seminar I was offering in American women writers. The canon, for him, conferred excellence; Chopin's exclusion demonstrated only her lesser worth. As far as he was concerned, I could no more justify giving English-department credit for the study of Chopin than I could dare publicly to question Shakespeare's genius. Through hindsight, I have now come to view that discussion as not only having posed fruitless oppositions but also having entirely evaded the much more profound problem lurking just beneath the surface of our disagreement. That is, that the fact of canonization puts any work beyond questions of establishing its merit and, instead, invites students to offer only increasingly more ingenious readings and interpretations, the purpose of which is to validate the greatness already imputed by canonization.

Had I only understood it for what it was then, into this circular and self-serving set of assumptions I might have interjected some statement of my right to question why *any* text is revered and my need to know what it tells us about "how we live, how we have been living, how we have been led to imagine ourselves, [and] how our language has trapped as well as liberated us."[31] The very fact of our critical training within the strictures imposed by an established canon of major works and authors, however, repeatedly deflects us from such questions. Instead, we find ourselves endlessly responding to the riposte that the overwhelmingly male presence among canonical authors was only an accident of history and never intentionally sexist, coupled with claims to the "obvious" aesthetic merit of those canonized texts. It is, as I say, a fruitless exchange, serving more to obscure than to expose the territory being protected and dragging us, again and again, through the minefield.

It is my contention that current hostilities might be transformed into a true dialogue with our critics if we at last made explicit what appear, to this observer, to constitute the three crucial propositions to which our special interests inevitably give rise. They are, moreover, propositions which, if handled with care and intelligence, could breathe new life into now moribund areas of our profession: (1) literary history (and with that, the historicity of literature) is a fiction; (2) insofar as we are taught how to read, what we engage are not texts but paradigms; and finally, (3) since the grounds upon which we assign aesthetic value to texts are never infallible, unchangeable, or universal, we must reexamine not only our aesthetics but, as well, the inherent biases and assumptions informing the critical methods which (in part) shape our aesthetic responses. For the sake of brevity, I will not attempt to offer the full arguments for each but, rather, only sufficient elaboration to demonstrate what I see as their intrinsic relation to the potential scope of and present challenge implied by feminist literary study.

1. *Literary history (and with that, the historicity of literature) is a fiction.* To begin with, an established canon functions as a model by which to chart the continuities and discontinuities, as well as the influences upon and the interconnections between works, genres, and authors. That model we tend to forget, however, is of our own making. It will take a very different shape, and explain its inclusions and exclusions in very different ways, if the reigning critical ideology believes that new literary forms result from some kind of ongoing internal dialectic within preexisting styles and traditions or if, by contrast, the ideology declares that literary change is dependent upon societal development and therefore determined by upheavals in the social and economic organization of the culture at large.[32] Indeed, whenever in the previous century of English and American literary scholarship one alternative replaced the other, we saw dramatic alterations in canonical "wisdom."

This suggests, then, that our sense of a "literary history," and, by extension, our confidence in a "historical" canon, is rooted not so much in any definitive understanding of the past as it is in our need to call up and utilize the past on behalf of a better understanding of the present. Thus, to paraphrase David Couzens Hoy, it becomes necessary "to point out that the understanding of art and literature is such an essential aspects of the present's self-understanding that this self-understanding conditions what even gets taken" as constituting that artistic and literary past. To quote Hoy fully, "this continual reinterpretation of the past goes hand in hand with the continual reinterpretation by the present of itself."[33] In our own time, uncertain as to which, if any, model truly accounts for our canonical choices or accurately explains literary history, and pressured further by the feminists' call for some justification of the criteria by which women's writings were largely excluded from both that canon and history, we suffer what Harold Bloom has called "a remarkable dimming" of "our mutual sense of canonical standards."[34]

Into this apparent impasse, feminist literary theorists implicitly introduce the observation that our choices and evaluations of current literature have the effect either of solidifying or of reshaping our sense of the past. The authority of any established canon, after all, is reified by our perception that current work seems to grow almost inevitably out of it (even in opposition or rebellion), and is called into question when what we read appears to have little or no relation to what we recognize as coming before. So, were the larger critical community to begin to attend seriously to the recent outpouring of fine literature by women, this would surely be accompanied by a concomitant researching of the past, by literary historians, in order to account for the present phenomenon. In that process, literary history would itself be altered: works by seventeenth-, eighteenth-, or nineteenth-century women to which we had not previously attended might be given new importance as "precursors" or as prior influences upon present-day authors; while selected male writers might also be granted new prominence as figures whom the women today, or even yesterday, needed to reject. I am arguing, in other words, that the choices we make in the present inevitably alter our sense of the past that led to them.

Related to this is the feminist challenge to that patently mendacious critical fallacy that we read the "classics" in order to reconstruct the past "the way it really was," and that we read Shakespeare and Milton in order to apprehend the meanings that they intended. Short of time machines or miraculous resurrections, there is simply no way to know, precisely or surely, what "really was," what Homer intended when he sang, or Milton when he dictated. Critics more acute than I have already pointed up the impossibility of grounding a reading in the imputation of authorial intention because the further removed the author is from us, so too must be her or his systems of knowledge and belief, points of view, and structures of vision (artistic and otherwise).[35] (I omit here the difficulty of finally either proving or disproving the imputation of intentionality because, inescapably, the only appropriate authority is unavailable: deceased.) What we have really come to mean when we speak of competence in reading historical texts, therefore, is the ability to recognize literary conventions which have survived through time—so as to remain operational in the mind of the reader—and, where these are lacking, the ability to translate (or perhaps transform?) the text's ciphers into more current and recognizable shapes. But we never really reconstruct the past in its own terms. What we gain when we read the "classics," then, is neither Homer's Greece nor George Eliot's England *as they knew it* but, rather, an approximation of an already fictively inputed past made available, through our interpretative strategies, for present concerns. Only by understanding this can we put to rest that recurrent delusion that the "continuing relevance" of the classics serves as "testimony to perennial features of human experience."[36] The only "perennial feature" to which our ability to read and reread texts written in previous centuries testifies is our inventiveness—in the sense that all of literary history is a fiction which we daily re-create as we reread it. What distinguishes feminists in this regard is their desire to alter and extend what we take as historically relevant from out of that vast storehouse of our literary inheritance and, further, feminists' recognition of the storehouse for what it really is: a resource for remodeling our literary history, past, present, and future.

2. *Insofar as we are taught how to read, what we engage are not texts but paradigms.* To pursue the logical consequences of the first proposition leads, however uncomfortably, to the conclusion that we appropriate meaning from a text according to what we need (or desire), or in other words, according to the critical assumptions or predispositions (conscious or not) that we bring to it. And we appropriate different meanings, or report different gleanings, at different times—even from the same text—according to our changed assumptions, circumstances, and requirements. This, in essence, constitutes the heart of the second proposition. For insofar as literature is itself a social institution, so, too, reading is a highly socialized—or learned—activity. What makes it so exciting, of course, is that it can be constantly relearned and refined, so as to provide either an individual or an entire reading community, over time, with infinite variations of the same text. It *can* provide that, but, I must add, too often it does not. Frequently our reading habits become fixed, so that each successive reading experience functions, in effect, normatively, with one particular kind of novel stylizing our expectations of those to follow, the stylistic devices of any favorite author (or group of authors) alerting us to the presence or absence of those devices in the works of others, and so on. "Once one has read his first poem," Murray Krieger has observed, "he turns to his second and to the others that will follow thereafter with an increasing series of preconceptions about the sort of activity in which he is indulging. In matters of literary

experience, as in other experiences," Krieger concludes, "one is a virgin but once."[37]

For most readers, this is a fairly unconscious process, and not unnaturally, what we are taught to read well and with pleasure, when we are young predisposes us to certain specific kinds of adult reading tastes. For the professional literary critic, the process may be no different, but it is at least more conscious. Graduate schools, at their best, are training grounds for competing interpretative paradigms or reading techniques: affective stylistics, structuralism, and semiotic analysis, to name only a few of the more recent entries. The delight we learn to take in the mastery of these interpretative strategies is then often mistakenly construed as our delight in reading specific texts, especially in the case of works that would otherwise be unavailable or even offensive to us. In my own graduate career, for example, with superb teachers to guide me, I learned to take great pleasure in *Paradise Lost,* even though, as both a Jew and a feminist, I can subscribe neither to its theology nor to its hierarchy of sexual valuation. If, within its own terms (as I have been taught to understand them), the text manipulates my sensibilities and moves me to pleasure—as I will affirm it does—then, at least in part, that must be because, in spite of my real-world alienation from many of its basic tenets, I have been able to enter that text through interpretative strategies which allow me to displace less comfortable observations with others to which I have been taught pleasurably to attend. Though some of my teachers may have called this process "learning to read the text properly," I have now come to see it as learning to effectively manipulate the critical strategies which they taught me so well. Knowing, for example, the poem's debt to epic conventions, I am able to discover in its echoes and reworkings of both lines and situations from Virgil and Homer; placing it within the ongoing Christian debate between Good and Evil, I comprehend both the philosophic and the stylistic significance of Satan's ornate rhetoric as compared with God's majestic simplicity in Book III. But in each case, an interpretative model, already assumed, had guided my discovery of the evidence for it.[38]

When we consider the implications of these observations for the processes of canon formation and for the assignment of aesthetic value, we find ourselves locked in a chicken-and-egg dilemma, unable easily to distinguish as primary the importance of *what* we read as opposed to *how* we have learned to read it. For, simply put, we read well, and with pleasure, what we already know how to read; and what we know how to read is to a large extent dependent upon what we have already read (works from which we developed our expectations and learned our interpretative strategies). What we then choose to read—and, by extension, teach and thereby "canonize"—usually follows upon our previous reading. Radical breaks are tiring, demanding, uncomfortable, and sometimes wholly beyond our comprehension.

Though the argument is not usually couched in precisely these terms, a considerable segment of the most recent feminist rereadings of women writers allows the conclusion that, where those authors have dropped out of sight, it may be due not to any lack of merit in the work but, instead, to an incapacity of predominantly male readers to properly interpret and appreciate women's texts—due, in large part, to a lack of prior acquaintance. The fictions that women compose about the worlds they inhabit may owe a debt to prior, influential works by other women or, simply enough, to the daily experience of the writer herself or, more usually, to some combination of the two. The reader coming upon such fiction with knowledge of neither its informing literary traditions nor its real-world contexts will find himself hard pressed, though he may recognize the words on the page, to competently decipher its intended meanings. And this is what makes the recent studies by Spacks, Moers, Showalter, Gilbert and Gubar, and others so crucial. For, by attempting to delineate the connections and interrelations that make for a female literary tradition, they provide us invaluable aids for recognizing and understanding the unique literary traditions and sex-related contexts out of which women write.

The (usually male) reader who, both by experience and by reading, has never made acquaintance with those contexts—historically, the lying-in room, the parlor, the nursery, the kitchen, the laundry, and so on—will necessarily lack the capacity to fully interpret the dialogue or action embedded therein; for, as every good novelist knows, the meaning of any character's action or statement is inescapably a function of the specific situation in which it is embedded.[39] Virginia Woolf therefore quite properly anticipated the male reader's disposition to write off what he could not understand, abandoning women's writings as offering "not merely a difference of view, but a view that is weak, or trivial, or sentimental because it differs from his own." In her 1929 essay "Women and Fiction," Woolf grappled most obviously with the ways in which male writers and male subject matter had already preempted the language of literature. Yet she was also tacitly commenting on the problem of (male) audience and conventional reading expectations when she speculated that the woman writer might well "find that she is perpetually wishing to alter the established values [in literature]—to make serious what appears insignificant to a man, and trivial what is to him important."[40] "The 'competence' necessary for understanding [a] literary message . . . depends upon a great number of codices," after all; as Cesare Segre has pointed out, to be competent, a reader must either share or at least be familiar with, "in addition to the code language . . . the codes of custom, of society, and of conceptions of the world"[41] (what Woolf meant by "values"). Males ignorant of women's "values" or conceptions of the world will, necessarily, be poor readers of works that in any sense recapitulate their codes.

The problem is further exacerbated when the language of the literary text is largely dependent upon figuration. For it can be argued, as Ted Cohen has shown, that while "in general, and with some obvious qualifications . . . all literal use of language is accessible to all whose language it is . . . figurative use can be inaccessible to all but those who share information about one another's knowledge, beliefs, intentions, and attitudes."[42] There was nothing fortuitous, for example, in Charlotte Perkins Gilman's decision to situate the progressive mental breakdown and increasing incapacity of the protagonist of "The Yellow Wallpaper" in an upstairs room that had once served as a nursery (with barred windows, no less). But a reader unacquainted with the ways in which women have traditionally inhabited a household might not take the initial description of the setting as semantically relevant, and the progressive infantilization of the adult protagonist would thereby lose some of its symbolic implications. Analogously, the contemporary poet who declares, along with Adrienne Rich, the need for "a whole new poetry beginning here" is acknowledging that the materials available for symbolization and figuration from women's contexts will necessarily differ from those that men have traditionally utilized.

> *Vision begins to happen in such a life*
> *as if a woman quietly walked away*
> *from the argument and jargon in a room*
> *and sitting down in the kitchen, began turning in her lap*
> *bits of yarn, calico and velvet scraps,*
>
> . . .
>
> *pulling the tenets of a life together*
> *with no mere will to mastery,*
> *only care for the many-lived, unending*
> *forms in which she finds herself.*[43]

What, then, is the fate of the woman writer whose competent reading community is composed only of members of her own sex? And what, then, the response of the male critic who, on first looking into Virginia Woolf or Doris Lessing, finds all of the interpretative strategies at his command inadequate to a full and pleasurable deciphering of their pages? Historically, the result has been the diminished status of women's products and their consequent absence from major canons. Nowadays, however, by pointing out that the act of "interpreting language is no more sexually neutral than language use or the language system itself," feminist students of language like Nelly Furman help us better understand the crucial linkage between our gender and our interpretative, or reading, strategies. Insisting upon "the contribution of the . . . reader [in] the active attribution of significance to formal signifiers,"[44] Furman and others promise to shake us all—female and male alike—out of our canonized and conventional aesthetic assumptions.

3. *Since the grounds upon which we assign aesthetic value to texts are never infallible, unchangeable, or universal, we must reexamine not only our aesthetics but, as well, the inherent biases and assumptions informing the critical methods which (in part) shape our aesthetic responses.* I am, on the one hand, arguing that men will be better readers, or appreciators, of women's books when they have read more of them (as women have always been taught to become astute readers of men's texts). On the other hand, it will be noted, the emphasis of my remarks shifts the act of critical judgment from assigning aesthetic valuations to texts and directs it, instead, to ascertaining the adequacy of any interpretative paradigm to a full reading of both female and male writing. My third proposition—and, I admit, perhaps the most controversial—thus calls into question that recurrent tendency in criticism to establish norms for the evaluation of literary works when we might better serve the cause of literature by developing standards for evaluating the adequacy of our critical methods.[45] This does not mean that I wish to discard aesthetic valuation. The choice, as I see it, is not between retaining or discarding aesthetic values; rather, the choice is between having some awareness of what constitutes (at least in part) the bases of our aesthetic responses and going without such an awareness. For it is my view that insofar as aesthetic responsiveness continues to be an integral aspect of our human response system—in part spontaneous, in part learned and educated—we will inevitably develop theories to help explain, formalize, or even initiate those responses.

In challenging the adequacy of received critical opinion or the imputed excellence of established canons, feminist literary critics are essentially seeking to discover how aesthetic value is assigned in the first place, where it resides (in the text or in the reader), and, most important, what validity may really be claimed by our aesthetic "judgments." What ends do those judgments serve, the feminist asks; and what conceptions of the world or ideological stances do they (even if unwittingly) help to perpetuate? In so doing, she points out, among other things, that any response labeled "aesthetic" may as easily designate some immediate experienced moment or event as it may designate a species of nostalgia, a yearning for the components of a simpler past when the world seemed known or at least understandable. Thus the value accorded an opera or a Shakespeare play may well reside in the viewer's immediate viewing pleasure, or it may reside in the play's nostalgic evocation of a once comprehensible and ordered world. At the same time, the feminist confronts, for example, the reader who simply cannot entertain the possibility that women's worlds are symbolically rich, the reader who, like the male characters in Susan Glaspell's 1917 short story "A Jury of Her Peers," has already assumed the innate "insignificance of kitchen things."[46] Such a reader, she knows, will prove himself unable to assign significance to fictions that attend to "kitchen things" and will, instead, judge such fictions as trivial and as aesthetically wanting. For her to take useful issue with such a reader, she must make clear that what appears to be a dispute about aesthetic merit is, in reality, a dispute about the *contexts of judgment;* and what is at issue, then, is the adequacy of the prior assumptions and reading habits brought to bear on the text. To put it bluntly: we have had enough pronouncements of aesthetic valuation for a time; it is now our task to evaluate the imputed norms and normative reading patterns that, in part, led to those pronouncements.

By and large, I think I have made my point. Only to clarify it do I add this coda: when feminists turn their attention to the works of male authors which have traditionally been accorded high aesthetic value and, where warranted, follow Olsen's advice that we assert our "right to say: this is surface, this falsifies reality, this degrades,"[47] such statements do not necessarily mean that we will end up with a diminished canon. To question the source of the aesthetic pleasures we have gained from reading Spenser, Shakespeare, Milton, and so on does not imply that we must deny those pleasures. It means only that aesthetic response is once more invested with epistemological, ethical, and moral concerns. It means, in other words, that readings of *Paradise Lost* which analyze its complex hierarchal structures but fail to note the implications of gender within that hierarchy; or which insist upon the inherent (or even inspired) perfection of Milton's figurative language but fail to note the consequences, for Eve, of her specifically gender-marked weakness, which, like the flowers she attends, requires "propping up"; or which concentrate on the poem's thematic reworking of classical notions of martial and epic prowess into Christian (moral) heroism but fail to note that Eve is stylistically edited out of that process—all such readings, however useful, will no longer be deemed wholly adequate. The pleasures we had earlier learned to take in the poem will not be diminished thereby, but they will become part of an altered reading attentiveness.

These three propositions I believe to be at the theoretical core of most current feminist literary criticism, whether acknowledged as such or not. If I am correct in this, then that criticism represents more than a profoundly skeptical stance toward all other preexisting and contemporaneous schools and methods, and more than an impassioned demand that the variety and variability of women's literary expression be taken into full account, rather than written off as caprice and exception, the irregularity in an otherwise regular design. It represents that locus in literary study where, in unceasing effort, female self-consciousness turns in upon itself, attempting to grasp the deepest conditions of its own unique and multiplicitous realities, in the hope, eventually, of altering the very forms through which the culture perceives, expresses, and knows itself. For, if what the larger women's movement looks for in the future is a transformation of the structures of primarily male power which now order our society, then the feminist literary critic demands that we understand the ways in which those structures have been—and continue to be—reified by our literature and by our literary criticism. Thus, along with other "radical" critics and critical schools, though our focus remains the power of the word to both structure and mirror human experience, our overriding commitment is to a radical alteration—an improvement, we hope—in the nature of that experience.

What distinguishes our work from those similarly oriented "social consciousness" critiques, it is said, is its lack of systematic coherence. Pitted against, for example, psychoanalytic or Marxist readings, which owe a decisive share of their persuasiveness to their apparent internal consistency as a system, the aggregate of feminist literary criticism appears woefully deficient in system, and painfully lacking in program. It is, in fact, from all quarters, the most telling defect alleged against us, the most explosive threat in the minefield. And my own earlier observation that, as of 1976, feminist literary criticism appeared "more like a set of interchangeable strategies than any coherent school or shared goal orientation" has been taken by some as an indictment, by others as a statement of impatience. Neither was intended. I felt then, as I do now, that this would "prove both its strength *and* its weakness,"[48] in the sense that the apparent disarray would leave us vulnerable to the kind of objection I have just alluded to; while the fact of our diversity would finally place us securely where, all along, we should have been: camped out, on the far side of the minefield, with the other pluralists and pluralisms.

In our heart of hearts, of course, most critics are really structuralists (whether or not they accept the label) because what we are seeking are patterns (or structures) that can order and explain the otherwise inchoate; thus, we invent, or believe we discover, relational patternings in the texts we read which promise transcendence from difficulty and perplexity to clarity and coherence. But, as I have tried to argue in these pages, to the imputed "truth" or "accuracy" of these findings the feminist must oppose the painfully obvious truism that what is attended to in a literary work, and hence what is reported about it, is often determined not so much by the work itself as by the critical technique or aesthetic criteria through which it is filtered or, rather, read and decoded. All the feminist is asserting, then, is her own equivalent right to liberate new (and perhaps different) significances from these same texts; and at the same time, her right to choose which features of a text she takes as relevant because she is, after all, asking new and different questions of it. In the process, she claims neither definitiveness nor structural completeness for her different readings and reading systems, but only their usefulness in recognizing the particular achievements of woman-as-author and their applicability in conscientiously decoding woman-as-sign.

That these alternate foci of critical attentiveness will render alternate readings or interpretations of the same text—even among feminists—should be no cause for alarm. Such developments illustrate only the pluralist contention that "in approaching a text of any complexity . . . the reader must choose to emphasize certain aspects which seem to him crucial," and that "in fact, the variety of readings which we have for many works is a function of the selection of crucial aspects made by the variety of readers." Robert Scholes, from whom I have been quoting, goes so far as to assert that "there is no single 'right' reading for any complex literary work," and, following the Russian formalist school, he observes that "we do not speak of readings that are simply true or false, but of readings that are more or less rich, strategies that are more or less appropriate."[49] Because those who share the term "feminist" nonetheless practice a diversity of critical strategies, leading, in some cases, to quite different readings, we must acknowledge among ourselves that sister critics, "having chosen to tell a different story, may in their interpretation identify different aspects of the meanings conveyed by the same passage."[50]

Adopting a "pluralist" label does not mean, however, that we cease to disagree; it means only that we entertain the possibility that different readings, even of the same text, may be differently useful, even illuminating, within different contexts of inquiry. It means, in effect, that we enter a dialectical process of examining, testing, even trying out the contexts—be they prior critical assumptions or explicitly stated ideological stances (or some combination of the two)—that led to the disparate readings. Not all will be equally acceptable to every one of us, of course, and even those prior assumptions or ideologies that are acceptable may call for further refinement or clarification. But at the very least, because we will have grappled with the assumptions that led to it, we will be better able to articulate *why* we find a particular reading or interpretation adequate or inadequate. This kind of dialectical process, moreover, not only makes us more fully aware of what criticism is, and how it functions; it also gives us access to its future possibilities, making us conscious, as R. P. Blackmur put it, "of what we have done," "of what can be done next, or done again."[51] or, I would add, of what can be done differently. To put it still another way: just because we will no longer tolerate the specifically sexist omissions and oversights of earlier critical schools and methods does not mean that, in their stead, we must establish our own "party line."

In my view, our purpose is not and should not be the formulation of any single reading method or potentially Procrustean set of critical procedures nor, even less, the generation of prescriptive categories for some dreamed-of non-sexist literary canon.[52] Instead, as I see it, our task is to initiate nothing less than a playful pluralism, responsive to the possibilities of multiple critical schools and methods, but captive of none, recognizing that the many tools needed for our analysis will necessarily be largely inherited and only partly of our own making. Only by employing a plurality of methods will we protect ourselves from the temptation of so oversimplifying any text—and especially those particularly offensive to us—that we render ourselves unresponsive to what Scholes has called "its various systems of meaning and their interaction."[53] Any text we deem worthy of our critical attention is usually, after all, a locus of many and varied kinds of (personal, thematic, stylistic, structural, rhetorical) relationships. So, whether we tend to treat a text as a *mimesis,* in which words are taken to be re-creating or representing viable worlds; or whether we prefer to treat a text as a kind of equation of communication, in which decipherable messages are passed from writers to readers; and whether we locate meaning as inherent in the text, the act of reading, or in some collaboration between reader and text—whatever our predilection, let us not generate from it a straightjacket that limits the scope of possible analysis. Rather, let us generate an ongoing dialogue of competing potential possibilities—among feminists and, as well, between feminists and nonfeminist critics.

The difficulty of what I describe does not escape me. The very idea of pluralism seems to threaten a kind of chaos for the future of literary inquiry while, at the same time, it seems to deny the hope of establishing some basic conceptual model which can organize all data—the hope which always begins any analytical exercise. My effort here, however, has been to demonstrate the essential delusions that inform such objections: if literary inquiry has historically escaped chaos by establishing canons, then it has only substituted one mode of arbitrary action for another—and in this case, at the expense of half the population. And if feminists openly acknowledge ourselves as pluralists, then we do not give up the search for patterns of opposition and connection—probably the basis of thinking itself; what we give up is simply the arrogance of claiming that our work is either exhaustive or definitive. (It is, after all, the identical arrogance we are asking our nonfeminist colleagues to abandon.) If this kind of pluralism appears to threaten both the present coherence of and the inherited aesthetic criteria for a canon of "greats," then, as I have earlier argued, it is precisely that threat which alone can free us from the prejudices, the strictures, and the blind spots of the past. In feminist hands, I would add, it is less a threat than a promise.

What unites and repeatedly invigorates feminist literary criticism, then, is neither dogma nor method but an acute and impassioned *attentiveness* to the ways in which primarily male structures of power are inscribed (or encoded) within our literary inheritance; the consequences of that encoding for women—as characters, as readers, and as writers; and, with that, a shared analytic *concern* for the implications of that encoding not only for a better understanding of the past but also for an improved reordering of the present and future. If that concern identifies feminist literary criticism as one of the many academic arms of the larger women's movement, then that attentiveness, within the halls of academe, poses no less a challenge for change, generating as it does the three propositions explored here. The critical pluralism that inevitably follows upon those three propositions, however, bears little resemblance to what Robinson has called "the greatest bourgeois theme of all, the myth of pluralism, with its consequent rejection of ideological commitment as 'too simple' to embrace the (necessarily complex) truth."[54] Only ideological commitment could have gotten us to enter the minefield, putting in jeopardy our careers and our livelihood. Only the power of ideology to transform our conceptual worlds, and the inspiration of that ideology to liberate long-suppressed energies and emotions, can account for our willingness to take on critical tasks that, in an earlier decade, would have been "abandoned in despair or apathy."[55] The fact of differences among us proves only that, despite our shared commitments, we have nonetheless refused to shy away from complexity, preferring to disagree openly rather than to give up either intellectual honesty or hard-won insights.

Finally, I would argue, pluralism informs feminist literary inquiry not simply as a description of what already exists but, more importantly, as the only critical stance consistent with the current status of the larger women's movement. Segmented and variously focused, the different women's organizations neither espouse any single system of analysis nor, as a result, express any wholly shared, consistently articulated ideology. The ensuing loss in effective organization and political clout is a serious one, but it has not been paralyzing; in spite of our differences, we have united to act in areas of clear mutual concern (the push for the Equal Rights Amendment is probably the most obvious example). The trade-off, as I see it, has made possible an ongoing and educative dialectic of analysis and proffered solutions, protecting us thereby from the inviting traps of reductionism and dogma. And so long as this dialogue remains active, both our politics and our criticism will be free of dogma—but never, I hope, of feminist ideology, in all its variety. For, "whatever else ideologies may be—projections of unacknowledged fears, disguises for ulterior motives, phatic expressions of group solidarity" (and the women's movement, to date, has certainly been all of these, and more)—whatever ideologies express, they are, as Geertz astutely observes, "most distinctively, maps of problematic social reality and matrices for the creation of collective conscience." And despite the fact that "ideological advocates . . . tend as much to obscure as to clarify the true nature of the problems involved," as Geertz notes, "they at least call attention to their existence and, by polarizing issues, make continued neglect more difficult. Without Marxist attack, there would have been no labor reform; without Black Nationalists, no deliberate speed."[56] Without Seneca Falls, I would add, no enfranchisement of women, and without "consciousness raising," no feminist literary criticism nor, even less, women's studies.

Ideology, however, only truly manifests its power by ordering the *sum* of our actions.[57] If feminist criticism calls anything into question, it must be that dog-eared myth of intellectual neutrality. For what I take to be the underlying spirit or message of any consciously ideologically premised criticism—that is, that ideas are important *because* they determine the ways we live, or want to live, in the world—is vitiated by confining those ideas to the study, the classroom, or the pages of our books. To write chapters decrying the sexual stereotyping of women in our literature, while closing our eyes to the sexual harassment of our women students and colleagues; to display Katherine Hepburn and Rosalind Russell in our courses on "The Image of the Independent Career Women in Film," while managing not to notice the paucity of female administrators on our own campus; to study the women who helped make universal enfranchisement a political reality, while keeping silent about our activist colleagues who are denied promotion or tenure; to include segments on "Women in the Labor Movement" in our American studies or women's studies courses, while remaining willfully ignorant of the department secretary fired for her efforts to organize a clerical workers' union; to glory in the delusions of "merit," "privilege," and "status" which accompany campus life in order to insulate ourselves from the millions of women who labor in poverty—all this is not merely hypocritical; it destroys both the spirit and the meaning of what we are about. It puts us, however unwittingly, in the service of those who laid the minefield in the first place. In my view, it is a fine thing for many of us, individually, to have traversed the minefield; but that happy circumstance will only prove of lasting importance if, together, we expose it for what it is (the male fear of sharing power and significance with women) and deactivate its components, so that others, after us, may literally dance through the minefield.

NOTES

"Dancing Through the Minefield" was the winner of the 1979 Florence Howe Essay Contest, which is sponsored by the Women's Caucus of the Modern Language Association.

Some sections of this essay were composed during the time made available to me by a grant from the Rockefeller Foundation, for which I am most grateful.

This essay intentionally deals with white feminist critics only, because it was originally conceived as the first of a two-essay dialogue with myself. A second essay, which was to have dealt with black and Third World American feminist literary critics, is now part of a comprehensive study of feminist criticism in progress, to be called *Dancing Through the Minefield.*

[1]Mary Ellman, *Thinking About Women* (New York: Harcourt, Brace & World, 1968).

[2]See Clifford Gertz, "Ideology as a Cultural System," *The Interpretation of Cultures: Selected Essays* (New York: Basic Books, 1973), p. 232.

[3]Ibid., p. 204.

[4]Lillian S. Robinson, "Cultural Criticism and thc *Horror Vacui,*" *College English* 33 (October 1972); reprinted as "The Critical Task" in her *Sex, Class, and Culture* (Bloomington: Indiana University Press, 1978), p. 51.

[5]Elaine Showalter, *A Literature of Their Own: British Women Novelists From Brontë to Lessing* (Princeton, N.J.: Princeton University Press, 1977), p. 36.

[6]Adrienne Rich, "When We Dead Awaken: Writing as Re-Vision," *College English* 34 (October 1972); reprinted in *Adrienne Rich's Poetry,* ed. Barbara Charlesworth Gelpi and Albert Gelpi (New York: W. W. Norton, 1975), p. 90.

[7]Kate Millett, *Sexual Politics* (Garden City, N.Y.: Doubleday, 1970).

[8]Rebecca Harding Davis, *Life in the Iron Mills,* originally published in the *Atlantic Monthly,* April 1861; reprinted with "A Biographical Interpretation" by Tillie Olsen (Old Westbury, N.Y.: Feminist Press, 1972). Charlotte Perkins Gilman, "The Yellow Wallpaper," originally published in the *New England Magazine,* May 1892; reprinted with an Afterword by Elaine R. Hedges (Old Westbury, N.Y.: Feminist Press, 1973).

[9]Nina Baym, *Woman's Fiction: A Guide to Novels by and about Women in America, 1820–1870* (Ithaca, N.Y.: Cornell University Press, 1978).

[10]In her *Feminine Consciousness in the Modern British Novel* (Urbana: University of Illinois Press, 1975), p. 3, Sydney Janet Kaplan explains that she is using the term "feminine consciousness" "not simply as some general attitude of women toward their own femininity, and not as something synonymous with a particular sensibility among female writers. I am concerned with it as a literary device: a method of characterization of females in fiction."

[11]Patricia Meyer Spacks, *The Female Imagination* (New York: Avon Books, 1975), p. 6.

[12]Ellen Moers, *Literary Women: The Great Writers* (Garden City, N.Y.: Doubleday, 1976).

[13]Showalter, *A Literature of Their Own,* p. 11.

[14]Jean E. Kennard, *Victims of Convention* (Hamden, Conn.: Archon Books, 1978), pp. 164, 18, 14.

[15]See Millett, *Sexual Politics,* pt. 3, "The Literary Reflection," pp. 235–361.

[16]The phrase is Geertz's; see "Ideology as a Cultural System," p. 214.

[17]Lillian S. Robinson, "Criticism—and Self-Criticism," *College English* 36 (January 1974), and "Criticism: Who Needs It?" in *The Uses of Criticism,* ed. A. P. Foulkes

(Bern and Frankfurt: Lang, 1976); both reprinted in *Sex, Class, and Culture,* pp. 67, 80.

[18]Rich, "When We Dead Awaken," p. 90.

[19]Judith Fetterley, *The Resisting Reader: A Feminist Approach to American Fiction* (Bloomington: Indiana University Press, 1978).

[20]Tillie Olsen, *Silences* (New York: Delacorte Press, 1978), pp. 239–40.

[21]See Cheris Kramer, Barrie Thorne, and Nancy Henley, "Perspectives on Language and Communication," Review Essay, *Signs* 3 (Summer 1978): 646.

[22]See Adrienne Rich's discussion of the difficulty in finding authentic language for her experience as a mother in *Of Woman Born: Motherhood as Experience and Institution* (New York: W. W. Norton, 1976), p. 15.

[23]Nelly Furman, "The Study of Women and Language: Comment on Vol. 3, no. 3," *Signs* 4 (Fall 1978): 184.

[24]Again, my phrasing comes from Geertz, "Thick Description: Toward an Interpretive Theory of Culture," *Interpretation of Cultures,* p. 9.

[25]Julia Penelope Stanley and Susan W. Robbins, "Toward a Feminist Aesthetic," *Chrysalis,* no. 6 (1977), p. 63.

[26]Hélène Cixous, "The Laugh of the Medusa," trans. Keith Cohen and Paula Cohen, *Signs* 1 (Summer 1976): 887.

[27]In *The Madwoman in the Attic: The Woman Writer and the Nineteenth-Century Literary Imagination* (New Haven, Conn.: Yale University Press, 1979), Sandra M. Gilbert and Susan Gubar suggest that women's writings are in some sense "palimpsestic" in that their "surface designs conceal or obscure deeper, less accessible (and less socially acceptable) levels of meaning" (p. 73). It is, in their view, an art designed "both to express and to camouflage" (p. 81).

[28]Consider, for example, Robert Boyers's reductive and inaccurate generalization that "what distinguishes ordinary books and articles about women from feminist writing is the feminist insistence on asking the same questions of every work and demanding ideologically satisfactory answers to those questions as a means of evaluating it," in "A Case Against Feminist Criticism," *Partisan Review* 43 (1976): 602. It is partly as a result of such misconceptions that we have the paucity of feminist critics who are granted a place in English departments that otherwise pride themselves on the variety of their critical orientations.

[29]Ambivalent though he is about the literary continuity that begins with Homer, Harold Bloom nonetheless somewhat ominously prophesies "that the first true break . . . will be brought about in generations to come, if the burgeoning religion of Liberated Woman spreads from its clusters of enthusiasts to dominate the West," in *A Map of Misreading* (New York: Oxford University Press, 1975), p. 33. On p. 36, he acknowledges that while something "as violent [as] a quarrel would ensue if I expressed my judgment" on Robert Lowell and Norman Mailer, "it would lead to something more intense than quarrels if I expressed my judgment upon . . . the 'literature of Women's Liberation.' "

[30]Kennard, *Victims of Convention,* p. 14.

[31]Rich, "When We Dead Awaken," p. 90.

[32]The first is a proposition currently expressed by some structuralists and formalist critics; the best statement of the second probably appears in Georg Lukacs, *Writer and Critic* (New York: Grosset & Dunlap, 1970), p. 119.

[33]David Couzens Hoy, "Hermeneutic Circularity, Indeterminacy, and Incommensurability," *New Literary History* 10 (Fall 1978): 166–67.

[34]Bloom, *Map of Misreading,* p. 36.

[35]John Dewey offered precisely this argument in 1934 when he insisted that a work of art "is recreated every time it is esthetically experienced. . . . It is absurd to ask what an artist 'really' meant by his product: he himself would find different meanings in it at different days and hours and in different stages of his own development." Further, he explained, "It is simply an impossibility that any one today should experience the Parthenon as the devout Athenian contemporary citizen experienced it, any more than the religious statuary of the twelfth century can mean, esthetically, even to a good Catholic today just what it meant to the worshipers of the old period." *Art as Experience* (New York: Capricorn Books, 1958), pp. 108–9.

[36]Charles Altieri, "The Hermeneutics of Literary Indeterminacy: A Dissent from the New Orthodoxy," *New Literary History* 10 (Fall 1978): 90.

[37]Murray Krieger, *Theory of Criticism: A Tradition and Its System* (Baltimore: Johns Hopkins University Press, 1976), p. 6.

[38]See Stanley E. Fish, "Normal Circumstances, Literal Language, Direct Speech Acts, the Ordinary, the Everyday, the Obvious, What Goes without Saying, and Other Special Cases," *Critical Inquiry* 4 (Summer 1978): 627–28.

[39]Ibid., p. 643.

[40]Virginia Woolf, "Women and Fiction," *Granite and Rainbow: Essays* (London: Hogarth Press, 1958), p. 81.

[41]Cesare Segre, "Narrative Structures and Literary History," *Critical Inquiry* 3 (Winter 1976): 272–73.

[42]Ted Cohen, "Metaphor and the Cultivation of Intimacy," *Critical Inquiry* 5 (Fall 1978): 9.

[43]From Adrienne Rich's "Transcendental Etude," *The Dream of a Common Language: Poems 1974–1977* (New York: W. W. Norton, 1978), pp. 76–77.

[44]Furman, "Study of Women and Language," p. 184.

[45]"A recurrent tendency in criticism is the establishment of false norms for the evaluation of literary works," notes Robert Scholes in *Structuralism in Literature: An Introduction* (New Haven, Conn.: Yale University Press, 1974), p. 131.

[46]For a full discussion of the Glaspell short story that takes this problem into account, please see my "A Map for Rereading: Gender and the Interpretation of Literary Texts," in this volume, pp. 46–62.

[47]Olsen, *Silences,* p. 45.

[48]Annette Kolodny, "Literary Criticism," Review Essay, *Signs* 2 (Winter 1976): 420.

[49]Scholes, *Structuralism in Literature,* pp. 144–45. These comments appear within his explication of Tzvetan Todorov's theory of reading.

[50]I borrow this concise phrasing of pluralistic modesty from M. H. Abrams's "The Deconstructive Angel," *Critical Inquiry* 3 (Spring 1977): 427. Indications of the pluralism that was to mark feminist inquiry were to be found in the diversity of essays collected by Susan Koppelman Cornillon for her early and groundbreaking anthology, *Images of Women in Fiction: Feminist Perspectives* (Bowling Green, Ohio: Bowling Green University Popular Press, 1972).

[51]R. P. Blackmur, "A Burden for Critics," *Hudson Review* 1 (Summer 1948): 171. Blackmur, of course, was referring to the way in which criticism makes us conscious of how art functions; I use his wording here because I am arguing that that same awareness must also be focused on the critical act itself. "Consciousness," he avers, "is the way we feel the critic's burden."

[52]I have earlier elaborated my objection to prescriptive categories for literature in

"The Feminist as Literary Critic," Critical Response, *Critical Inquiry* 2 (Summer 1976): 827–28.

[53]Scholes, *Structuralism in Literature,* pp. 151–52.

[54]Lillian S. Robinson, "Dwelling in Decencies: Radical Criticism and the Feminist Perspective," *College English* 32 (May 1971); reprinted in *Sex, Class, and Culture,* p. 11.

[55]"Ideology bridges the emotional gap between things as they are and as one would have them be, thus ensuring the performance of roles that might otherwise be abandoned in despair or apathy," Geertz comments in "Ideology as a Cultural System," p. 205.

[56]Ibid., pp. 220, 205.

[57]I here follow Frederic Jameson's view in *The Prison-House of Language: A Critical Account of Structuralism and Russian Formalism* (Princeton, N.J.: Princeton University Press, 1974), p. 107: "Ideology would seem to be that grillwork of form, convention, and belief which orders our actions."

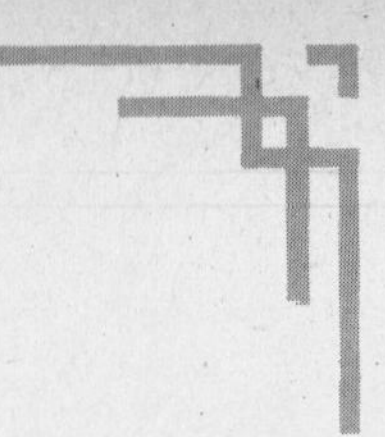

Toward a Black Feminist Criticism

Barbara Smith

I do not know where to begin. Long before I tried to write this I realized that I was attempting something unprecedented, something dangerous, merely by writing about Black women writers from a feminist perspective and about Black lesbian writers from any perspective at all. These things have not been done. Not by white male critics, expectedly. Not by Black male critics. Not by white women critics who think of themselves as feminists. And most crucially not by Black women critics, who, although they pay the most attention to Black women writers as a group, seldom use a consistent feminist analysis or write about Black lesbian literature. All segments of the literary world—whether establishment, progressive, Black, female, or lesbian—do not know, or at least act as if they do not know, that Black women writers and Black lesbian writers exist.

For whites, this specialized lack of knowledge is inextricably connected to their not knowing in any concrete or politically transforming way that Black women of any description dwell in this place. Black women's existence, experience, and culture and the brutally complex systems of oppression which shape these are in the "real world" of white and/or male consciousness beneath consideration, invisible, unknown.

This invisibility, which goes beyond anything that either Black men or white women experience and tell about in their writing, is one reason it is so difficult for me to know where to start. It seems overwhelming to break such a massive silence. Even more numbing, however, is the realization that so many of the women who will read this have not yet noticed us missing either from their reading matter, their politics, or their lives. It is galling that ostensible feminists and acknowledged lesbians have been so blinded to the implications of any womanhood that is not white womanhood and that they have yet to struggle with the deep racism in themselves that is at the source of this blindness.

I think of the thousands and thousands of books, magazines, and articles which have been devoted, by this time, to the subject of women's writing and I am filled with rage at the fraction of those pages that mention Black and other Third World women. I finally do not know how to begin because in 1977 I want to be writing this for a Black feminist publication, for Black women who know and love these writers as I do and who, if they do not yet know their names, have at least profoundly felt the pain of their absence.

The conditions that coalesce into the impossibilities of this essay have as much to do with politics as with the practice of literature. Any discussion of Afro-American writers can rightfully begin with the fact that for most of the time we have been in this country we have been categorically denied not only literacy but the most minimal possibility of a decent human life. In her landmark essay, "In Search of Our Mothers' Gardens," Alice Walker discloses how the political, economic, and social restrictions of slavery and racism have historically stunted the creative lives of Black women.[1]

At the present time I feel that the politics of feminism have a direct relationship to the state of Black women's literature. A viable, autonomous Black feminist movement in this country would open up the space needed for the exploration of Black women's lives and the creation of consciously Black woman–identified art. At the same time a redefinition of the goals and strategies of the white feminist movement would lead to much-needed change in the focus and content of what is now generally accepted as women's culture.

I want to make in this essay some connections between the politics of Black women's lives, what we write about, and our situation as artists. In order to do this I will look at how Black women have been viewed critically by outsiders, demonstrate the necessity for Black feminist criticism, and try to understand what the existence or nonexistence of Black lesbian writing reveals about the state of Black women's culture and the intensity of *all* Black women's oppression.

The role that criticism plays in making a body of literature recognizable and real hardly needs to be explained here. The necessity for nonhostile and perceptive analysis of works written by persons outside the "mainstream" of white/male cultural rule has been proven by the Black cultural resurgence of the 1960s and 1970s and by the even more recent growth of feminist literary scholarship. For books to be real and remembered they have to be talked about. For books to be understood they must be examined in such a way that the basic intentions of the writers are at least considered. Because of racism Black literature has usually been viewed as a discrete subcategory of American literature, and there have been Black critics of Black literature who did much to keep it alive long before it caught the attention of whites. Before the advent of specifically feminist criticism in this decade, books by white women, on the other hand, were not clearly perceived as the cultural manifestation of an oppressed people. It took the surfacing of the second wave of the North American feminist movement to expose the fact that these works contain a stunningly accurate record of the impact of patriarchal values and practice upon the lives of women, and more significantly, that literature by women provides essential insights into female experience.

In speaking about the current situation of Black women writers, it is important to remember that the existence of a feminist movement was an essential precondition to the growth of feminist literature, criticism, and women's studies, which focused at the beginning almost entirely upon investigations of literature. The fact that a parallel Black feminist movement has been much slower in evolving cannot help but have impact upon the situation of Black women writers and artists and explains in part why during this very same period we have been so ignored.

There is no political movement to give power or support to those who want to examine Black women's experience through studying our history, literature, and culture. There is no political presence that demands a minimal level of consciousness and respect from those who write or talk about our lives. Finally, there is not a developed body of Black feminist political theory whose assumptions could be used in the study of Black women's art. When Black women's books are dealt with at all, it is usually in the context of Black literature, which largely ignores the implications of sexual politics. When white women look at Black women's works they are of course ill-equipped to deal with the subtleties of racial politics. A Black feminist approach to literature that embodies the realization that the politics of sex as well as the politics of race and class are crucially interlocking factors in the works of Black women writers is an absolute necessity. Until a Black feminist criticism exists we will not even know what these writers mean. The citations from a variety of critics which follow prove that without a Black feminist critical perspective not only are books by Black women misunderstood, they are destroyed in the process.

Jerry H. Bryant, *The Nation's* white male reviewer of Alice Walker's *In Love and Trouble: Stories of Black Women,* wrote in 1973:

> The subtitle of the collection, "Stories of Black Women," is probably an attempt by the publisher to exploit not only

> black subjects but feminine ones. There is nothing feminist about these stories, however.[2]

Blackness and feminism are to his mind mutually exclusive and peripheral to the act of writing fiction. Bryant of course does not consider that Walker might have titled the work herself, nor did he apparently read the book, which unequivocally reveals the author's feminist consciousness.

In *The Negro Novel in America,* a book that Black critics recognize as one of the worst examples of white racist pseudoscholarship, Robert Bone cavalierly dismisses Ann Petry's classic, *The Street.* He perceives it to be "a superficial social analysis" of how slums victimize their Black inhabitants. He further objects:

> It is an attempt to interpret slum life in terms of *Negro* experience, when a larger frame of reference is required. As Alain Locke has observed, "*Knock on Any Door* is superior to *The Street* because it designates class and environment, rather than mere race and environment, as its antagonist."[3]

Neither Robert Bone nor Alain Locke, the Black male critic he cites, can recognize that *The Street* is one of the best delineations in literature of how sex, race, *and* class interact to oppress Black women.

In her review of Toni Morrison's *Sula* for the *New York Times Book Review* in 1973, putative feminist Sara Blackburn makes similarly racist comments:

> Toni Morrison is far too talented to remain only a marvelous recorder of the black side of provincial American life. If she is to maintain the large and serious audience she deserves, she is going to have to address a riskier contemporary reality than this beautiful but nevertheless distanced novel. *And if she does this, it seems to me that she might easily transcend that early and unintentionally limiting classification "black woman writer" and take her place among the most serious, important and talented American novelists now working.*[4] [Italics mine]

Recognizing Morrison's exquisite gift, Blackburn unashamedly asserts that Morrison is "too talented" to deal with mere Black folk, particularly those double nonentities, Black women. In order to be accepted as "serious," "important," "talented," and "American," she must obviously focus her efforts upon chronicling the doings of white men.

The mishandling of Black women writers by whites is paralleled more often by their not being handled at all, particularly in feminist criticism. Although Elaine Showalter in her review essay on literary criticism for *Signs* states that "the best work being produced today [in feminist criticism] is exacting and cosmopolitan," her essay is neither. If it were, she would not have failed to mention a single Black or Third World woman writer, whether "major" or "minor," to cite her questionable categories. That she also does not even hint that lesbian writers of any color exist renders her purported overview virtually meaningless. Showalter obviously thinks that the identities of being Black and female are mutually exclusive, as this statement illustrates:

> Furthermore, there are other literary subcultures (black American novelists, for example) whose history offers a precedent for feminist scholarship to use.[5]

The idea of critics like Showalter *using* Black literature is chilling, a case of barely disguised cultural imperialism. The final insult is that she footnotes the preceding remark by pointing readers to works on Black literature by white males Robert Bone and Roger Rosenblatt!

Two recent works by white women, Ellen Moers's *Literary Women: The Great Writers* and Patricia Meyer Spacks's *The Female Imagination,* evidence the same racist flaw.[6] Moers includes the names of four Black and one Puertorriqueña writer in her seventy pages of bibliographical notes and does not deal at all with Third World women in the body of her book. Spacks refers to a comparison between Negroes *(sic)* and women in Mary Ellmann's *Thinking About Women* under the index entry "blacks, women and." "*Black Boy* (Wright)" is the preceding entry. Nothing follows. Again there is absolutely no recognition that Black and female identity ever coexist, specifically in a group of Black women writers. Perhaps one can assume that these women do not know who Black women writers are, that like most Americans they have little opportunity to learn about them. Perhaps. Their ignorance seems suspiciously selective, however, particularly in the light of the dozens of truly obscure white women writers they are able to unearth. Spacks was herself employed at Wellesley College at the same time that Alice Walker was there teaching one of the first courses on Black women writers in the country.

I am not trying to encourage racist criticism of Black women writers like that of Sara Blackburn, to cite only one example. As a beginning I would at least like to see in print white women's acknowledgment of the contradictions of who and what are being left out of their research and writing.[7]

Black male critics can also *act* as if they do not know that Black women writers exist and are, of course, hampered by an inability to comprehend Black women's experience in sexual as well as racial terms. Unfortunately there are also those who are as virulently sexist in their treatment of Black women writers as their white male counterparts. Darwin Turner's discussion of Zora Neale Hurston in his *In a Minor Chord: Three Afro-American Writers and Their Search for Identity* is a frightening example of the near assassination of a great Black woman writer.[8] His descriptions of her and her work as "artful," "coy," "irrational," "superficial," and "shallow" bear no relationship to the actual quality of her achievements. Turner is completely insensitive to the sexual political dynamics of Hurston's life and writing.

In a recent interview the notoriously misogynist writer Ishmael Reed comments in this way upon the low sales of his newest novel:

> . . . but the book only sold 8000 copies. I don't mind giving out the figure: 8000. Maybe if I was one of those young *female* Afro-American writers that are so hot now, I'd sell more. You know, fill my books with ghetto women who can *do no wrong*. . . . But come on, I think I could have sold 8000 copies by myself.[9]

The politics of the situation of Black women are glaringly illuminated by this statement. Neither Reed nor his white male interviewer has the slightest compunction about attacking Black women in print. They need not fear widespread public denunciation since Reed's statement is in perfect agreement with the values of a society that hates Black people, women, and Black women. Finally the two of them feel free to base their actions on the premise that Black women are powerless to alter either their political or their cultural oppression.

In her introduction to "A Bibliography of Works Written by American Black Women" Ora Williams quotes some of the reactions of her colleagues toward her efforts to do research on Black women:

> Others have reacted negatively with such statements as, "I really don't think you are going to find very much written," "Have 'they' written anything that is any good?" and, "I wouldn't go overboard with this woman's lib thing." When discussions touched on the possibility of teaching a course in which emphasis would be on the literature by Black women, one response was, "Ha, ha. That will certainly be the most nothing course ever offered!"[10]

A remark by Alice Walker capsulizes what all the preceding examples indicate about the position of Black women writers and the reasons for the damaging criticism about them. She responds to her interviewer's question, "Why do you think that the black woman writer has been so ignored in

America? Does she have even more difficulty than the black male writer, who perhaps has just begun to gain recognition?" Walker replies:

> There are two reasons why the black woman writer is not taken as seriously as the black male writer. One is that she's a woman. Critics seem unusually ill-equipped to intelligently discuss and analyze the works of black women. Generally, they do not even make the attempt; they prefer, rather, to talk about the lives of black women writers, not about what they write. And, since black women writers are not—it would seem—very likable—until recently they were the least willing worshippers of male supremacy—comments about them tend to be cruel.[11]

A convincing case for Black feminist criticism can obviously be built solely upon the basis of the negativity of what already exists. It is far more gratifying, however, to demonstrate its necessity by showing how it can serve to reveal for the first time the profound subtleties of this particular body of literature.

Before suggesting how a Black feminist approach might be used to examine a specific work, I will outline some of the principles that I think a Black feminist critic could use. Beginning with a primary commitment to exploring how both sexual and racial politics and Black and female identity are inextricable elements in Black women's writings, she would also work from the assumption that Black women writers constitute an identifiable literary tradition. The breadth of her familiarity with these writers would have shown her that not only is theirs a verifiable historical tradition that parallels in time the tradition of Black men and white women writing in this country, but that thematically, stylistically, aesthetically, and conceptually Black women writers manifest common approaches to the act of creating literature as a direct result of the specific political, social, and economic experience they have been obliged to share. The way, for example, that Zora Neale Hurston, Margaret Walker, Toni Morrison, and Alice Walker incorporate the traditional Black female activities of rootworking, herbal medicine, conjure, and midwifery into the fabric of their stories is not mere coincidence, nor is their use of specifically Black female language to express their own and their characters' thoughts accidental. The use of Black women's language and cultural experience in books *by* Black women *about* Black women results in a miraculously rich coalescing of form and content and also takes their writing far beyond the confines of white/male literary structures. The Black feminist critic would find innumerable commonalities in works by Black women.

Another principle which grows out of the concept of a tradition and which would also help to strengthen this tradition would be for the critic to look first for precedents and insights in interpretation within the works of other Black women. In other words she would think and write out of her own identity and not try to graft the ideas or methodology of white/male literary thought upon the precious materials of Black women's art. Black feminist criticism would by definition be highly innovative, embodying the daring spirit of the works themselves. The Black feminist critic would be constantly aware of the political implications of her work and would assert the connections between it and the political situation of all Black women. Logically developed, Black feminist criticism would owe its existence to a Black feminist movement while at the same time contributing ideas that women in the movement could use.

Black feminist criticism applied to a particular work can overturn previous assumptions about it and expose for the first time its actual dimensions. At the "Lesbians and Literature" discussion at the 1976 Modern Language Association convention Bertha Harris suggested that if in a woman writer's work a sentence refuses to do what it is supposed to do, if there are strong images of women and if there is a refusal to be linear, the result is innately lesbian literature. As usual, I wanted to see if these ideas might be applied to the Black women writers that I know and quickly realized that many of their works were, in Harris's sense, lesbian. Not because women are "lovers," but because they are the central figures, are positively portrayed and have pivotal relationships with one another. The form and language of these works are also nothing like what white patriarchal culture requires or expects.

I was particularly struck by the way in which Toni Morrison's novels *The Bluest Eye* and *Sula* could be explored from this new perspective.[12] In both works the relationships between girls and women are essential, yet at the same time physical sexuality is overtly expressed only between men and women. Despite the apparent heterosexuality of the female characters, I discovered in rereading *Sula* that it works as a lesbian novel not only because of the passionate friendship between Sula and Nel but because of Morrison's consistently critical stance toward the heterosexual institutions of male-female relationships, marriage, and the family. Consciously or not, Morrison's work poses both lesbian and feminist questions about Black women's autonomy and their impact upon each other's lives.

Sula and Nel find each other in 1922 when each of them is twelve, on the brink of puberty and the discovery of boys. Even as awakening sexuality "clotted their dreams," each girl desires "a someone" obviously female with whom to share her feelings. Morrison writes:

> . . . for it was in dreams that the two girls had met. Long before Edna Finch's Mellow House opened, even before

> they marched through the chocolate halls of Garfield Primary School . . . they had already made each other's acquaintance in the delirium of their noon dreams. They were solitary little girls whose loneliness was so profound it intoxicated them and sent them stumbling into Technicolored visions that always included a presence, a someone who, quite like the dreamer, shared the delight of the dream. When Nel, an only child, sat on the steps of her back porch surrounded by the high silence of her mother's incredibly orderly house, feeling the neatness pointing at her back, she studied the poplars and fell easily into a picture of herself lying on a flower bed, tangled in her own hair, waiting for some fiery prince. He approached but never quite arrived. But always, watching the dream along with her, were some smiling sympathetic eyes. Someone as interested as she herself in the flow of her imagined hair, the thickness of the mattress of flowers, the voile sleeves that closed below her elbows in gold-threaded cuffs.
>
> Similarly, Sula, also an only child, but wedged into a household of throbbing disorder constantly awry with things, people, voices and the slamming of doors, spent hours in the attic behind a roll of linoleum galloping through her own mind on a gray-and-white horse tasting sugar and smelling roses in full view of someone who shared both the taste and the speed.
>
> So when they met, first in those chocolate halls and next through the ropes of the swing, they felt the ease and comfort of old friends. Because each had discovered years before that they were neither white nor male, and that all freedom and triumph was forbidden to them, they had set about creating something else to be. Their meeting was fortunate, for it let them use each other to grow on. Daughters of distant mothers and incomprehensible fathers (Sula's because he was dead; Nel's because he wasn't), they found in each other's eyes the intimacy they were looking for. (Pp. 51–52)

As this beautiful passage shows, their relationship, from the very beginning, is suffused with an erotic romanticism. The dreams in which they are initially drawn to each other are actually complementary aspects of the same sensuous fairy tale. Nel imagines a "fiery prince" who never quite arrives while Sula gallops like a prince "on a gray-and-white horse."[13] The "real world" of patriarchy requires, however, that they channel this energy away from each other to the opposite sex. Lorraine Bethel explains this dynamic in her essay "Conversations With Ourselves: Black Female Relationships in Toni Cade Bambara's *Gorilla, My Love* and Toni Morrison's *Sula*"

> I am not suggesting that Sula and Nel are being consciously sexual, or that their relationship has an overt lesbian nature. I am suggesting, however, that there is a certain sensuality in their interactions that is reinforced by the mirror-like nature of their relationship. Sexual exploration and coming of age is a natural part of adolescence. Sula and Nel discover men together, and though their flirtations with males are an important part of their sexual exploration, the sensuality that they experience in each other's company is equally important.[14]

Sula and Nel must also struggle with the constrictions of racism upon their lives. The knowledge that "they were neither white nor male" is the inherent explanation of their need for each other. Morrison depicts in literature the necessary bonding that has always taken place between Black women for the sake of barest survival. Together the two girls can find the courage to create themselves.

Their relationship is severed only when Nel marries Jude, an unexceptional young man who thinks of her as "the hem—the tuck and fold that hid his raveling edges" (p. 83). Sula's inventive wildness cannot overcome social pressure or the influence of Nel's parents who "had succeeded in rubbing down to a dull glow any sparkle or splutter she had" (p. 83). Nel falls prey to convention while Sula escapes it. Yet at the wedding which ends the first phase of their relationship, Nel's final action is to look past her husband toward Sula,

> a slim figure in blue, gliding, with just a hint of a strut, down the path towards the road. . . . Even from the rear Nel could tell that it was Sula and that she was smiling; that something deep down in that litheness was amused. (P. 85)

When Sula returns ten years later, her rebelliousness full-blown, a major source of the town's suspicions stems from the fact that although she is almost thirty, she is still unmarried. Sula's grandmother, Eva, does not hesitate to bring up the matter as soon as she arrives. She asks:

> "When you gone to get married? You need to have some babies. It'll settle you. . . . Ain't no woman got no business floatin' around without no man." (P. 92)

Sula replies: "I don't want to make somebody else. I want to make myself" (p. 92). Self-definition is a dangerous activity for any woman to engage in, especially a Black one, and it expectedly earns Sula pariah status in Medallion.

Morrison clearly points out that it is the fact that Sula has not been tamed or broken by the exigencies of heterosexual family life which most galls the others:

> Among the weighty evidence piling up was the fact that Sula did not look her age. She was near thirty and, unlike them, had lost no teeth, suffered no bruises, developed no ring of fat at the waist or pocket at the back of her neck. (P. 115)

In other words she is not a domestic serf, a woman run down by obligatory childbearing or a victim of battering. Sula also sleeps with the husbands of the town once and then discards them, needing them even less than her own mother did for sexual gratification and affection. The town reacts to her disavowal of patriarchal values by becoming fanatically serious about their own family obligations, as if in this way they might counteract Sula's radical criticism of their lives.

Sula's presence in her community functions much like the presence of lesbians everywhere to expose the contradictions of supposedly "normal" life. The opening paragraph of the essay "The Woman-Identified Woman" has amazing relevance as an explanation of Sula's position and character in the novel. It asks:

> What is a lesbian? A lesbian is the rage of all women condensed to the point of explosion. She is the woman who, often beginning at an extremely early age, acts in accordance with her inner compulsion to be a more complete and freer human being than her society—perhaps then, but certainly later—cares to allow her. These needs and actions, over a period of years, bring her into painful conflict with people, situations, the accepted ways of thinking, feeling and behaving, until she is in a state of continual war with everything around her, and usually with herself. She may not be fully conscious of the political implications of what for her began as personal necessity, but on some level she has not been able to accept the limitations and oppression laid on her by the most basic role of her society—the female role.[15]

The limitations of the *Black* female role are even greater in a racist and sexist society, as is the amount of courage it takes to challenge them. It is no wonder that the townspeople see Sula's independence as imminently dangerous.

Morrison is also careful to show the reader that despite their years of separation and their opposing paths, Nel and Sula's relationship retains its primacy for each of them. Nell feels transformed when Sula returns and thinks:

> It was like getting the use of an eye back, having a cataract removed. Her old friend had come home. Sula. Who made her laugh, who made her see old things with new eyes, in whose presence she felt clever, gentle and a little raunchy. (P. 95)

Laughing together in the familiar "rib-scraping" way, Nel feels "new, soft and new" (p. 98). Morrison uses here the visual imagery which symbolizes the women's closeness throughout the novel.

Sula fractures this closeness, however, by sleeping with Nel's husband, an act of little import according to her system of values. Nel, of course, cannot understand. Sula thinks ruefully:

> Nel was the one person who had wanted nothing from her, who had accepted all aspects of her. Now she wanted everything, and all because of *that.* Nel was the first person who had been real to her, whose name she knew, who had seen as she had the slant of life that made it possible to stretch it to its limits. Now Nel was one of *them.* (Pp. 119–20)

Sula also thinks at the realization of losing Nel about how unsatisfactory her relationships with men have been and admits:

> She had been looking all along for a friend, and it took her a while to discover that a lover was not a comrade and could never be—for a woman. (P. 121)

The nearest that Sula comes to actually loving a man is in a brief affair with Ajax and what she values most about him is the intellectual companionship he provides, the brilliance he "allows" her to show.

Sula's feelings about sex with men are also consistent with a lesbian interpretation of the novel. Morrison writes:

> She went to bed with men as frequently as she could. It was the only place where she could find what she was looking for: *misery and the ability to feel deep sorrow. . . .* During the lovemaking she found and needed to find the cutting edge.

> When she left off cooperating with her body and began to assert herself in the act, particles of strength gathered in her like steel shavings drawn to a spacious magnetic center, forming a tight cluster that nothing, it seemed, could break. *And there was utmost irony and outrage in lying under someone, in a position of surrender, feeling her own abiding strength and limitless power.* . . . When her partner disengaged himself, she looked up at him in wonder trying to recall his name . . . waiting impatiently for him to turn away . . . *leaving her to the postcoital privateness in which she met herself, welcomed herself, and joined herself in matchless harmony.* (Pp. 122–23; italics mine)

Sula uses men for sex which results, not in communion with them, but in her further delving into self.

Ultimately the deepest communion and communication in the novel occurs between two women who love each other. After their last painful meeting, which does not bring reconciliation, Sula thinks as Nel leaves her:

> "So she will walk on down that road, her back so straight in that old green coat . . . thinking how much I have cost her and never remember the days when we were two throats and one eye and we had no price." (P. 147)

It is difficult to imagine a more evocative metaphor for what women can be to each other, the "pricelessness" they achieve in refusing to sell themselves for male approval, the total worth that they can only find in each other's eyes.

Decades later the novel concludes with Nel's final comprehension of the source of the grief that has plagued her from the time her husband walked out:

> "All that time, all that time, I thought I was missing Jude." And the loss pressed down on her chest and came up into her throat. "We was girls together," she said as though explaining something. "O Lord, Sula," she cried, "girl, girl, girlgirlgirl."
>
> It was a fine cry—loud and long—but it had no bottom and it had no top, just circles and circles of sorrow. (P. 174)

Again Morrison exquisitely conveys what women, Black women, mean to each other. This final passage verifies the depth of Sula and Nel's relationship and its centrality to an accurate interpretation of the work.

Sula is an exceedingly lesbian novel in the emotions expressed, in the definition of female character, and in the way that the politics of heterosexuality are portrayed. The very meaning of lesbianism is being expanded in literature, just as it is being redefined through politics. The confusion that many readers have felt about *Sula* may well have a lesbian explanation. If one sees Sula's inexplicable "evil" and nonconformity as the evil of not being male-identified, many elements in the novel become clear. The work might be clearer still if Morrison had approached her subject with the consciousness that a lesbian relationship was at least a possibility for her characters. Obviously Morrison did not *intend* the reader to perceive Sula and Nel's relationship as inherently lesbian. However, this lack of intention only shows the way in which heterosexist assumptions can veil what may logically be expected to occur in a work. What I have tried to do here is not to prove that Morrison wrote something that she did not, but to point out how a Black feminist critical perspective at least allows consideration of this level of the novel's meaning.

In her inteıview in *Conditions: One* Adrienne Rich talks about unconsummated relationships and the need to reevaluate the meaning of intense yet supposedly nonerotic connections between women. She asserts:

> We need a lot more documentation about what actually happened: I think we can also imagine it, because we know it happened—we know it out of our own lives.[16]

Black women are still in the position of having to "imagine," discover, and verify Black lesbian literature because so little has been written from an avowedly lesbian perspective. The near nonexistence of Black lesbian literature which other Black lesbians and I so deeply feel has everything to do with the politics of our lives, the total suppression of identity that all Black women, lesbian or not, must face. This literary silence is again intensified by the unavailability of an autonomous Black feminist movement through which we could fight our oppression and also begin to name ourselves.

In a speech, "The Autonomy of Black Lesbian Women," Wilmette Brown comments upon the connection between our political reality and the literature we must invent:

> Because the isolation of Black lesbian women, given that we are superfreaks, given that our lesbianism defies both the sexual identity that capital gives us and the racial identity that capital gives us, the isolation of Black lesbian women from heterosexual Black women is very profound. Very profound. I have searched throughout Black history, Black literature, whatever, looking for some women that I could see

> were somehow lesbian. Now I know that in a certain sense they were all lesbian. But that was a very painful search.[17]

Heterosexual privilege is usually the only privilege that Black women have. None of us have racial or sexual privilege, almost none of us have class privilege; maintaining "straightness" is our last resort. Being out, particularly out in print, is the final renunciation of any claim to the crumbs of "tolerance" that nonthreatening "ladylike" Black women are sometimes fed. I am convinced that it is our lack of privilege and power in every other sphere that allows so few Black women to make the leap that many white women, particularly writers, have been able to make in this decade, not merely because they are white or have economic leverage, but because they have had the strength and support of a movement behind them.

As Black lesbians we must be out not only in white society but in the Black community as well, which is at least as homophobic. That the sanctions against Black lesbians are extremely high is well illustrated in this comment by Black male writer Ishmael Reed. Speaking about the inroads that whites make into Black culture, he asserts:

> In Manhattan you find people actively trying to impede intellectual debate among Afro-Americans. The powerful "liberal/radical/existentialist" influences of the Manhattan literary and drama establishment speak through tokens, like for example that ancient notion of the *one* black ideologue (who's usually a Communist), the *one* black poetess (who's usually a feminist lesbian).[18]

To Reed, "feminist" and "lesbian" are the most pejorative terms he can hurl at a Black woman and totally invalidate anything she might say, regardless of her actual politics or sexual identity. Such accusations are quite effective for keeping in line Black women writers who are writing with integrity and strength from any conceivable perspective, but especially ones who are actually feminist and lesbian. Unfortunately Reed's reactionary attitude is all too typical. A community which has not confronted sexism, because a widespread Black feminist movement has not required it to, has likewise not been challenged to examine its heterosexism. Even at this moment I am not convinced that one can write explicitly as a Black lesbian and live to tell about it.

Yet there are a handful of Black women who have risked everything for truth. Audre Lorde, Pat Parker, and Ann Allen Shockley have at least broken ground in the vast wilderness of works that do not exist.[19] Black feminist criticism will again have an essential role not only in creating a climate in which Black lesbian writers can survive, but in undertaking the total reassessment of Black literature and literary history needed to reveal the Black woman–identified women that Wilmette Brown and so many of us are looking for.

Although I have concentrated here upon what does not exist and what needs to be done, a few Black feminist critics have already begun this work. Gloria T. Hull at the University of Delaware has discovered in her research on Black women poets of the Harlem Renaissance that many of the women who are considered "minor" writers of the period were in constant contact with each other and provided both intellectual stimulation and psychological support for each other's work. At least one of these writers, Angelina Weld Grimké, wrote many unpublished love poems to women. Lorraine Bethel, a recent graduate of Yale College, has done substantial work on Black women writers, particularly in her senior essay, "This Infinity of Conscious Pain: Blues Lyricism and Hurston's Black Female Folk Aesthetic and Cultural Sensibility in *Their Eyes Were Watching God,*" in which she brilliantly defines and uses the principles of Black feminist criticism. Elaine Scott at the State University of New York at Old Westbury is also involved in highly creative and politically resonant research on Hurston and other writers.

The fact that these critics are young and, except for Hull, unpublished merely indicates the impediments we face. Undoubtedly there are other women working and writing whom I do not even know, simply because there is no place to read them. As Michele Wallace states in her article "A Black Feminist's Search for Sisterhood":

> We exist as women who are Black who are feminists, each stranded for the moment, working independently because there is not yet an environment in this society remotely congenial to our struggle—[or our thoughts].[20]

I only hope that this essay is one way of breaking our silence and our isolation, of helping us to know each other.

Just as I did not know where to start I am not sure how to end. I feel that I have tried to say too much and at the same time have left too much unsaid. What I want this essay to do is lead everyone who reads it to examine *everything* that they have ever thought and believed about feminist culture and to ask themselves how their thoughts connect to the reality of Black women's writing and lives. I want to encourage in white women, as a first step, a sane accountability to all the women who write and live on this soil. I want most of all for Black women and Black lesbians somehow not to be so alone. This last will require the most expansive of revolutions as well as many new words to tell us how to make this revolution real. I finally want to express how much easier both my waking and my sleeping hours would be if there were one book in existence that would tell me something specific about my life. One book based in Black feminist and Black lesbian experience, fiction or nonfiction. Just one work to reflect the reality that I and the Black women whom I love are trying to create. When such a book exists then each of us will not only know better how to live, but how to dream.

NOTES

[1]Alice Walker, "In Search of Our Mothers' Gardens," in *Ms.*, May 1974, and in *Southern Exposure* 4, no. 4, *Generations: Women in the South* (Winter 1977): 60–64.

[2]Jerry H. Bryant, "The Outskirts of a New City," *The Nation*, November 12, 1973, p. 502.

[3]Robert Bone, *The Negro Novel in America* (New Haven, Conn.: Yale University Press, 1958), p. 180. *Knock on Any Door* is a novel by Black writer Willard Motley.

[4]Sara Blackburn, "You Still Can't Go Home Again," *New York Times Book Review*, December 30, 1973, p. 3.

[5]Elaine Showalter, "Literary Criticism," Review Essay, *Signs* 1 (Winter 1975): 460, 445.

[6]Ellen Moers, *Literary Women: The Great Writers* (Garden City, N.Y.: Anchor Books, 1977); Patricia Meyer Spacks, *The Female Imagination* (New York: Avon Books, 1976).

[7]An article by Nancy Hoffman, "White Women, Black Women: Inventing an Adequate Pedagogy," *Women's Studies Newsletter* 5 (Spring 1977): 21–24, gives valuable insights into how white women can approach the writing of Black women.

[8]Darwin T. Turner, *In a Minor Chord: Three Afro-American Writers and Their Search for Identity* (Carbondale and Edwardsville: Southern Illinois University Press, 1971).

[9]John Domini, "Roots and Racism: An Interview with Ishmael Reed," *Boston Phoenix*, April 5, 1977, p. 20.

[10]Ora Williams, "A Bibliography of Works Written by American Black Women," *College Language Association Journal* 15 (March 1972): 355. There is an expanded book-length version of this bibliography: *American Black Women in the Arts and Social Sciences: A Bibliographic Survey* (Metuchen, N.J.: Scarecrow Press, 1973; rev. and expanded ed., 1978).

[11]John O'Brien, ed., *Interviews with Black Writers* (New York: Liveright, 1973), p. 201.

[12]Toni Morrison, *The Bluest Eye* (1970; reprint ed., New York: Pocket Books, 1972, 1976) and *Sula* (New York: Alfred A. Knopf, 1974). All subsequent references to this work will be designated in the text.

[13]My sister, Beverly Smith, pointed out this connection to me.

[14]Lorraine Bethel, "Conversations With Ourselves: Black Female Relationships in Toni Cade Bambara's *Gorilla, My Love* and Toni Morrison's *Sula,*" unpublished paper written at Yale University, 1976, 47 pp. Bethel has worked from a premise similar to mine in a much more developed treatment of the novel.

[15]New York Radicalesbians, "The Woman-Identified Woman," in *Lesbians Speak Out* (Oakland, Calif.: Women's Press Collective, 1974), p. 87.

[16]Elly Bulkin, "An Interview With Adrienne Rich: Part I," *Conditions: One* 1 (April 1977): 62.

[17]Wilmette Brown, "The Autonomy of Black Lesbian Women," manuscript of speech delivered July 24, 1976, in Toronto, Canada, p. 7.

[18]Domini, "Roots and Racism," p. 18.

[19]Audre Lorde, *New York Head Shop and Museum* (Detroit: Broadside Press, 1974); *Coal* (New York: W. W. Norton, 1976); *Between Our Selves* (Point Reyes, Calif.: Eidolon Editions, 1976); *The Black Unicorn* (New York: W. W. Norton, 1978).

Pat Parker, *Child of Myself* (Oakland, Calif.: Women's Press Collective, 1972 and 1974); *Pit Stop* (Oakland, Calif.: Women's Press Collective, 1973); *Womanslaughter* (Oakland, Calif.: Diana Press, 1978); *Movement in Black* (Oakland, Calif.: Diana Press, 1978).

Ann Allen Shockley, *Loving Her* (Indianapolis: Bobbs-Merrill, 1974).

There is at least one Black lesbian writers' collective, Jemima, in New York. They do public readings and have available a collection of their poems. They can be contacted c/o Boyce, 41-11 Parsons Boulevard, Flushing, N.Y. 11355.

[20]Michele Wallace, "A Black Feminist's Search for Sisterhood," *Village Voice*, July 28, 1975, p. 7.

New Directions for Black Feminist Criticism

Deborah E. McDowell

What is commonly called literary history," writes Louise Bernikow, "is actually a record of choices. Which writers have survived their times and which have not depends upon who noticed them and chose to record their notice."[1] Women writers have fallen victim to arbitrary selection. Their writings have been "patronized, slighted, and misunderstood by a cultural establishment operating according to male norms out of male perceptions."[2] Both literary history's "sins of omission" and literary criticism's inaccurate and partisan judgments of women writers have come under attack since the early 1970s by feminist critics.[3] To date, no one has formulated a precise or complete definition of feminist criticism, but since its inception, its theorists and practitioners have agreed that it is a "corrective, unmasking the omissions and distortions of the past—the errors of a literary critical tradition that arise from and reflect a culture created, perpetuated, and dominated by men."[4]

These early theorists and practitioners of feminist literary criticism were largely white females who, wittingly or not, perpetrated against the Black woman writer the same exclusive practices they so vehemently decried in white male scholars. Seeing the experiences of white women, particularly white middle-class women, as normative, white female scholars proceeded blindly to exclude the work of Black women writers from literary anthologies and critical studies. Among the most flagrant examples of this chauvinism is Patricia Meyer Spacks's *The Female Imagination.* In a weak defense of her book's exclusive focus on women in the Anglo-American literary tradition, Spacks quotes Phyllis Chesler (a white female psychologist): "I have no theory to offer of Third World female psychology in America. . . . As a white woman, I'm reluctant and unable to construct theories about experiences I haven't had."[5] But, as Alice Walker observes, "Spacks never lived in nineteenth-century Yorkshire, so why theorize about the Brontës?"[6]

Not only have Black women writers been "disenfranchised" from critical works by white women scholars on the "female tradition," but they have also been frequently excised from those on the Afro-American literary tradition by Black scholars, most of whom are males. For example, Robert Stepto's *From Behind the Veil: A Study of Afro-American Narrative* purports to be "a history . . . of the historical consciousness of an Afro-American art form—namely, the Afro-American written narrative."[7] Yet, Black women writers are conspicuously absent from the table of contents. Though Stepto does have a token two-page discussion of Zora Neale Hurston's *Their Eyes Were Watching God* in which he refers to it as a "seminal narrative in Afro-American letters,"[8] he did not feel that the novel merited its own chapter or the thorough analysis accorded the other works he discusses.

When Black women writers are neither ignored altogether nor merely given honorable mention, they are critically misunderstood and summarily dismissed. In *The Negro Novel in America,* for example, Robert Bone's reading of Jessie Fauset's novels is both partisan and superficial and might explain the reasons Fauset remains obscure. Bone argues that Fauset is the foremost member of the "Rear Guard" of writers "who lagged behind," clinging to established literary traditions. The "Rear Guard" drew their source material from the Negro middle class in their efforts "to orient Negro art toward white opinion," and "to apprise educated whites of the existence of respectable Negroes." Bone adds that Fauset's emphasis on the Black middle class results in novels that are "uniformly sophomoric, trivial and dull."[9]

While David Littlejohn praises Black fiction since 1940, he denigrates the work of Fauset and Nella Larsen. He maintains that "the newer writers are obviously writing as men, for men," and are avoiding the "very close and steamy" writing that is the result of "any subculture's taking itself too seriously, defining the world and its values exclusively in the terms of its own restrictive norms and concerns."[10] This "phallic criticism,"[11] to use Mary Ellman's term, is based on masculine-centered values and definitions. It has dominated the criticism of Black women writers and has done much to guarantee that most would be, in Alice Walker's words, "casually pilloried and consigned to a sneering oblivion."[12]

Suffice it to say that the critical community has not favored Black women writers. The recognition among Black female critics and writers that white women, white men, and Black men consider their experiences as normative and Black women's experiences as deviant has given rise to Black feminist criticism. Much as in white feminist criticism, the critical postulates of Black women's literature are only skeletally defined. Although there is no concrete definition of Black feminist criticism, a handful of Black female scholars have begun the necessary enterprise of resurrecting forgotten Black women writers and revising misinformed critical opinions of them. Justifiably enraged by the critical establishment's neglect and mishandling of Black women writers, these critics are calling for, in the words of Barbara Smith, "nonhostile and perceptive analysis of works written by persons outside the 'mainstream' of white/-male cultural rule."[13]

Despite the urgency and timeliness of the enterprise, however, no substantial body of Black feminist criticism—either in theory or practice—exists, a fact which might be explained partially by our limited access to and control of the media.[14] Another explanation for the paucity of Black feminist criticism, notes Barbara Smith, is the lack of a "developed body of Black feminist political theory whose assumptions could be used in the study of Black women's art."

Despite the strained circumstances under which Black feminist critics labor, a few committed Black female scholars have broken necessary ground. For the remainder of this essay I would like to focus on selected writings of Black feminist critics, discussing their strengths and weaknesses and suggesting new directions toward which the criticism might move and pitfalls that it might avoid.

Unfortunately, Black feminist scholarship has been decidedly more practical than theoretical, and the theories developed thus far have often lacked sophistication and have been marred by slogans, rhetoric, and idealism. The articles that attempt to apply these theoretical tenets often lack precision and detail. These limitations are not without reason. As Dorin Schumacher observes, "the feminist critic has few philosophical shelters, pillars, or guideposts," and thus "feminist criticism is fraught with intellectual and professional risks, offering more opportunity for creativity, yet greater possibility of errors."[15]

The earliest theoretical statement on Black feminist criticism is Barbara Smith's "Toward a Black Feminist Criticism." Though its importance as a groundbreaking piece of scholarship cannot be denied, it suffers from lack of precision and detail. In justifying the need for a Black feminist aesthetic, Smith argues that "a Black feminist approach to literature that embodies the realization that the politics of sex as well as the politics of race and class are crucially interlocking factors in the works of Black women writers is an absolute necessity." Until such an approach exists, she continues, "we will not even know what these writers mean."

Smith points out that "thematically, stylistically, aesthetically, and conceptually Black women writers manifest common approaches to the act of creating literature as a direct result of the specific political, social, and economic experience they have been obliged to share." She offers, as an example, the incorporation of rootworking, herbal medicine, conjure, and midwifery in the stories of Zora Neale Hurston, Margaret Walker, Toni Morrison, and Alice Walker. While these folk elements certainly do appear in the work of these writers, they also appear in the works of certain Black male writers, a fact that Smith omits. If Black women writers use these elements differently from Black male writers, such a distinction must be made before one can effectively articulate the basis of a Black feminist aesthetic.

Smith maintains further that Zora Neale Hurston, Margaret Walker, Toni Morrison, and Alice Walker use a "specifically black female language to express their own and their characters' thoughts," but she fails to describe or to provide examples of this unique language. Of course, we have come recently to acknowledge that "many of our habits of language usage are sex-derived, sex-associated, and/or sex-distinctive," that "the ways in which men and women internalize and manipulate language" are undeniably sex-related.[16] But this realization in itself simply paves the way for further investigation that can begin by exploring some critical questions. For example, is there a monolithic Black female language? Do Black female high school dropouts, welfare mothers, college graduates, and Ph.D.s share a common language? Are there regional variations in this common language? Further, some Black male critics have tried to describe the uniquely "Black linguistic elegance"[17] that characterizes Black poetry. Are there noticeable differences between the languages of Black females and Black males? These and other questions must be addressed with precision if current feminist terminology is to function beyond mere critical jargon.

Smith turns from her discussion of the commonalities among Black women writers to describe the nature of her critical enterprise. "Black feminist criticism would by definition be highly innovative," she maintains. "Applied to a particular work [it] can overturn previous assumptions about [the work] and expose for the first time its actual dimensions." Smith then proceeds to demonstrate this critical postulate by interpreting Toni Morrison's *Sula* as a lesbian novel, an interpretation she believes is maintained in "the emotions expressed, in the definition of female character and in the way that the politics of heterosexuality are portrayed." Smith vacillates between arguing forthrightly for the validity of her interpretation and recanting or overqualifying it in a way that undercuts her own credibility.

According to Smith, "if in a woman writer's work a sentence refuses to do what it is supposed to do, if there are strong images of women and if there is a refusal to be linear, the result is innately lesbian literature." She adds, "because of Morrison's consistently critical stance toward the heterosexual institutions of male-female relationships, marriage, and the family," *Sula* works as a lesbian novel. This definition of lesbianism is vague and imprecise; it subsumes far more Black women writers, particularly contemporary ones, than not into the canon of Lesbian writers. For example, Jessie Fauset, Nella Larsen, and Zora Neale Hurston all criticize major socializing institutions, as do Gwendolyn Brooks, Alice Walker, and Toni Cade Bambara. Further, if we apply Smith's definition of lesbianism, there are probably a few Black male writers who qualify as well. All of this is to say that Smith has simultaneously oversimplified and obscured the issue of lesbianism. Obviously aware of the delicacy of her position, she interjects that "the very meaning of lesbianism is being expanded in literature." Unfortunately, her qualification does not strengthen her argument. One of the major tasks ahead of Black feminist critics who write from a lesbian perspective, then, is to define lesbianism and lesbian literature precisely. Until they can offer a definition which is not vacuous, their attempts to distinguish Black lesbian writers from those who are not will be hindered.[18]

Even as I call for firmer definitions of lesbianism and lesbian literature, I question whether a lesbian aesthetic is not finally a reductive approach to the study of Black women's literature which possibly ignores other equally important aspects of the literature. For example, reading *Sula* solely from a lesbian perspective overlooks the novel's density and complexity, its skillful blend of folklore, omens, and dreams, its metaphorical and symbolic richness. Although I do not quarrel with Smith's appeal for fresher, more innovative approaches to Black women's literature, I suspect that "innovative" analysis is pressed to the service of an individual political persuasion. One's personal and political presuppositions enter into one's critical judgments. Nevertheless, we should heed Annette Kolodny's warning for feminist critics to

> be wary of reading literature as though it were polemic. . . . If when using literary materials to make what is essentially a political point, we find ourselves virtually rewriting a text, ignoring certain aspects of plot or characterization, or over-simplifying the action to fit our "political" thesis, then we are neither practicing an honest criticism nor saying anything useful about the nature of art (or about the art of political persuasion, for that matter).

Alerting feminist critics to the dangers of political ideology yoked with aesthetic judgment is not synonymous with denying that feminist criticism is a valid and necessary cultural and political enterprise. Indeed, it is both possible and useful to translate ideological positions into aesthetic ones, but if the criticism is to be responsible, the two must be balanced.

Because it is a cultural and political enterprise, feminist critics, in the main, believe that their criticism can effect social change. Smith certainly argues for socially relevant criticism in her conclusion that "Black feminist criticism would owe its existence to a Black feminist movement while at the same time contributing ideas that women in the movement could use." This is an exciting idea in itself, but we should ask: What ideas, specifically, would Black feminist criticism contribute to the movement? Further, even though the proposition of a fruitful relationship between political activism and the academy is an interesting (and necessary) one, I doubt its feasibility. I am not sure that either in theory or in practice Black feminist criticism will be able to alter significantly circumstances that have led to the oppression of Black women. Moreover, as Lillian Robinson pointedly remarks, there is no assurance that feminist aesthetics "will be productive of a vision of art or of social relations that is of the slightest use to the masses of women, or even one that acknowledges the existence and struggle of such women."[20] I agree with Robinson that "ideological criticism must take place in the context of a political movement that can put it to work. The revolution is simply not going to be made by literary journals."[21] I should say that I am not arguing a defeatist position with respect to the social and political uses to which feminist criticism can be put. Just as it is both possible and useful to translate ideological positions into aesthetic ones, it must likewise be possible and useful to translate aesthetic positions into the machinery for social change.

Despite the shortcomings of Smith's article, she raises critical issues on which Black feminist critics can build. There are many tasks ahead of these critics, not the least of which is to attempt to formulate some clear definitions of what Black feminist criticism is. I use the term here simply to refer to Black female critics who analyze the works of Black female writers from a feminist or political perspective. But the term can also apply to any criticism written by a Black woman regardless of her subject or perspective—a book written by a male from a feminist or political perspective, a book written by a Black woman or about Black women authors in general, or any writings by women.[22]

In addition to defining the methodology, Black feminist critics need to determine the extent to which their criticism intersects with that of white feminist critics. Barbara Smith and others have rightfully challenged white women scholars to become more accountable to Black and Third World women writers, but will that require white women to use a different set of critical tools when studying Black women writers? Are white women's theories predicated upon culturally specific values and assumptions? Andrea Benton

Rushing has attempted to answer these questions in her series of articles on images of Black women in literature. She maintains, for example, that critical categories of women, based on analyses of white women characters, are Euro-American in derivation and hence inappropriate to a consideration of Black women characters.[23] Such distinctions are necessary and, if held uniformly, can materially alter the shape of Black feminist scholarship.

Regardless of which theoretical framework Black feminist critics choose, they must have an informed handle on Black literature and Black culture in general. Such a grounding can give this scholarship more texture and completeness and perhaps prevent some of the problems that have had a vitiating effect on the criticism.

This footing in Black history and culture serves as a basis for the study of the literature. Termed "contextual" by theoreticians, this approach is often frowned upon if not dismissed entirely by critics who insist exclusively upon textual and linguistic analysis. Its limitations notwithstanding, I firmly believe that the contextual approach to Black women's literature exposes the conditions under which literature is produced, published, and reviewed. This approach is not only useful but necessary to Black feminist critics.

To those working with Black women writers prior to 1940, the contextual approach is especially useful. In researching Jessie Fauset, Nella Larsen, and Zora Neale Hurston, for example, it is useful to determine what the prevalent attitudes about Black women were during the time that they wrote. There is much information in the Black "little" magazines published during the Harlem Renaissance. An examination of *The Messenger,* for instance, reveals that the dominant social attitudes about Black women were strikingly consistent with traditional middle-class expectations of women. *The Messenger* ran a monthly symposium for some time entitled "Negro Womanhood's Greatest Needs." While a few female contributors stressed the importance of women being equal to men socially, professionally, and economically, the majority emphasized that a woman's place was in the home. It was her duty "to cling to the home [since] great men and women evolve from the environment of the hearthstone."[24]

One of the most startling entries came from a woman who wrote:

> The New Negro Woman, with her head erect and spirit undaunted, is resolutely marching forward, ever conscious of her historic and noble mission of doing her bit toward the liberation of her people in particular and the human race in general. Upon her shoulders rests the big task to create and keep alive, in the breast of black men, a holy and consuming passion to break with the slave traditions of the past; to

> spurn and overcome the fatal, insidious inferiority complex of the present, which . . . bobs up ever and anon, to arrest the progress of the New Negro Manhood Movement; and to fight with increasing vigor, with dauntless courage, unrelenting zeal and intelligent vision for the attainment of the stature of a full man, a free race and a new world.[25]

Not only does the contributor charge the Black woman with a formidable task, but she also sees her solely in relation to Black men.

This information enhances our understanding of what Fauset, Larsen, and Hurston confronted in attempting to offer alternative images of Black women. Moreover, it helps to clarify certain textual problems and ambiguities of their work. Though Fauset and Hurston, for example, explored feminist concerns, they leaned toward ambivalence. Fauset especially is alternately forthright and cagey, radical and traditional, on issues that confront women. Her first novel, *There Is Confusion* (1924), is flawed by an unanticipated and abrupt reversal in characterization that brings the central female character more in line with a feminine norm. Similarly, in her last novel, *Seraph on the Swanee* (1948), Zora Neale Hurston depicts a female character who shows promise for growth and change, for a departure from the conventional expectations of womanhood, but who in the end apotheosizes marriage, motherhood, and domestic servitude.

These two examples alone clearly capture the tension between social pressure and artistic integrity which is felt, to some extent, by all women writers. As Tillie Olsen points out, the fear of reprisal from the publishing and critical arenas is a looming obstacle to the woman writer's coming into her own authentic voice. "Fear—the need to please, to be safe—in the literary realm too. Founded fear. Power is still in the hands of men. Power of validation, publication, approval, reputation. . . .[26]

While insisting on the validity, usefulness, and necessity of contextual approaches to Black women's literature, the Black feminist critic must not ignore the importance of rigorous textual analysis. I am aware of many feminist critics' stubborn resistance to the critical methodology handed down by white men. Although the resistance is certainly politically consistent and logical, I agree with Annette Kolodny that feminist criticism would be "shortsighted if it summarily rejected all the inherited tools of critical analysis simply because they are male and western." We should, rather, salvage what we find useful in past methodologies, reject what we do not, and, where necessary, move toward "inventing new methods of analysis."[27] Particularly useful is Lillian Robinson's suggestion that "a radical kind of textual criticism . . . could usefully study the way the texture of sentences, choice of metaphors, patterns of exposition and narrative relate to [feminist] ideology."[28]

This rigorous textual analysis involves, as Barbara Smith recommends, isolating as many thematic, stylistic, and linguistic commonalities among Black women writers as possible. Among contemporary Black female novelists, the thematic parallels are legion. In Alice Walker and Toni Morrison, for example, the theme of the thwarted female artist figures prominently.[29] Pauline Breedlove in Morrison's *The Bluest Eye,* for example, is obsessed with ordering things:

> Jars on shelves at canning, peach pits on the step, sticks, stones, leaves. . . . Whatever portable plurality she found, she organized into neat lines, according to their size, shape or gradations of color. . . . She missed without knowing what she missed—paints and crayons.[30]

Similarly, Eva Peace in *Sula* is forever ordering the pleats in her dress. And Sula's strange and destructive behavior is explained as "the consequence of an idle imagination."

> Had she paints, clay, or knew the discipline of the dance, or strings; had she anything to engage her tremendous curiosity and her gift for metaphor, she might have exchanged the restlessness and preoccupation with whim for an activity that provided her with all she yearned for. And like any artist with no form, she became dangerous.[31]

Likewise, Meridian's mother in Alice Walker's novel *Meridian* makes artificial flowers and prayer pillows too small for kneeling.

The use of "clothing as iconography"[32] is central to writings by Black women. For example, in one of Jessie Fauset's early short stories, "The Sleeper Wakes" (1920), Amy, the protagonist, is associated with pink clothing (suggesting innocence and immaturity) while she is blinded by fairy-tale notions of love and marriage. However, after she declares her independence from her racist and sexist husband, Amy no longer wears pink. The imagery of clothing is abundant in Zora Neale Hurston's *Their Eyes Were Watching God* (1937). Janie's apron, her silks and satins, her head scarves, and finally her overalls all symbolize various stages of her journey from captivity to liberation. Finally, in Alice Walker's *Meridian,* Meridian's railroad cap and dungarees are emblems of her rejection of conventional images and expectations of womanhood.

A final theme that recurs in the novels of Black women writers is the motif of the journey. Though one can also find this same motif in the works of Black male writers, they do not use it in the same way as do Black female writers.[33] For example, the journey of the Black male character in works by Black men takes him underground. It is a "descent into the underworld,"[34] and is primarily political and social in its implications. Ralph Ellison's *Invisible Man,* Imamu Amiri Baraka's *The System of Dante's Hell,* and Richard Wright's "The Man Who Lived Underground" exemplify this quest. The Black female's journey, on the other hand, though at times touching the political and social, is basically a personal and psychological journey. The female character in the works of Black women is in a state of becoming "part of an evolutionary spiral, moving from victimization to consciousness."[35] The heroines in Zora Neale Hurston's *Their Eyes Were Watching God,* in Alice Walker's *Meridian,* and in Toni Cade Bambara's *The Salt Eaters* are emblematic of this distinction.

Even though isolating such thematic and imagistic commonalities should continue to be one of the Black feminist critic's most urgent tasks, she should beware of generalizing on the basis of too few examples. If one argues authoritatively for the existence of a Black female "consciousness" or "vision" or "literary tradition," one must be sure that the parallels found recur with enough consistency to support these generalizations. Further, Black feminist critics should not become obsessed in searching for common themes and images in Black women's works. As I pointed out earlier, investigating the question of "female" language is critical and may well be among the most challenging jobs awaiting the Black feminist critic. The growing body of research on gender-specific uses of language might aid these critics. In fact, wherever possible, feminist critics should draw on the scholarship of feminists in other disciplines.

An equally challenging and necessary task ahead of the Black feminist critic is a thoroughgoing examination of the works of Black male writers. In her introduction to *Midnight Birds,* Mary Helen Washington argues for the importance of giving Black women writers their due first:

> Black women are searching for a specific language, specific symbols, specific images with which to record their lives, and, even though they can claim a rightful place in the Afro-American tradition and the feminist tradition of women writers, it is also clear that, for purposes of liberation, black women writers will first insist on their own name, their own space.[36]

I likewise believe that the immediate concern of Black feminist critics must be to develop a fuller understanding of Black women writers who have not received the critical attention Black male writers have. Yet, I cannot advocate indefinitely such a separatist position, for the countless thematic, stylistic, and imagistic parallels between Black male and female writers must be examined. Black feminist critics should explore these parallels in an effort to determine the ways in which these commonalities are manifested differently in Black women's writing and the ways in which they coincide with writings by Black men.

Of course, there are feminist critics who are already examining Black male writers, but much of the scholarship has been limited to discussions of the negative images of Black women found in the works of these authors.[37] Although this scholarship served an important function in pioneering Black feminist critics, it has virtually run its course. Feminist critics run the risk of plunging their work into cliché and triviality if they continue merely to focus on how Black men treat Black women in literature. Hortense Spillers offers a more sophisticated approach to this issue in her discussion of the power of language and myth in female relations in James Baldwin's *If Beale Street Could Talk.* One of Spillers's most cogent points is that "woman-freedom, or its negation, is tied to the assertions of myth, or ways of saying things."[38]

Black feminist criticism is a knotty issue, and while I have attempted to describe it, to call for clearer definitions of its methodology, to offer warnings of its limitations, I await the day when Black feminist criticism will expand to embrace other modes of critical inquiry. In other words, I am philosophically opposed to what Annis Pratt calls "methodolatry." Wole Soyinka has offered one of the most cogent defenses against critical absolutism. He explains:

> The danger which a literary ideology poses is the act of consecration—and of course excommunication. Thanks to the tendency of the modern consumer-mind to facilitate digestion by putting in strict categories what are essentially fluid operations of the creative mind upon social and natural phenomena, the formulation of a literary ideology tends to congeal sooner or later into instant capsules which, administered also to the writer, may end by asphyxiating the creative process.[39]

Whether Black feminist criticism will or should remain a separatist enterprise is a debatable point. Black feminist critics ought to move from this issue to consider the specific language of Black women's literature, to describe the ways Black women writers employ literary devices in a distinct way, and to compare the way Black women writers create their own mythic structures. If they focus on these and other pertinent issues, Black feminist critics will have laid the cornerstone for a sound, thorough articulation of the Black feminist aesthetic.

NOTES

[1]Louise Bernikow, *The World Split Open: Four Centuries of Women Poets in England and America, 1552–1950* (New York: Vintage Books, 1974), p. 3.

[2]William Morgan, "Feminism and Literary Study: A Reply to Annette Kolodny," *Critical Inquiry* 2 (Summer 1976): B11.

[3]The year 1970 was the beginning of the Modern Language Association's Commission on the Status of Women, which offered panels and workshops that were feminist in approach.

[4]Statement by Barbara Desmarais quoted in Annis Pratt, "The New Feminist Criticisms: Exploring the History of the New Space," in *Beyond Intellectual Sexism: A New Woman, A New Reality,* ed. Joan I. Roberts (New York: David McKay, 1976), p. 176.

[5]Patricia Meyer Spacks, *The Female Imagination* (New York: Avon Books, 1976), p. 5. Ellen Moers, *Literary Women: The Great Writers* (Garden City, N.Y.: Anchor Books, 1977) is another example of what Alice Walker terms "white female chauvinism."

[6]Alice Walker, "One Child of One's Own—An Essay on Creativity," *Ms.,* August 1979, p. 50.

[7]Robert Stepto, *From Behind the Veil: A Study of Afro-American Narrative* (Urbana: University of Illinois Press, 1979), p. x. Other sexist critical works include Donald B. Gibson, ed., *Five Black Writers* (New York: New York University Press, 1970), a collection of essays on Wright, Ellison, Baldwin, Hughes, and Leroi Jones, and Jean Wagner, *Black Poets of the United States: From Paul Lawrence Dunbar to Langston Hughes,* trans. Kenneth Douglas (Urbana: University of Illinois Press, 1973).

[8]Stepto, *From Behind the Veil,* p. 166.

[9]Robert Bone, *The Negro Novel in America* (1958; reprint ed., New Haven, Conn.: Yale University Press, 1972), pp. 97, 101.

[10]David Littlejohn, *Black on White: A Critical Survey of Writing by American Negroes* (New York: Viking Press, 1966), pp. 48–49.

[11]Ellman's concept of "phallic criticism" is discussed in a chapter of the same name in her *Thinking About Women* (New York: Harcourt, Brace & World, 1968), pp. 28–54.

[12]Introduction to *Zora Neale Hurston: A Literary Biography* by Robert Hemenway (Urbana: University of Illinois Press, 1976), p. xiv. Although Walker makes this observation specifically about Hurston, it is one that can apply to a number of Black women writers.

[13]Barbara Smith, "Toward a Black Feminist Criticism," in this volume, pp. 168–85.

[14]See Evelyn Hammonds, "Toward a Black Feminist Aesthetic," *Sojourner,* October 1980, p. 7, for a discussion of the limitations on Black feminist critics. She correctly points out that Black feminist critics "have no newspapers, no mass-marketed magazines or journals that are explicitly oriented toward the involvement of women of color in the feminist movement."

[15]Dorin Schumacher, "Subjectivities: A Theory of the Critical Process," in *Feminist Literary Criticism: Explorations in Theory,* ed. Josephine Donovan (Lexington: University Press of Kentucky, 1975), p. 34.

[16]Annette Kolodny, "The Feminist as Literary Critic," Critical Response, *Critical Inquiry* 2 (Summer 1976): 824–25. See also Cheris Kramer, Barrie Thorne, and Nancy Henley, "Perspectives on Language and Communication," *Signs* 3 (Spring 1978): 638–51, and Nelly Furman, "The Study of Women and Language: Comment on Vol. 3, no. 3," *Signs* 4 (Fall 1978): 152–85.

[17]Stephen Henderson, *Understanding the New Black Poetry: Black Speech and Black Music as Poetic References* (New York: William Morrow, 1973), pp. 31–46.

[18]Some attempts have been made to define or at least discuss lesbianism. See Adrienne Rich's two essays, "It Is the Lesbian in Us . . ." and "The Meaning of Our Love for Woman Is What We Have," in *On Lies, Secrets and Silence* (New York: W. W. Norton, 1979), pp. 199–202 and 223–30, respectively. See also Bertha Harris's "*What We Mean to Say:* Notes Toward Defining the Nature of Lesbian Literature," *Heresies* 1 (Fall 1977): 5–8, and Blanche Cook's " 'Women Alone Stir My Imagination': Lesbianism and the Cultural Tradition," *Signs* 4 (Summer 1979): 718–39. Also, at least one bibliography of Black lesbian writers has been compiled. See Ann Allen Shockley's "The Black Lesbian in American Literature: An Overview," *Conditions: Five* 2 (Fall 1979): 133–42.

[19]Annette Kolodny, "Some Notes on Defining a 'Feminist Literary Criticism,' " *Critical Inquiry* 2 (Fall 1975): 90.

[20]Lillian S. Robinson, "Working Women Writing," *Sex, Class, and Culture* (Bloomington: Indiana University Press, 1978), p. 226.

[21]Robinson, "The Critical Task," *Sex, Class, and Culture,* p. 52.

[22]I am borrowing here from Kolodny, who makes similar statements in "Some Notes on Defining a 'Feminist Literary Criticism,' " p. 75.

[23]Andrea Benton Rushing, "Images of Black Women in Afro-American Poetry," in *The Afro-American Woman: Struggles and Images,* ed. Sharon Harley and Rosalyn Terborg-Penn (Port Washington, N.Y.: Kennikat Press, 1978), pp. 74–84. She argues that few of the stereotypic traits which Mary Ellman describes in *Thinking About Women* "seem appropriate to Afro-American images of black women." See also her "Images of Black Women in Modern African Poetry: An Overview," in *Sturdy Black Bridges: Visions of Black Women in Literature,* ed. Roseann P. Bell et al. (New York: Anchor Books, 1979), pp. 18–24. Rushing argues similarly that Mary Ann Ferguson's categories of women (the submissive wife, the mother angel or "mom," the woman on a pedestal, for example) cannot be applied to Black women characters, whose cultural imperatives are different from white women's.

[24]*The Messenger:* 9 (April 1927): 109.

[25]*The Messenger* 5 (July 1923): 757.

[26]Tillie Olsen, *Silences* (New York: Delacorte Press, 1978), p. 257.

[27]Kolodny, "Some Notes on Defining a 'Feminist Literary Criticism,' " p. 89.

[28]Lillian S. Robinson, "Dwelling in Decencies: Radical Criticism and Feminist Perspectives," in *Feminist Criticism,* ed. Cheryl Brown and Karen Olsen (Metuchen, N.J.: Scarecrow Press, 1978), p. 34.

[29]For a discussion of Toni Morrison's frustrated female artists see Renita Weems, "Artists Without Art Form: A Look at One Black Woman's World of Unrevered Black Women," *Conditions: Five* 2 (Fall 1979): 48–58. See also Alice Walker's classic essay, "In Search of Our Mothers' Gardens," *Ms.,* May 1974, for a discussion of Black women's creativity in general.

[30]Toni Morrison, *The Bluest Eye* (New York: Pocket Books, 1970), pp. 88–89.

[31]Toni Morrison, *Sula* (New York: Bantam Books, 1980), p. 105.

[32]Kolodny, "Some Notes on Defining a 'Feminist Literary Criticism,' " p. 86.

[33]In an NEH Summer Seminar at Yale University in the summer of 1980, Carolyn Naylor of Santa Clara University suggested this to me.

[34]For a discussion of this idea see Michael G. Cooke, "The Descent into the Underworld and Modern Black Fiction," *Iowa Review* 5 (Fall 1974): 72–90.

[35]Mary Helen Washington, *Midnight Birds: Stories of Contemporary Black Women Writers* (Garden City, N.Y.: Anchor Books, 1980), p. 43.

[36]Ibid., p. xvii.

[37]See Saundra Towns, "The Black Woman as Whore: Genesis of the Myth," *The Black Position* 3 (1974): 39–59, and Sylvia Keady, "Richard Wright's Women Characters and Inequality," *Black American Literature Forum* 10 (1976): 124–28, for example.

[38]Hortense Spillers, "The Politics of Intimacy: A Discussion," in Bell et al., eds., *Sturdy Black Bridges,* p. 88.

[39]Wole Soyinka, *Myth, Literature and the African World* (London: Cambridge University Press, 1976), p. 61.

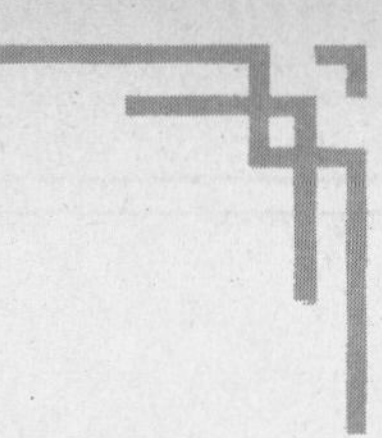

What Has Never Been

An Overview of Lesbian Feminist Literary Criticism

Bonnie Zimmerman

In the 1970s, a generation of lesbian feminist literary critics came of age. Some, like the lesbian professor in Lynn Strongin's poem "Sayre,"[1] had been closeted in the profession; many had "come out" as lesbians in the women's liberation movement. As academics and as lesbians, we cautiously began to plait together the strands of our existence: teaching lesbian literature, establishing networks and support groups, and exploring assumptions about a lesbian-focused literary criticism. Beginning with nothing, as we thought, this generation quickly began to expand the limitations of literary scholarship by pointing to what had been for decades "unspeakable"—lesbian existence—thus phrasing, in novelist June Arnold's words, "what has never been."[2] Our process has paralleled the development of feminist literary criticism—and, indeed, pioneering feminist critics and lesbian critics are often one and the same. As women in a male-dominated academy, we explored the way we write and read from a different or "other" perspective. As lesbians in a heterosexist academy, we have continued to explore the impact of "otherness," suggesting dimensions previously ignored and yet necessary to understand fully the female condition and the creative work born from it.

Lesbian critics in the 1980s may have more questions than answers, but the questions are important not only to lesbians but to all feminists teaching and criticizing literature. Does a woman's sexual and affectional preference influence the way she writes, reads, and thinks? Does lesbianism belong in the classroom and in scholarship? Is there a lesbian aesthetic distinct from a feminist aesthetic? What should be the role of the lesbian critic? Can we establish a lesbian "canon" in the way feminist critics have established a female canon? Can lesbian feminists develop insights into female creativity that might enrich all literary criticism? Different women, of course, answer these questions in different ways, but one set of assumptions underlies virtually all lesbian criticism: that a woman's identity is not defined only by her relation to a male world and male literary tradition (as feminist critics have demonstrated), that powerful bonds between women are a crucial factor in women's lives, and that the sexual and emotional orientation of a woman profoundly affects her consciousness and thus her creativity. Those critics who have consciously chosen to read as lesbians argue that this perspective can be uniquely liberating and can provide new insights into life and literature because it assigns the lesbian a specific vantage point from which to criticize and analyze the politics, language, and culture of patriarchy.

> We have the whole range of women's experience and the other dimension too, which is the unique viewpoint of the dyke. This extra dimension puts us a step outside of so-called normal life and lets us see how gruesomely abnormal it is. . . . [This perspective] can issue in a world-view that is distinct in history and uniquely liberating.[3]

The purpose of this essay is to analyze the current state of lesbian scholarship, to suggest how lesbians are exercising this unique world view, and to investigate some of the problems, strengths, and future needs of a developing lesbian feminist literary criticism.[4]

One way in which this unique world view takes shape is as a "critical consciousness about heterosexist assumptions."[5] Heterosexism is the set of values and structures that assumes heterosexuality to be the only natural form of sexual and emotional expression, "*the* perceptual screen provided by our [patriarchal] cultural conditioning."[6] Heterosexist assumptions abound in literary texts, such as feminist literary anthologies, that purport to be open-minded about lesbianism. When authors' biographies make special note of husbands, male mentors, and male companions, even when that author was primarily female-identified, but fail to mention the female companions of prominent lesbian writers—that is heterosexism. When anthologists ignore historically significant lesbian writers such as Renée Vivien and Radclyffe Hall—that is heterosexism. When anthologies include only the heterosexual or nonsexual works of a writer like Katherine Philips or Adrienne Rich who is celebrated for her lesbian or homoemotional poetry—that is heterosexism. When a topically organized anthology includes sections on wives, mothers, sex objects, young girls, aging women, and liberated women, but not lesbians—that is heterosexism. Heterosexism in feminist anthologies—like the sexism of androcentric collections—serves to obliterate lesbian existence and maintain the lie that women have searched for emotional and sexual fulfillment only through men—or not at all.

Lesbians have also expressed concern that the absence of lesbian material in women's studies journals such as *Feminist Studies, Women's Studies,* and *Women and Literature* indicates heterosexism either by omission or by design. Only in 1979 did lesbian-focused articles appear in *Signs* and *Frontiers.* Most lesbian criticism first appeared in alternative, nonestablishment lesbian journals, particularly *Sinister Wisdom* and *Conditions,* which are unfamiliar to many feminist scholars. For example, *Signs*'s first review article on literary criticism by Elaine Showalter (1975) makes no mention of lesbianism as a theme or potential critical perspective, not even to point out its absence. Annette Kolodny, in the second review article in *Signs* (1976), does call Jane Rule's *Lesbian Images* "a novelist's challenge to the academy and its accompanying critical community," and further criticizes the homophobia in then-current biographies, calling for "candor and sensitivity" in future work.[7] However, neither this nor subsequent review articles familiarize the reader with "underground" sources of lesbian criticism, some of which had appeared by this time, nor do they explicate lesbianism as a literary theme or critical perspective. Ironically, more articles on lesbian literature have appeared in traditional literary journals than in the women's studies press, just as for years only male critics felt free to mention lesbianism. Possibly, feminist critics continue to feel that they will be identified as "dykes," thus invalidating their work.

The perceptual screen of heterosexism is also evident in most of the acclaimed works of feminist literary criticism. None of the current collections of essays—such as *The Authority of Experience* or *Shakespeare's Sisters*—includes even a token article from a lesbian perspective. Ellen Moers's *Literary Women,* germinal work as it is, is homophobic as well as heterosexist. Lesbians, she points out, appear as monsters, grotesques, and freaks in works by Carson McCullers, Djuna Barnes (her reading of *Nightwood* is at the very least questionable), and Diane Arbus, but she seems to concur in this identification rather than call it into question or explain its historical context. Although her so-called defense of unmarried women writers against the "charge" of lesbianism does criticize the way in which this word has been used as a slur, she neither condemns such antilesbianism nor entertains the possibility that some women writers were, in fact, lesbians. Her chapter on "Loving Heroinism" is virtually textbook heterosexism, assuming as it does that women writers only articulate love for men.[8] Perceptual blinders also mar *The Female Imagination* by Patricia Meyers Spacks, which never uses the word "lesbian" (except in the index) or "lover" to describe either the "sexual ambiguity" of the bond between Jane and Helen in *Jane Eyre,* nor Margaret Anderson's relationship with a "beloved older woman." Furthermore, Spacks claims that Gertrude Stein, "whose life lack[ed] real attachments" (a surprise to Alice B. Toklas), also "denied whatever is special to women" (which lesbianism is not?).[9] This latter judgment is particularly ominous because heterosexuals often have difficulty accepting that a lesbian, especially a role-playing "butch," is in fact a woman. More care is demonstrated by Elaine Showalter who, in *A Literature of Their Own,* uncovers the attitudes toward lesbianism held by nineteenth-century writers Eliza Lynn Linton and Mrs. Humphrey Ward. However, she does not integrate lesbian issues into her discussion of the crucial generation of early-twentieth-century writers (Virginia Woolf, Vita Sackville-West, Dorothy Richardson, and Rosamond Lehmann among others; Radclyffe Hall is mentioned, but not *The Well of Loneliness*), all of whom wrote about sexual love between women. Her well-taken point that modern British novelists avoid lesbianism might have been balanced, however, by a mention of Maureen Duffy, Sybille Bedford, or Fay Weldon.[10] Finally, Sandra Gilbert and Susan Gubar's *The Madwoman in the Attic* does not even index lesbianism; the lone reference made in the text is to the possibility that "Goblin Market" describes "a covertly (if ambiguously) lesbian world." The authors' tendency to interpret all pairs of female characters as aspects of the self sometimes serves to mask a relationship that a lesbian reader might interpret as bonding or love between women.[11]

Lesbian critics, who as feminists owe much to these critical texts, have had to turn to other resources, first to develop a lesbian canon, and then to establish a lesbian critical perspective. Barbara Grier, who, as Gene Damon, reviewed books for the pioneering lesbian journal *The Ladder,* laid the groundwork for this canon with her incomparable but largely unknown *The Lesbian in Literature: A Bibliography.*[12] Equally obscure was Jeannette Foster's *Sex Variant Women in Literature,* self-published in 1956 after having been rejected by a university press because of its subject matter. An exhaustive chronological account of every reference to love between women from Sappho and Ruth to the fiction of the fifties, *Sex Variant Women* has proven to be an invaluable starting point for lesbian readers and scholars. Out of print almost immediately after its publication and lost to all but a few intrepid souls, it was finally reprinted by Diana Press in 1975.[13] A further resource and gathering point for lesbian critics was the special issue on lesbian writing and publishing in *Margins,* a review of small-press publications, which appeared in 1975, the first issue of a literary journal devoted entirely to lesbian writing. In 1976, its editor, Beth Hodges, produced a second special issue, this time in *Sinister Wisdom.*[14] Along with the growing visibility and solidarity of lesbians within the academic profession, and the increased availability of lesbian literature from feminist and mass-market presses, these two journal issues propelled lesbian feminist literary criticism to the surface.[15]

The literary resources available to lesbian critics form only part of the story, for lesbian criticism is equally rooted in political ideology. Although not all lesbian critics are activists, most have been strongly influenced by the politics of lesbian feminism. These politics travel the continuum from civil rights advocacy to separatism; however, most if not all lesbian feminists assume that lesbianism is a healthy life-style chosen by women in virtually all eras and all cultures, and thus strive to eliminate the stigma historically attached to lesbianism. One way to remove this stigma is to associate lesbianism with positive and desirable attributes, to divert women's attention away from male values and toward an exclusively female *communitas.* Thus, the influential Radicalesbians' essay "The Woman-Identified Woman" argues that lesbian feminism assumes "the primacy of women relating to women, of women creating a new consciousness of and with each other. . . . We see ourselves as prime, find our centers inside of ourselves."[16] Many lesbian writers and critics have also been influenced profoundly by the politics of separatism, which provides a critique of heterosexuality as a political institution rather than a personal choice, "because relationships between men and women are essentially political, they involve power and dominance."[17] As we shall see, the notion of "woman-identification," that is, the primacy of women bonding with women emotionally and politically, as well as the premises of separatism, that lesbians have a unique and critical place at the margins of patriarchal society, are central to much current lesbian literary criticism.

Unmasking heterosexist assumptions in feminist literary criticism has been an important but hardly primary task for lesbian critics. We are more concerned with the development of a unique lesbian feminist perspective or, at the very least, determining whether or not such a perspective is possible. In order to do so, lesbian critics have had to begin with a special question: "When is a text a 'lesbian text' or its writer a 'lesbian writer' "?[18] Lesbians are faced with this special problem of definition: presumably we know when a writer is a "Victorian writer" or a "Canadian writer." To answer this question, we have to determine how inclusively or exclusively we define "lesbian." Should we limit this appellation to those women for whom sexual experience with other women can be proven? This is an almost impossible historical task, as many have noted, for what constitutes proof? Women have not left obvious markers in their private writings. Furthermore, such a narrow definition "names" lesbianism as an exclusively sexual phenomenon, which, many argue, may be an inadequate construction of lesbian experience, both today and in less sexually explicit eras. This sexual definition of lesbianism also leads to the identification of literature with life, and thus can be an overly defensive and suspect strategy.

Nevertheless, lesbian criticism continues to be plagued with the problem of definition. One perspective insists that

> desire must be there and at least somewhat embodied. . . . That carnality distinguishes it from gestures of political sympathy for homosexuals and from affectionate friendships in which women enjoy each other, support each other, and commingle their sense of identity and well-being.[19]

A second perspective, which might be called a school, claims, on the contrary, that "the very meaning of lesbianism is being expanded in literature, just as it is being redefined through politics."[20] An articulate spokeswoman for this "expanded meaning" school of criticism is Adrienne Rich, who offers a compelling, inclusive definition of lesbianism:

> I mean the term *lesbian continuum* to include a range—through each woman's life and throughout history—of woman-identified experience; not simply the fact that a woman has had or consciously desired genital experience with another woman. If we expand it to embrace many more forms of primary intensity between and among women, including the sharing of a rich inner life, the bonding against male tyranny, the giving and receiving of practical and political support . . . we begin to grasp breadths of female history and psychology which have lain out of reach as a consequence of limited, mostly clinical, definitions of "lesbianism."[21]

This definition has the virtue of deemphasizing lesbianism as a static entity and of suggesting interconnections among the various ways in which women bond together. However, all-inclusive definitions of lesbianism risk blurring the distinctions between lesbian relationships and nonlesbian female friendships, or between lesbian identity and female-centered identity. Some lesbian writers would deny that there are such distinctions, but this position is reductive and of mixed value to those who are developing lesbian criticism and theory and who may need limited and precise definitions. In fact, reductionism is a serious problem in lesbian ideology. Too often, we identify lesbian and woman, or feminist; we equate lesbianism with any close bonds between women or with political commitment to women. These identifications can be fuzzy and historically questionable, as, for example, in the claim that lesbians have a unique relationship with nature or (as Rich also has claimed) that all female creativity is lesbian. By so reducing the meaning of lesbian, we have in effect eliminated lesbianism as a meaningful category.

A similar problem arises when lesbian theorists redefine lesbianism politically, equating it with strength, independence, and resistance to patriarchy. This new political definition then influences the interpretation of literature: "If in a woman writer's work a sentence refuses to do what it is supposed to do, if there are strong images of women and if there is a refusal to be linear, the result is innately lesbian literature."[22] The concept of an "innately" lesbian perspective or aesthetic allows the critic to separate lesbianism from biographical content, which is an essential development in lesbian critical theory. Literary interpretation will, of course, be supported by historical and biographical evidence, but perhaps lesbian critics should borrow a few insights from New Criticism. If a text lends itself to a lesbian reading, then no amount of biographic "proof" ought to be necessary to establish it as a lesbian text.[23] Barbara Smith, for example, interprets Toni Morrison's *Sula* as a lesbian novel, regardless of the author's affectional preference. But we need to be cautious about what we call "innately" lesbian. Why is circularity or strength limited to lesbians, or, similarly, why is love of nature or creativity? It is certainly not evident that women, let alone lesbians, are "innately" anything. And, although it might require a lesbian perspective to stress the dominant relationship between Nel and Sula ("All that time, all that time, I thought I was missing Jude"), it is difficult to imagine a novel so imbued with heterosexuality as lesbian.

Almost midway between the inclusive and exclusive approaches to a definition of lesbianism lies that of Lillian Faderman in her extraordinary overview, *Surpassing the Love of Man: Romantic Friendship and Love Between Women from the Renaissance to the Present.* Faderman's precise definition of lesbianism provides a conceptual framework for the four hundred years of literary history explored by the text:

> "Lesbian" describes a relationship in which two women's strongest emotions and affections are directed toward each other. Sexual contact may be a part of the relationship to a greater or lesser degree, or it may be entirely absent. By preference the two women spend most of their time together and share most aspects of their lives with each other.[24]

Broader than the exclusive definition of lesbianism—for Faderman argues that not all lesbian relationships may be fully embodied—but narrower than Rich's "lesbian continuum," this definition is both specific and discriminating. The book is slightly marred by a defensive, overexplanatory tone, caused, no doubt, by her attempt to neutralize the "intense charge of the word *lesbian*"; note, for example, that this charged word is omitted from the title.[25] Furthermore, certain problems remain with her framework, as with any that a lesbian critic or historian might establish. The historical relationship between genital sexuality and lesbianism remains unclear, and we cannot identify easily lesbianism outside a monogamous relationship. Nevertheless, despite problems in definition that may be inherent in lesbian studies, the strength of *Surpassing the Love of Men* is partially the precision with which Faderman defines her topic and chooses her texts and subjects.

This problem of definition is exacerbated by the problem of silence. One of the most pervasive themes in lesbian criticism is that woman-identified writers, silenced by a homophobic and misogynistic society, have been forced to adopt coded and obscure language and internal censorship. Emily Dickinson counseled us to "tell all the truth/but tell it slant," and critics are now calculating what price we have paid for slanted truth. The silences of heterosexual women writers may become lies for lesbian writers, as Rich warns: "a life 'in the closet' [may] spread into private life, so that lying (described as *discretion*) becomes an easy way to avoid conflict or complication."[26] Gloria T. Hull recounts the moving story of just such a victim of society, the black lesbian poet Angelina Weld Grimké, whose "convoluted life and thwarted sexuality" marked her slim output of poetry with images of self-abnegation, diminution, sadness, and the wish for death. The lesbian writer who is working-class or a woman of color may be particularly isolated, shackled by conventions and, ultimately, silenced "with [her] real gifts stifled within."[27] What does a lesbian writer do when the words cannot be silenced? Critics are pointing to the codes and strategies for literary survival adopted by many women. For example, Willa Cather may have adopted her characteristic male persona in order to express safely her emotional and erotic feelings for other women.[28] Thus, a writer some critics call antifeminist or at least disappointing may be better appreciated when her lesbianism is taken into account. Similarly, many ask whether Gertrude Stein cultivated obscurity, encoding her lesbianism in order to express hidden feelings and evade potential enemies. Or, on the other hand, Stein may have been always a declared lesbian, but a victim of readers' (and scholars') unwillingness or inability to pay her the close and sympathetic attention she requires.[29]

The silence of "Shakespeare's [lesbian] sister" has meant that modern writers have had little or no tradition with which to nurture themselves. Feminist critics such as Moers, Showalter, and Gilbert and Gubar have demonstrated the extent and significance of a female literary tradition, but the lesbian writer developed her craft alone (and perhaps this is the significance of the title of *the* lesbian novel about novel writing, *The Well of Loneliness*). Elly Bulkin's much-reprinted article on lesbian poetry points out that lesbian poets "have their work shaped by the simple fact of their having begun to write without knowledge of such history and with little or no hope of support from a woman's and/or lesbian writing community."[30] If white women can at least imagine a lesbian literature, the black lesbian writer, as Barbara Smith demonstrates, is even more hampered by the lack of tradition: "Black women are still in the position of having to 'imagine,' discover and verify Black lesbian literature because so little has been written from an avowedly lesbian perspective."[31] Blanche Wiesen Cook points out further that all lesbians are affected by this absence of tradition and role models, or the limiting of role models to Hall's Stephen Gordon. She also reminds us that our lesbian foremothers and networks were not simply lost and forgotten; rather, our past has been "erased," obliterated by the actions of a hostile society.[32]

It would appear then that lesbian critics are faced with a set of problems that make our work particularly delicate and problematic, requiring caution, sensitivity, and flexibility as well as imagination and risk. Lesbian criticism begins with the establishment of the lesbian text: the creation of language out of silence. The critic must first define the term "lesbian" and then determine its applicability to both writer and text, sorting out the relation of literature to life. Her definition of lesbianism will influence the texts she identifies as lesbian, and, except for the growing body of literature written from an explicitly lesbian perspective since the development of a lesbian political movement, it is likely that many will disagree with various identifications of lesbian texts. It is not only *Sula* that may provoke controversy, but even the "coded" works of lesbian writers like Gertrude Stein. The critic will need to consider whether a lesbian text is one written by a lesbian (and if so, how do we determine who is a lesbian?), one written about lesbians (which might be by a heterosexual woman or a man), or one that expresses a lesbian "vision" (which has yet to be satisfactorily outlined). But despite the problems raised by definition, silence and coding, and absence of tradition, lesbian critics have begun to develop a critical stance. Often this stance involves peering into shadows, into the spaces between words, into what has been unspoken and barely imagined. It is a perilous critical adventure with results that may violate accepted norms of traditional criticism, but that may also transform our notions of literary possibility.

One of the first tasks of this emerging lesbian criticism has been to provide lesbians with a tradition, even if a retrospective one. Jane Rule, whose *Lesbian Images* appeared about the same time as *Literary Women,* first attempted to establish this tradition.[33] Although her text is problematic, relying over much on biographical evidence and derivative interpretations and including some questionable writers (such as Dorothy Baker) while omitting others, *Lesbian Images* was a milestone in lesbian criticism. Its importance is partially suggested by the fact that it took five years for another complete book—Faderman's—to appear on lesbian literature. In a review of *Lesbian Images,* I questioned the existence of a lesbian "great tradition" in literature, but now I think I was wrong.[34] Along with Rule, Dolores Klaich in *Woman Plus Woman* and Louise Bernikow in the introduction to *The World Split Open* have explored the possibility of a lesbian tradition,[35] and recent critics such as Faderman and Cook in particular have begun to define that tradition, who belongs to it, and what links the writers who can be identified as lesbians. Cook's review of lesbian literature and culture in the early twentieth century proposes "to analyze the literature and attitudes out of which the present lesbian feminist works have emerged, and to examine the continued denials and invalidation of the lesbian experience."[36] Focusing on the recognized lesbian networks in France and England that included Virginia Woolf, Vita Sackville-West, Ethel Smythe, Gertrude Stein, Radclyffe Hall, Natalie Barney, and Romaine Brooks, Cook provides an important outline of a lesbian cultural tradition and an insightful analysis of the distortions and denials of homophobic scholars, critics, and biographers.

Faderman's *Surpassing the Love of Men,* like her earlier critical articles, ranges more widely through a literary tradition of romantic love between women (whether or not one calls that "lesbian") from the sixteenth to the twentieth centuries. Her thesis is that passionate love between women was labeled neither abnormal nor undesirable—probably because women were perceived to be asexual—until the sexologists led by Krafft-Ebing and Havelock Ellis "morbidified" female friendship around 1900.

Although she does not always clarify the dialectic between idealization and condemnation that is suggested in her text, Faderman's basic theory is quite convincing. Most readers, like myself, will be amazed at the wealth of information about women's same-sex love that Faderman has uncovered. She rescues from heterosexual obscurity Mary Wollstonecraft, Mary Wortley Montagu, Anna Seward, Sarah Orne Jewett, Edith Somerville, "Michael Field," and many others, including the Scottish schoolmistresses whose lesbian libel suit inspired Lillian Hellman's play *The Children's Hour.* Faderman has also written on the theme of same-sex love and romantic friendship in poems and letters of Emily Dickinson; in novels by Henry James, Oliver Wendell Holmes, and Henry Wadsworth Longfellow; and in popular magazine fiction of the early twentieth century.[37]

Faderman is preeminent among those critics who are attempting to establish a lesbian tradition by rereading writers of the past previously assumed to be heterosexual or "spinsters." As songwriter Holly Near expresses it: "Lady poet of great acclaim/ I have been misreading you/ I never knew your poems were meant for me."[38] It is in this area of lesbian scholarship that the most controversy—and some of the most exciting work—occurs. Was Mary Wollstonecraft's passionate love for Fanny Blood, recorded in *Mary, A Fiction,* lesbian? Does Henry James dissect a lesbian relationship in *The Bostonians*? Did Emily Dickinson address many of her love poems to a woman, not a man? How did Virginia Woolf's relationships with Vita Sackville-West and Ethel Smythe affect her literary vision? Not only are some lesbian critics increasingly naming such women and relationships "lesbian," they are also suggesting that criticism cannot fail to take into account the influence of sexual and emotional orientation on literary expression.

In the establishment of a self-conscious literary tradition, certain writers have become focal points both for critics and for lesbians in general, who affirm and celebrate their identity by "naming names," establishing a sense of historical continuity and community through the knowledge that incontrovertibly great women were also lesbians. Foremost among these heroes (or "heras") are the women who created the first self-identified lesbian feminist community in Paris during the early years of the twentieth century. With Natalie Barney at its hub, this circle included such notable writers as Colette, Djuna Barnes, Radclyffe Hall, Renée Vivien, and, peripherally, Gertrude Stein. Contemporary lesbians—literary critics, historians, and lay readers—have been drawn to their mythic and mythmaking presence, seeing in them a vision of lesbian society and culture that may have existed only once before —on the original island of Lesbos.[39] More interest, however, has been paid to their lives so far than to their art. Barnes's portraits of decadent, tormented lesbians and homosexuals in *Nightwood* and silly, salacious ones in *The Ladies Almanack* often prove troublesome to lesbian readers and critics.[40] However, Elaine Marks's perceptive study of French lesbian writers traces a tradition and how it has changed, modified by circumstance and by feminism, from the Sappho of Renée Vivien to the Amazons of Monique Wittig.[41]

The problems inherent in reading lesbian literature primarily for role modeling is most evident with Hall—the most notorious of literary lesbians —whose archetypal "butch," Stephen Gordon, has bothered readers since the publication of *The Well of Loneliness.* Although one critic praises it as "the standard by which all subsequent similar works are measured," most contemporary lesbian feminists would, I believe, agree with Faderman's harsh condemnation that it "helped to wreak confusion in young women."[42] Such an extraliterary debate is not limited to lesbian novels and lesbian characters; I am reminded of the intense disappointment expressed by many feminists over

George Eliot's disposal of Dorothea Brooke in *Middlemarch.* In both cases, the cry is the same: Why haven't these writers provided us with appropriate role models? Cook may be justified in criticizing Hall for creating a narrow and debilitating image for lesbians who follow, but my reading of the novel (and that of Catharine Stimpson in an excellent study of the lesbian novel) convinces me that both Hall's hero and her message are highly complex.[43] In looking to writers for a tradition, we need to recognize that the tradition may not always be a happy one. Women like Stephen Gordon exist alongside characters like Molly Bolt, in Rita Mae Brown's *Rubyfruit Jungle,* but lesbians may also question whether the incarnation of a "politically correct" but elusive and utopian mythology provides our only appropriate role model.

As with Hall, many readers and critics are strongly antipathetic to Stein, citing her reactionary and antifeminist politics and her role-playing relationship with Alice B. Toklas. However, other critics, by carefully analyzing Stein's actual words, establish, convincingly to my reading, that she did have a lesbian and feminist perspective, calling into question assumptions about coding and masculine role playing. Cynthia Secor, who is developing an exciting lesbian feminist interpretation of Stein, argues that her novel *Ida* attempts to discover what it means to be a female person, and that the author profited from her position on the boundaries of patriarchal society: "Stein's own experience as a lesbian gives her a critical distance that shapes her understanding of the struggle to be one's self. Her own identity is not shaped as she moves into relation with a man." Similarly, Elizabeth Fifer points out that Stein's situation encouraged her to experiment with parody, theatricality, role playing, and "the diversity of ways possible to look at homosexual love and at her love object." Deirdre Vanderlinde finds in *Three Lives* "one of the earliest attempts to find a new language in which to say, 'I, woman-loving woman, exist.' " Catharine Stimpson places more critical emphasis on Stein's use of masculine pronouns and conventional language, but despite what may have been her compromise, Stimpson feels that female bonding in Stein provides her with a private solution to woman's mind-body split.[44]

Along with Stein, Dickinson's woman-identification has drawn the most attention from recent critics, and has generated considerable controversy between lesbian and other feminist critics. Faderman insists that Dickinson's love for women must be considered homosexual, and that critics must take into account her sexuality (or affectionality). Like most critics who accept this lesbian identification of Dickinson, she points to Susan Gilbert Dickinson as Emily's primary romantic and sexual passion. Both Faderman and Bernikow thus argue that Dickinson's "muse" was sometimes a female figure as well as a male.[45] Some of this work can be justifiably criticized for too closely identifying literature with life; however, by altering our awareness of what is *possible*

—namely, that Dickinson's poetry was inspired by her love for a woman—we also can transform our response to the poetry. Paula Bennett daringly suggests that Dickinson's use of crumbs, jewels, pebbles, and similar objects was an attempt to create "clitoral imagery." In a controversial paper on the subject, Nadean Bishop argues forcefully that the poet's marriage poems must be reread in light of what she considers to have been Dickinson's consummated sexual relationship with her sister-in-law.[46]

The establishment of a lesbian literary tradition, a "canon," as my lengthy discussion suggests, has been the primary task of critics writing from a lesbian feminist perspective. But it is not the only focus to emerge. For example, lesbian critics, like feminist critics in the early seventies, have begun to analyze the images, stereotypes, and mythic presence of lesbians in fiction by or about lesbians. Bertha Harris, a major novelist as well as a provocative and trailblazing critic, considers the lesbian to be the prototype of the monster and "the quintessence of all that is female; and female enraged . . . a lesbian is . . . that which has been unspeakable about women."[47] Harris offers this monstrous lesbian as a female archetype who subverts traditional notions of female submissiveness, passivity, and virtue. Her "tooth-and-claw" image of the lesbian is ironically similar to that of Ellen Moers, although from a lesbian rather than a heterosexual point of view. But the very fact that Moers presents the lesbian-as-monster in a derogatory context and Harris in a celebratory one suggests that there is an important dialectic between how the lesbian articulates herself and how she is articulated and objectified by others. Popular culture, in particular, exposes the objectifying purpose of the lesbian-as-monster image, such as the lesbian vampire first created by Joseph Sheridan LeFanu's 1871 ghost story "Carmilla" and revived in early 1970s "B" films as a symbolic attack on women's struggle for self-identity.[48] Other critics also have analyzed the negative symbolic appearance of the lesbian in literature. Ann Allen Shockley, reviewing black lesbian characters in American fiction, notes that "within these works exists an undercurrent of hostility, trepidation, subtlety, shadiness, and in some instances, ignorance culling forth homophobic stereotypes."[49] Homophobic stereotypes are also what Judith McDaniel and Maureen Brady find in abundance in recent commercial fiction (such as *Kinflicks, A Sea Change, Some Do,* and *How to Save Your Own Life*) by avowedly feminist novelists. Although individuals might disagree with McDaniel and Brady's severe criticism of specific novels, their over-all argument is unimpeachable. Contemporary feminist fiction, by perpetuating stereotyped characters and themes (such as the punishment theme so dear to prefeminist lesbian literature), serves to "disempower the lesbian."[50] Lesbian as well as heterosexual writers present the lesbian as Other, as Julia Penelope Stanley discovered in prefeminist fiction: "the lesbian character creates for herself a mythology of darkness, a world in which she moves through dreams and shadows."[51] Lesbian critics may wish to avoid this analysis of the lesbian as Other because we no longer wish to dwell upon the cultural violence done against us. Yet this area must be explored until we strip these stereotypes of their inhibiting and dehumanizing presence in our popular culture and social mythology.

Lesbian critics have also delved into the area of stylistics and literary theory. If we have been silenced for centuries and speak an oppressor's tongue, then liberation for the lesbian must begin with language. Some writers may have reconciled their internal censor with their speech by writing in code, but many critics maintain that modern lesbian writers, because they are uniquely alienated from the patriarchy, experiment with its literary style and form. Julia Penelope Stanley and Susan Wolfe, considering such diverse writers as Virginia Woolf, Gertrude Stein, Kate Millett, and Elana Dykewoman, claim that "a feminist aesthetic, as it emerges out of women's evolution, grounds itself in female consciousness and in the unrelenting language of process and change."[52] In this article, the authors do not call their feminist aesthetic a lesbian feminist aesthetic, although all the writers they discuss are, in fact, lesbians. Susan Wolfe later confronted this fact: "Few women who continue to identify with men can risk the male censure of 'women's style,' and few escape the male perspective long enough to attempt it."[53] Through examples from Kate Millett, Jill Johnston, and Monique Wittig, she illustrates her contention that lesbian literature is characterized by the use of the continuous present, unconventional grammar, and neologism; and that it breaks boundaries between art and the world, between events and our perceptions of them, and between past, present, and the dream world. It is, as even the proponents of this theory admit, highly debatable that all lesbian writers are modernists, or that all modernists are lesbians. If Virginia Woolf wrote in nonlinear, stream-of-consciousness style because she was a lesbian (or "woman-identified") how does one explain Dorothy Richardson, whose *Pilgrimage,* despite one lesbian relationship, is primarily heterosexual? If both Woolf and Richardson can be called "feminist" stylists, then how does one explain the nonlinear experimentation of James Joyce or Alain Robbe-Grillet, for example? The holes that exist in this theory should not, however, detract from the highly suggestive overlap between experimental and lesbian writers. Nor should we ignore the clear evidence that many contemporary, self-conscious lesbian writers (such as Wittig, Johnston, Bertha Harris, and June Arnold) are choosing an experimental style as well as content.

This development of a self-conscious lesbian literature and literary theory in recent years has led a number of critics to investigate the unifying themes and values of current literature. Such an attempt has been made by Elly Bulkin, who traces the various sources of contemporary lesbian poetry, analyzes "the range of lesbian voices," and advises feminist teachers how to teach lesbian poetry. Mary Carruthers, in asking why so much contemporary feminist poetry is also lesbian, observes that the "lesbian love celebrated in contemporary women's poetry requires an affirmation of the value of femaleness, women's bodies, women's sexuality—in women's language."[54] Jane Gurko and Sally Gearhart compare contemporary lesbian and gay male literature, attempting to discern to what extent one or the other transforms heterosexual ideology. They claim that, unlike gay male literature, lesbian literature "does express a revolutionary model of sexuality which in its structure, its content, and its practice defies the fundamental violent assumptions of patriarchal culture."[55] There is a danger in this attempt to establish a characteristic lesbian vision or literary value system, one that is well illustrated by this article. In an attempt to say *this* is what defines a lesbian literature, we are easily tempted to read selectively, omitting what is foreign to our theories. Most contemporary lesbian literature does embrace a rhetoric of nonviolence, but this is not universally true; for example, M. F. Beal's *Angel Dance* is a lesbian hard-boiled detective novel, and Monique Wittig's *Le Corps lesbien* is infused with a violent eroticism that is nonetheless intensely nonpatriarchal. Violence, role playing, disaffection, unhappiness, suicide, and self-hatred, to name a few "taboo" subjects, all exist within the lesbian culture, and a useful criticism will have to effectively analyze these as *lesbian* themes and issues, regardless of ideological purity.

Lesbian feminist criticism faces a number of concerns that must be addressed as it grows in force and clarity. Among these concerns is the fact that this criticism is dominated by the politics of lesbian separatism. This is exemplified by the following statement from *Sinister Wisdom,* a journal that has developed a consistent and articulate separatist politics:

> "Lesbian consciousness" is really a point of view, a view from the boundary. And in a sense every time a woman draws a circle around her psyche, saying "this is a room of *my own,*" and then writes from within that "room," she's inhabiting lesbian consciousness.[56]

The value of separatism, which, I believe, has always provided the most exciting theoretical developments in lesbian ideology, is precisely this marginality: lesbian existence "on the periphery of patriarchy."[57] Separatism provides criticism, as it did for lesbian politics, a cutting edge and radical energy that keep us moving forward rather than backward from either fear or complacency. Those critics who maintain a consciously chosen position on the boundaries (and not one imposed by a hostile society) help to keep lesbian and feminist criticism radical and provocative, preventing both from becoming another arm of the established truth. At the same time, it is essential that separatist criticism does not itself become an orthodoxy and thus repetitive, empty, and resistant to change. Lesbian criticism, as Kolodny has argued about feminist criticism, has more to gain from resisting dogma than from monotheism.[58] Understandably, those critics and scholars willing to identify themselves publicly as lesbians also have tended to hold radical politics of marginality. Exposing oneself to public scrutiny as a lesbian may in fact entail marginality through denial of tenure or loss of job, and those lesbians willing to risk these consequences usually have a political position that justifies their risk. However, to me it seems imperative that lesbian criticism develop diversity in theory and approach. Much as lesbians, even more than heterosexual feminists, may mistrust systems of thought developed by and associated with men and male values, we may, in fact, enrich our work through the insights of Marxist, structuralist, semiotic, or even psychoanalytic criticism. Perhaps "male" systems of thought are incompatible with a lesbian literary vision, but we will not know until we attempt to integrate these ideas into our work.[59]

Similarly, lesbian criticism and cultural theory in general can only gain by developing a greater specificity, historically and culturally. We have tended to write and act as if lesbian experience—which is perceived as that of a contemporary, white middle-class feminist—is universal and unchanging. Although most lesbians know that this is not the case, we too often forget to apply rigorous historical and cross-cultural tools to our scholarship. Much of this ahistoricity occurs around the shifting definitions of lesbianism from one era and one culture to another. To state simply that Wollstonecraft "was" a lesbian because she passionately loved Fanny Blood, or Susan B. Anthony was a lesbian because she wrote amorous letters to Anna Dickinson, without accounting for historical circumstances, may serve to distort or dislocate the actual meaning of these women's lives (just as it is distorting to *deny* their love for women). There are also notable differences between the institution of the *berdache* (the adoption by one sex of the opposite gender role) in Native American tribes; *faute de mieux* lesbian activity tolerated in France (as in Colette's *Claudine* novels); idyllic romantic friendships (such as that of the famous Ladies of Llangollen); and contemporary self-conscious lesbianism. I do believe that there is a common structure—a lesbian "essence"—that may be located in all these specific historical existences, just as we may speak of a widespread, perhaps universal, structure of marriage or the family. However, in each of these cases—lesbianism, marriage, the family—careful attention to history teaches us that differences are as significant as similarities, and vital information about female survival may be found in the different ways in which women have responded to their historical situation. This tendency toward simplistic universalism is accompanied by what I see as a dangerous development of biological determinism and a curious revival of the nineteenth-century feminist notion of female (now lesbian) moral superiority—that women are uniquely caring and superior to inherently violent males. Although only an undertone in some criticism and literature, any such sociobiological impulse should be questioned at every appearance.

The denial of meaningful differences between women is being challenged, particularly around the issue of racism. Bulkin has raised criticisms about the racism of white lesbian feminist theory. She has written:

> If I can put together—or think someone else can put together—a viable piece of feminist criticism or theory whose base is the thought and writing of white women/lesbians and expect that an analysis of racism can be tacked on or dealt with later as a useful addition, it is a measure of the extent to which I partake of that white privilege.[60]

Implicit in the criticism of Bulkin and other antiracist writers is the belief that lesbians, because of their experience of stigma and exclusion from the feminist mainstream, ought to be particularly sensitive to the dynamic between oppression and oppressing. White lesbians who are concerned about eradicating racism in criticism and theory have been greatly influenced as well by the work of several black lesbian feminist literary critics, such as Gloria T. Hull, Barbara Smith, and Lorraine Bethel.[61] Such concern is not yet present over the issue of class, although the historical association of lesbianism with upper-class values has often been used by left-wing political groups and governments to deny legitimacy to homosexual rights and needs. Lesbian critics studying the Barney circle, for example, might analyze the historical connections between lesbianism and class status. Lesbian critics might also develop comparisons between the literatures of various nationalities, because the lesbian canon is of necessity cross-national. We have barely explored the differences between American, English, French, and German lesbian literature (although *Surpassing the Love of Men* draws some distinctions), let alone non-Western literature. The paucity of lesbian scholars trained in these literatures has so far prevented the development of a truly international lesbian literary canon.

As lesbian criticism matures, we may anticipate the development of ongoing and compelling political and practical concerns. At this time, for example, lesbians are still defining and discovering texts. We are certainly not as badly off as we were in the early seventies when the only lesbian novels in print were *The Well of Loneliness, Rubyfruit Jungle,* and Isabel Miller's *Patience and Sarah.* However, texts published prior to 1970 are still difficult to find, and even *The Well of Loneliness* is intermittently available at the whim of publishers.[62] Furthermore, the demise of Diana Press and the apparent slowdown of Daughters (two of the most active lesbian publishing houses) leaves many major works unavailable, possibly forever. As the boom in gay literature subsides, teachers of literature will find it very difficult to unearth teachable texts. Scholars have the excellent Arno Press series, *Homosexuality: Lesbians and Gay Men in Society, History, and Literature,* but, as Faderman's monumental scholarship reveals, far more lesbian literature exists than anyone has suspected. This literature needs to be unearthed, analyzed, explicated, perhaps translated, and made available to readers.

As lesbian critics, we also need to address the exclusion of lesbian literature from not merely the traditional but also the feminist canon. Little lesbian literature has been integrated into the mainstream of feminist texts, as evidenced by what is criticized, collected, and taught. It is a matter of serious concern that lesbian literature is omitted from anthologies or included in mere token amounts, or that critical works and Modern Language Association panels still exclude lesbianism. It may as yet be possible for heterosexual feminists to claim ignorance about lesbian literature; however, lesbian critics should make it impossible for that claim to stand much longer. Lesbianism is still perceived as a minor and somewhat discomforting variation within the female life-cycle, when it is mentioned at all. Just as we need to integrate lesbian material and perspectives into the traditional and feminist canons, we might also apply lesbian theory to traditional literature. Feminists have not only pointed out the sexism in many canonical works, but have also provided creative and influential rereadings of these works; similarly, lesbians might contribute to the rereading of the classics. For example, *The Bostonians,* an obvious text, has been reread often from a lesbian perspective, and we could reinterpret D. H. Lawrence's antifeminism or Doris Lessing's compromised feminism (particularly in *The Golden Notebook*) by relating these attitudes to their fear of or discomfort with lesbianism. Other texts or selections of texts —such as Rossetti's "Goblin Market" or the relationship between Lucy Snowe and Ginevra Fanshawe in *Villette*—might reveal a subtext that could be called lesbian. Just as few texts escape a feminist re-vision, few might evade a lesbian transformation.

This last point—that there is a way in which we might "review" literature as lesbians—brings me to my conclusion. In a brief period of a few years, critics have begun to demonstrate the existence of a distinct lesbian aesthetic, just as feminists have outlined elements of a female aesthetic. Certain components of this aesthetic or critical perspective are clear:

> Perhaps lesbian feminist criticism [or literature, I would add] is a political or thematic perspective, a kind of imagination that can see beyond the barriers of heterosexuality, role stereotypes, patterns of language and culture that may be repressive to female sexuality and expression.[63]

A lesbian artist very likely would express herself differently about sexuality, the body, and relationships. But are there other—less obvious—unifying themes, ideas, and imagery that might define a lesbian text or subtext? How, for example, does the lesbian's sense of outlaw status affect her literary vision? Might lesbian writing, because of the lesbian's position on the boundaries, be characterized by a particular sense of freedom and flexibility or, rather, by images of violently imposed barriers, the closet? Or, in fact, is there a dialectic between freedom and imprisonment unique to lesbian writing? Do lesbians have a special perception of suffering and stigma, as so much prefeminist literature seems to suggest? What about the "muse," the female symbol of literary creativity: do women writers create a lesbian relationship with their muse as May Sarton asserts? If so, do those writers who choose a female muse experience a freedom from inhibition because of that fact, or might there be a lack of creative tension in such a figurative same-sex relationship? I feel on solid ground in asserting that there are certain topics and themes that define lesbian culture, and that we are beginning to define a lesbian symbolism. Lesbian literature may present a unified tradition of thematic concerns such as that of unrequited longing, a longing of almost cosmic totality because the love object is denied not by circumstance or chance but by necessity. The tension between romantic love and genital sexuality takes a particular form in woman-to-woman relationships, often articulated through musings on the difference between purity and impurity (culminating in Colette's study of variant sexuality, *The Pure and the Impure*). Lesbian literature approaches the theme of development or the quest in a manner different from that of men or heterosexual women.[64] Lesbian literature, like lesbian culture in general, is particularly flexible on issues of gender and role identification; even *The Well of Loneliness* hints at the tragedy of rigid gender roles. Because of this flexibility, lesbian artists and writers have always been fascinated with costuming, because dress is an external manifestation of gender roles lesbians often reject.[65] As we read and reread literature from a lesbian perspective, I am confident we will continue to expand our understanding of the lesbian literary tradition and a lesbian aesthetic.

This essay has suggested the vigor of lesbian criticism and its value to all feminists in raising awareness of entrenched heterosexism in existing texts, clarifying the lesbian traditions in literature through scholarship and reinterpretation, pointing out barriers that have stood in the way of free lesbian expression, explicating the recurring themes and values of lesbian literature, and exposing the dehumanizing stereotypes of lesbians in our culture. Many of the issues that face lesbian critics—resisting dogma, expanding the canon, creating a nonracist and nonclassist critical vision, transforming our readings of traditional texts, and exploring new methodologies—are the interests of all feminist critics. Because feminism concerns itself with the removal of limitations and impediments in the way of female imagination, and lesbian criticism helps to expand our notions of what is *possible* for women, then all women would grow by adopting for themselves a lesbian vision. Disenfranchised groups have had to adopt a double vision for survival; one of the political transformations of recent decades has been the realization that enfranchised groups—men, whites, heterosexuals, the middle class—would do well to adopt that double vision for the survival of us all. Lesbian literary criticism simply restates what feminists already know, that one group cannot name itself "humanity" or even "woman": "We're not trying to become part of the old order misnamed 'universal' which has tabooed us; we are transforming the meaning of 'universality.' "[66] Whether lesbian criticism will survive depends as much upon the external social climate as it does upon the creativity and skill of its practitioners. If political attacks on gay rights and freedom grow; if the so-called Moral Majority wins its fight to eliminate gay teachers and texts from the schools (it would be foolhardy to believe they will exempt universities); and if the academy, including feminist teachers and scholars, fails to support lesbian scholars, eradicate heterosexist values and assumptions, and incorporate the insights of lesbian scholarship into the mainstream; then current lesbian criticism will probably suffer the same fate as did Jeannette Foster's *Sex Variant Women* in the fifties. Lesbian or heterosexual, we will all suffer from that loss.

NOTES

An earlier version of this paper was presented at the first annual convention of the National Women's Studies Association, Lawrence, Kansas, May 1979.

[1]Lynn Strongin, "Sayre," in *Rising Tides: Twentieth Century American Women Poets,* ed. Laura Chester and Sharon Barba (New York: Washington Square Press, 1973), p. 317.

[2]June Arnold, "Lesbian Fiction," in *Lesbian Writing and Publishing,* a special issue of *Sinister Wisdom* 2 (Fall 1976): 28.

[3]Sandy Boucher, "Lesbian Artists," in *Lesbian Art and Artists,* a special issue of *Heresies* 3 (Fall 1977): 48.

[4]This survey is limited to published and unpublished essays in literary criticism that present a perspective either sympathetic to lesbianism or explicitly lesbian in orientation. It is limited to literature and to theoretical articles (not book reviews). The sexual preference of the authors is, for the most part, irrelevant; this is an analysis of lesbian feminist ideas, not authors. Although the network of lesbian critics is well developed, some major unpublished papers may have escaped my attention.

[5]Elly Bulkin, " 'Kissing Against the Light': A Look at Lesbian Poetry," *Radical Teacher* 10 (December 1978): 8. This article was reprinted in *College English* and *Women's Studies Newsletter;* an expanded version is available from the Lesbian-Feminist Study Clearinghouse, Women's Studies Program, University of Pittsburgh, Pittsburgh, Penn. 15260.

[6]Julia Penelope [Stanley], "The Articulation of Bias: Hoof in Mouth Disease," paper presented at the convention of the National Council of Teachers of English, San Francisco, November 1979, pp. 4–5. On the same panel, I presented a paper, "Heterosexism in Literary Anthologies," which develops some of the points of this paragraph.

[7]Annette Kolodny, "Literary Criticism," Review Essay, *Signs* 2 (Winter 1976): 416, 419.

[8]Ellen Moers, *Literary Women: The Great Writers* (Garden City, N.Y.: Doubleday, 1976), pp. 108–9, 145.

[9]Patricia Meyer Spacks, *The Female Imagination* (New York: Avon Books, 1976), pp. 89, 214, 363.

[10]Elaine Showalter, *A Literature of Their Own: British Women Novelists From Brontë to Lessing* (Princeton, N.J.: Princeton University Press, 1977), pp. 178, 229, 316.

[11]Sandra M. Gilbert and Susan Gubar, *The Madwoman in the Attic: The Woman Writer and the Nineteenth-Century Literary Imagination* (New Haven, Conn.: Yale University Press, 1979), p. 567. Regarding another issue—their analysis of Emily Dickinson's poem no. 1722—Nadean Bishop says, "It is hard to fathom how Sandra Gilbert and Susan Gubar could take this erotic representation of lesbian love-making to be an 'image of the chaste moon goddess Diana,' who does not have hand or tender tongue or inspire incredulity." See Nadean Bishop, "Renunciation in the Bridal Poems of Emily Dickinson," paper presented at the National Women's Studies Association, Bloomington, Indiana, May 16–20, 1980. One other major critical study, Judith Fetterley's *The Resisting Reader: A Feminist Approach to American Fiction* (Bloomington: Indiana University Press, 1978), is uniquely sensitive to lesbianism in its interpretation of *The Bostonians.*

[12]Gene Damon, Jan Watson, and Robin Jordan, *The Lesbian in Literature: A Bibliography* (1967; reprint ed., Reno, Nev.: Naiad Press, 1975).

[13]Jeannette Foster, *Sex Variant Women in Literature* (1956; reprint ed., Balti-

more: Diana Press, 1975). See also Karla Jay, "The X-Rated Bibliographer: A Spy in the House of Sex," in *Lavender Culture,* ed. Karla Jay and Allen Young (New York: Harcourt Brace Jovanovich, 1978), pp. 257–61.

[14]Beth Hodges, ed., *Lesbian Writing and Publishing,* a special issue of *Margins* 23 (August 1975). Beth Hodges, ed., *Lesbian Literature and Publishing,* a special issue of *Sinister Wisdom* 2 (Fall 1976).

[15]In addition, networks of lesbian critics, teachers, and scholars were established through panels at the Modern Language Association's annual conventions and at the Lesbian Writer's Conference in Chicago, which began in 1974 and continued for several years. Currently, networking continues through conferences, journals, and other institutionalized outlets. The Lesbian-Feminist Study Clearinghouse reprints articles, bibliographies, and syllabi pertinent to lesbian studies. See note 5 for the address. The Lesbian Herstory Archives collects all material documenting lesbian lives past or present; their address is P.O. Box 1258, New York, N. Y. 10001. *Matrices: A Lesbian-Feminist Research Newsletter* is a network of information about research projects, reference materials, calls for papers, bibliographies, and so forth. There are several regional editors; the managing editor is Bobby Lacy, 4000 Randolph, Lincoln, Neb. 68510.

[16]Radicalesbians, "The Woman-Identified Woman," in *Radical Feminism,* ed. Anne Koedt, Ellen Levine, and Anita Rapone (New York; Quadrangle Books, 1973). This article is extensively reprinted in women's studies anthologies.

[17]Charlotte Bunch, "Lesbians in Revolt," in *Lesbianism and the Women's Movement,* ed. Nancy Myron and Charlotte Bunch (Baltimore: Diana Press, 1975), p. 30.

[18]Susan Sniader Lanser, "Speaking in Tongues: *Ladies Almanack* and the Language of Celebration," *Frontiers* 4 (Fall 1979): 39.

[19]Catharine R. Stimpson, "Zero Degree Deviancy: A Study of the Lesbian Novel," unpublished paper, p. 2. This article was published, as "Zero Degree Deviancy: The Lesbian Novel in English," in *Critical Inquiry* 8 (Winter 1981): 363–80.

[20]Barbara Smith, "Toward a Black Feminist Criticism," in this volume, p. 181. It is sometimes overlooked that Smith's pathbreaking article on black feminist criticism is also a lesbian feminist analysis.

[21]Adrienne Rich, "Compulsory Heterosexuality and Lesbian Existence," *Signs* 5 (Summer 1980): 648–49.

[22]Bertha Harris, quoted by Smith, "Toward a Black Feminist Criticism," p. 175.

[23]Supportive historical and biographical information about women writers can be found in a number of recent articles, in addition to those cited elsewhere in this essay. See, for example, Judith Schwarz, "*Yellow Clover:* Katherine Lee Bates and Katherine Coman," pp. 59–67; Josephine Donovan, "The Unpublished Love Poems of Sarah Orne Jewett," pp. 26–31; and Margaret Cruikshank, "Geraldine Jewsbury and Jane Carlyle," pp. 60–64, all in *Lesbian History,* a special issue of *Frontiers* 4 (Fall 1979).

[24]Lillian Faderman, *Surpassing the Love of Men: Romantic Friendship and Love Between Women from the Renaissance to the Present* (New York: William Morrow, 1981), pp. 17–18.

[25]Adrienne Rich, " 'It Is the Lesbian in Us . . . ,' " *On Lies, Secrets, and Silence* (New York: W. W. Norton, 1979), p. 202.

[26]Rich, "Women and Honor: Some Notes on Lying (1975)," *On Lies, Secrets, and Silence,* p. 190.

[27]Gloria T. Hull, " 'Under the Days': The Buried Life and Poetry of Angelina

Weld Grimké," in *The Black Women's Issue,* a special issue of *Conditions: Five* 2 (1979): 23, 20.

[28]Joanna Russ, "To Write 'Like a Woman': Transformations of Identity in Willa Cather," paper presented at the MLA convention, San Francisco, December 1979. On coding in other writers, see Ann Cothran and Diane Griffin Crowder, "An Optical Thirst for Invisible Water: Image Structure, Codes and Recording in Colette's *The Pure and the Impure,*" paper presented at the MLA convention, New York, December 1978; and Annette Kolodny, "The Lady's Not For Spurning: Kate Millett and the Critics," *Contemporary Literature* 17 (Fall 1976) 541–62.

[29]Two male critics—Edmund Wilson and Robert Bridgman—first suggested the connection between Stein's obscurity and her lesbianism. Jane Rule in *Lesbian Images* (see note 33 below) and Dolores Klaich in *Woman Plus Woman* (see note 35) both follow their analysis. Cynthia Secor has argued that Stein did declare her lesbianism in her writing: "Can We Call Gertrude Stein a Non-Declared Lesbian Writer?" paper presented at the MLA convention, San Francisco, December 1979. For more on Stein, see note 44 below.

[30]Bulkin, " 'Kissing Against the Light,' " p. 8.

[31]Smith, "Toward a Black Feminist Criticism," p. 181.

[32]Blanche Wiesen Cook, " 'Women Alone Stir My Imagination': Lesbianism and the Cultural Tradition," *Signs* 4 (Summer 1979): 718–39. A curious example of contemporary denial of lesbianism—the obliteration of the lesbian tradition such as it is—is found in Judith Hallett, "Sappho and Her Social Context: Sense and Sensuality," *Signs* 4 (Spring 1979): 447–64. Sappho, of course, personifies "lesbian existence," indeed lesbian *possibility,* as well as female poetic creativity. Hallett, however, essentially denies Sappho's love for women with her conclusion that "she did not represent herself in her verses as having expressed homosexual feelings physically." One might certainly argue that no other possible interpretation can exist for Sappho's "He is more than a hero" (Mary Barnard's translation). Eva Stigers, in "Romantic Sensuality, Poetic Sense: A Response to Hallett on Sappho" (same issue, pp. 464–71), contends that Sappho "chose female homosexual love as the vehicle because lesbian love offered the most receptive setting for romantic *eros.*" This interpretation may more accurately reflect the perspective of the nineteenth-century Romantic poets who rediscovered Sappho. However, Stiger's argument that Sappho used lesbian love to create an alternate world in which male values are not dominant and in which to explore the female experience provides a starting point for a feminist analysis of Sappho's influence on her modern lesbian followers. A fine exposition of this "Sappho model" in French lesbian literature is provided by Elaine Marks in her essay "Lesbian Intertextuality" (see note 41 below).

[33]Jane Rule, *Lesbian Images* (Garden City, N. Y.: Doubleday, 1975).

[34]Bonnie Zimmerman, "The New Tradition," *Sinister Wisdom* 2 (Fall 1976): 34–41.

[35]Dolores Klaich, *Woman Plus Woman: Attitudes Toward Lesbianism* (New York: William Morrow, 1974); Louise Bernikow, *The World Split Open: Four Centuries of Women Poets in England and America, 1552–1950* (New York: Vintage Books, 1974).

[36]Cook, "Women Alone Stir My Imagination," p. 720.

[37]See Lillian Faderman's articles: "The Morbidification of Love Between Women by Nineteenth-Century Sexologists," *Journal of Homosexuality* 4 (Fall 1978): 73–90; "Emily Dickinson's Letters to Sue Gilbert," *Massachusetts Review* 18 (Summer 1977): 197–225; "Emily Dickinson's Homoerotic Poetry," *Higginson Journal* 18 (1978): 19–27; "Female Same-Sex Relationships in Novels by Longfellow, Holmes, and

James," *New England Quarterly* 60 (September 1978): 309–32; and "Lesbian Magazine Fiction in the Early Twentieth Century," *Journal of Popular Culture* 11 (Spring 1978): 800–17.

[38]Holly Near, "Imagine My Surprise," on *Imagine My Surprise!* (Redwood Records, 1978).

[39]See Klaich, *Woman Plus Woman,* chap. 6. Also see Bertha Harris, "The More Profound Nationality of their Lesbianism: Lesbian Society in Paris in the 1920's," *Amazon Expedition* (New York: Times Change Press, 1973), pp. 77–88; and Gayle Rubin's Introduction to Renée Vivien's *A Woman Appeared to Me,* trans. Jeanette Foster (Reno, Nev.: Naiad Press, 1976).

[40]For example, see Lanser, "Speaking in Tongues."

[41]Marks, "Lesbian Intertextuality," in *Homosexualities and French Literature,* ed. George Stambolian and Elaine Marks (Ithaca, N.Y.: Cornell University Press, 1979), pp. 353–77.

[42]Lillian Faderman and Ann Williams, "Radclyffe Hall and the Lesbian Image," *Conditions: One* 1 (April 1977): 40; and Sybil Korff Vincent, "Nothing Fails Like Success: Radclyffe Hall's *The Well of Loneliness,*" unpublished paper.

[43]Stimpson, "Zero Degree Deviancy," pp. 8–17.

[44]Cynthia Secor, "*Ida,* A Great American Novel," *Twentieth-Century Literature* 24 (Spring 1978): 99; Elizabeth Fifer, "Is Flesh Advisable? The Interior Theater of Gertrude Stein," *Signs* 4 (Spring 1979): 478; Deirdre Vanderlinde, "Gertrude Stein: Three Lives," paper presented at the MLA convention, San Francisco, December 1979, p. 10; and Catharine R. Stimpson, "The Mind, and Body and Gertrude Stein," *Critical Inquiry* 3 (Spring 1977): 489–506. Like Stimpson on Stein, Lanser, in "Speaking in Tongues," suggests that Djuna Barnes in *Ladies Almanack* "writes through the lesbian body, celebrating not the abstraction of a sexual preference, but female sexuality and its lesbian expression."

[45]Lillian Faderman and Louise Bernikow, "Comment on Joanne Feit Diehl's 'Come Slowly—Eden,'" *Signs* 4 (Fall 1978): 188–95. For another perspective on woman as muse, see my paper "'The Dark Eye Beaming': George Eliot, Sara Hennell, and the Female Muse," presented at the 1980 MLA convention, "George Eliot and the Female Tradition" (1977), and Arlene Raven and Ruth Iskin, "Through the Peephole: Toward a Lesbian Sensibility in Art," *Chrysalis,* no. 4 (1977), pp. 19–31. Contemporary lesbian interpretations of Dickinson were anticipated by Rebecca Patterson in *The Riddle of Emily Dickinson* (Boston: Houghton Mifflin, 1951).

[46]Paula Bennett, "The Language of Love: Emily Dickinson's Homoerotic Poetry," *Gai Saber* 1 (Spring 1977): 13–17; Bennett, "Emily Dickinson and the Value of Isolation," *Dickinson Studies* 36 (1979): 13–17. Bennett's paper presented at the 1979 MLA convention; and Bishop, "Renunciation in the Bridal Poems."

[47]Bertha Harris, "*What we mean to say:* Notes Toward Defining the Nature of Lesbian Literature," *Heresies* 1 (Fall 1977): 7–8. Also Harris, "The Purification of Monstrosity: The Lesbian as Literature," paper presented at the MLA convention, New York, December 1974.

[48]Bonnie Zimmerman, "'Daughters of Darkness': Lesbian Vampires," *Jump Cut,* no. 24–25 (March 1981), pp. 23–24. See also Jane Caputi, "'Jaws': Fish Stories and Patriarchal Myth," *Sinister Wisdom* 7 (Fall 1978): 66–81.

[49]Ann Allen Shockley, "The Black Lesbian in American Literature: An Overview," *Conditions: Five* 2 (Fall 1979): 136.

[50]Maureen Brady and Judith McDaniel, "Lesbians in the Mainstream: Images of Lesbians in Recent Commercial Fiction," *Conditions: Six* 2 (Summer 1980): 83.

[51]Julia Penelope Stanley, "Uninhabited Angels: Metaphors for Love," *Margins* 23 (August 1975): 8.

[52]Julia Penelope Stanley and Susan J. Wolfe, "Toward a Feminist Aesthetic," *Chrysalis,* no. 6 (1978), p. 66.

[53]Susan J. Wolfe, "Stylistic Experimentation in Millett, Johnston, and Wittig," paper presented at the MLA convention, New York, December 1978, p. 3. On lesbian stylistics, see Lanser, "Speaking in Tongues"; and Martha Rosenfield, "Linguistic Experimentation in Monique Wittig's *Le Corps lesbien,*" paper presented at the 1978 MLA convention.

[54]Mary Carruthers, "Imagining Women: Notes Toward a Feminist Poetic," *Massachusetts Review* 20 (Summer 1979): 301.

[55]Jane Gurko and Sally Gearhart, "The Sword and the Vessel Versus the Lake on the Lake: A Lesbian Model of Nonviolent Rhetoric," paper presented at the 1979 MLA convention, p. 3.

[56]Harriet Desmoines, "Notes for a Magazine II," *Sinister Wisdom* 1 (July 1976): 29.

[57]Wolfe, "Stylistic Experimentation," p. 16.

[58]Annette Kolodny, "Dancing Through the Minefield: Some Observations on the Theory, Practice and Politics of a Feminist Literary Criticism," in this volume, pp. 144–167.

[59]For example, a panel at the 1980 MLA convention in Houston, "Literary History and the New Histories of Sexuality," presented gay and lesbian perspectives on contemporary French philosophies.

[60]Elly Bulkin, "Racism and Writing: Some Implications for White Lesbian Critics," *Sinister Wisdom* 13 (Spring 1980): 16.

[61]A highly recommended resource on black lesbians is *The Black Women's Issue, Conditions: Five* 2, no. 2, edited by Lorraine Bethel and Barbara Smith (Fall 1979). Two additional publications have recently appeared: Cherríe Moraga and Gloria Anzaldúa, eds., *This Bridge Called My Back: Writings by Radical Women of Color* (Watertown, Mass.: Persephone Press, 1981), and J. R. Roberts, *Black Lesbians: An Annotated Bibliography* (Tallahassee, Fla.: Naiad Press, 1981).

[62]In a response to my complaint about *The Well of Loneliness* being out of print, an editor at Washington Square Press remarked that "the existence in any mass-market form of a minor work of fiction is itself something of a wonder" (personal correspondence, January 29, 1981). This attitude does not bode well for readers and teachers of lesbian literature.

[63]Judith McDaniel, "Lesbians and Literature," *Sinister Wisdom* 2 (Fall 1976): 2.

[64]See my essay "Existing from Patriarchy: The Lesbian Novel of Deveopment," in *The Voyage In: Fictions of Female Development*, ed. Elizabeth Abel, Marianne Hirsch, and Elizabeth Langland (Hanover, N.H.: University Press of New England, 1983), pp. 244–57.

[65]This idea was suggested by John Biren (JEB) in her slide show "Lesbian Images in Photography 1850–1980." JEB can be contacted through Glad Hag Books, Box 2934, Main City Station, Washington, D.C. 20013.

[66]Elly Bulkin, "An Interview with Adrienne Rich: Part II," *Conditions: Two* 1, no. 2 (October 1977): 58.

Are Women's Novels Feminist Novels?

Rosalind Coward

Over recent years we have been witness to a strange phenomenon, the emergence of what we may loosely call the "feminist novel." This phenomenon has involved the immense commercial success and popular appeal of some novels which claim explicit allegiance to the women's liberation movement. Some of these novels, like Marilyn French's *The Women's Room* and Sara Davison's *Loose Change,* even use the practice of "consciousness-raising" as a framing device. These novels have been published alike by feminist publishing groups and commercial publishers, yet the number printed of such novels is far in excess of the number printed of other forms of feminist writing: magazines, journals, and political tracts. Accompanying the appearance of novels like these has been a practice, initiated by feminist publishing groups, of reprinting novels written by women who have fallen into relative oblivion. All these novels are read with pleasure and interest by feminists; they are frequently discussed informally. It seems as though, unlike many other contemporary political movements, feminism is accompanied by the development of a "feminist culture"—something which is not confined to literature but is also evidenced by the proliferation of feminist theater and film groups.

Yet in the informal networks in which the phenomena like the "feminist novel" are discussed, responses are rarely unambiguous. No one is quite sure about the political validity of the admixture of conventional entertainment with a serious political message. Many are suspicious of the commercial success of "the novel that changes lives" and are eager to demonstrate how these novels are ultimately "not feminist." This has been the fate of Erica Jong's

Fear of Flying. Others question the nature of the popular appeal of these novels, when other aspects of feminist political involvement are so readily ridiculed in the media through designations like "bra-burners" or "women's libbers." Is it that these novels are carrying out subversive politicization, drawing women into structures of consciousness-raising without their knowing it? Or is it that the accounts of women's experiences they offer in fact correspond more closely to popular sentiment than they do to feminist aspirations? These are not insignificant questions. They relate to debates over what effective feminist politics are; whether ideological practices like literature, theater, or film can be political; and finally, whether it is the centrality these novels attribute to women's experience which would justify their designation as "feminist."

To begin to address these questions at all, we are confronted with the need for a systematic approach to representational practices like literature. For we need to know certain things which go beyond whether we like or enjoy a book. Firstly, we need to know about the institutions which make a piece of writing available; about the financial and ideological policies of the publishing groups; about the audience which is being created through various marketing strategies; about the patterns of consumption of writing created through, for example, cheap mass paperbacks or hardbacks for libraries. Secondly, we need to examine other institutional practices which determine *how* we come to read a piece of writing in a particular way. Thus we need to consider how the institution of "literary criticism" and its diffusion through the education system determine how certain pieces of writing are designated as "literature" or "potboiler," making distinctions on the basis of nebulous notions like "quality." Finally, we need to consider practices internal to the text which determine how we read a piece of writing. All pieces of writing are texts; books, pamphlets, duplicated sheets are all simply words—language—on a page. Yet definite practices in writing make it quite clear what we are reading. Writing conventions are so rigid that we instantly know whether we are reading a page of "theory" or a page from a John Le Carré novel. Language is used in certain ways to gain certain effects. Thus, fiction (in general) is characterized by narrative form—beginning, middle, and end.

Within fiction there are very definite genres, practices which are internal to the text and backed up by institutions of marketing. These are conventions of writing, like romance, the detective novel, science fiction, which determine to a large extent *how* a text is read. A statement like "She took the 4:50 train from Paddington" would invite totally different attention in different genres. In a detective novel, we would expect every sentence to resonate with a potential significance. Its significance will ultimately be revealed, but with careful attention to each statement and its connection with other statements we may be able to decipher the significance before the detective does. Yet in a so-called realist novel, such a statement would rarely be invested with this level of significance. It would be careful detail to make the novel more plausible, or perhaps be used to convey psychological characteristics, like the woman's punctuality or obsession with detail.

Although "texts" are only words on a page, they come to have very precise meanings and to convey a definite sense of what they are representing. Codes within the texts and marketing practices determine what statements or forms of statements are appropriate to a certain convention of representing reality. In science fiction the following statement can occur (from *The Nomads of Gor*):

> There were four major tribes of Wagon People living off their herds of constantly moving bosk, riding their savage, fighting kaiila, the women secured in the wagons they called Home.[1]

The statement draws on certain stereotypes of the nomadic horde, marked for the reader by the name of the people, "the wagon people," and by their "constantly moving" herds. Other information is also given; the horde is savage—they ride savage fighting animals; it is chauvinistic—the women are secured in the wagons; and finally it is primitive—they have a pathetic conception of "home." But the statement also employs definite conventions of science fiction, to ensure we read it as fantasy. One of these is the convention of invented names—herds of "bosk," fighting "kaiila." Even in this initial statement we know that this is not a novel of colonial life, where we might have been told "the tribesmen ride horses which they call 'kaiila.' " What is at stake here is a consideration of all practices of writing as constructions or versions of "reality." The *Nomads of Gor* example is an extreme case, exposing how conventions of language are used to construct a version of reality. But it is no less true for novels which claim to reflect reality; they too rely on definite constructions and conventions of what is and is not appropriate to build up a particular sense of reality. Often it is when the novel claims to be most naturalistic that it contains very definite ideologies. A feminist approach to literature has exposed how supposedly "truthful" and "honest" accounts of "reality" rely on distinct ideologies, in particular of what men and women should be like. For example, where critics have championed D. H. Lawrence for his honest accounts of sexuality, feminists have exposed these accounts as phallocratic and degrading representations of women. In other words there are no neutral conventions in novelistic writing; all accounts of reality are versions of reality. As feminists we have to be constantly alerted to *what* reality is being constructed, and *how* representations are achieving this construction. In this respect, reading a novel can be a political activity, similar to activities which have always been important to feminist politics in general. This involves the contesting of natural attitudes, the challenging of agreed definitions—definitions which feminists have long recognized to be an integral aspect of the oppression of women in this society. Thus even novels which have a surface commitment to feminism should be interrogated as to by what representations of sexuality, of maleness and femaleness, they achieve their version of reality.

Attempts have been made to develop this approach to literature from within Marxism and feminism—an approach which seeks to understand the literary text in all its complexity. This new approach questions the institutions of reading, the practices of writing (such as genre), and the production of the text itself as something which is neither the creation of an inspired individual nor simply a reflection of social conditions. This approach has already opened out onto more general questions about the nature and effectivity of ideological practices. As such, it has always conceived of itself as highly political, since it raises issues which Marxists and feminists consider important—questions of the nature of ideology, its mode of functioning, and its hold on the individual.[2]

For these reasons Rebecca O'Rourke's article "Summer Reading" in *Feminist Review* (no. 2, 1979) was something of a disappointment, since it merely indicates issues of importance without ever pursuing them, and apparently ignores the attempts that have been made to develop a systematic and political analysis of texts. She begins by briefly examining the traditional institutions of literary criticism in which feminists have attempted to work, and signals the need for feminists to engage with contemporary developments of women's writing and feminist publishing. But the article then settles down to accounts of various writings, to "demonstrate the diversity and range of women's writings." Because the article simply draws the reader's attention to the multitude of new or reprinted novels, it fails to engage with more interesting questions about feminist writings, grouping together such different writers as Michèle Roberts and Stella Gibbons under the category "women writers." It would be difficult to find much in common between these two writers. Michèle Roberts's *A Piece of the Night* employs a self-consciously political approach to experience and writing, using the quasi-autobiographical "voice" of woman so characteristic of recent feminist novels. *Cold Comfort Farm* could not be more different. It is a witty satire on "twilight romances," such as *Precious Bane* by Mary Webb, in which the middle-class heroine, Flora, sorts out the filth and disorder of the semiproletarianized inhabitants of the farm. Delightful though the novel is, it surely belongs more properly to the tradition of right-wing humorists like Nancy Mitford than to a nebulous tradition of "women's writing" which is supposed to be of interest to feminists.

It is important to distinguish between novels like these, not in order to designate one text as progressive in a crude moralistic way—far from it—but because with the increase of feminist involvement in cultural politics we cannot leave unasked the question of *how* representations work. O'Rourke admits to the pleasure experienced in reading what are in many ways politically reactionary books, only to justify that pleasure by the fact that these books were written by women. It would be far more important to understand what these pleasures are, how they can be used and transformed.

There are two reasons why O'Rourke does not engage with issues like these. The first, which I have already indicated, is the appeal to a supposedly self-defining tradition of women's writing. Although she points to important differences between particular women writers, and locates the specific historical traditions in which these different writers are found, O'Rourke suggests that these differences are overridden by the importance of their all being *women* writers. It is with this supposed unified category of women's writing that I would want to disagree. Secondly, having raised some general issues about feminist criticism at the outset of the article, in her treatment of the fiction in question O'Rourke relies on traditional literary critical assumptions which tend to exclude many important questions. Literary criticism tends to assume that what is at issue is a correct reading of a pregiven text, for which the critic's subjective sensitivity is required to evaluate various texts as in some way representing "quality" or being poetic. Literary criticism, as practiced by the dominant tradition of establishment critics, usually depends upon an individual response to a text—a search for the correct interpretation of its meaning—and also assumes that writing represents reality in an unproblematic way. It thereby excludes from consideration the social context of the text and the practices of writing and ideology which make it up. Traditionally, Marxist criticism has not transcended the central relationship between text and critic that characterizes bourgeois criticism. It has tended frequently to read novels, for instance, in terms of their "representativeness"; it sees them in terms of whether they typify a particular social class or group. This tradition of Marxist criticism, although imputing a social determination of the text frequently absent in establishment criticism, has not fundamentally challenged the role of the literary critic and has not adequately explored how the text itself is constructed by writing practices and what ideologies are involved in it. By providing us with a "feminist reading" of these novels O'Rourke draws, apparently uncritically, on some of the assumptions embedded in these different schools of literary criticism and does not engage systematically with the questions posed at the beginning of her article.

To consider these traditions of criticism is not simply an academic quibble. These approaches represent serious divergences about how texts can be analyzed, and these differences are not without effects. In fact, the failure to treat literature in a systematic way can lead to dubious conclusions. O'Rourke's comments on the commercial success of what she calls women-centered writing can be used to illustrate how different treatments of the literary text can have very different conclusions. For example:

> The willingness of mainstream publishers to print and reprint the work of women must in part be their response to the creation, through the women's movement, of a feminist audience whose choice of reading is women centred. Much as we might regret who makes the profit on these works, we have to be grateful for this extension of available works for us to read.[3]

This raises a number of questions about the phenomenon of the "feminist novel," and in this passage O'Rourke seems to be assuming certain answers to these questions. Firstly, is she suggesting that writing which is women-centered should necessarily be of interest to feminists? Would this also imply that perhaps women-centered writing is feminist? Secondly, is she suggesting that the widespread popularity of women-centered novels can tell us anything about how widespread a "feminist consciousness" now is? Thirdly, is she assuming that commercial publishers are cashing in on this and making profits which should go to a feminist cause? And lastly, is she suggesting that even if we regret these profits we should welcome a wider availability of more progressive works for "us" to read?

If O'Rourke is indeed working with assumptions such as these—though elsewhere in "Summer Reading" this is by no means clear—then I would want to disagree with her. The questions she has raised are of importance in the development of an adequate approach to literature, but they can be considered in a quite different way.

Women-Centered Writing

It is just not possible to say that women-centered writings have any necessary relationship to feminism. Women-centered novels are by no means a new phenomenon. The Mills and Boon romantic novels are written by, read by, marketed for, and are all about women. Yet nothing could be further from the aims of feminism than these fantasies based on the sexual, racial, and class submission which so frequently characterize these novels. The plots and elements are frequently so predictable that cynics have suggested that Mills and Boon's treasured authors might well be computers. Yet the extraordinary rigidity of the formula of the novels, where the heroine invariably finds material success through sexual submission and marriage, does not prevent these publishers having a larger sales than Pan and Penguin. The average print run for each novel is 115,000. While Mills and Boon may have a highly individual market, their formulas are not so radically different from romance fiction in general. Such immensely popular writers as Mary Stewart and Georgette Heyer invariably have the experience of the heroine at the center, and concentrate on the vagaries of her emotions as the principal substance of the novel. In the cinema, the equivalent of the romantic novel is melodrama, and melodrama is often promoted as "women's pictures," suggesting that they are directed towards women as well as being about women. Indeed, it would not be stretching credibility too far to suggest that the consciousness of the individual heroine has been a principal narrative device of the English novel in the last century, a fact which may well have contributed to the relative presence of women writers in this field.

While this all shows how misguided it would be to mark a book of interest to feminism because of the centrality it attributes to women's experiences, it could be argued that what we loosely call feminist novels are qualitatively different. But to make such a claim it would be necessary to specify in what way "women-centered" writing, allying itself with feminist politics, did mark itself out as different. Some of the so-called feminist novels like *The Women's Room* and *A Piece of the Night* do make explicit their allegiance to the women's liberation movement. However, many of the others in roughly the same genre do not. *Fear of Flying, Kinflicks,* and *Loose Change* all fall into this category. Yet the encounter with the milieu and aspirations of feminism often forms a central element in the narrative of these novels. And, the practice of consciousness-raising—the reconstruction of personal histories within a group of women—sometimes forms the structure of the novel. Then there is a further category. Here we find novels like Kate Millett's *Sita* whose feminist commitment is guaranteed not so much by the content of the book as by the other theoretical and political writings of the author. And finally, there is a whole host of novels which are adopted as honorary "feminist novels," taking in such different writers as Doris Lessing, Fay Weldon, and Alison Lurie. Their writings deal not so much with the milieu of contemporary feminism as with charting the experience of women's oppression.

Now, there is a certain convention within all these novels which does clearly mark them off from the romance genre, for example. One striking feature is the frequency with which we encounter the quasi-autobiographical structure. *The Women's Room, Fear of Flying, Kinflicks, Sita* all foreground the writer struggling to turn her experience into literature, even if this figure loiters in the background in godlike omnipotence as in *The Women's Room.* Moreover, the "voice" of the central protagonist, if not presenting itself directly as the author's voice, frequently offers itself as "representative" of women in general, first claiming sexual experience as a vital terrain of all women's experience, sometimes also making generalities as to the oppressive nature of that experience. The distinctiveness of the genre has attracted attention; a *Sunday Times* color supplement heading shows one response to the self-consciously "representative" nature of these novels:

> Liberating the Libido. Getting sex straight was an essential first step along the noisy road to liberation; writing about it could be the next leap forward. Books by women surveying sex, and novels by women whose heroines savour sex are selling like hotdogs in America—beating men into second place and turning the authoresses into millionairesses at the drop of a hard-sell dust-jacket.

I have raised this here in order to show that we do have a recognizable group of novels whose roots are, in a variety of ways, in the women's liberation movement but that their relation to feminism is not the necessary outcome of taking women's experience as central. But other questions arise in relation to this statement, questions whether the "representativeness" these novels claim is simply a reflection of "feminist consciousness," or a propaganda device towards such a consciousness, or whether we have to be more cautious in analyzing their structure and effects.

The Commercial Success of the Novels That Change Lives

O'Rourke seems to imply that the widespread success of these novels can be attributed to a widespread diffusion of "feminist consciousness." In fact, the disparity between the print runs of these novels and political texts gives rise to the exactly opposite suspicion in more cynical minds. Perhaps the kind of writing involved in *Kinflicks* or *The Women's Room* corresponds more closely to the structures of popular fiction rather than satisfying the incipient feminism of the population. The fact is that the space occupied by these novels is not so radically different from the conventional structures which make up the "novelistic." In other words, that space of themes, modes of writing, hierarchies of appropriate statements which constitute these "feminist novels" is not so utterly unlike those of popular fiction in general. We can isolate several aspects of this correspondence.

A dominant element in contemporary fiction has been that of the "confessional" novel—the structuring of the novel, and the significant events of the narrative, around the voice of a principal protagonist describing her or his life. Novels like J. D. Salinger's *Catcher in the Rye* or *Lucky Jim* by

Kingsley Amis bear an exceptionally strong resemblance to feminist works such as Alice Munro's *Lives of Girls and Women* in this respect. But the similarity does not end here. For this structure has increasingly been characterized by the absolute centrality given to the experience of adolescence and young adulthood. In particular the experiences of this period have come to be almost synonymous with sexual experience. In drawing attention to the reception of feminist writers by the bourgeois press, I have already hinted how this preoccupation with the confession of sexual experience is one of the most characteristic features of contemporary feminist writings. Like the confessional novel in general, the novels by feminists also present the experience of sexuality as the significant experience of the novel. Whereas in romantic fiction (and indeed quite often in "the classics") it was the events leading to marriage, or events disrupting love, which occupied the position of significant events, increasingly sexual experience is becoming sufficient.

Certain points can be made about the confessional form of these novels and their preoccupation with sexuality. An obvious point is that speaking about sexuality, a preoccupation with sexuality, is not in and of itself progressive. Feminists have been involved for too long now in the analysis of images and ideologies to be conned into thinking that accounts of sexuality are progressive just because they take women's sexuality as their central concern. Criticism of pornography, which frequently highlights the sexual experiences of women, is just one example of representations of sexuality which feminists have actually contested.

It has been suggested that the centrality which the confession of sexuality has assumed and which is now an integral part of our culture does not in fact represent a radical break with the past. Michel Foucault, for example, has suggested that it represents a continuation of certain practices of dealing with sexuality which have been part of Western culture for several centuries.[4] He argues that sexuality has never been "repressed" as such but has been the object of a variety of discourses for several centuries. In the past these discourses were frequently directed towards the control or negation of certain sexual practices, as with the medical and educational discourses of the Victorian period: they nevertheless had sexuality as their object. In Catholic countries, he suggests that the practice of the church confessional was taken over into scientific and social discourses, where once again sexuality became an object to be interrogated, spoken about, controlled. Again and again, whatever the explicit aim of the discourses, sexuality was taken to be the element which revealed the "true" and "essential" nature of people. Foucault sees within this concern with sexuality the workings of power; the identity of the subject is found through discourses which multiply areas of pleasure and attention only to control, classify, subject. To deny a sudden rupture in the history of sexuality—from repression to liberation—does not mean that we have to go along with Foucault in suggesting that there have not been radical changes in the representations of sexuality themselves. For women, discourses on sexuality have changed importantly. That the equation of female sexuality with the illicit and disgusting is no longer a dominant representation, and that the possibilities of sexual enjoyment are no longer focused on motherhood, are changes for which feminism has fought.

Nevertheless, these ideas are useful in this context. They indicate how the centrality which sexuality has assumed in the novel, either coyly in romantic preoccupations or explicitly in the confession of sexual experiences, has definite correspondences with other social practices. Within the novel, the "confession" has appeared, structured by traditions, specific to the novel. In particular it has been influenced by the importance of narrative, which organizes a series of events or experiences as significant and progressing towards a meaningful conclusion. This space of time, or narrative, is one in which the central character or characters undergo an experience or series of experiences which radically affect their lives or transform their attitudes. The effect of this structure is to create a distinct ideology of knowledge and indeed life—that experience brings knowledge and possibly wisdom. But where women have been, and are, the central focus of the novel, a variation occurs. That variation is that the only space where knowledge or understanding for women is produced is across sexual experience—love, marriage, divorce, or just sex. In romance, for example, the significant space is that of encounter, love, (possibly) a hindrance, and marriage; understanding is finding the proper mate. It is rare to find a novel such as Jane Austen's *Emma* where the sentimental lesson is combined with an intellectual lesson, that of discretion. An examination of novelistic practices—customs of the single central character, "realistic" writing, the delineation of time as progressive and significant—would require a lengthy article, but it is sufficient to bring them forward here to indicate that women-centered novels are *not* the product of a feminist audience. Nor can we say that the structures of the realist novel are neutral and that they can just be filled with a feminist content. Indeed, it could be argued that the emergence of this particular form of "women's writing," with its emphasis on sexual experience as the source of significant experience, might have the effect of confirming women as bearers of sentiment, experience, and romance (albeit disillusioned).

It is quite clear that there are compelling similarities between "novels that change lives" and contemporary fictional conventions, which should warn us against any simple designation of these novels as feminist. This does not mean that we cannot say anything about the emergence of this group of novels in their specificity, nor does it mean that there is nothing progressive about these novels. First of all, it is clear that female sexuality (as distinct from just female emotions) is becoming more and more an object to be interrogated, in a variety of social practices—film, sociological, psychological, and "sexological" studies. The novel's own history—its confessional form, and its highlighting of sexual events as significant time—make it particularly responsive to this preoccupation. And this preoccupation undoubtedly at a certain level represents a response to a problem: what is female sexual pleasure? Thus, though feminist writing may well be compromised by its uncritical use of the conventional forms of the novel, it is also an important presence in a popular form of fiction.

But it would also be limited to suggest that all the novels which we loosely designate feminist never escape beyond defining women entirely by their sexuality. Occasionally some go beyond the limits of the conventional novelistic forms and preoccupations. Doris Lessing and Fay Weldon, for example, both occasionally disrupt the conventions of the central narrative voice or character, and their writings suddenly become a myriad of historical, social, and sexual concerns which do not "belong" to an individual subjectivity. Where sexuality is treated as political, this is occasionally the outcome, and is one of the most interesting aspects of novels like these.

It is by paying attention to practices of writing, conventions of genre, and their relation to other forms of writing that we can differentiate between novels and assess their political effects. And it is only in conjunction with an analysis of the conventions internal to the text that we can understand marketing strategies.

Publishing Practices and Women-Centered Novels

Rebecca O'Rourke suggests that commercial publishers are cashing in on feminism. I have already suggested that we cannot designate many of the novels she discusses as feminist in any simple sense. And a cursory glance at the marketing of these "women-centered" novels by commercial publishers confirms my view that they are often directed towards the popular fiction market. Look at the difference between the "sensationalist" cover of *Kinflicks* (a cover which many found incongruous with the content of the book) and the restful paintings which characterize the publications of the feminist publishing groups—paintings which lay claim for the novels as "classics."

There are undoubtedly important considerations in the relationship between commercial publishing groups and political movements, both socialist and feminist. You would have to be blind not to notice how the publication by commercial publishing houses of "women's studies" texts has proliferated. These sections clearly have a commercial viability, but their existence is no less the product of hard-fought battles of feminists within more conventional publishing groups. The kinds of numbers printed of "academic" feminist books are minimal compared with, say, *Kinflicks* (about 4,000 versus 50,000), but the issue seems to be similar. It is just not enough to regret the profits of commercial firms. In fact, such profits should be welcomed if they encourage groups with a mass market to invest in other such books. The question is much rather what is the relationship of the practice of reading, both of fiction and nonfiction, with political movements, in what way are texts effective, and, most important, which ones are. The passive relation which O'-Rourke assumes (that is, that these novels simply provide pleasure for the already converted) would surely be a cause for pessimism.

The Politics of Literature

Finally O'Rourke suggests that despite the regrettable fact that commercial publishers are making profits from profeminist texts, these texts should be welcomed as an "extension of available works for us to read." There are several points which could be made in relation to this assessment. Firstly, many of the texts which are mentioned already *were* available in certain forms. Many local libraries had countless copies of Mary Webb, Stella Gibbons, Winifred Holtby, and others. There is indeed a shift in forms of availability, in that these novels are being made available for feminists to buy as attractive commodities, but we should be clear that the "us" in question must be the ranks of feminists who prefer to own a novel rather than borrow from the public library, and have the cash to dispose of in this way. Secondly, many of these works have been available in different forms of media which are far more popular than the novel. Mary Webb was a popular source of cinema melodrama at one point (for example *Gone to Earth,* directed by Michael Powell in 1952); *South Riding* has been a TV serial and also a film (directed by Victor Saville in 1939); *Cold Comfort Farm* was televised. While the experience of different forms of the media can be quite different, it is nevertheless clear that there has been access to some of these writers and their ideas for a considerable time. What in fact has changed is the designation of these novels as having "literary significance" and their reintroduction as purchasable commodities. Thirdly, the assessment that these novels are to be welcomed as an extension of texts for "us" to read represents a fundamentally different approach to the question of the politics of literature from mine. These points of disagreement are not trivial quibbles. They are serious questions for feminism, asking what is the nature of the intervention of *feminist* publishers in the women's movement; what is its relation to commercial publishing; and, most important, in what way, if any, are we to relate the account of the "representative experience" of women in novels to feminist political questions. Of the first question, there are many ways in which the feminist publishers can be welcomed in much the same way Rebecca O'Rourke welcomes them—for giving space to young and committed feminist writers such as Michèle Roberts, for printing translations and American writings which have had little circulation, and so on. However, O'Rourke's account leaves no room for regret for the heavily "literary" bias of the ventures of Virago and the Women's Press—an emphasis which has, ironically, left many academic and political tracts to the province of commercial publishers.

On the second question, which is more difficult, it is to be regretted that O'Rourke can be read to imply that to describe experience typical of women was sufficient to justify calling that account "feminist." For this question is one that has been absolutely central to the women's movement, and it is still problematic and unresolved. It relates to the experience which is central to consciousness-raising. Consciousness-raising founded itself very much on the notion of "representative experience," hence the claim that "the personal is political." This slogan always rests on the swivel between two meanings. It is both the claim that what is political is more than just the governmental and the regulation of relations between the classes (as socialists often suggested), but also that to speak the personal and experiential was to go beyond it and to discover its "representativeness," which would show the workings of ideology and its relation to objective, material structures of oppression.

Yet it has frequently been recognized within feminism that consciousness-raising is never sufficient as a politics. Consciousness-raising groups frequently run into trouble themselves, where women find themselves experiencing antagonism and rivalries which had been assumed to be the private property of men. And, even when these groups do provide immense personal strength, support, and the experience of nonhierarchical collective work, they have difficulty in transforming this into any kind of effective politics. In fact, the politics which has tended to result from the assumption of this basis of unity has been a politics which assumes that men are equally united and "other" to women—they are inevitably different from and antagonistic towards women. For the most part, consciousness-raising no longer forms the heart of feminism; small groups which do still have a central place in feminist politics are now often either campaigning groups or study groups. But the question of how to articulate the discoveries of consciousness-raising with struggles over financial, legal, and other forms of social and sexual oppression is still crucial. For consciousness-raising and a variety of feminist writings demonstrated how oppression was not exclusively the effect of economic and legal discrimination. Oppression is also something which exists in personal relationships, in the relationships in the home, between "maleness" and "femaleness" (whether this occurs between men and women, or two people of the same sex), between parents and children. And the fight around these "ideological" relations is a fight of enormous importance for feminists. But it is a fight which cannot be waged by an appeal to the common experience of womankind. People are always crossed by a multitude of other interpellations, involving definite forms of recognition. Class background, racial difference, and educational differences all are sources of different experience. None of these factors is sufficient to generate a politics which corresponds to these experiences. Someone brought up in Stoke-on-Trent might experience a form of recognition in an Arnold Bennett novel, a recognition perhaps more powerful than that provoked by *The Women's Room,* yet this would in no way cause the reader to espouse Bennett's politics. In other words, the relationship between so-called representative experience and feminist politics is a much more problematic relation than that implied by Rebecca O'Rourke. Feminism can never be the product of the identity of women's experiences and interests—there is no such unity. Feminism must always be the alignment of women in a political movement with particular political aims and objectives. It is a grouping unified by its *political interests,* not its common experiences.

Finally, I think it is only if we raise such questions—questions of the institutions, politics of those institutions, the representations produced and circulated within those institutions and the assessment of those representations—that we can make any claim at all to a "feminist reading." And to ignore these questions is to neglect a vital tradition of feminism. Images, representations, words, are part of feminism's stock-in-trade. More than any other radical movement, feminism is aware of the material effects of images and words and the oppression or resistance which can be involved in them. This concern has motivated campaigns against oppressive stereotypes, has led to political and theoretical writing on the role of ideology seriously challenging earlier Marxist traditions, and has led to the strong presence of feminists in cultural politics—film, theater and literature. It would be a shame to consign this impressive tradition to the bourgeois literary critics and to suggest, that the novel is not an arena of political struggle but something we read on holiday when "real" politics are put aside with the boots and banners for a fortnight.

NOTES

The author would like to acknowledge the help of Judy Holder and the *Feminist Review* collective with this piece. Some of these ideas are explored further in *Female Desire* (London: Paladin, 1984).

[1]John Norman, *The Nomads of Gor* (London: Tandem, 1972).

[2]I refer to the tradition of semiological analysis, typified by the work of Roland Barthes, especially in *Mythologies,* trans. Annette Lavers (New York: Hill & Wang, 1972), and *S/Z,* trans. Richard Miller (New York: Hill & Wang, 1974). See also his *Image-Music-Text,* trans. Stephen Heath (New York: Hill & Wang, 1978). In Britain

this work has been developed primarily in the magazines *Screen* and *Screen Education,* publications of the Society for Education in Film and Television, 29 Old Compton Street, London WC1. For an application of this work to specifically feminist questions, see Judith Williamson, *Decoding Advertisements: Ideology and Meaning in Advertising* (Bridgeport, Conn.: Merrimack, 1978), and Jo Spence, "Class, Gender, Women," *Screen Education* (Winter 1978). For a discussion of issues relating to semiology, see Rosalind Coward and John Ellis, *Language and Materialism: Developments in Semiology and the Theory of the Subject* (London and New York: Routledge & Kegan Paul, 1977).

[3]Rebecca O'Rourke, "Summer Reading," *Feminist Review,* no. 2 (1979), p. 3.

[4]Michel Foucault, *The History of Sexuality,* vol. 1, *An Introduction,* trans. Robert Hurley (New York: Pantheon Books, 1978).

III

Women's Writing and Feminist Critical Theories

Feminist Criticism in the Wilderness

Elaine Showalter

Pluralism and the Feminist Critique

Women have no wilderness in them,
They are provident instead
Content in the tight hot cell of
their hearts
To eat dusty bread.

LOUISE BOGAN, "Women"

In a splendidly witty dialogue of 1975, Carolyn Heilbrun and Catharine Stimpson identified two poles of feminist literary criticism. The first of these modes, righteous, angry, and admonitory, they compared to the Old Testament, "looking for the sins and errors of the past." The second mode, disinterested and seeking "the grace of imagination," they compared to the New Testament. Both are necessary, they concluded, for only the Jeremiahs of ideology can lead us out of the "Egypt of female servitude" to the promised land of humanism.[1] Matthew Arnold also thought that literary critics might perish in the wilderness before they reached the promised land of disinterestedness; Heilbrun and Stimpson were neo-Arnoldian as befitted members of the Columbia and Barnard faculties. But if, in the 1980s, feminist literary critics are still wandering in the wilderness, we are in good company; for, as Geoffrey Hartman tells us, *all* criticism is in the wilderness.[2] Feminist critics may be startled to find ourselves in this band of theoretical pioneers, since in the American literary tradition the wilderness has been an exclusively masculine domain. Yet between feminist ideology and the liberal ideal of disinterestedness lies the wilderness of theory, which we too must make our home.

Until very recently, feminist criticism has not had a theoretical basis; it has been an empirical orphan in the theoretical storm. In 1975, I was persuaded that no theoretical manifesto could adequately account for the varied methodologies and ideologies which called themselves feminist reading or writing.[3] By the next year, Annette Kolodny had added her observation that feminist literary criticism appeared "more like a set of interchangeable strategies than any coherent school or shared goal orientation."[4] Since then, the expressed goals have not been notably unified. Black critics protest the "massive silence" of feminist criticism about black and Third-World women writers and call for a black feminist aesthetic that would deal with both racial and sexual politics. Marxist feminists wish to focus on class along with gender as a crucial determinant of literary production.[5] Literary historians want to uncover a lost tradition. Critics trained in deconstructionist methodologies wish to "synthesize a literary criticism that is both textual and feminist."[6] Freudian and Lacanian critics want to theorize about women's relationship to language and signification.

An early obstacle to constructing a theoretical framework for feminist criticism was the unwillingness of many women to limit or bound an expressive and dynamic enterprise. The openness of feminist criticism appealed particularly to Americans who perceived the structuralist, post-structuralist, and deconstructionist debates of the 1970s as arid and falsely objective, the epitome of a pernicious masculine discourse from which many feminists wished to escape. Recalling in *A Room of One's Own* how she had been prohibited from entering the university library, the symbolic sanctuary of the male *logos,* Virginia Woolf wisely observed that while it is "unpleasant to be locked out . . . it is worse, perhaps, to be locked in." Advocates of the antitheoretical position traced their descent from Woolf and from other feminist visionaries, such as Mary Daly, Adrienne Rich, and Marguerite Duras, who had satirized the sterile narcissism of male scholarship and celebrated women's fortunate exclusion from its patriarchal methodolatry. Thus for some, feminist criticism was an act of resistance to theory, a confrontation with existing canons and judgments, what Josephine Donovan calls "a mode of negation within a fundamental dialectic." As Judith Fetterley declared in her book, *The Resisting Reader,* feminist criticism has been characterized by "a resistance to codification and a refusal to have its parameters prematurely set." I have discussed elsewhere, with considerable sympathy, the suspicion of monolithic systems and the rejection of scientism in literary study that many feminist critics have voiced. While scientific criticism struggled to purge itself of the subjective, feminist criticism reasserted the authority of experience.[7]

Yet it now appears that what looked like a theoretical impasse was actually an evolutionary phase. The ethics of awakening have been succeeded, at least in the universities, by a second stage characterized by anxiety about the isolation of feminist criticism from a critical community increasingly theoretical in its interests and indifferent to women's writing. The question of how feminist criticism should define itself with relation to the new critical theories and theorists has occasioned sharp debate in Europe and the United States. Nina Auerbach has noted the absence of dialogue and asks whether feminist criticism itself must accept responsibility:

> Feminist critics seem particularly reluctant to define themselves to the uninitiated. There is a sense in which our sisterhood has become too powerful; as a school, our belief in ourself is so potent that we decline communication with the networks of power and respectability we say we want to change.[8]

But rather than declining communication with these networks, feminist criticism has indeed spoken directly to them, in their own media: *PMLA, Diacritics, Glyph, Tel Quel, New Literary History,* and *Critical Inquiry.* For the feminist critic seeking clarification, the proliferation of communiqués may itself prove confusing.

There are two distinct modes of feminist criticism, and to conflate them (as most commentators do) is to remain permanently bemused by their theoretical potentialities. The first mode is ideological; it is concerned with the feminist as *reader,* and it offers feminist readings of texts which consider the images and stereotypes of women in literature, the omissions and misconceptions about women in criticism, and woman-assign in semiotic systems. This is not all feminist reading can do; it can be a liberating intellectual act, as Adrienne Rich proposes:

> A radical critique of literature, feminist in its impulse, would take the work first of all as a clue to how we live, how we have been living, how we have been led to imagine ourselves, how our language has trapped as well as liberated us, how the very act of naming has been till now a male prerogative, and how we can begin to see and name—and therefore live —afresh.[9]

This invigorating encounter with literature, which I will call *feminist reading* or the *feminist critique,* is in essence a mode of interpretation, one of many which any complex text will accommodate and permit. It is very difficult to propose theoretical coherence in an activity which by its nature is so eclectic and wide-ranging, although as a critical practice feminist reading has certainly been very influential. But in the free play of the interpretive field, the feminist critique can only compete with alternative readings, all of which have the built-in obsolescence of Buicks, cast away as newer readings take their place. As Kolodny, the most sophisticated theorist of feminist interpretation, has conceded:

> All the feminist is asserting, then, is her own equivalent right to liberate new (and perhaps different) significances from these same texts; and, at the same time, her right to choose which features of a text she takes as relevant because she is, after all, asking new and different questions of it. In the process, she claims neither definitiveness nor structural completeness for her different readings and reading systems, but only their usefulness in recognizing the particular achievements of woman-as-author and their applicability in conscientiously decoding woman-as-sign.

Rather than being discouraged by these limited objectives, Kolodny found them the happy cause of the "playful pluralism" of feminist critical theory, a pluralism which she believes to be "the only critical stance consistent with the current status of the larger women's movement."[10] Her feminist critic dances adroitly through the theoretical minefield.

Keenly aware of the political issues involved and presenting brilliant arguments, Kolodny nonetheless fails to convince me that feminist criticism must altogether abandon its hope "of establishing some basic conceptual model." If we see our critical job as interpretation and reinterpretation, we must be content with pluralism as our critical stance. But if we wish to ask questions about the process and the contexts of writing, if we genuinely wish to define ourselves to the uninitiated, we cannot rule out the prospect of theoretical consensus at this early stage.

All feminist criticism is in some sense revisionist, questioning the adequacy of accepted conceptual structures, and indeed most contemporary American criticism claims to be revisionist too. The most exciting and comprehensive case for this "revisionary imperative" is made by Sandra Gilbert: at its most ambitious, she asserts, feminist criticism "wants to decode and demystify all the disguised questions and answers that have always shadowed the connections between textuality and sexuality, genre and gender, psychosexual identity and cultural authority."[11] But in practice, the revisionary feminist critique is redressing a grievance and is built upon existing models. No one would deny that feminist criticism has affinities to other contemporary critical practices and methodologies and that the best work is also the most fully informed. Nonetheless, the feminist obsession with correcting, modifying, supplementing, revising, humanizing, or even attacking male critical theory keeps us dependent upon it and retards our progress in solving our own theoretical problems. What I mean here by "male critical theory" is a concept of creativity, literary history, or literary interpretation based entirely on male experience and put forward as universal. So long as we look to androcentric models for our most basic principles—even if we revise them by adding the feminist frame of reference—we are learning nothing new. And when the process is so one-sided, when male critics boast of their ignorance of feminist criticism, it is disheartening to find feminist critics still anxious for approval from the "white fathers" who will not listen or reply. Some feminist critics have taken upon themselves a revisionism which becomes a kind of homage; they have made Lacan the ladies' man of *Diacritics* and have forced Pierre Macherey into those dark alleys of the psyche where Engels feared to tread. According to Christiane Makward, the problem is even more serious in France than in the United States: "If neofeminist thought in France seems to have ground to a halt," she writes, "it is because it has continued to feed on the discourse of the masters."[12]

It is time for feminist criticism to decide whether between religion and revision we can claim any firm theoretical ground of our own. In calling for a feminist criticism that is genuinely women centered, independent, and intellectually coherent, I do not mean to endorse the separatist fantasies of radical feminist visionaries or to exclude from our critical practice a variety of intellectual tools. But we need to ask much more searchingly what we want to know and how we can find answers to the questions that come from *our* experience. I do not think that feminist criticism can find a usable past in the androcentric critical tradition. It has more to learn from women's studies than from English studies, more to learn from international feminist theory than from another seminar on the masters. It must find its own subject, its own system, its own theory, and its own voice. As Rich writes of Emily Dickinson, in her poem "I Am in Danger—Sir—," we must choose to have the argument out at last on our own premises.

Defining the Feminine: Gynocritics and the Woman's Text

> *A woman's writing is always feminine; it cannot help being feminine; at its best it is most feminine; the only difficulty lies in defining what we mean by feminine.*
>
> VIRGINIA WOOLF

> *It is impossible to* define *a feminine practice of writing, and this is an impossibility that will remain, for this practice will*

> *never be theorized, enclosed, encoded—which doesn't mean that it doesn't exist.*
>
> Hélène Cixous, "The Laugh of the Medusa"

In the past decade, I believe, this process of defining the feminine has started to take place. Feminist criticism has gradually shifted its center from revisionary readings to a sustained investigation of literature by women. The second mode of feminist criticism engendered by this process is the study of women *as writers,* and its subjects are the history, styles, themes, genres, and structures of writing by women; the psychodynamics of female creativity; the trajectory of the individual or collective female career; and the evolution and laws of a female literary tradition. No English term exists for such a specialized critical discourse, and so I have invented the term "gynocritics." Unlike the feminist critique, gynocritics offers many theoretical opportunities. To see women's writing as our primary subject forces us to make the leap to a new conceptual vantage point and to redefine the nature of the theoretical problem before us. It is no longer the ideological dilemma of reconciling revisionary pluralisms but the essential question of difference. How can we constitute women as a distinct literary group? What is *the difference* of women's writing?

Patricia Meyer Spacks, I think, was the first academic critic to notice this shift from an androcentric to a gynocentric feminist criticism. In *The Female Imagination* (1975), she pointed out that few feminist theorists had concerned themselves with women's writing. Simone de Beauvoir's treatment of women writers in *The Second Sex* "always suggests an a priori tendency to take them less seriously than their masculine counterparts"; Mary Ellmann, in *Thinking about Women,* characterized women's literary success as escape from the categories of womanhood; and, according to Spacks, Kate Millett, in *Sexual Politics,* "has little interest in woman imaginative writers."[13] Spacks' wide-ranging study inaugurated a new period of feminist literary history and criticism which asked, again and again, how women's writing had been different, how womanhood itself shaped women's creative expression. In such books as Ellen Moers's *Literary Women* (1976), my *A Literature of Their Own* (1977), Nina Baym's *Woman's Fiction* (1978), Sandra Gilbert and Susan Gubar's *The Madwoman in the Attic* (1979), and Margaret Homans's *Women Writers and Poetic Identity* (1980), and in hundreds of essays and papers, women's writing asserted itself as the central project of feminist literary study.

This shift in emphasis has also taken place in European feminist criticism. To date, most commentary on French feminist critical discourse has stressed its fundamental dissimilarity from the empirical American orientation, its unfamiliar intellectual grounding in linguistics, Marxism, neo-Freudian and Lacanian psychoanalysis, and Derridean deconstruction. Despite these differences, however, the new French feminisms have much in common with radical American feminist theories in terms of intellectual affiliations and rhetorical energies. The concept of *écriture féminine,* the inscription of the female body and female difference in language and text, is a significant theoretical formulation in French feminist criticism, although it describes a Utopian possibility rather than a literary practice. Hélène Cixous, one of the leading advocates of *écriture féminine,* has admitted that, with only a few exceptions, "there has not yet been any writing that inscribes femininity," and Nancy Miller explains that *écriture féminine* "privileges a textuality of the avant-garde, a literary production of the late twentieth century, and it is therefore fundamentally a hope, if not a blueprint, for the future."[14] Nonetheless, the concept of *écriture féminine* provides a way of talking about women's writing which reasserts the *value* of the feminine and identifies the theoretical project of feminist criticism as the analysis of difference. In recent years, the translations of important work by Julia Kristeva, Cixous, and Luce Irigaray and the excellent collection *New French Feminisms* have made French criticism much more accessible to American feminist scholars.[15]

English feminist criticism, which incorporates French feminist and Marxist theory but is more traditionally oriented to textual interpretation, is also moving toward a focus on women's writing.[16] The emphasis in each country falls somewhat differently: English feminist criticism, essentially Marxist, stresses oppression; French feminist criticism, essentially psychoanalytic, stresses repression; American feminist criticism, essentially textual, stresses expression. All, however, have become gynocentric. All are struggling to find a terminology that can rescue the feminine from its stereotypical associations with inferiority.

Defining the unique difference of women's writing, as Woolf and Cixous have warned, must present a slippery and demanding task. Is difference a matter of style? Genre? Experience? Or is it produced by the reading process, as some textual critics would maintain? Spacks calls the difference of women's writing a "delicate divergency," testifying to the subtle and elusive nature of the feminine practice of writing. Yet the delicate divergency of the woman's text challenges us to respond with equal delicacy and precision to the small but crucial deviations, the cumulative weightings of experience and exclusion, that have marked the history of women's writing. Before we can chart this history, we must uncover it, patiently and scrupulously; our theories must be firmly grounded in reading and research. But we have the opportunity, through gynocritics, to learn something solid, enduring, and real about the relation of women to literary culture.

Theories of women's writing presently make use of four models of difference: biological, linguistic, psychoanalytic, and cultural. Each is an effort to define and differentiate the qualities of the woman writer and the woman's text; each model also represents a school of gynocentric feminist criticism with its own favorite texts, styles, and methods. They overlap but are roughly sequential in that each incorporates the one before. I shall try now to sort out the various terminologies and assumptions of these four models of difference and evaluate their usefulness.

Women's Writing and Woman's Body

More body, hence more writing.

Cixous, "The Laugh of the Medusa"

Organic or biological criticism is the most extreme statement of gender difference, of a text indelibly marked by the body: anatomy is textuality. Biological criticism is also one of the most sibylline and perplexing theoretical formulations of feminist criticism. Simply to invoke anatomy risks a return to the crude essentialism, the phallic and ovarian theories of art, that oppressed women in the past. Victorian physicians believed that women's physiological functions diverted about twenty percent of their creative energy from brain activity. Victorian anthropologists believed that the frontal lobes of the male brain were heavier and more developed than female lobes and thus that women were inferior in intelligence.

While feminist criticism rejects the attribution of literal biological inferiority, some theorists seem to have accepted the *metaphorical* implications of female biological difference in writing. In *The Madwoman in the Attic,* for example, Gilbert and Gubar structure their analysis of women's writing around metaphors of literary paternity. "In patriarchal western culture," they maintain, ". . . the text's author is a father, a progenitor, a procreator, an aesthetic patriarch whose pen is an instrument of generative power like his penis." Lacking phallic authority, they go on to suggest, women's writing is profoundly marked by the anxieties of this difference: "If the pen is a metaphorical penis, from what organ can females generate texts?"[17]

To this rhetorical question Gilbert and Gubar offer no reply; but it is a serious question of much feminist theoretical discourse. Those critics who, like myself, would protest the fundamental analogy might reply that women generate texts from the brain or that the word-processor, with its compactly coded microchips, its inputs and outputs, is a metaphorical womb. The metaphor of literary paternity, as Auerbach has pointed out in her review of *The Madwoman,* ignores "an equally timeless and, for me, even more oppressive metaphorical equation between literary creativity and childbirth."[18] Certainly metaphors of literary *maternity* predominated in the eighteenth and nineteenth centuries; the process of literary creation is analogically much more similar to gestation, labor, and delivery than it is to insemination. Describing Thackeray's plan for *Henry Esmond,* for example, Douglas Jerrold jovially remarked, "You have heard, I suppose, that Thackeray is big with twenty parts, and unless he is wrong in his time, expects the first installment at Christmas."[19] (If to write is metaphorically to give birth, from what organ can males generate texts?)

Some radical feminist critics, primarily in France but also in the United States, insist that we must read these metaphors as more than playful; that we must seriously rethink and redefine biological differentiation and its relation to women's writing. They argue that "women's writing proceeds from the body, that our sexual differentiation is also our source."[20] In *Of Woman Born,* Rich explains her belief that

> female biology . . . has far more radical implications than we have yet come to appreciate. Patriarchal thought has limited female biology to its own narrow specifications. The feminist vision has recoiled from female biology for these reasons; it will, I believe, come to view our physicality as a resource rather than a destiny. In order to live a fully human life, we require not only *control* of our bodies . . . we must touch the unity and resonance of our physicality, the corporeal ground of our intelligence.[21]

Feminist criticism written in the biological perspective generally stresses the importance of the body as a source of imagery. Alicia Ostriker, for example, argues that contemporary American women poets use a franker, more pervasive anatomical imagery than their male counterparts and that this insistent body language refuses the spurious transcendence that comes at the price of denying the flesh. In a fascinating essay on Whitman and Dickinson, Terence Diggory shows that physical nakedness, so potent a poetic symbol of authenticity for Whitman and other male poets, had very different connotations for Dickinson and her successors, who associated nakedness with the objectified or sexually exploited female nude and who chose instead protective images of the armored self.[22]

Feminist criticism which itself tries to be biological, to write from the critic's body, has been intimate, confessional, often innovative in style and form. Rachel Blau DuPlessis's "Washing Blood," the introduction to a special issue of *Feminist Studies* on the subject of motherhood, proceeds, in short lyrical paragraphs, to describe her own experience in adopting a child, to recount her dreams and nightmares, and to meditate upon the "healing unification of body and mind based not only on the lived experiences of motherhood as a social institution . . . but also on a biological power speaking through us."[23] Such criticism makes itself defiantly vulnerable, virtually bares its throat to the knife, since our professional taboos against self-revelation are so strong. When it succeeds, however, it achieves the power and the dignity of art. Its existence is an implicit rebuke to women critics who continue to write, according to Rich, "from somewhere outside their female bodies." In comparison to this flowing confessional criticism, the tight-lipped Olympian intelligence of such texts as Elizabeth Hardwick's *Seduction and Betrayal* or Susan Sontag's *Illness as Metaphor* can seem arid and strained.

Yet in its obsessions with the "corporeal ground of our intelligence," feminist biocriticism can also become cruelly prescriptive. There is a sense in which the exhibition of bloody wounds becomes an initiation ritual quite separate and disconnected from critical insight. And as the editors of the journal *Questions féministes* point out, "it is . . . dangerous to place the body at the center of a search for female identity. . . . The themes of otherness and of the Body merge together, because the most visible difference between men and women, and the only one we know for sure to be permanent . . . is indeed the difference in body. This difference has been used as a pretext to 'justify' full power of one sex over the other" (trans. Yvonne Rochette-Ozzello, *NFF*, p. 218). The study of biological imagery in women's writing is useful and important as long as we understand that factors other than anatomy are involved in it. Ideas about the body are fundamental to understanding how women conceptualize their situation in society; but there can be no expression of the body which is unmediated by linguistic, social, and literary structures. The difference of woman's literary practice, therefore, must be sought (in Miller's words) in "the body of her writing and not the writing of her body."[24]

Women's Writing and Women's Language

> *The women say, the language you speak poisons your glottis tongue palate lips. They say, the language you speak is made up of words that are killing you. They say, the language you speak is made up of signs that rightly speaking designate what men have appropriated.*
>
> Monique Wittig, *Les Guérillères*

Linguistic and textual theories of women's writing ask whether men and women use language differently; whether sex differences in language use can be theorized in terms of biology, socialization, or culture; whether women can create new languages of their own; and whether speaking, reading, and writing are all gender marked. American, French, and British feminist critics have all drawn attention to the philosophical, linguistic, and practical problems of women's use of language, and the debate over language is one of the most exciting areas in gynocritics. Poets and writers have led the attack on what Rich calls "the oppressor's language," a language sometimes criticized as sexist, sometimes as abstract. But the problem goes well beyond reformist efforts to purge language of its sexist aspects. As Nelly Furman explains, "It is through the medium of language that we define and categorize areas of difference and similarity, which in turn allow us to comprehend the world around us. Male-centered categorizations predominate in American English and subtly shape our understanding and perception of reality; this is why attention is increasingly directed to the inherently oppressive aspects for women of a male-constructed language system."[25] According to Carolyn Burke, the language system is at the center of French feminist theory:

> The central issue in much recent women's writing in France is to find and use an appropriate female language. Language is the place to begin: a *prise de conscience* must be followed by a *prise de la parole*. . . . In this view, the very forms of the dominant mode of discourse show the mark of the dominant masculine ideology. Hence, when a woman writes or speaks herself into existence, she is forced to speak in something like a foreign tongue, a language with which she may be personally uncomfortable.[26]

Many French feminists advocate a revolutionary linguism, an oral break from the dictatorship of patriarchal speech. Annie Leclerc, in *Parole de femme,* calls on women "to invent a language that is not oppressive, a language that does not leave speechless but that loosens the tongue" (trans. Courtivron, *NFF,* p. 179). Chantal Chawaf, in an essay on "La chair linguistique," connects biofeminism and linguism in the view that women's language and a genuinely feminine practice of writing will articulate the body:

> In order to reconnect the book with the body and with pleasure, we must disintellectualize writing. . . . And this language, as it develops, will not degenerate and dry up, will not go back to the fleshless academicism, the stereotypical and servile discourses that we reject.
>
> . . . Feminine language must, by its very nature, work on life passionately, scientifically, poetically, politically in order to make it invulnerable. [Trans. Rochette-Ozzello, *NFF,* pp. 177–78]

But scholars who want a women's language that *is* intellectual and theoretical, that works *inside* the academy, are faced with what seems like an impossible paradox, as Xavière Gauthier has lamented: "As long as women remain silent, they will be outside the historical process. But, if they begin to speak and write *as men do,* they will enter history subdued and alienated; it is a history that, logically speaking, their speech should disrupt" (trans. Marilyn A. August, *NFF,* pp. 162–63). What we need, Mary Jacobus has proposed, is a women's writing that works within "male" discourse but works "ceaselessly to deconstruct it: to write what cannot be written," and according to Shoshana Felman, "the challenge facing the woman today is nothing less than to 'reinvent' language, . . . to speak not only against, but outside of the specular phallogocentric structure, to establish a discourse the status of which would no longer be defined by the phallacy of masculine meaning."[27]

Beyond rhetoric, what can linguistic, historical, and anthropological research tell us about the prospects for a women's language? First of all, the concept of a women's language is not original with feminist criticism; it is very ancient and appears frequently in folklore and myth. In such myths, the essence of women's language is its secrecy; what is really being described is the male fantasy of the enigmatic nature of the feminine. Herodotus, for example, reported that the Amazons were able linguists who easily mastered the languages of their male antagonists, although men could never learn the women's tongue. In *The White Goddess,* Robert Graves romantically argues that a women's language existed in a matriarchal stage of prehistory; after a great battle of the sexes, the matriarchy was overthrown and the women's language went underground, to survive in the mysterious cults of Eleusis and Corinth and the witch covens of Western Europe. Travelers and missionaries in the seventeenth and eighteenth centuries brought back accounts of "women's languages" among American Indians, Africans, and Asians (the differences in linguistic structure they reported were usually superficial). There is some ethnographic evidence that in certain cultures women have evolved a private form of communication out of their need to resist the silence imposed upon them in public life. In ecstatic religions, for example, women, more frequently than men, speak in tongues, a phenomenon attributed by anthropologists to their relative inarticulateness in formal religious discourse. But such ritualized and unintelligible female "languages" are scarcely cause for rejoicing; indeed, it was because witches were suspected of esoteric knowledge and possessed speech that they were burned.[28]

From a political perspective, there are interesting parallels between the feminist problem of a women's language and the recurring "language issue" in the general history of decolonization. After a revolution, a new state must decide which language to make official: the language that is "psychologically immediate," that allows "the kind of force that speaking one's mother tongue permits"; or the language that "is an avenue to the wider community of modern culture," a community to whose movements of thought only "foreign" languages can give access.[29] The language issue in feminist criticism has emerged, in a sense, after our revolution, and it reveals the tensions in the women's movement between those who would stay outside the academic establishments and the institutions of criticism and those who would enter and even conquer them.

The advocacy of a women's language is thus a political gesture that also carries tremendous emotional force. But despite its unifying appeal, the concept of a women's language is riddled with difficulties. Unlike Welsh, Breton, Swahili, or Amharic, that is, languages of minority or colonized groups, there is no mother tongue, no genderlect spoken by the female population in a society, which differs significantly from the dominant language. English and American linguists agree that "there is absolutely no evidence that would suggest the sexes are preprogrammed to develop structurally different linguistic systems." Furthermore, the many specific differences in male and female speech, intonation, and language use that have been identified cannot be explained in terms of "two separate sex-specific languages" but need to be considered instead in terms of styles, strategies, and contexts of linguistic performance.[30] Efforts at quantitative analysis of language in texts by men or women, such as Mary Hiatt's computerized study of contemporary fiction, *The Way Women Write* (1977), can easily be attacked for treating words apart from their meanings and purposes. At a higher level, analyses which look for "feminine style" in the repetition of stylistic devices, image patterns, and syntax in women's writing tend to confuse innate forms with the overdetermined results of literary choice. Language and style are never raw and instinctual but are always the products of innumerable factors, of genre, tradition, memory, and context.

The appropriate task for feminist criticism, I believe, is to concentrate on women's access to language, on the available lexical range from which words can be selected, on the ideological and cultural determinants of expression. The problem is not that language is insufficient to express women's consciousness but that women have been denied the full resources of language and have been forced into silence, euphemism, or circumlocution. In a series of drafts for a lecture on women's writing (drafts which she discarded or suppressed), Woolf protested against the censorship which cut off female access to language. Comparing herself to Joyce, Woolf noted the differences between their verbal territories: "Now men are shocked if a woman says what she feels (as Joyce does). Yet literature which is always pulling down blinds is not literature.

All that we have ought to be expressed—mind and body—a process of incredible difficulty and danger."[31]

"All that we have ought to be expressed—mind and body." Rather than wishing to limit women's linguistic range, we must fight to open and extend it. The holes in discourse, the blanks and gaps and silences, are not the spaces where female consciousness reveals itself but the blinds of a "prison-house of language." Women's literature is still haunted by the ghosts of repressed language, and until we have exorcised those ghosts, it ought not to be in language that we base our theory of difference.

Women's Writing and Woman's Psyche

Psychoanalytically oriented feminist criticism locates the difference of women's writing in the author's psyche and in the relation of gender to the creative process. It incorporates the biological and linguistic models of gender difference in a theory of the female psyche or self, shaped by the body, by the development of language, and by sex-role socialization. Here too there are many difficulties to overcome; the Freudian model requires constant revision to make it gynocentric. In one grotesque early example of Freudian reductivism, Theodor Reik suggested that women have fewer writing blocks than men because their bodies are constructed to facilitate release: "Writing, as Freud told us at the end of his life, is connected with urinating, which physiologically is easier for a woman—they have a wider bladder."[32] Generally, however, psychoanalytic criticism has focused not on the capacious bladder (could this be the organ from which females generate texts?) but on the absent phallus. Penis envy, the castration complex, and the Oedipal phase have become the Freudian coordinates defining women's relationship to language, fantasy, and culture. Currently the French psychoanalytic school dominated by Lacan has extended castration into a total metaphor for female literary and linguistic disadvantage. Lacan theorizes that the acquisition of language and the entry into its symbolic order occurs at the Oedipal phase in which the child accepts his or her gender identity. This stage requires an acceptance of the phallus as a privileged signification and a consequent female displacement, as Cora Kaplan has explained:

> The phallus as a signifier has a central, crucial position in language, for if language embodies the patriarchal law of the culture, its basic meanings refer to the recurring process by which sexual difference and subjectivity are acquired. . . . Thus the little girl's access to the Symbolic, i.e., to language

> and its laws, is always negative and/or mediated by intro-subjective relation to a third term, for it is characterized by an identification with lack.[33]

In psychoanalytic terms, "lack" has traditionally been associated with the feminine, although Lac(k)anian critics can now make their statements linguistically. Many feminists believe that psychoanalysis could become a powerful tool for literary criticism, and recently there has been a renewed interest in Freudian theory. But feminist criticism based in Freudian or post-Freudian psychoanalysis must continually struggle with the problem of feminine disadvantage and lack. In *The Madwoman in the Attic,* Gilbert and Gubar carry out a feminist revision of Harold Bloom's Oedipal model of literary history as a conflict between fathers and sons and accept the essential psychoanalytic definition of the woman artist as displaced, disinherited, and excluded. In their view, the nature and "difference" of women's writing lies in its troubled and even tormented relationship to female identity; the woman writer experiences her own gender as "a painful obstacle or even a debilitating inadequacy." The nineteenth-century woman writer inscribed her own sickness, her madness, her anorexia, her agoraphobia, and her paralysis in her texts; and although Gilbert and Gubar are dealing specifically with the nineteenth century, the range of their allusion and quotation suggests a more general thesis:

> Thus the loneliness of the female artist, her feelings of alienation from male predecessors coupled with her need for sisterly precursors and successors, her urgent sense of her need for a female audience together with her fear of the antagonism of male readers, her culturally conditioned timidity about self-dramatization, her dread of the patriarchal authority of art, her anxiety about the impropriety of female invention—all these phenomena of "inferiorization" mark the woman writer's struggle for artistic self-definition and differentiate her efforts at self-creation from those of her male counterpart.[34]

In "Emphasis Added," Miller takes another approach to the problem of negativity in psychoanalytic criticism. Her strategy is to expand Freud's view of female creativity and to show how criticism of women's texts has frequently been unfair because it has been based in Freudian expectations. In his essay "The Relation of the Poet to Daydreaming" (1908), Freud maintained that the unsatisfied dreams and desires of women are chiefly erotic; these are the desires that shape the plots of women's fiction. In contrast, the dominant fantasies behind men's plots are egoistic and ambitious as well as erotic. Miller shows how women's plots have been granted or denied credibility in terms of their conformity to this phallocentric model and that a gynocentric reading reveals a repressed egoistic/ambitious fantasy in women's writing as well as in men's. Women's novels which are centrally concerned with fantasies of romantic love belong to the category disdained by George Eliot and other serious women writers as "silly novels"; the smaller number of women's novels which inscribe a fantasy of power imagine a world for women outside of love, a world, however, made impossible by social boundaries.

There has also been some interesting feminist literary criticism based on alternatives to Freudian psychoanalytic theory: Annis Pratt's Jungian history of female archetypes, Barbara Rigney's Laingian study of the divided self in women's fiction, and Ann Douglas's Eriksonian analysis of inner space in nineteenth-century women's writing.[35] And for the past few years, critics have been thinking about the possibilities of a new feminist psychoanalysis that does *not* revise Freud but instead emphasizes the development and construction of gender identities.

The most dramatic and promising new work in feminist psychoanalysis looks at the pre-Oedipal phase and at the process of psychosexual differentiation. Nancy Chodorow's *The Reproduction of Mothering: Psychoanalysis and the Sociology of Gender* (1978) has had an enormous influence on women's studies. Chodorow revises traditional psychoanalytic concepts of differentiation, the process by which the child comes to perceive the self as separate and to develop ego and body boundaries. Since differentiation takes place in relation to the mother (the primary caretaker), attitudes toward the mother "emerge in the earliest differentiation of the self"; "the mother, who is a woman, becomes and remains for children of both genders the other, or object."[36] The child develops core gender identity concomitantly with differentiation, but the process is not the same for boys and girls. A boy must learn his gender identity negatively as being not-female, and this difference requires continual reinforcement. In contrast, a girl's core gender identity is positive and built upon sameness, continuity, and identification with the mother. Women's difficulties with feminine identity come after the Oedipal phase, in which male power and cultural hegemony give sex differences a transformed value. Chodorow's work suggests that shared parenting, the involvement of men as primary caretakers of children, will have a profound effect on our sense of sex difference, gender identity, and sexual preference.

But what is the significance of feminist psychoanalysis for literary criticism? One thematic carry-over has been a critical interest in the mother-daughter configuration as a source of female creativity.[37] Elizabeth Abel's bold investigation of female friendship in contemporary women's novels uses

Chodorow's theory to show how not only the relationships of women characters but also the relationship of women writers to each other are determined by the psychodynamics of female bonding. Abel too confronts Bloom's paradigm of literary history, but unlike Gilbert and Gubar she sees a "triadic female pattern" in which the Oedipal relation to the male tradition is balanced by the woman writer's pre-Oedipal relation to the female tradition. "As the dynamics of female friendship differ from those of male," Abel concludes, "the dynamics of female literary influence also diverge and deserve a theory of influence attuned to female psychology and to women's dual position in literary history."[38]

Like Gilbert, Gubar, and Miller, Abel brings together women's texts from a variety of national literatures, choosing to emphasize "the constancy of certain emotional dynamics depicted in diverse cultural situations." Yet the privileging of gender implies not only the constancy but also the immutability of these dynamics. Although psychoanalytically based models of feminist criticism can now offer us remarkable and persuasive readings of individual texts and can highlight extraordinary similarities between women writing in a variety of cultural circumstances, they cannot explain historical change, ethnic difference, or the shaping force of generic and economic factors. To consider these issues, we must go beyond psychoanalysis to a more flexible and comprehensive model of women's writing which places it in the maximum context of culture.

Women's Writing and Women's Culture

> *I consider women's literature as a specific category, not because of biology, but because it is, in a sense, the literature of the colonized.*
>
> CHRISTIANE ROCHEFORT,
> "The Privilege of Consciousness"

A theory based on a model of women's culture can provide, I believe, a more complete and satisfying way to talk about the specificity and difference of women's writing than theories based in biology, linguistics, or psychoanalysis. Indeed, a theory of culture incorporates ideas about women's body, language, and psyche but interprets them in relation to the social contexts in which they occur. The ways in which women conceptualize their bodies and their sexual and reproductive functions are intricately linked to their cultural environments. The female psyche can be studied as the product or construction of cultural forces. Language, too, comes back into the picture, as we consider the social dimensions and determinants of language use, the shaping of linguistic behavior by cultural ideals. A cultural theory acknowledges that there are important differences between women as writers: class, race, nationality, and history are literary determinants as significant as gender. Nonetheless, women's culture forms a collective experience within the cultural whole, an experience that binds women writers to each other over time and space. It is in the emphasis on the binding force of women's culture that this approach differs from Marxist theories of cultural hegemony.

Hypotheses of women's culture have been developed over the last decade primarily by anthropologists, sociologists, and social historians in order to get away from masculine systems, hierarchies, and values and to get at the primary and self-defined nature of female cultural experience. In the field of women's history, the concept of women's culture is still controversial, although there is agreement on its significance as a theoretical formulation. Gerda Lerner explains the importance of examining women's experience in its own terms:

> Women have been left out of history not because of the evil conspiracies of men in general or male historians in particular, but because we have considered history only in male-centered terms. We have missed women and their activities, because we have asked questions of history which are inappropriate to women. To rectify this, and to light up areas of historical darkness we must, for a time, focus on a *woman-centered* inquiry, considering the possibility of the existence of a female culture *within* the general culture shared by men and women. History must include an account of the female experience over time and should include the development of feminist consciousness as an essential aspect of women's past. This is the primary task of women's history. The central question it raises is: What would history be like if it were seen through the eyes of women and ordered by values they define?[39]

In defining female culture, historians distinguish between the roles, activities, tastes, and behaviors prescribed and considered appropriate for women and those activities, behaviors, and functions actually generated out of women's lives. In the late-eighteenth and nineteenth centuries, the term "woman's sphere" expressed the Victorian and Jacksonian vision of separate roles for men and women, with little or no overlap and with women subordinate. Woman's sphere was defined and maintained by men, but women frequently internalized its precepts in the American "cult of true womanhood" and the English "feminine ideal." Women's culture, however, redefines women's "activities and goals from a woman-centered point of view. . . . The term implies an assertion of equality and an awareness of sisterhood, the communality of women." Women's culture refers to "the broad-based communality of values, institutions, relationships, and methods of communication" unifying nineteenth-century female experience, a culture nonetheless with significant variants by class and ethnic group (*MFP,* pp. 52, 54).

Some feminist historians have accepted the model of separate spheres and have seen the movement from woman's sphere to women's culture to women's-rights activism as the consecutive stages of an evolutionary political process. Others see a more complex and perpetual negotiation taking place between women's culture and the general culture. As Lerner has argued:

> It is important to understand that "woman's culture" is not and should not be seen as a subculture. It is hardly possible for the majority to live in a subculture. . . . Women live their social existence within the general culture and, whenever they are confined by patriarchal restraint or segregation into separateness (which always has subordination as its purpose), they transform this restraint into complementarity (asserting the importance of woman's function, even its "superiority") and redefine it. Thus, women live a duality—as members of the general culture and as partakers of women's culture. [*MFP,* p. 52]

Lerner's views are similar to those of some cultural anthropologists. A particularly stimulating analysis of female culture has been carried out by two Oxford anthropologists, Shirley and Edwin Ardener. The Ardeners have tried to outline a model of women's culture which is not historically limited and to provide a terminology for its characteristics. Two essays by Edwin Ardener, "Belief and the Problem of Women" (1972) and "The 'Problem' Revisited" (1975), suggest that women constitute a *muted group,* the boundaries of whose culture and reality overlap, but are not wholly contained by, the *dominant (male) group.* A model of the cultural situation of women is crucial to understanding both how they are perceived by the dominant group and how they perceive themselves and others. Both historians and anthropologists emphasize the incompleteness of androcentric models of history and culture and the inadequacy of such models for the analysis of female experience. In the past, female experience which could not be accommodated by androcentric models was treated as deviant or simply ignored. Observation from an exterior point of view could never be the same as comprehension from within. Ardener's model also has many connections to and implications for current feminist literary theory, since the concepts of perception, silence, and silencing are so central to discussions of women's participation in literary culture.[40]

By the term "muted," Ardener suggests problems both of language and of power. Both muted and dominant groups generate beliefs or ordering ideas of social reality at the unconscious level, but dominant groups control the forms or structures in which consciousness can be articulated. Thus muted groups must mediate their beliefs through the allowable forms of dominant structures. Another way of putting this would be to say that all language is the language of the dominant order, and women, if they speak at all, must speak through it. How then, Ardener asks, "does the symbolic weight of that other mass of persons express itself?" In his view, women's beliefs find expression through ritual and art, expressions which can be deciphered by the ethnographer, either female or male, who is willing to make the effort to perceive beyond the screens of the dominant structure.[41]

Let us now look at Ardener's diagram of the relationship of the dominant and the muted group:

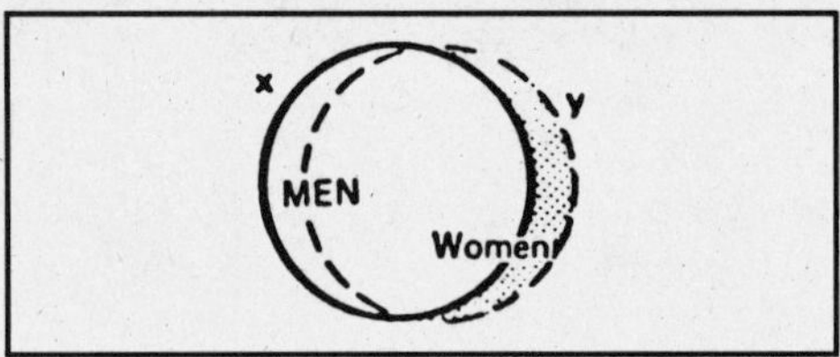

Unlike the Victorian model of complementary spheres, Ardener's groups are represented by intersecting circles. Much of muted circle Y falls within the boundaries of dominant circle X; there is also a crescent of Y which is outside the dominant boundary and therefore (in Ardener's terminology) "wild." We can think of the "wild zone" of women's culture spatially, experientially, or metaphysically. Spatially it stands for an area which is literally no-man's-land, a place forbidden to men, which corresponds to the zone in X which is off limits to women. Experientially it stands for the aspects of the female life-style which are outside of and unlike those of men; again, there is a corresponding zone of male experience alien to women. But if we think of the wild zone metaphysically, or in terms of consciousness, it has no corresponding male space since all of male consciousness is within the circle of the dominant structure and thus accessible to or structured by language. In this sense, the "wild" is always imaginary; from the male point of view, it may simply be the projection of the unconscious. In terms of cultural anthropology, women know what the male crescent is like, even if they have never seen it, because it becomes the subject of legend (like the wilderness). But men do not know what is in the wild.

For some feminist critics, the wild zone, or "female space," must be the address of a genuinely women-centered criticism, theory, and art, whose shared project is to bring into being the symbolic weight of female consciousness, to make the invisible visible, to make the silent speak. French feminist critics would like to make the wild zone the theoretical base of women's difference. In their texts, the wild zone becomes the place for the revolutionary women's language, the language of everything that is repressed, and for the revolutionary women's writing in "white ink." It is the Dark Continent in which Cixous's laughing Medusa and Wittig's *guérillères* reside. Through voluntary entry into the wild zone, other feminist critics tell us, a woman can write her way out of the "cramped confines of patriarchal space."[42] The images of this journey are now familiar in feminist quest fictions and in essays about them. The writer/heroine, often guided by another woman, travels to the "mother country" of liberated desire and female authenticity; crossing to the other side of the mirror, like Alice in Wonderland, is often a symbol of the passage.

Many forms of American radical feminism also romantically assert that women are closer to nature, to the environment, to a matriarchal principle at once biological and ecological. Mary Daly's *Gyn/Ecology* and Margaret Atwood's novel *Surfacing* are texts which create this feminist mythology. In English and American literature, women writers have often imagined Amazon Utopias, cities or countries situated in the wild zone or on its border: Elizabeth Gaskell's gentle *Cranford* is probably an Amazon Utopia; so is Charlotte Perkins Gilman's *Herland* or, to take a recent example, Joanna Russ's *Whileaway.* A few years ago, the feminist publishing house Daughters, Inc. tried to create a business version of the Amazon Utopia; as Lois Gould reported in the *New York Times Magazine* (2 January 1977), "They believe they are building the working models for the critical next stage of feminism: full independence from the control and influence of "male-dominated" institutions—the news media, the health, education, and legal systems, the art, theater, and literary worlds, the banks."

These fantasies of an idyllic enclave represent a phenomenon which feminist criticism must recognize in the history of women's writing. But we must also understand that there can be no writing or criticism totally outside of the dominant structure; no publication is fully independent from the economic and political pressures of the male-dominated society. The concept of a woman's text in the wild zone is a playful abstraction: in the reality to which we must address ourselves as critics, women's writing is a "double-voiced discourse" that always embodies the social, literary, and cultural heritages of both the muted and the dominant.[43] And insofar as most feminist critics are also women writing, this precarious heritage is one we share; every step that feminist criticism takes toward defining women's writing is a step toward self-understanding as well; every account of a female literary culture and a female literary tradition has parallel significance for our own place in critical history and critical tradition.

Women writing are not, then, *inside* and *outside* of the male tradition; they are inside two traditions simultaneously, "undercurrents," in Ellen Moers's metaphor, of the mainstream. To mix metaphors again, the literary estate of women, as Myra Jehlen says, "suggests . . . a more fluid imagery of interacting juxtapositions, the point of which would be to represent not so much the territory, as its defining borders. Indeed, the female territory might well be envisioned as one long border, and independence for women, not as a separate country, but as open access to the sea." As Jehlen goes on to explain, an aggressive feminist criticism must poise itself on this border and must see women's writing in its changing historical and cultural relation to that other body of texts identified by feminist criticism not simply as literature but as "men's writing."[44]

The difference of women's writing, then, can only be understood in terms of this complex and historically grounded cultural relation. An important aspect of Ardener's model is that there are muted groups other than women; a dominant structure may determine many muted structures. A black American woman poet, for example, would have her literary identity formed by the dominant (white male) tradition, by a muted women's culture, and by a muted black culture. She would be affected by both sexual and racial politics in a combination unique to her case; at the same time, as Barbara Smith points out, she shares an experience specific to her group: "Black women writers constitute an identifiable literary tradition . . . thematically, stylistically, aesthetically, and conceptually. Black women writers manifest common approaches to the act of creating literature as a direct result of the specific political, social, and economic experience they have been obliged to share."[45] Thus the first task of a gynocentric criticism must be to plot the precise cultural locus of female literary identity and to describe the forces that intersect an individual woman writer's cultural field. A gynocentric criticism would also situate women writers with respect to the variables of literary culture, such as modes of production and distribution, relations of author and audience, relations of high to popular art, and hierarchies of genre.

Insofar as our concepts of literary periodization are based on men's writing, women's writing must be forcibly assimilated to an irrelevant grid; we discuss a Renaissance which is not a renaissance for women, a Romantic period in which women played very little part, a modernism with which women conflict. At the same time, the ongoing history of women's writing has been suppressed, leaving large and mysterious gaps in accounts of the development of genre. Gynocentric criticism is already well on the way to providing us with another perspective on literary history. Margaret Anne Doody, for example, suggests that "the period between the death of Richardson and the appearance of the novels of Scott and Austen" which has "been regarded as a dead period, a dull blank" is in fact the period in which late eighteenth-century women writers were developing "the paradigm for women's fiction of the nineteenth century—something hardly less than the paradigm of the nineteenth-century novel itself."[46] There has also been a feminist rehabilitation of the female gothic, a mutation of a popular genre once believed marginal but now seen as part of the great tradition of the novel.[47] In American literature, the pioneering work of Ann Douglas, Nina Baym, and Jane Tompkins, among others, has given us a new view of the power of women's fiction to feminize nineteenth-century American culture.[48] And feminist critics have made us aware that Woolf belonged to a tradition other than modernism and that this tradition surfaces in her work precisely in those places where criticism has hitherto found obscurities, evasions, implausibilities, and imperfections.[49]

Our current theories of literary influence also need to be tested in terms of women's writing. If a man's text, as Bloom and Edward Said have maintained, is fathered, then a woman's text is not only mothered but parented; it confronts both paternal and maternal precursors and must deal with the problems and advantages of both lines of inheritance. Woolf says in *A Room of One's Own* that "a woman writing thinks back through her mothers." But a woman writing unavoidably thinks back through her fathers as well; only male writers can forget or mute half of their parentage. The dominant culture need not consider the muted, except to rail against "the woman's part" in itself. Thus we need more subtle and supple accounts of influence, not just to explain women's writing but also to understand how men's writing has resisted the acknowledgment of female precursors.

We must first go beyond the assumption that women writers either imitate their male predecessors or revise them and that this simple dualism is adequate to describe the influences on the woman's text. I. A. Richards once commented that the influence of G. E. Moore had had an enormous negative impact on his work: "I feel like an obverse of him. Where there's a hole in him, there's a bulge in me."[50] Too often women's place in literary tradition is translated into the crude topography of hole and bulge, with Milton, Byron, or Emerson the bulging bogeys on one side and women's literature from Aphra Behn to Adrienne Rich a pocked moon surface of revisionary lacunae on the other. One of the great advantages of the women's-culture model is that it shows how the female tradition can be a positive source of strength and solidarity as well as a negative source of powerlessness; it can generate its own experiences and symbols which are not simply the obverse of the male tradition.

How can a cultural model of women's writing help us to read a woman's text? One implication of this model is that women's fiction can be read as a double-voiced discourse, containing a "dominant" and a "muted" story, what Gilbert and Gubar call a "palimpsest." I have described it elsewhere as an object/field problem in which we must keep two alternative oscillating texts simultaneously in view: "In the purest feminist literary criticism we are . . . presented with a radical alteration of our vision, a demand that we see meaning in what has previously been empty space. The orthodox plot recedes, and another plot, hitherto submerged in the anonymity of the background, stands out in bold relief like a thumbprint." Miller too sees "another text" in women's fiction, "more or less muted from novel to novel" but "always there to be read."[51]

Another interpretative strategy for feminist criticism might be the contextual analysis that the cultural anthropologist Clifford Geertz calls "thick description." Geertz calls for descriptions that seek to understand the meaning of cultural phenomena and products by "sorting out the structures of signification . . . and determining their social ground and import."[52] A genuinely "thick" description of women's writing would insist upon gender and upon a female literary tradition among the multiple strata that make up the force of meaning in a text. No description, we must concede, could ever be thick enough to account for all the factors that go into the work of art. But we could work toward completeness, even as an unattainable ideal.

In suggesting that a cultural model of women's writing has considerable usefulness for the enterprise of feminist criticism, I don't mean to replace psychoanalysis with cultural anthropology as the answer to all our theoretical problems or to enthrone Ardener and Geertz as the new white fathers in place of Freud, Lacan, and Bloom. No theory, however suggestive, can be a substitute for the close and extensive knowledge of women's texts which constitutes our essential subject. Cultural anthropology and social history can perhaps offer us a terminology and a diagram of women's cultural situation. But feminist critics must use this concept in relation to what women actually write, not in relation to a theoretical, political, metaphoric, or visionary ideal of what women ought to write.

I began by recalling that a few years ago feminist critics thought we were on a pilgrimage to the promised land in which gender would lose its power, in which all texts would be sexless and equal, like angels. But the more precisely we understand the specificity of women's writing not as a transient by-product of sexism but as a fundamental and continually determining reality, the more clearly we realize that we have misperceived our destination. We may never reach the promised land at all; for when feminist critics see our task as the study of women's writing, we realize that the land promised to us is not the serenely undifferentiated universality of texts but the tumultuous and intriguing wilderness of difference itself.

NOTES

[1]Carolyn G. Heilbrun and Catharine R. Stimpson, "Theories of Feminist Criticism: A Dialogue," in *Feminist Literary Criticism,* ed. Josephine Donovan (Lexington: University Press of Kentucky, 1975), p. 64. I also discuss this distinction in my "Toward a Feminist Poetics," in this volume, pp. 125–143; a number of the ideas in the first part of the present essay are raised more briefly in the earlier piece.

[2]No women critics are discussed in Geoffrey Hartman's *Criticism in the Wilderness: The Study of Literature Today* (New Haven, Conn.: Yale University Press, 1980), but he does describe a feminine spirit called "the Muse of Criticism": "more a governess than a Muse, the stern daughter of books no longer read under trees and in the fields" (p. 175).

[3]See my "Literary Criticism," Review Essay, *Signs* 1 (Winter 1975): 435–60.

[4]Annette Kolodny, "Literary Criticism," Review Essay, *Signs* 2 (Winter 1976): 420.

[5]On black criticism, see Barbara Smith, "Toward a Black Feminist Criticism," in this volume, pp. 168–85, and Mary Helen Washington, "New Lives and New Letters: Black Women Writers at the End of the Seventies," *College English* 43 (January 1981): 1–11. On Marxist criticism, see the Marxist-Feminist Literature Collective's "Women's Writing," *Ideology and Consciousness* 3 (Spring 1978): 27–48, a collectively written analysis of several nineteenth-century women's novels which gives equal weight to gender, class, and literary production as textual determinants.

[6]Margaret Homans, *Women Writers and Poetic Identity: Dorothy Wordsworth, Emily Brontë, and Emily Dickinson* (Princeton, N.J.: Princeton University Press, 1980), p. 10.

[7]Josephine Donovan, "Afterward: Critical Revision," *Feminist Literary Criticism,* p. 74. Judith Fetterley, *The Resisting Reader: A Feminist Approach to American Fiction* (Bloomington: Indiana University Press, 1978), p. viii. See my "Toward a Feminist Poetics," pp. 125–43. *The Authority of Experience* is the title of an anthology edited by Arlyn Diamond and Lee R. Edwards (Amherst, Mass.: University of Massachusetts Press, 1977).

[8]Nina Auerbach, "Feminist Criticism Reviewed," in *Gender and Literary Voice,* ed. Janet Todd (New York: Holmes & Meier, 1980), p. 258.

[9]Adrienne Rich, "When We Dead Awaken: Writing as Re-Vision," *On Lies, Secrets, and Silence* (New York: W. W. Norton, 1979), p. 35.

[10]Annette Kolodny, "Dancing through the Minefield: Some Observations on the Theory, Practice, and Politics of a Feminist Literary Criticism," in this volume, p. 00. The complete theoretical case for a feminist hermeneutics is outlined in Kolodny's essays, including "Some Notes on Defining a 'Feminist Literary Criticism,'" *Critical Inquiry* 2 (Autumn 1975): 75–92; "A Map for Rereading; or, Gender and the Interpretation of Literary Texts," in this volume, pp. 46–62; and "The Theory of Feminist Criticism" (paper delivered at the National Center for the Humanities Conference on Feminist Criticism, Research Triangle Park, N.C., March 1981).

[11]Sandra M. Gilbert, "What Do Feminist Critics Want? A Postcard from the Volcano," in this volume, p. 36.

[12]Christiane Makward, "To Be or Not to Be. . . . A Feminist Speaker," in *The Future of Difference,* ed. Hester Eisenstein and Alice Jardine (Boston: G. K. Hall,

1980), p. 102. On Lacan, see Jane Gallop, "The Ladies' Man," *Diacritics* 6 (Winter 1976): 28–34; on Macherey, see the Marxist-Feminist Literature Collective's "Women's Writing."

[13]Patricia Meyer Spacks, *The Female Imagination* (New York: Alfred A. Knopf, 1975), pp. 19, 32.

[14]Hélène Cixous, "The Laugh of the Medusa," trans. Keith and Paula Cohen, *Signs* 1 (Summer 1976): 878. Nancy K. Miller, "Emphasis Added: Plots and Plausibilities in Women's Fiction," in this volume, pp. 339–60.

[15]For an overview, see Domna C. Stanton, "Language and Revolution: The Franco-American Dis-Connection," in Eisenstein and Jardine, *Future of Difference,* pp. 73–87, and Elaine Marks and Isabelle de Courtivron, eds., *New French Feminisms* (Amherst: University of Massachusetts Press, 1979); all further references to *New French Feminisms,* abbreviated *NFF,* will hereafter be included with translator's name parenthetically in the text.

[16]Two major works are the manifesto of the Marxist-Feminist Literature Collective, "Women's Writing," and the papers from the Oxford University lectures on women and literature, Mary Jacobus, ed., *Women Writing and Writing about Women* (New York: Barnes & Noble Imports, 1979).

[17]Sandra M. Gilbert and Susan Gubar, *The Madwoman in the Attic: The Woman Writer and the Nineteenth-Century Literary Imagination* (New Haven, Conn.: Yale University Press, 1979), pp. 6, 7.

[18]Nina Auerbach, review of *Madwoman, Victorian Studies* 23 (Summer 1980): 506.

[19]Douglas Jerrold, quoted in Kathleen Tillotson, *Novels of the Eighteen-Forties* (London: Oxford University Press, 1961), p. 39 n. James Joyce imagined the creator as female and literary creation as a process of gestation; see Richard Ellmann, *James Joyce: A Biography* (London: Oxford University Press, 1959), pp. 306–8.

[20]Carolyn G. Burke, "Report from Paris: Women's Writing and the Women's Movement," *Signs* 3 (Summer 1978): 851.

[21]Adrienne Rich, *Of Woman Born: Motherhood as Experience and Institution* (New York: W. W. Norton, 1976), p. 62. Biofeminist criticism has been influential in other disciplines as well: e.g., art critics, such as Judy Chicago and Lucy Lippard, have suggested that women artists are compelled to use a uterine or vaginal iconography of centralized focus, curved lines, and tactile or sensuous forms. See Lippard, *From the Center: Feminist Essays on Women's Art* (New York: E. P. Dutton, 1976).

[22]See Alicia Ostriker, "Body Language: Imagery of the Body in Women's Poetry," in *The State of the Language,* ed. Leonard Michaels and Christopher Ricks (Berkeley: University of California Press, 1980), pp. 247–63, and Terence Diggory, "Armoured Women, Naked Men: Dickinson, Whitman, and Their Successors," in *Shakespeare's Sisters: Feminist Essays on Women Poets,* ed. Sandra M. Gilbert and Susan Gubar (Bloomington: Indiana University Press, 1979), pp. 135–50.

[23]Rachel Blau DuPlessis, "Washing Blood," *Feminist Studies* 4 (June 1978): 10. The entire issue is an important document of feminist criticism.

[24]Nancy K. Miller, "Women's Autobiography in France: For a Dialectics of Identification," in *Women and Language in Literature and Society,* ed. Sally McConnell-Ginet, Ruth Borker, and Nelly Furman (New York: Praeger, 1980), p. 271.

[25]Nelly Furman, "The Study of Women and Language: Comment on Vol. 3, No. 3," *Signs* 4 (Autumn 1978): 182.

[26]Burke, "Report from Paris," p. 844.

[27]Jacobus, "The Difference of View," in *Women's Writing and Writing about Women,* pp. 12–13. Shoshana Felman, "Women and Madness: The Critical Phallacy," *Diacritics* 5 (Winter 1975): 10.

[28]On women's language, see Sarah B. Pomeroy, *Goddesses, Whores, Wives, and Slaves: Women in Classical Antiquity* (New York: Schocken Books, 1976), p. 24; Sally McConnell-Ginet, "Linguistics and the Feminist Challenge," in *Women and Language,* p. 14; and Ioan M. Lewis, *Ecstatic Religion* (1971), cited in Shirley Ardener, ed., *Perceiving Women* (New York: Halsted Press, 1978), p. 50.

[29]Clifford Geertz, *The Interpretation of Cultures* (New York: Basic Books, 1973), pp. 241–42.

[30]McConnell-Ginet, "Linguistics and the Feminist Challenge," pp. 13, 16.

[31]Virginia Woolf, "Speech, Manuscript Notes," *The Pargiters: The Novel-Essay Portion of the Years 1882–1941,* ed. Mitchell A. Leaska (New York: New York Public Library, 1977), p. 164.

[32]Quoted in Erika Freeman, *Insights: Conversations with Theodor Reik* (Englewood Cliffs, N.J.: Prentice-Hall, 1971), p. 166. Reik goes on, "But what the hell, writing! The great task of a woman is to bring a child into the world."

[33]Cora Kaplan, "Language and Gender," unpublished paper, University of Sussex, 1977, p. 3.

[34]Gilbert and Gubar, *Madwoman in the Attic,* p. 50.

[35]See Annis Pratt, "The New Feminist Criticisms," in *Beyond Intellectual Sexism: A New Woman, a New Reality,* ed. Joan I. Roberts (New York: Longman, 1976); Barbara H. Rigney, *Madness and Sexual Politics in the Feminist Novel: Studies in Brontë, Woolf, Lessing, and Atwood* (Madison: University of Wisconsin Press, 1978); and Ann Douglas, "Mrs. Sigourney and the Sensibility of the Inner Space," *New England Quarterly* 45 (June 1972): 163–81.

[36]Nancy Chodorow, "Gender, Relation, and Difference in Psychoanalytic Perspective," in Eisenstein and Jardine, *Future of Difference,* p. 11. See also Chodorow et al., "On *The Reproduction of Mothering:* A Methodological Debate," *Signs* 6 (Spring 1981): 482–514.

[37]See, e.g., *The Lost Tradition: Mothers and Daughters in Literature,* ed. Cathy M. Davidson and E. M. Broner (New York: Frederick Ungar, 1980); this work is more engaged with myths and images of matrilineage than with redefining female identity.

[38]Elizabeth Abel, "(E)Merging Identities: The Dynamics of Female Friendship in Contemporary Fiction by Women," *Signs* 6 (Spring 1981): 434.

[39]Gerda Lerner, "The Challenge of Women's History," *The Majority Finds Its Past: Placing Women in History* (New York: Oxford University Press, 1979); all further references to this book, abbreviated *MFP,* will hereafter be included parenthetically in the text.

[40]See, e.g., Tillie Olsen, *Silences* (New York: Delacorte Press, 1978); Sheila Rowbotham, *Woman's Consciousness, Man's World* (New York: Penguin Books, 1974), pp. 31–37; and Marcia Landy, "The Silent Woman: Towards a Feminist Critique," in Diamond and Edwards, *Authority of Experience* (n. 7 above), pp. 16–27.

[41]Edwin Ardener, "Belief and the Problem of Women," in S. Ardener, *Perceiving Women* (note 28 above), p. 3.

[42]Mari McCarty, "Possessing Female Space: 'The Tender Shoot,'" *Women's Studies* 8 (1981): 368.

[43]Susan Lanser and Evelyn Torton Beck, "[Why] Are There No Great Women Critics? And What Difference Does It Make?" in *The Prism of Sex: Essays in the*

Sociology of Knowledge, ed. Beck and Julia A. Sherman (Madison: University of Wisconsin Press, 1979), p. 86.

[44]Myra Jehlen, "Archimedes and the Paradox of Feminist Criticism," *Signs* 6 (Fall 1981): 582.

[45]Smith, "Black Feminist Criticism," p. 000. See also Gloria T. Hull, "Afro-American Women Poets: A Bio-Critical Survey," in Gilbert and Gubar, *Shakespeare's Sisters,* pp. 165–82, and Elaine Marks, "Lesbian Intertextuality," in *Homosexualities and French Literature,* ed. Marks and George Stambolian (Ithaca, N.Y.: Cornell University Press, 1979).

[46]Margaret Anne Doody, "George Eliot and the Eighteenth-Century Novel," *Nineteenth-Century Fiction* 35 (December 1980): 267–68.

[47]See, e.g., Judith Wilt, *Ghosts of the Gothic: Austen, Eliot, and Lawrence* (Princeton, N.J.: Princeton University Press, 1980).

[48]See Ann Douglas, *The Feminization of American Culture* (New York: Alfred A. Knopf, 1977); Nina Baym, *Woman's Fiction: A Guide to Novels by and about Women in America, 1820–1870* (Ithaca, N.Y.: Cornell University Press, 1978); and Jane P. Tompkins, "Sentimental Power: *Uncle Tom's Cabin* and the Politics of Literary History," in this volume, pp. 000–00.

[49]See, e.g., the analysis of Woolf in Sandra M. Gilbert, "Costumes of the Mind: Transvestism as Metaphor in Modern Literature," *Critical Inquiry* 7 (Winter 1980): 391–417.

[50]I. A. Richards, quoted in John Paul Russo, "A Study in Influence: The Moore-Richards Paradigm," *Critical Inquiry* 5 (Summer 1979): 687.

[51]Showalter, "Literary Criticism," p. 435; Miller, "Emphasis Added," p. 000. To take one example, whereas *Jane Eyre* had always been read in relation to an implied "dominant" fictional and social mode and had thus been perceived as flawed, feminist readings foreground its muted symbolic strategies and explore its credibility and coherence in its own terms. Feminist critics revise views like those of Richard Chase, who describes Rochester as castrated, thus implying that Jane's neurosis is penis envy, and G. Armour Craig, who sees the novel as Jane's struggle for superiority, to see Jane instead as healthy within her own system, that is, a *women's* society. See Chase, "The Brontës; or, Myth Domesticated," in *Jane Eyre* (New York: W.W. Norton, 1971), pp. 462–71; Craig, "The Unpoetic Compromise: On the Relation between Private Vision and Social Order in Nineteenth-Century English Fiction," in *Self and Society,* ed. Mark Schorer (New York, 1956), pp. 30–41; Nancy Pell, "Resistance, Rebellion, and Marriage: The Economics of *Jane Eyre,*" *Nineteenth-Century Fiction* 31 (March 1977): 397–420; Helene Moglen, *Charlotte Brontë: The Self Conceived* (New York: W. W. Norton, 1977); Adrienne Rich, "*Jane Eyre:* The Temptations of a Motherless Woman," *MS,* October 1973; and Maurianne Adams, "*Jane Eyre:* Woman's Estate," in Diamond and Edwards, *Authority of Experience,* pp. 137–59.

[52]Geertz, *Interpretation of Cultures,* p. 9.

For the Etruscans

Rachel Blau DuPlessis

Thinking smugly, "She shouldn't be working on Woolf." 1964. "Doesn't she know that she'd better not work on a woman?" Why was I lucky to know this. What was the threat? Dickinson? Marginality? Nin? I bought Nin's book, I threw it out. What! Didn't want it, might confront

> The great difficulties in understanding the language . . . not . . . from an inability to read the script, every letter of which is now clearly understood. It is as if books were discovered, printed in our own Roman letters, so that one could articulate the words without trouble, but written in an unknown language with no known parallels.[1]

myself. 1979. The general feeling (of the dream) was that I was free of the testers. However, I was entirely obligated to take and pass their test. My relationship to the testers is—? 1965. My big ambition, my hemmed and nervous space. Her uncompromising, oracular poems. Her fluid, decisive writing. Her dream life, surfacing. Not even to read this? to read with contempt? "This is a Blossom of the Brain—/ A small—italic Seed" (Dickinson, no. 945).

What is going on here? 1968. Is the female aesthetic simply an (1978) enabling myth? Fish on one foot, hook on the other, angling for ourselves. Woolf: catching "something about the body."[2] Crash. MOM! WHAT! "You never buy what I like! Only what YOU like! (Fig Newtons.)

* * *

A golden bough. The torch is passed on. His son clutches his hand, his crippled father clings to his back, three male generations leave the burning city. The wife, lost. Got lost in burning. No one knows what happened to her, when they became the Romans.

She became the Etruscans?

> Even so, there is nothing to prevent those with a special aptitude for cryptography from tackling Etruscan, which is the last of the important languages to require translating.[3]

Sheepish, I am sheepish and embarrassed to mention this

that for me it was always the herding. The herding, the bonding, the way you can speak their language but also have a different language or different needs so hard to say this. Always: I have heard this story from many sources—they bond and clump outside your door and never "ask you to lunch" or they talk and be wonderful, lambent, but when you walk up "they turn away" or "they turn on you, teasing, making sexual jokes"

all headed in the same direction, herding and glistening, of course some don't. But it has been difficult for these to separate from the rest. Probably the reward system?

To translate ourselves from our disguises. The enthralled sexuality, the knife-edge brilliance, the intellectual dowdiness, evasions, embarrassments, imprecisions, deferments; smug primness with which there is no dialogue. Combativeness straight into malice. Invisibility, visibility, crossing the legs, uncrossing them. Knights in shining amour. Daddy to the rescue. "Imposing" sex on the situation. "Not imposing" "sex" on the "situation." "Doesn't she know she'd better not work on a woman?" She'd better now work on a woman. "I bid you take a wisp from the wool of their precious fleece."[4] The golden fleece. The golden bough. The female quest?

Frankly, it was *The Golden Notebook* (1966). Which pierced my heart with its two-headed arrow.

How to be? How to be-have? I remember one preceptor who brought her little white dog to school and trotted it up and down the fourth floor of Hamilton Hall. What delightful, charming, adorable girls! The temptation of Eve was fruit, of Mary, lambs. Thinking that they followed *you* to school.

* * *

It is, after all, always the meaning, the reading of difference that matters, and meaning is culturally engendered and sustained. Not to consider the body as some absolute (milk, blood, breasts, clitoris) for no "body" is unmediated. Not body but the "body" of psychosocial fabrications of difference. Or again, of sameness. Or again, of their relation. The contexts in which are formed and reinforced gendered human beings, produced in the family, in institutions of gender development, in the forms of sexual preference, in the division of labor by gender, especially the structure of infant care, in the class and conditions of the families in which we are psychologically born, and in the social maintenance of the sexes through life's stages and in any historical era.[5] And as such, these differing experiences do surely produce (some) different consciousnesses, different cultural expressions, different relations to realms of symbols and symbol users. Different "language," metaphorical; different uses of the grammatical and expressive resources of language (verb parts, questions, intonation, pronouns).

> *Stein says we no longer have the words people used to have*
> *so we have to make them new in some way but women haven't*
> *had them at all and how can you deconstruct a language you*
> *never constructed or it was never constructed by others like*
> *you, or with you in mind?*[6] Frances Jaffer

And therefore there is female aesthetic, but not *a* female aesthetic, not one single constellation of strategies.

I am watering cattle, who are thirsty. A frisky Holstein, pointed face and horns with pink tips, pokes me, playful, calling attention to herself. I must establish that she is not male (1978). I pick up her little curtain. There. Fleshy pink udders, she is pink, black

and white. I have watered the cattle and they have given me a guide.

Etruscan, the last important language.

What holds civilization intact? The presence of apparently voiceless Others, "thoughtless" Others, powerless Others against which the Law, the Main, the Center, even the Diffusions of power are defined.

> **Throughout the ages the problem of woman has puzzled**
> **people of every kind. . . . You too will have pondered this**

> **question insofar as you are men. From the women among you that is not to be expected, for you yourselves are the riddle.[7]**

A special aptitude for cryptography. The only ones barred from the riddle. Ha ha. His gallantry is hardest to bear. Not to think about the riddle is to remain the riddle. To break with what I have been told I am, and I am able to? am unable disabled disbarred *un sous-développé, comme tu dis, un sous-capable*[8] The Etruscan language can be heard, if one chooses to mouth it, but not comprehended. Pondering is not to be expected, so why bother?

What happens at the historical moment when the voiceless and powerless seek to unravel their riddle? (For Caliban does seize his voice, reject the magician of civilization in Césaire's writing of Shakespeare's *Tempest.*) ANS.: We are cutting into the deep heart, the deepest heart of cultural compacts. They have already lost our allegiance. Something is finished.

Now did I go downstairs, now did I cut up a pear, eight strawberries, now did I add some cottage cheese thinking to get some more or even some ricotta at the Italian Market so that I could make lasagna so that when B. comes back from New York he would have something nice and so I wouldn't have to cook again for days; now did I put some sugar on the fruit and then fill the sugar bowl because it was almost empty; now did I hang two bath mats out on the line, they are washed only once a year and it was today that I washed them; now did I and do I wonder that there are words that repeat in a swaying repetitive motion. Deliberately breaking the flow of thought, when it comes to change, and with food, with dust. With food and dust.

> **must here snatch time to remark how discomposing it is for her biographer that this culmination and peroration should be dashed from us on a laugh casually like this; but the truth is that when we write of a woman, everything is out of place—culminations and perorations; the accent never falls where it does with a man.[9]**

I dreamed I was an artist; my medium was cottage cheese.

For the woman artist is not privileged or mandated to find her self-in-world except by facing (affronting?) and mounting an enormous struggle with the cultural fictions—myths, narratives, iconographies, languages—which heretofore have delimited the representation of women. And which are culturally and psychically saturating.

* * *

To define then. "Female aesthetic": the production of formal, epistemological, and thematic strategies by members of the group Woman, strategies born in struggle with much of already existing culture, and overdetermined by two elements of sexual difference—by women's psychosocial experiences of gender asymmetry and by women's historical status in an (ambiguously) nonhegemonic group.

All the animals, and I knew they were thirsty. They were mine, and were very thirsty. I had to give them

Something I call an emotional texture, a structural expression of mutuality. Writers know their text as a form of intimacy, of personal contact, whether conversations with the reader or with the self. Letters, journals, voices are sources for this element,

> see "no reason why one should not write as one speaks, familiarly, colloquially"[10]

expressing the porousness and nonhierarchic stances of intimate conversation in both structure and function. Like *Orlando,* like Griffin's *Voices,* like *The Golden Notebook,* these may be antiphonal many-voiced works, beguilingly, passionately subjective, seeing emotional commitment as an adventure. (As our form of adventure?)[11]

"What a secret language we talk, Undertones, overtones, nuances, abstractions, symbols. Then we return to Henry with an incandescence which frightens him."[12]

"addressing the reader, making herself and her reader part of the narrative . . . an offhand, conversational manner"[13]

> *I find myself more and more attracted to the porous, the statement that permits interpretation (penetration?) rather than positing an absolute. Not vagueness—I want each component to be clear—but a whole that doesn't pretend to be ultimate, academic.*[14]

Not positing oneself as the only, sol(e) authority. Sheep of the sun. Meaning, a statement that is open to the reader, not better than the reader, not set apart from; not seeking the authority of the writer. Not even seeking the authority of the writing. (Reader could be writer, writer reader. Listener could be teacher.)

* * *

Assuming for the moment. That this description is true? or that we could find these traits and name them. One way of proving that the female aesthetic can exist would be to find reasons for the existence of this poetics in the gender experiences specific to women, in sexual difference. Deena Metzger speaks of a denial of competition and aggression in women, suggesting that these lead to nonhierarchic forms of mutuality.[15] But female competition of course exists (jealous, "she's said it all"; sibling, "she was there first"; smug, "she should know better than choosing to work on a woman"), wherever there are special rewards for some women at the expense of others. Or just because we are no better than anyone else. Jean Baker Miller and Carol Gilligan argue similarly that roles and functions of women engender a different psychological orientation. Shaped by nurturance, women take both donor and recipient roles, using tactics of giving and receiving. Shaped by the interdependent and relational, women are led to "a more contextual mode of judgment and a different moral understanding."[16]

The second trait is both/and vision. This is the end of the either-or, dichotomized universe, proposing monism (is this really the name for what we are proposing? or is it dialectics?) in opposition to dualism, a dualism pernicious because it valorizes one side above another, and makes a hierarchy where there were simply twain.

> a " 'shapeless' shapeliness," said Dorothy Richardson, the "unique gift of the feminine psyche." "Its power to do what the shapely mentalities of men appear incapable of doing for themselves, to act as a focus for divergent points of view. . . . The characteristic . . . of being all over the place and in all camps at once. . . ."[17]

A both/and vision born of shifts, contraries, negations, contradictions; linked to personal vulnerability and need. Essay and sermon. A both/and vision that embraces movement, situational. (I don't mean: opportunistic, slidy.) Structurally, such a writing might say different things, not settle on one, which is final. This is not a condition of "not choosing," since choice exists always in what to represent and in the rhythms of presentation. It is nonacademic; for in order to make a formal presentation, one must have chosen among theses: this is the rhetorical demand. Cannot, in formal argument, say both yes and no, if yes and no are given equal value under the same conditions. Either one or the other has to prevail. But say, in a family argument? where both, where all, are right? generates another model of discourse.

* * *

If one does not just rest silent, stuff the mouth with food.

* * *

Lessing has built "Dialogue" on an either-or opposition which becomes a both/and vision of the female. He: the tower, is nihilism, the abyss, rigidity, isolation, and control; is courage, reason, and a sickness. She: the leaf, a vulval shape. She is infused with an irrational happiness, sensuality, pleasure, and openness to community. Has common sense, does not drive a philosophical position to the end and bind herself to it. This female mode of seeing holds to one side of a polarity (a "feminine" side) yet is simultaneously that force which includes and transcends male nihilism and rationality.[18] A constellated integrative form. This vision contains feminine, transcends masculine, asserts female as synthesis. Makes me very nervous (are we "just" valorizing our idealized selves?). This structure is parallel to the double status of Mrs. Ramsay in Lily's painting (and in Woolf's *To the Lighthouse*), as one side of the masculine-feminine polarity, fit only to be surpassed; at the same time, as that stroke in the middle, the one unifying lighthouse stroke, which is love and ambition, mother and child, death and pleasure: the female synthesis.

Of the voices of Woolf's essay *Three Guineas,* one takes the trial tone: rational, legalistic, logical. The other voice discourses loosely, inventive, chatty, exploring every nook and cranny. As for facts—anecdote is authority. But as the Antigone reference ripens, and we talk of women defying the laws of the state, both masculine and feminine are sublated in a heroic, intransigent but unauthoritarian voice which combines reason and emotion, logic and defiance. This is the noncontractual voice of the Outsiders, (ambiguously) nonhegemonic

> who speak the last of the important languages to require translating.
>
> **A constant alternation between time and its "truth," identity and its loss, history and the timeless, signless, extra-phenomenal things that produce it. An impossible dialectic: a permanent alternation: never the one without the other. It is not certain that anyone here and now is capable of it. A [psycho]analyst conscious of history and politics? A politician tuned into the unconscious? A woman perhaps . . .[19]**

This both/and vision, the contradictory movement between the logically irreconcilable, must have several causes. Perhaps it is based on the bisexual oscillation within female psychosexual development. Nancy Chodorow shows how the Oedipal configuration occurs differently in girls and boys and that, because of the way the sexes are reproduced in the family, most women retain men as erotic objects and women as emotional objects. This oscillation between men and women, father and mother, pervades her emotional (and thus aesthetic) life. And do we also value the K-Mart version of this structure: conflict avoidance. Everybody is right. Feel like a chameleon, taking coloration—

Insider-outsider social status will also help to dissolve an either-or dualism. For the woman finds she is irreconcilable things: an outsider by her gender position, by her relation to power; may be an insider by her social position, her class. She can be both. Her ontological, her psychic, her class position all cause doubleness. Doubled consciousness. Doubled understandings. How then could she neglect to invent a form which produces this incessant, critical, splitting motion. To invent this form. To invent the theory for this form.

Following, the "female aesthetic" will produce artworks that incorporate contradiction and nonlinear movement into the heart of the text.

An art object may then be nonhierarchic, showing "an organization of material in fragments," breaking climactic structures, making an even display of elements over the surface with no climactic place or moment, since the materials are "organized into many centers."[20]

Monique Wittig's *Les Guérillères,* a form of verbal quilt. We hear her lists, her unstressed series, no punctuation even, no pauses, no setting apart, and so everything joined with no subordination, no ranking. It is radical parataxis. Something droning. Nothing epitomizes another. If fruits are mentioned, many are named, for unlike symbolism, where one stands for the many, here the many stand for the many. Hol-Stein, one of the thirsty animals.

May also be a form of sexuality, that multifocal female body and its orgasmic capacity, where orgasms vary startlingly and are multiple. And how we think about the body.

> *She began to think about "climax" and "anticlimax"—what these mean in female and male associations.*[21] *The language of criticism: "lean, dry, terse, powerful, strong, spare, linear, focused, explosive"—god forbid it should be "limp"!! But—"soft, moist, blurred, padded, irregular, going around in circles," and other descriptions of* our bodies—the very abyss of aesthetic judgment, danger, the wasteland for artists!
>
> Frances Jaffer

Multiclimactic, multiple centers of attention: *Orlando, Between the Acts* where the cows, the rain intervene in art, where the border between life and art is down, is down!

The anti-authoritarian ethics occurs on the level of structure. We call all this "new" ("new form," "new book," "new way of writing," layered and "strudled," Metzger says), that use of the word "new" which, for centuries, has signaled antithesis to dominant values.[22] And which coincides with the thrilling ambition to write a great, encyclopedic, holistic work, the ambition to get everything in, inclusively, reflexively, monumentally.

Moreover there looms ahead of me the shadow of some kind of form which a diary might attain to. I might in the course of time learn what it is that one can make of this loose, drifting material of life; finding another use for it than the use I put it to, so much more consciously and scrupulously, in fiction. What sort of diary should I like mine to be? Something loose knit and yet not slovenly, so elastic that it will embrace anything, solemn, slight or beautiful that comes into my mind. I should like it to resemble some deep old desk, or capacious hold-all, in which one flings a mass of odds and ends without looking them through.[23]

The form of the desk, the tote bag, the journal. Interesting that for Woolf it was the form of a journal, and for Pound too it began as a "rag bag," a market mess of spilled fish, but became the form of *Analects,* of codes, a great man's laws. The *Cantos.* For Williams, it was the form of antiquarian history, local lore, wonders, layered in the City. *Paterson.* For both the male writers, a geopolitical stance, and this may have happened in a turn from the female, a reassertion of the polarized sexes. For the woman, it is a diary: her bag, her desk.

We intend to find ourselves. In the burning city.

The holistic sense of life without the exclusionary wholeness of art. These holistic forms: inclusion, apparent nonselection, because selection is censorship of the unknown, the between, the data, the germ, the interstitial, the bit of sighting that the writer cannot place. Holistic work: great tonal shifts, from polemic to essay to lyric. A self-questioning, the writer built into the center of the work, the questions at the center of the writer, the discourses doubling, retelling the same, differently. And not censored: love, politics, children, dreams, close talk. The first Tampax in world literature. A room where clippings paper the walls.

* * *

of course I am describing *The Golden Notebook* again. Again.

The artwork produced with this poetics distinguishes itself by the fact that it claims a social function and puts moral change and emotional vulnerability at the center of the experience for the reader.[24]

A possible definition? "female aesthetic" tackling Etruscan the doubling of doubleness cottage cheese the riddle our riddle sphinx to sphinx sexual difference artistic production I am hungry—K-Mart *The Golden Notebook* (ambiguously) nonhegemonic

Artistic production. The making, the materials the artist faced, collected, resolved. A process of makings, human choice and necessity. Any work is made to meet itself at the crossroads. Any work is a strategy to resolve, transpose, reweight, dilute, arrange, substitute contradictory material from culture, from society, from personal life. And (the) female aesthetic? Various and possibly contradictory strategies of response and invention shared by women in response to gender experiences.

Take Nin. Her diary as form and process is a stratagem to solve a contradiction often present in acute form for women: between the desire to please, making woman an object, and the desire to reveal, making her a subject. The culturally sanctioned relationship to art and artists which Nin continually imagines (ornament, inspiration, sexual and psychic reward) is in conflict with the direct relationship she seeks as artist, colleague, fellow worker. And Nin's diary as fact and artifact transposes these conflicting forces, reveals and protects simultaneously, allowing her to please others (by showing male friends specially prepared sections) while writing to please herself. Double, sometimes duplicitous needs.

These experiences of difference which produce different consciousnesses, different cultural expression, different relation to realms of symbols and to symbol users.

And therefore, and therefore, there is female aesthetic

> "from this [difference in priorities between men and women] spring not only marked differences of plot and incident, but infinite differences in selection, method and style"[25]

as there is male

> "It is a commonplace of criticism that only the male myths are valid or interesting; a book as fine (and well-structured) as *Jane Eyre* fails *even to be seen* by many critics because it grows out of experiences—events, fantasies, wishes, fears, daydreams, images of self—entirely foreign to their own."[26]

Female aesthetic begins when women take, investigate, the structures of feeling that are ours. And trying to take them, find also the conflict between these often inchoate feelings (coded as resistances, coded as the thirsty animals) and patriarchal structures of feeling—romantic thralldom, fear of male anger, and of our own weaknesses of nerve. Essentialist? No. We are making a creation, not a discovery.[27]

Yet it is also clear that there would be many reasons not to see female work as different. Why might someone object?

First, a desire to say that great art is not made by the factoring out of the sexes, is "androgynous" as Woolf uses the term in the twenties. The desire to state that greatness is (must be?) universal, that anything else is special pleading. The fear that to notice gender in any way becomes destructive to women. Thus the disincentive: if gender categories have always been used so destructively, our use of them, is it not "playing into their hands"? (There can be no greater proof of gender difference than this argument.)

> "Another reason women don't like their art to be seen through their bodies is that women have been sex objects all along and to let your art be seen that way is just falling right back into the same old rut."[28]

Women may then respond with a strategy of self-chosen, proud ghettoization (Richardson's "feminine psyche") or may respond as Woolf did. In that (neo-Freudian) context, Woolf's argument for androgyny is a situational triumph, rejecting the ghettos, stating that woman's art contains the man, contains the woman, has access to both.

Where then is (the) "female aesthetic"? In both, in all these strategies of response to difference. Even if, even when, contradictory.

Then, there is the desire at all costs to avoid special pleading, anything that looks like women have gotten by because of our sex (ambiguous word: meaning, our gender, meaning, our sexuality). This is a rejection of the stance of the courtesan for the firm-chinned professional, who does not (in dress, in manner, in talk) call attention to her "sex." She has her babies bravely between semesters. She fears being ghettoized. Being patronized. But it happened anyway. Any way. And she did not "control" it.

Another fear: that any aesthetic is bound to be misused, misappropriated, and this one is surely extremely vulnerable, with its blurring of all the elements we have firmly regarded as setting art apart: blurring between art and life, blurring between social creativity and "high" art, blurring between one's journal and one's poem, blurring between the artifact and the immersion in experience. Such exact polarities.[29]

I am hungry. I am very very hungry. Have I always been this empty?

I see that the next day I wrote in my journal. I would love someone (me?) to write a wonderful novel using the aesthetics you speak of—that are in my little list—mutuality, porousness, intimacy, recontacting a both/and, using both sides of the brain, nonhierarchic, anti- or multiclimactic, wholistic, lacking distance . . . perhaps didactic—but I think this person would have to be a particularly strong and careful artist. I have to tell you that I don't love one single novel that has come out of the 1960–70s women's movement. I don't think there is anyone concerned enough about either language or the real details of daily life. My sense is that everyone has been in a rush. (I feel in this rush too sometimes. Who wants to be a poor nobody at forty?) Sure there are wonderful moments here and there in different pieces of fiction. But no one has been concerned enough about FORM for me. None of this conflicts with what you said in our workshop. It's just another vantage point. Or perhaps also a corrective, in the sense that I fear too many women can take your aesthetic and churn out crap in three easy lessons. It's really like petit-point to get so close to one's subject, keep it porous, open, multiclimactic, and still keep it art.

Carol Ascher

The possible characteristics of a female aesthetic that you suggested seemed familiar and true certainly of my own work. Therefore I wanted to find out something else *and maybe offer something else (if only doubts or impatience with the deterministic limitation of nonhierarchic, layered, "porously intimate," subjective, etc. work) but felt disappointed and thwarted.* Mira Schor

In my essays' psychic and speculative search for contradictions, for wholeness, linear and constellated forms coexist. The work is metonymic (based on juxtaposition) and metaphoric (based on resemblance).[30] It is at once analytic and associative, visceral and intellectual, law and body. The struggle with cultural hegemony, and the dilemmas of that struggle, are articulated in a voice that does not seek authority of tone or stasis of position but rather seeks to express the struggle in which it is immersed.

As for female aesthetic? this essay points to one set of responses. One. Only. One among several possibilities.[31] Of course, for descriptive purposes, the actual traits matter, but more important are the functions I postulate, the functioning of the traits to express, confirm, illuminate, distort, evade, situations that have a gender valence.

But to test whether this is true, whether what you are calling women's themes do appear in women's writing, would you not have to use objective methods, devise objective tests of this knowledge? Mirra Komarovsky

We have covered the whole range of the anxiety inherent in scientific methodology—from Mirra's comment that the individual scholar must prove her thesis to have validation for more than herself (by the "objective," "scientific" method), to my concern that to define a female aesthetic is to establish a rigid norm of female creativity, which repeats the patriarchal tyranny of an "objective" absolute way of doing things. Lou Roberts

Can I prove it? I can prove that different social groups produce differences in cultural expression. I can prove that women are a social group. I can point to examples of differences in our relation to the symbolic order and in our cultural expression.

But I cannot prove that only women, that women only, use this aesthetic. And this failure is actually the strongest proof of all.

Women are (ambiguously) nonhegemonic because as a group, generally, we are outside the dominant systems of meaning, value, and power, as these saturate us, as they are "organized and lived."[32] To talk of society and culture as involving "hegemonic" practices does not mean that a hegemony is a ten-ton stone falling from nowhere to crush you into some shape.

Hegemony is not to be understood at the level of mere opinion or mere manipulation. It is a whole body of practices and expectations; our assignments of energy, our ordinary understanding of the nature of [people] and of [their] world. It is a set of meanings and values which as they are

experienced as practices appear as reciprocally confirming. It thus constitutes a sense of reality for most people in the society . . . but . . . is not, except in the operation of a moment of abstract analysis, in any sense a static system.[33]

A hegemony, as a set of practices, has "continually to be renewed, recreated, defended and modified" as well as "continually resisted, limited, altered, challenged."[34]

Women, in a generally nonhegemonic position, barred from or quota'd into the cultural institutions of renewal, defense, and modification.

> *the "mainstream" of European intellectual history was carried on without us. The clerical status of scholars in the Middle Ages automatically excluded women from the formal training which would fit them for the learned world, and as you know, this situation was not rectified in modern times until very recently. Moreover, self-study was for most women virtually impossible because the formal training was carried on in a highly technical Latin (and Greek after the humanist movement), unintelligible even to the ordinary literate lay person.*

Yet still (Margery of Kemp, Christine de Pisane)

> *At least once before in Western history, women did make a substantial contribution to the formation of what might—in the context of our workshop—be called a nonpatriarchal language, the "mother-tongue" which they spoke in contrast to the formal language of scholars.* Jo Ann McNamara

While it is generally asserted and assumed that women belong to the majority, to hegemony, I could suggest that women are virtually always (ambiguously) nonhegemonic. A great number are formed by residual social practices: ethnic, kin-based, male- and child-centered female communities. Some may be emergent, "alternative or oppositional to the dominant elements."[35]

Why are women as a group (ambiguously) nonhegemonic? A woman may be joined to a dominant system of meanings and practices by her race (say, white), yet not by her gender; she may be joined via her class, but not by her gender; joined thru her sexual preference, but not her gender. May be oppositional, with many sources of alternative conditions (working-class, black), but still oriented in ideology and consciousness towards hegemonic norms. (June Jordan's poem "If you saw a Negro lady" speaks of this possibility.)

(Ambiguously) nonhegemonic. For women, then, existing in the dominant system of meanings and values that structure culture and society may be a painful, or amusing, double dance, clicking in, clicking out—the divided consciousness. For this, the locus classicus is Woolf.

Again if one is a woman one is often surprised by a sudden splitting off of consciousness, say in walking down Whitehall, when from being the natural inheritor of that civilization, she becomes, on the contrary, outside of it, alien and critical.[36]

That shifting focus, bringing the world into different perspectives, is the ontological situation of women because it is our social situation, our relationship to power, our relationship to language.

What we here have been calling (the) female aesthetic turns out to be a specialized name for any practices available to those groups—nations, genders, sexualities, races, classes—all social practices which wish to criticize, to differentiate from, to overturn the dominant forms of knowing and understanding with which they are saturated.

Nineteenth-century Russian fiction has analogues with women's writing; both are nonhegemonic practices " 'pointless' or 'plotless' narratives stuffed with strange minutiae, and not obeying the accepted laws of dramatic development, lyrical in the wrong places, condensed in the wrong places, overly emotional, obsessed with things we do not understand, perhaps even grotesque."[37]

Négritude has analogues with women's aesthetic practices.

Consider then the white European standing before an object, before the exterior world, before Nature, before the *Other.* A man of will, a warrior, a bird of prey, a pure act of watching, the white European distinguishes himself from the object. He holds the object at a distance, he immobilizes it, he fixes it. Equipped with his instruments of precision, he dissects it in a cold analysis. Moved by the will to power, he kills the Other and, in a centripetal movement, he makes it a means to use for his own practical ends. He *assimilates* it. . . . The black African is first of all in his colour as if standing in the primordial night. He does not see the object, he *feels* it. He

is like one of those worms of the Third Day, a pure sensing field, Subjectively, at the end of his sensing organs, he discovers the Other. . . . So the black African sympathizes with, and identifies with the Other.[38]

For blacks excluded from a Western world of whiteness will affirm a connection to rhythms of earth, sensuality, intuition, subjectivity, and this will sound precisely as some women writers do.

High modernists are the most problematic nonhegemonic group, because they make a conservative, sometimes *fascisante* criticism of bourgeois culture, with "positive" values ascribed to hierarchical social order, sometimes buttressed by religion, but also, astonishingly, linked to peasant-based agriculture (as opposed, of course, to our urban, industrial morass). These writers constitute themselves as a group-against, whose common bond is opposition to the social basis on which their world in fact rested. Modernists show the strength of a politicized culture based on a shared revulsion to World War I, on one hand, and to the Russian Revolution on the other. This set of individuals with residual values (Eliot, Pound, Yeats, Lewis, Lawrence) depends on responses to a once-existing, and somewhat mythologized, social basis in peasantry and patriarch. Aristocrat, head, *il capo.* A revolution from the right.

Literature by women, in its ethical and moral position, has analogues with the equally nonhegemonic modernism in its subversive critique of culture. (Most —Woolf, Lessing, H. D.—are in no way right-wing; this more than just an "interesting observation.") In women's writing, as in modernist, there is a didactic element, related to the project of cultural transformation, of establishing values. In women's writing, as in modernist, there is an encyclopedic impulse, in which the writer invents a new and total culture, symbolized by and announced in a long work, like the modern long poem.

And contemporary women have produced just such works, often in the encyclopedic form of essay, compendia, polemic, collage, sacred and critical texts and images: Susan Griffin's *Woman and Nature;* Judy Chicago's *The Dinner Party;* Tillie Olsen's *Silences;* Mary Daly's *Gyn/Ecology.*[39]

Then, literature by women, in its phenomenological position, is associated with postmodernism, and with the democratic tolerance and realism of Williams, or the generative blankness and fecundity of Stevens. A list of the characteristics of postmodernism would be a list of the traits of women's writing: inwardness, illumination in the here and now (Levertov); use of the continuous present (Stein); the foregrounding of consciousness (Woolf); the muted, multiple, or absent *telos;* a fascination with process; a horizontal world; a decentered universe where "man" (indeed) is no longer privileged. But women reject this position as soon as it becomes politically quietistic or shows ancient gender values. For when the phenomenological exploration of self-in-world turns up a world that devalues the female self, when that exploration moves along the tacit boundaries of a social status quo, she cannot just "let it be," but must transform values, rewrite culture, subvert structures.

As my political analysis became more sophisticated, as I became a Marxist shaped by the Frankfurt School and then a feminist, I was able to present a theoretical explanation for my intuitions **(they were mine, and were thirsty).** *I understood that, at least for middle-class Americans under late capitalism, the form (structure, "language") of the culture is the sustaining force of social domination. But though I was implicated in those forms, I also knew—perhaps because of my somewhat marginal position as a woman, a petite bourgeoise?* **(She became the Etruscans?)**—*that I recognized these forms to be, not self-evident and natural, but intolerable and changeable, and that occasionally I discovered, and tried to transmit through my teaching and writing* **(printed in our Roman letters),** *examples and visions of how things could be other and better. It's been clearer and clearer to me, since I've been a feminist* **(some ricotta at the Italian Market)** *that we women were never completely integrated into the structures of capitalism* **((ambiguously) nonhegemonic)** *and that our difference* **(a vulval shape),** *whether only psychosocial or somehow biological as well, has given us a privileged position* **(horns with pink tips)** *from which to rebel and to envision alternatives. What's difficult, though, is to believe in those glimmers* **(entirely obligated to take and pass their test),** *to hold fast to them, even more, to model them out and explore them. And this is the importance to me of women's writing* **(her diary, her bag, her desk).** *If it's really the forms, the language, which dominate us, then disrupting them as radically as possible can give us hope and possibilities. What I'd like to try to understand and explain to other people* **(you yourselves are the riddle)** *is how the form of women's writing is, if ambiguously* **(of double, sometimes duplicitious needs)** *nonetheless profoundly revolutionary (as are, in their confusing ways, modernism and postmodernism, also written from positions of marginality to the dominant culture).*

But I've also been thinking recently that we need a writer who would be for feminism what Brecht was for modernism—who understands, to put it a little crudely, that literature doesn't change things, people do **(a process of makings, human choice and necessity).** *Our literature and thinking still seem quietistic to me, in that they require us to understand and respond, but not to* *act on our understanding, certainly not to act collectively* **(a room where clippings paper the walls).** *Moreover, I think we haven't even grasped the most radical implications of feminism for a theory which mediates back to practice: that we have a vision which men have barely glimpsed of what dialectical thought is really about—about a total, specific, feeling and thinking subject, present in her interaction with "objective" materials, overcoming the division between thought and action.* **(The golden bough. The golden fleece. The female quest?)**

I've been angry recently that, while theory proliferates, we have given up on what was compelling about the late sixties and early seventies—that feeling of infinite possibility which challenged us to think and live differently. So many of those experiments have fallen by the wayside, victim to the economic situation and our own discouragement and exhaustion. Sara Lennox

Exploration not in service of reconciling self to world, but creating a new world for a new self

given our revolutionary desire (that feeling of infinite possibility) for a nonpatriarchal order, in the symbolic realm and in the realms of productive, personal, and political relations.

for the Etruscans

NOTES

"For the Etruscans" is a shortened and revised version of what was said at Workshop 9, Barnard College, Scholar and Feminist Conference in 1979, and what was published in *The Future of Difference: The Scholar and the Feminist,* ed. Hester Eisenstein and Alice Jardine (Boston: G. K. Hall, 1980). For this text, I have also drawn on the version written for delivery at SUNY-Buffalo early in 1980. I have avoided the anachronistic temptation to alter opinions or to respond to commentary on the work, though I have updated some of the notes.

With special thanks to Carol Ascher, Frances Jaffer, Sara Lennox, Jo Ann McNamara, Lou Roberts, Mira Schor, and Louise Yelin for their own letters and notes on Workshop 9, not all of which are retained in this version of the essay.

My source of inspiration for this kind of writing was Robert Duncan's *H. D. Book* (chapters scattered in little magazines through the past decades), Virginia Woolf's essays, and my own letters. But (and) many people have reinvented the essay.

[1]Ellen Macnamara, *Everyday Life of the Etruscans* (London: B. T. Batsford, 1973), p. 181.

[2]Virginia Woolf, "Professions for Women," *The Death of the Moth and Other Essays* (1942; reprint ed., New York: Harcourt Brace Jovanovich, 1974), p. 240.

[3]James Wellard, *The Search for the Etruscans* (New York: Saturday Review Press, 1973), p. 192.

[4]The second task of Psyche. See Erich Neumann, *Amor and Psyche: The Psychic Development of the Feminine: A Commentary on the Tale by Apuleius,* trans. Ralph Manheim (1952; reprint ed., Princeton, N.J.: Princeton University Press, 1971). See also Rachel Blau DuPlessis, "Psyche, or Wholeness," *Massachusetts Review* 20 (Spring 1979): 77–96.

[5]Sources for this summary include Gayle Rubin, "The Traffic in Women: Notes on the 'Political Economy' of Sex," in *Toward an Anthropology of Women,* ed. Rayna [Rapp] Reiter (New York: Monthly Review Press, 1975), pp. 157–210; Nancy Chodorow, *The Reproduction of Mothering: Psychoanalysis and the Sociology of Gender* (Berkeley: University of California Press, 1978); Dorothy Dinnerstein, *The Mermaid and the Minotaur: Sexual Arrangements and Human Malaise* (New York: Harper & Row, 1976); Juliet Mitchell, *Psychoanalysis and Feminism: Freud, Reich, Laing, and Women* (New York: Vintage Books, 1975).

[6]Frances Jaffer, "Procedures for Having Lunch," unpublished manuscript.

[7]Sigmund Freud, *New Introductory Lectures on Psycho-Analysis,* trans. W. J. H. Sprott (New York: W. W. Norton, 1933), pp. 154–55.

[8]Aimé Césaire, *Une tempête, Adaptation de "La Tempête" de Shakespeare pour un théâtre nègre* (Paris: Editions du Seuil, 1969), p. 88.

[9]Virginia Woolf, *Orlando* (1928; reprint ed., New York: New American Library, 1960), p. 204.

[10]Virginia Woolf, "Mrs. Thrale," *The Moment and Other Essays* (1949; reprint ed., New York: Harcourt Brace Jovanovich, 1974), p. 52.

[11]B. Ruby Rich, "The Films of Yvonne Rainer," *Chrysalis: A Magazine of Women's Culture,* no. 2 (1977), pp. 115–27.

[12]Anaïs Nin, *The Diary of Anaïs Nin,* vol. 1, *1931–1934,* ed. Gunther Stuhlmann (New York: Swallow Press and Harcourt, Brace & World, 1966), p. 34.

[13]Julia Penelope Stanley and Susan J. Wolfe (Robbins), "Toward a Feminist Aesthetic," *Chrysalis,* no. 6 (1978), p. 68.

[14]Anita Barrows, "Form and Fragment," typescript, pp. 7–8, in Lynda Koolish, "A Whole New Poetry Beginning Here" (Ph.D. thesis, Stanford University, 1981), pp. 7–8.

[15]Deena Metzger, "In Her Image," *Heresies* 1 (May 1977): 2.

[16]Jean Baker Miller, *Toward a New Psychology of Women* (Boston: Beacon Press, 1976), p. 51; Carol Gilligan, *In a Different Voice: Psychological Theory and Women's Development* (Cambridge, Mass.: Harvard University Press, 1982), p. 22.

[17]Dorothy Richardson, "Leadership in Marriage," *New Adelphi,* 2nd ser. 2 (June–August 1929): 247.

[18]Doris Lessing, "Dialogue," *A Man and Two Women* (New York: Popular Library, 1958).

[19]Julia Kristeva, *About Chinese Women,* trans. Anita Barrows (New York: Urizen Books, 1977; first published in 1974), p. 38.

[20]Sheila de Bretteville, cited in Metzger, "In Her Image," p. 5.

[21]Combining two citations from Jaffer, the second from a letter in response to Workshop 9, the first, from a review of *Literary Women,* by Ellen Moers, *Chrysalis,* no. 1 (1977), p. 136.

[22]Metzger, "In Her Image," p. 7.

[23]Virginia Woolf, *A Writer's Diary,* ed. Leonard Woolf (New York: Harcourt, Brace, 1953), p. 13 (dated 1919).

[24]At this point in the original essay, I discussed the mother-daughter relations and the imbedded fictional artwork in *Kunstlerromane* by women such as Lessing, Woolf, Gilman, Olsen, Stead. The argument was based on a (then unpublished) chapter of

my *Writing Beyond the Ending: Narrative Strategies of Twentieth-Century Women Writers* (Bloomington: Indiana University Press, 1985); it can best be consulted there.

[25]Virginia Woolf, "Women Novelists," *Contemporary Writers* (New York: Harcourt, Brace & World, 1965), p. 27. Review dates from 1918.

[26]Joanna Russ, "What Can a Heroine Do? Or Why Women Can't Write," in *Images of Women in Fiction: Feminist Perspectives,* ed. Susan Koppelman Cornillon (Bowling Green, Ohio: Bowling Green University Popular Press, 1972), p. 14.

[27]Analysis of "Essentialism" as a philosophic concept made by Sybil Cohen to the Delaware Valley Women's Studies Consortium, April 1984.

[28]Lucy Lippard, *From the Center: Feminist Essays on Women's Art* (New York: E. P. Dutton, 1976), p. 92.

[29]Confirmation of these strategies in Barbara Currier Bell and Carol Ohmann, "Virginia Woolf's Criticism: A Polemical Preface," in *Feminist Literary Criticism: Explorations in Theory,* ed. Josephine Donovan (Lexington: University Press of Kentucky, 1975), pp. 48–60; and in Melissa Meyer and Miriam Schapiro, "Waste Not/Want Not: Femmage," *Heresies,* no. 4 (1978), pp. 66–69.

[30]Roman Jakobson, "Linguistics and Poetics," in *Style in Language,* ed. Thomas A. Sebeok (Cambridge, Mass.: MIT Press, 1960), pp. 350–77.

[31]Because locating just one set of strategies, my description is, necessarily, completely incomplete. It does not deal with an absolutely parallel, but aesthetically opposite use of the oracular, gnarled, compressed tactics, suggesting the difficulty of articulation, not its fluidity: Emily Dickinson. Marianne Moore. Laura Riding. Mina Loy. As Jeanne Kammer has said: "There emerges a complex psychology of linguistic parsimony related to a professional identity. Haunted by the specter of the sweet-singing 'poetess,' the woman poet may have come to the 'modern' style of the early decades of the twentieth century by a very different route than her male counterparts" ("The Art of Silence and the Forms of Women's Poetry," in *Shakespeare's Sisters: Feminist Essays on Women Poets,* ed. Sandra Gilbert and Susan Gubar [Bloomington: Indiana University Press, 1979], p. 156).

[32]Raymond Williams, "Base and Superstructure in Marxist Cultural Theory," *New Left Review* 82 (November–December 1973): 9.

[33]Ibid.

[34]Raymond Williams, *Marxism and Literature* (Oxford: Oxford University Press, 1977), p. 112.

[35]Ibid., p. 124.

[36]Virginia Woolf, *A Room of One's Own* (New York: Harcourt, Brace, 1929), p. 101. Compare Richard Wright's observation in 1956: "First of all, my position is a split one. I'm black. I'm a man of the West. These hard facts condition, to some degree, my outlook. I see and understand the West; but I also see and understand the non- or anti-Western point of view. . . . This contradiction of being both Western and a man of color creates a distance, so to speak, between me and my environment. . . . Me and my environment are one, but that oneness has in it, at its very heart, a schism." In *Présence Africaine,* no. 8–9–10 (November 1956), the proceedings of the First International Conference of Negro Writers and Artists, cited in *The Black Writer in Afriea and the Americas,* ed. Lloyd W. Brown (Los Angeles: Hennessey & Ingalls, 1973), p. 27.

[37]Russ, "What Can a Heroine Do?" in Cornillon, pp. 14–15.

[38]Léopold Sédar Senghor, *Liberté* I, cited in *Selected Poems/Poésies Choisies,* trans. and intro. C. Williamson (London: Rex Collings, 1976), pp. 12–13. *Négritude* (a black aesthetic) is a controversial concept: distinguished writers and critics oppose it (Wole Soyinka, Ralph Ellison) and embrace it (James Baldwin, Senghor).

[39]Susan Griffin, *Woman and Nature: The Roaring Inside Her* (New York: Harper & Row, 1978); Judy Chicago, *The Dinner Party: A Symbol of Our Heritage* (Garden City, N.Y.: Anchor Press, 1979); Tillie Olsen, *Silences* (New York: Delacorte Press, 1978); Mary Daly, *Gyn/Ecology: The Metaethics of Radical Feminism* (Boston: Beacon Press, 1978).

"The Blank Page" and the Issues of Female Creativity

Susan Gubar

When the "Mona Lisa" was stolen from the Louvre in Paris in 1911 and was missing for two years, more people went to stare at the blank space than had gone to look at the masterpiece in the 12 previous years.

BARBARA CARTLAND, *Book of Useless Information*

"The female genital, like the blank page anticipating the poem, is an absence, a not me, which I occupy."

SANDRA MCPHERSON, "Sentience,"
The Year of Our Birth

Consider for a moment Ovid's story of Pygmalion: a king, shocked at the vices of the female disposition, creates a beautiful statue, significantly an ivory statue white as snow, with which he falls in love. Pygmalion brings his lovely statue presents, dresses it, bedecks it with jewels, fondles its curves, takes it to bed, and prays to Venus that his wife be (or be like) his "ivory girl." When he feels the ivory under his fingers soften, "as wax grows soft in sunshine, made pliable by handling," Pygmalion is astonished with joy: "It is a body!"[1] Not only has he created life, he has created female life as he would like it to be—pliable, responsive, purely physical. Most important, he has evaded the humiliation, shared by many men, of acknowledging that it is *he* who is really created out of and from the *female* body.

Our culture is steeped in such myths of male primacy in theological, artistic, and scientific creativity. Christianity, as feminist theologians have shown us, is based on the power of God the Father, who creates the natural world of generation out of nothing.[2] Literary men like Coleridge, Shelley, Keats, and Ruskin describe the author as priest, prophet, warrior, legislator, or emperor, reinforcing the idea most lucidly articulated by Gerard Manley Hopkins that "the male quality is the creative gift."[3] The example of scientific overreachers from the Faust of Marlowe and Goethe and Mann to the most recent DNA biologists implies that scientific ingenuity also seeks to usurp the generative powers of the womb, even as it tries to re-create the female in the male's image. But if the creator is a man, the creation itself is the female, who, like Pygmalion's ivory girl, has no name or identity or voice of her own. Margaret Atwood's prose poem about two boys who construct a woman out of mud ("She began at the neck and ended at the knees and elbows: they stuck to essentials") seems far removed from Ovid's ivory girl. Yet the boys continually "repair her, making her hips more spacious, enlarging her breasts with their stone nipples," as they make use of "her brown wormy flesh" ("They would take turns, they were not jealous, she preferred them both"):[4] both the ivory girl and the mud woman are products of the male imagination, objects created for the use of men. As Simone de Beauvoir has demonstrated in *The Second Sex,* the phallus as the transcendent incarnate turns woman's self into an object, an other.[5]

Woman is not simply an object, however. If we think in terms of the production of culture, she is an art object: she is the ivory carving or mud replica, an icon or doll, but she is not the sculptor. Lest this seem fanciful, we should remember that until very recently women have been barred from art schools as students yet have always been acceptable as models. Both Laura and Beatrice were turned into characters by the poems they inspired. A poet as sensitive as Chaucer to this reification of the female allowed Criseyde to recognize and lament her own dilemma: "Allas, of me, unto the worldes ende,/Shall neyther ben ywriten nor ysonge/No good word; for these bokes wol me shende" (bk. 5, st. 152). Like the words written about her, she fears she will be "rolled on many a tongue!"[6] Shakespeare also studied this entrapment of the woman: looking at Desdemona, whom he imagines dishonest, Othello asks, "Was this fair paper, this most goodly book,/Made to write 'whore' upon?" (4. 2. 71–72).[7] The appropriation of the female "read" or "written" into textuality makes one wonder about many another heroine's fate. On more than one occasion, Dorothea Brooke in *Middlemarch* bemoans her inability to become a poet; how much of a comfort is Will Ladislaw's assurance to her that "You *are* a poem"?[8] Ezra Pound quotes a similar line to the poet H. D.: "You are a poem, though your poem's naught."[9] When the metaphors of literary creativity are filtered through a sexual lens, female sexuality is often identified with textuality.

We can see this clearly in Henry James's *Portrait of a Lady,* where the ideal *jeune fille* is described as "a sheet of blank paper." So "fair and smooth a page would be covered with an edifying text," we are told, whereas the experienced woman who is "written over in a variety of hands" has a "number of unmistakable blots" upon her surface.[10] In *To the Lighthouse,* egotistical Mr. Ramsay sees his wife in a window "as an illustration, a confirmation of something on the printed page to which one returns, fortified and satisfied."[11] In Conrad's *Victory,* Axel Heyst saves a girl called Lena (after the seductress Magdalena) from "murdering silence" in an all-female orchestra by renaming her Alma (soul). Converted from artist to accompanist to accomplice, she seems "like a script in an unknown language" or "like any writing to an illiterate." Looking at her Heyst feels like "a man looking this way and that on a piece of writing which he was unable to decipher, but which may be big with some revelation."[12] From *The Waste Land,* in which a woman's hair "glow[s] into words," to *The Great Gatsby,* in which the "black rivulets" of mascara on a weeping woman lead to the "humorous suggestion . . . that she sing the notes on her face," the female body has been feared for its power to articulate itself.[13] More recently, Ishmael Reed describes sex in this way: "He got good into her Book tongued her every passage thumbing her leaf and rubbing his hands all over her binding."[14] And John Berryman sums up the implications of this metaphor when he concludes a sequence of sonnets written to his mistress with the emphatic admission, "You are the text."[15]

In fact contemporary critics not infrequently write about the act of reading in sexual terms. A "passage" of a text is a way of knowing a "corpus" or "body" of material that should lead us on, tease us—but not too obviously. "Knowing" a book is not unlike sexual knowing, as Roland Barthes has demonstrated in *The Pleasure of the Text,* his erotics of reading.[16] Not only do we experience gratification orally as we "devour" books voraciously, we also respond subliminally to the "rhythms" of the plot, looking forward to a "climax." Furthermore, Claude Lévi-Strauss implies that the female must be identified with language used by men in the perpetuation of culture when he explains in *Structural Anthropology* that women are "*circulated* between clans, lineages, or families, in place of *the words of the group,* which are *circulated* between individuals."[17] Similarly, William Gass argues that "ordinary language ought to be like the gray inaudible wife who services the great man: an ideal engine, utterly self-effacing, devoted without remainder to its task; but when language is used as an art it is no longer used merely to communicate. It demands to be treated as a thing, inert and voiceless."[18] The connection between women and words is less explicit but just as significant in David Lodge's *Language of Fiction.* Lodge asserts that the medium of fiction "is never virgin: words come to the writer already violated by other men."[19] This corrupt lexicon presumably can be redeemed by the semantics of the text, for its seminal meaning is almost always closely associated with the seed or semen of the author's mind brooding on the repository of the page that bodies this meaning forth: Pound, for example, describes ideal creativity as a result of "the balance of the ejector [male] and retentive media [female]."[20] And in an effort to criticize what he calls phallocentrism, Jacques Derrida describes the literary process in terms of the identification of the pen with the penis, the hymen with the page. As Gayatri Spivak explains in her introduction to *Of Grammatology,* "The hymen is the always folded . . . space in which the pen writes its dissemination."[21]

This model of the pen-penis writing on the virgin page participates in a long tradition identifying the author as a male who is primary and the female as his passive creation—a secondary object lacking autonomy, endowed with often contradictory meaning but denied intentionality. Clearly this tradition excludes woman from the creation of culture, even as it reifies her as an artifact within culture. It is therefore particularly problematic for those women who want to appropriate the pen by becoming writers. Especially in the nineteenth century, women writers, who feared their attempts at the pen were presumptuous, castrating, or even monstrous, engaged in a variety of strategies to deal with their anxiety about authorship. Sandra M. Gilbert and I discuss some of these strategies in *The Madwoman in the Attic.* But just as important as the anxiety the male pen produces in the would-be woman writer is the horror she experiences at having been defined as his creation. Indeed, this problem seems to explain the coherence of nineteenth- and twentieth-century writing by women. Isak Dinesen's short story "The Blank Page" addresses this question with brilliant clarity.[22] This story can be used to illustrate how woman's image of herself as text and artifact has affected her attitudes toward her physicality and how these attitudes in turn shape the metaphors through which she imagines her creativity.

Briefly, the story of "The Blank Page" centers on the sisters of a Carmelite order of nuns who grow flax to manufacture the most exquisite linen in Portugal. This linen is so fine that it is used for the bridal sheets of all the neighboring royal houses. After the wedding night, it is solemnly and publicly displayed to attest to the virginity of the princess and is then reclaimed by the convent, where the central piece of the stained sheet "which bore witness to the honor of a royal bride" is mounted, framed, and hung in a long gallery with a plate identifying the name of the princess. These "faded markings" on the sheets are of special interest to female pilgrims who journey to the remote country convent, for "each separate canvas with its coroneted name-plate has a story to tell, and each has been set up in loyalty to the story." But pilgrims and sisters alike are especially fascinated by the framed canvas over the one nameless plate which displays the blank, snow-white sheet that gives the story its title.

Before approaching the mysterious promise of this blank page, let us consider the framed, bloodied sheets in the convent gallery, which is both a museum of women's paintings (each sheet displays a unique, abstract design and is mounted in a heavy frame) and a library of women's literary works (the bloodstains are the ink on these woven sheets of paper). Collected and cherished by a female community that has seen better days, a kind of paradigmatic women's studies department, these bloodstained marks illustrate at least two points about female anatomy and creativity: first, many women experience their own bodies as the only available medium for their art, with the result that the distance between the woman artist and her art is often radically diminished; second, one of the primary and most resonant metaphors provided by the female body is blood, and cultural forms of creativity are often experienced as a painful wounding. Although I will deal with each point separately, they are clearly related, for the woman artist who experiences herself as killed into art may also experience herself as bleeding into print.

As to my first point, the objects of art in "The Blank Page" are quite literally made out of the bodies of the royal princesses whose internal fluids are the print and the paint. Not only are artist and art object physically linked but also the canvases in the nuns' gallery are a direct response to the princesses' private lives. Royal ladies and highborn spinsters would proceed "on a pilgrimage which was by nature both sacred and secretly gay" to read the canvas bearing the name of a princess they had once served and to review the bride's life as a wife and mother. The stained pages are therefore biographical remnants of otherwise mute existences, a result of and response to life rather than an effort at producing an independent aesthetic object. Indeed, were the female community less sensitive to the significance of these signs, such stained sheets would hardly be considered art at all. Dinesen implies that woman's use of her own body in the creation of art results in forms of expression devalued or totally invisible to eyes trained by traditional aesthetic standards. She also seems to imply that, within the life of domesticity assigned the royal princess from birth, the body is the only accessible medium for self-expression.

Certainly women's limited options—expressed in the parable by the fact that all royal (privileged) women marry while all single women are nuns—have shaped the art they create. Unable to train themselves as painters, unable to obtain the space or income to become sculptors, gifted women in these areas have had to work in private, using the only materials at hand—their bodies, their selves. If, as Dinesen implies, female creativity has had to express itself within the confines of domesticity (in part because of the emphasis on the personal in female socialization), women could at the least paint their own faces, shape their own bodies, and modulate their own vocal tones to become the glass of fashion and the mold of form. To make up, for such women, means not only making up stories but making up faces. In terms of the Pygmalion myth with which I began, the woman who cannot become an artist can nevertheless turn herself into an artistic object.

Nowhere is this better illustrated than in the novels of George Eliot, in which many female characters squander their creativity on efforts to reconstruct their own images. From Hetty Sorrel in *Adam Bede* (1859), who peers at her earrings and ribbons in a blotched mirror as she sits at a dressing table where the brass handles hurt her knees, to Gwendolen Harleth in *Daniel Deronda* (1876), who poses as Saint Cecilia in a glass exquisitely framed in black and gold, Eliot analyzes the ways in which women's creativity has been deformed by being channeled into self-destructive narcissism. Eliot criticizes the idea that beauty is an index of moral integrity by demonstrating how narcissism infantilizes the female, turning her from an autonomous person into a character in search of an author (or a page in search of a pen, to keep up the metaphor with which I began). Such a woman is always and only "becoming"—that is, she is beautiful but she is also always imagining some future identity that she is unable to realize by herself.

Hetty, for example, is like a hopeful child waiting to be adopted and adapted by Arthur Donnithorne. Gwendolen's case is even clearer. After arranging at a party a series of *tableaux vivants* to gain the admiration of prospective suitors, she chooses to represent herself imitating a character who looks like a statue. Instead of turning back to life on cue, Gwendolen is terrified by a picture of a dead face that unexpectedly springs out of a movable panel before her eyes; when she returns to herself, she looks "like a statue into which a soul of Fear had entered: her pallid lips were parted; her eyes, usually narrowed under their long lashes, were dilated and fixed."[23] The dead face, Eliot implies, is Gwendolen's own. For in the process of turning herself into an artistic object, she makes herself autistic. Increasingly enmeshed in dreadful hallucinatory visions of her own distress, Gwendolen eventually is impelled to desire the death of her husband and her own death. Eliot's conviction that female creativity has been perverted (here as female narcissism and elsewhere in Eliot's fiction as enthrallment to male authority) helps us understand why she never wrote a *Kunstlerroman.*

Many female modernists have studied the deflection of female creativity from the production of art to the re-creation of the body,[24] but Edith Wharton, especially in *The House of Mirth* (1905), was most clearly influenced by

Eliot. Cynthia Griffin Wolff has already brilliantly shown how Wharton's first title, "A Moment's Ornament," captures "the decorative imperative of that aspect of femininity that Lily embodies and the ultimate fragility of a self that has grown out of that imperative."[25] Lily Bart's gracefulness, her stylish clothing, her belief in the power of her own beauty to do good, her use of furniture and nature as backdrop scenery, even the lines on her face she traces with dismay in the mirror justify Diana Trilling's view that "Lily herself possesses the quality of a fine work of art."[26] Because financially she cannot afford to maintain herself as a work of art without the money of a man, Lily's artful presentation resembles Gwendolen's; she too must attract a husband. Furthermore, the only man in the novel who could possibly save her from becoming a commodity on the marriage market is himself incapable of viewing her as anything but a collectible in the aesthetic market: "As a spectator, Lawrence Selden had always enjoyed Lily Bart," making "use of the 'argument from design,' " for he knows that "she must have cost a great deal to make" (p. 3). In fact, he believes that "even her weeping was an art" (p. 69). While he is correct that her self-presentation empties her of spontaneity and makes her relationships duplicitous, Selden only further imprisons her in this ornamental behavior by characterizing it as so uniquely her own.

Although Lily's art does not procure her security in the form of a husband, and although she is quite destitute on her deathbed at thirty years of age, Lily seems to triumph at the end of *The House of Mirth,* for her death is the logical extension of her life. Having turned herself into an artistic object, she now literally kills herself into art. Significantly, before taking the overdose that lulls her to sleep and death, Lily goes through her wardrobe of dresses which "still kept the long unerring lines, the sweep and amplitude of the great artist's stroke, and as she spread them out on the bed the scenes in which they had been worn rose vividly before her" (p. 211). She remembers specifically the party at which she, like Gwendolen, participated in *tableaux vivants;* when Lily turned herself into Reynolds's portrait of "Mrs. Lloyd," she looked "as though she had stepped, not out of, but into, Reynolds's canvas" (p. 131), thereby demonstrating to Selden and the other onlookers "the touch of poetry in her beauty" (p. 131).

While Lily waits in bed for the drug to bring oblivion, she thinks that there is "some word she had found" to tell Selden that would make everything well (p. 317). On entering her room, Selden sees "a narrow bed along the wall, and on the bed, with motionless hands and calm, unrecognizing face, the semblance of Lily Bart." He kneels by this semblance for a final moment, "drain[ing] their last moment to the lees; and in the silence there passed between them the word which made all clear" (p. 323). This word is Lily's dead body; for she is now converted completely into a script for his edification, a text not unlike the letters and checks she has left behind to vindicate her life. She submits to being thus defined, although she liberates her lover from such a degradation by destroying his letters. Lily's history, then, illustrates the terrors not of the word made flesh but of the flesh made word. In this respect, she illuminates the problems Wharton must have faced in her own efforts to create rather than be created—efforts not always successful, if we can trust the reported comments of as important a contemporary critic as Percy Lubbock, who, in comparing her to Henry James, quipped, "She was herself a novel of his, no doubt in his earliest manner."[27]

Like Kafka's victim in "In the Penal Colony," women have had to experience cultural scripts in their lives by suffering them in their bodies. This is why Maxine Hong Kingston writes so movingly about her resemblance to the mythic woman warrior who went into battle scarred by the thin blades which her parents literally used to write fine lines of script on her body.[28] For the artist, this sense that she is herself the text means that there is little distance between her life and her art. The attraction of women writers to personal forms of expression like letters, autobiographies, confessional poetry, diaries, and journals points up the effect of a life experienced as an art or an art experienced as a kind of life, as does women's traditional interest in cosmetics, fashion, and interior decorating. Many books by women writers (like Dorothy Richardson's *Pilgrimage* and Olive Schreiner's *From Man to Man*) cannot be finished because they are as ongoing and open-ended as the lives of their authors. The mythic lives of women artists from Emily Dickinson (who played out the Gothic fiction of the white-dressed maiden imprisoned in daddy's house) to Isadora Duncan (whose costumes and affairs and death express her creed as well as her autobiography does) also reveal the close identification experienced between the female artist and her art. Duncan's medium, dance, has always been acceptable for women, I suspect, because the body of the dancer becomes an instrument or icon on stage.

Not a few of the most exciting experiments of women artists, moreover, grow out of a self-conscious attempt to obliterate aesthetic distance. The insistence that the domestic is artistic is illustrated, for example, by Katherine Mansfield, who writes lovingly about the ways in which a kitchen is decorated with utensils and food.[29] It finds a kind of culmination in the performative art of Mierle Laderman Ukeles, whose "Maintenance Art Activity" consists in washing museum floors with a damp mop, over and over again, and even more to the purpose here, Carolee Schneemann, who reads from a long scroll she removes from her vagina in her performance of *Up To and Including Her Limits* (1975).[30] Writing about Eleanor Antin's videotape in which she applies makeup to the "canvas" of her face and her photo sequence in which she documents "carving" ten pounds off her body, Arlene Raven and Deborah

Marrow explain that "Antin's work is of the verb rather than the object" in its effort to illuminate how "in this culture women themselves are the art product."[31] Judy Chicago's *The Dinner Party* celebrates creative women who, refusing conventional definitions of the female, are in a privileged position to question the definitions of art that our culture accepts.[32] But *The Dinner Party* plates also imply that women, who have served, have been served up and consumed. They therefore remind us of the sacrificial nature of the body "dressed" as art. Indeed, in *The House of Mirth* the fashion plate often lifts a face "like an empty plate held up to be filled" (p. 45); Lily's beauty is described as a "glaze," (pp. 3 and 51), reminding us of the fragility and vulnerability of Chicago's "service."

The stain that darkens the reputation of a girl like Lily and the stains of vaginal imagery at the center of the porcelain plates turn us to my second point, the centrality of blood as a symbol furnished by the female body. Luce Irigaray has argued recently that women are made vulnerable by their inability to express their delirium: "Women do not manage to articulate their madness: they suffer it directly in their body."[33] In "The Blank Page," the sacrificial suffering of the inarticulate female body is revealed in the bloody ink print, which is the result of the hymen's penetration and which is so valued by the community; the high steward to the royal house proclaims, "*Virginem eam tenemus*—'we declare her to have been a virgin.' " While bloodstains can be a certification of freedom from pregnancy or the mark of entrance into puberty, in the Dinesen story they call to mind the more tragic associations of blood for women, especially for women writers. Unlike the blood of menstruation which presumably defiles like a curse or the blood of childbirth which is also taboo, the blood on the royal sheets is holy, for it certifies purity. By making the sheets into objects as sacred as altar cloths, the nuns sanctify the sacrifice of the virgin, and by reading the stains as if they were hieroglyphs, they imply that we must come to terms with the fact of blood before we can understand the nature of female art.

Lest this seem too Gothic a pronouncement, let me point to as pious and proper a poet as Christina Rossetti, for this Victorian conspicuously offers her song as a virginal blood sacrifice.[34] At least part of Rossetti's plan came from her sense that she was the model, not the painter, the character, not the author. She has been represented, moreover, "Not as she is, but as she fills his dream" ("In an Artist's Study"). Rossetti therefore experiences herself as "Dead before Death," to quote the title of a characteristic poem. In "From the Antique" she is explicit about her life's being "Doubly blank in a woman's lot." As in Dinesen's tale of the convent, Rossetti's speaker on the doorstep of "The Convent Threshold" feels caught between sexuality and chastity. Choosing to become a nun because there is mysterious "blood" between her lover and herself, she looks down to see her lily feet "soiled with mud,/With *scarlet* mud *which tells a tale*" (my italics). The same identification of bleeding with telling or singing appears in the vision of the suffering woman poet in "From House to Home." Beginning with a sense of sinfulness, of being stained, Rossetti transforms herself in a number of religious poems into the bride of Christ and into a female Christ (she had modeled for a painting of the Virgin Mary). Imitating his blood sacrifice, she testifies repeatedly to the "mark of blood" that distinguishes her door ("Despised and Rejected"). But this sign also recalls the tokens of virginity on the cloth brought before the elders of the city to redeem the honor of a slandered bride, as described and prescribed in Deuteronomy.[35]

The blood sacrifice of the royal princesses in Dinesen's story represents the sacrifice of virginity not through martyrdom but through marriage, although the stained sheets also seem to imply that marriage may be a martyrdom. The blood on the royal sheets is considered holy because it proves that the bride is a valuable property, given by father to husband for the production of sons. In other words, before the sheet is collected by the convent sisters and assumes the status of art, the bloodstains are a testimony to the woman's function as a silent token of exchange. But this blood wedding transforms the marriage bed into a kind of coffin in which the virgin is sacrificed. Dinesen may have considered her own marriage deathly because she believed her many illnesses in later life were related to the syphilis she unwittingly contracted from her husband, but she implies that many women in a patriarchy experience a dread of heterosexuality. The storyteller of "The Blank Page," who has told "one more than a thousand" tales, is thereby associated with Scheherazade, who told stories in the night to circumvent the death awaiting her after sexual initiation in the bridal chamber.[36] Not only a surrogate for her own body, her stories save the daughters of the land who have been threatened with penetration and execution by the misogynist king who is enraged by the infidelity of women.

The framed stained sheets imply, then, that all the royal princesses have been "framed" into telling the same story, namely, the story of their acquiescence as objects of exchange. The American poet H. D. treats this confinement as a primary plot (conspiracy) against women and an effective plot (burial mound) for women.[37] She has therefore dedicated her late poems to excavating the female by creating alternative scripts, as she explains in *Trilogy* (1944–46), where her muse carries "the blank pages/of the unwritten volume of the new."[38] In *Helen in Egypt* (1961), H. D. begins with a character who is a phantom because she has barely survived being turned into a heroine. Basing her epic on a seventh-century palinode by Stesichorus that claims Helen never got any farther than Egypt—it was merely an image of Helen that accompanied Paris to Troy to give the pretext for war—H. D. shows us a Helen haunted by stories told about the war, specifically, the blame heaped on her for presumably causing it and the role allotted to her as an object of exchange: war booty, gift, ransom.[39] Helen realizes at the beginning of H. D.'s revisionary epic that her own imagined role in the war was a sacrifice inflicted on her, that "the script was a snare" (p. 220). But it is terribly difficult for her to evade this snare or escape it, because, like Eliot's and Wharton's heroines and Dinesen's royal princesses, she feels that "*She herself is the writing*" (p. 91). She tries to rescue herself by considering other stories of growing up female, but these turn out to be the same story of the blood sacrifice of daughters and virgins: Iphigenia, Polyxena, Chryseis, Cassandra, and Persephone.

"Helen returns constantly to this theme of sacrifice" (p. 84) because the daughters "were all sacrificed in one way or another" (p. 173). Inside this blood factory, she mourns the "bridal pledge at the altar" as a "pledge to Death" (p. 73). Her blood consciousness harkens back to the mythic female artist, Philomela: raped by Tereus who cut out her tongue, Philomela took her revenge by weaving her story for all to see with "purple/On a white background."[40] In addition, Helen's blood consciousness also reaches forward to contemporary poems (by writers like May Swenson and Marge Piercy) in which the phallus is a weapon. The desecrated female body that feels like the self of the poet bleeds into print.[41] Anne Sexton therefore associates her female anatomy with the absence of control: in her female revision of *The Waste Land,* "Hurry Up Please It's Time," she identifies herself with Eliot's wasted working-class women, for she knows "I have ink but no pen." As a result, Sexton feels that her poems "leak" from her "like a miscarriage."[42] Likewise, Frida Kahlo, who presents herself as bound by red cords that are not only her veins and her roots but also her paint, is a painter whose tragic physical problems contributed to her feeling wounded, pierced and bleeding.[43]

Mired in stories of our own destruction, stories which we confuse with ourselves, how can women experience creativity? In Dinesen's story, the creation of female art feels like the destruction of the female body. Because of the forms of self-expression available to women, artistic creation often feels like a violation, a belated reaction to male penetration rather than a possessing and controlling. Not an ejaculation of pleasure but a reaction to rending, the blood on the royal marriage sheets seems to imply that women's paint and ink are produced through a painful wounding, a literal influence of male authority. If artistic creativity is likened to biological creativity, the terror of inspiration for women is experienced quite literally as the terror of being entered, deflowered, possessed, taken, had, broken, ravished—all words which illustrate the pain of the passive self whose boundaries are being violated. In fact, like their nineteenth-century foremothers, twentieth-century women often describe the emergence of their talent as an infusion from a male master rather than inspiration from or sexual commerce with a female muse. This phallic master causes the woman writer to feel her words are being expressed from her rather than by her. Like Mary Elizabeth Coleridge who sees her lips as a silent wound, or Charlotte Brontë who suffers from a "secret, inward wound" at the moment she feels the "pulse of Ambition," or Emily Dickinson who is bandaged as the empress of Calvary in some poems and as the wounded deer in others, women writers often dread the emergence of their own talents.[44]

If writing feels as if "the ink was pouring on to the sheets like blood," as it does for the heroine of Margaret Drabble's *The Waterfall,* then the poet can easily become frightened by her sense of victimization: "I was unnaturally aware of my own helpless subjugation to my gifts, my total inability to make a poem at will," Drabble's poet explains. "I resented this helplessness as I resented a woman's helplessness with a man."[45] The twentieth-century prototype of this anxious sense that poetry comes from being possessed and wounded is, of course, Sylvia Plath. Like Drabble's heroine, whose creativity is released by giving birth to a second child, Plath begins *Ariel* with a relatively cheerful poem about childbirth that seems to promise a more positive way of imagining creativity for women. But even here in "Morning Song," the new birth of morning seems converted into grief and mourning, for the child is a "New statue" and the parents "stand round blankly as walls." This statue, confined by blank walls, is transformed into the far more terrible wife of "The Applicant": "Naked as paper to start," she is "A living doll." Like Pygmalion's ivory girl, Atwood's mud woman, Eliot's living statues, Lily Bart who really is a living doll, or Sexton who is her own dead doll, Plath's wife is a kind of automaton in the clutches of someone else's will. Plath herself is not infrequently filled with a "thin/Papery feeling" which helps explain the thousands of paper dolls she played with as a child, and her poems lend sinister insight into Mansfield's perception that "Female dolls in their nakedness are the most female things on earth."[46] From Maggie Tulliver, who tortures her doll in the attic in *The Mill on the Floss,* to Pecola Breedlove in Toni Morrison's *The Bluest Eye,* who tortures herself because she cannot look like her doll, the heroines of women's fiction have played with dolls to define themselves.

Plath can only escape the dread that she has been created as an object (as she says in "Lady Lazarus," "I am your opus") by self-inflicted violence, by watching the bloodstain darkening the bandages, proving she is alive. A sense of helplessness seems inextricably related to the emergence of her voice: "By the roots of my hair some god got hold of me," Plath exclaims in "The Hanging Man"; "I sizzled in his blue volts like a desert prophet." As terrible as her muse is, however, her pain at his violation also proves she is alive. But the jolting words snapped out by these electric charges mean that the poetry Plath creates will kill her: "The blood jet is poetry,/There is no stopping it" ("Kindness"). She has had the blood sucked out of her by "Daddy," who "Bit [her] pretty red heart in two." While she has killed "The vampire who said he was you/And drank my blood for a year," she is still haunted by the black bat airs, and, having been bitten, she has herself become a bloodsucker, for "The blood flood is the flood of love" ("The Munich Mannequins"). The redness of the "Tulips" in her hospital bed therefore "talks to [her] wound, it corresponds." If she sees herself as "flat, ridiculous, a cut-paper shadow/Between the eye of the sun and the eyes of the tulips," she knows she will eventually fly into these eyes which are, of course, "the red/Eye, the cauldron of morning" ("Ariel"). The only way to escape papery perfection in "Stings" is to become the "red/Scar in the sky." At the end of *Ariel,* she is finally perfected into a statue: "The illusion of a Greek necessity/Flows in the scrolls of her toga" as she accepts her role as heroine in the tragedy that is not only her art but her life ("Edge"). The dialectic between perfection and blood destruction means finally that Plath's "Words" are "Axes" from whose rhythmic strokes she will never recover.[47]

Adrienne Rich also identifies blood with the female body: "Sometimes every/aperture of my body/leaks blood. I don't know whether/to pretend that this is natural." In other words, Rich is aware that even her most intimate attitudes toward her own blood have been defined by male voices:

You worship the blood
you call it hysterical bleeding
you want to drink it like milk
you dip your finger into it and write
you faint at the smell of it
you dream of dumping me into the sea.[48]

Rich seeks a way of experiencing the blood through her own sensibilities. In "Women," she sees three Fates who seem to represent her sense of women's progress in history: the first sister is sewing a costume for her role as Transparent Lady when "all her nerves will be visible"; the second is sewing "at the seam over her heart which has never healed entirely"; and the third is gazing "at a dark-red crust spreading westward far out on the sea."[49] Her beauty and her vision promise a time when women can authentically deny that our "wounds come from the same source as [our] power."[50] Refusing a poetry that implies performance, competition, or virtuosity, Rich strives in her most recent volume for "the musings of a mind/one with her body," within

. . . the many-lived, unending
forms in which she finds herself,
becoming now the sherd of broken glass
slicing light in a corner, dangerous
to flesh, now the plentiful, soft leaf
that wrapped round the throbbing finger,
soothes the wound.[51]

Rich's promise returns us to Dinesen's story, for the snow-white sheet of the nameless princess also seems to promise a breakthrough into new beginnings for new stories that can soothe the wound. The single and singular blank sheet that so fascinates pilgrims and nuns alike in the convent library-museum seems an alternative to the bloody sheets that surround it. Thus, in terms of the patriarchal identification of women with blankness and passivity with which we began, Dinesen's blank page becomes radically subversive, the result of one woman's defiance which must have cost either her life or her honor. Not a sign of innocence or purity or passivity, this blank page is a mysterious but potent act of resistance. The showing of the sheet, moreover, proves that the anonymous princess has forced some sort of acknowledgment or accommodation in the public realm. On a literal level, the blank sheet may mean any number of alternative scripts for women: Was this anonymous royal princess not a virgin on her wedding night? Did she, perhaps, run away from the marriage bed and thereby retain her virginity intact? Did she, like Scheherazade, spend her time in bed telling stories so as to escape the fate of her predecessors? Or again, maybe the snow-white sheet above the nameless plate tells the story of a young woman who met up with an impotent husband, or of a woman who learned other erotic arts, or of a woman who consecrated herself to the nun's vow of chastity but within marriage. Indeed, the interpretation of this sheet seems as impenetrable as the anonymous princess herself. Yet Dinesen's old storyteller, who learned her art from her grandmother much as her grandmother learned it from her own mother's mother, advises her audience to "look at this page, and recognize the wisdom of my grandmother and of all storytelling women!"

The storyteller says this, I think, first of all because the blank page contains all stories in no story, just as silence contains all potential sound and white contains all color. Tillie Olsen's *Silences* and Rich's *On Lies, Secrets, and Silences* teach us about the centrality of silence in women's culture, specifically the ways in which women's voices have gone unheard. While male writers like Mallarmé and Melville also explored their creative dilemmas through the trope of the blank page, female authors exploit it to expose how woman has been defined symbolically in the patriarchy as a tabula rasa, a lack, a negation, an absence. But blankness here is an act of defiance, a dangerous and risky refusal to certify purity. The resistance of the princess allows for self-expression, for she makes her statement by not writing what she is expected to write. Not to be written on is, in other words, the condition of new sorts of writing for women. The nuns and the storyteller recognize wisdom in the place where the uninitiated see nothing, in part by removing their attention from the traditional foreground to what is usually relegated to background, much as we might radically revise our understanding of the 1,001 blank days during which Scheherazade silently bore the king three sons whose surprise appearance at the end of the 1,001 nights wins her a reprieve from the death sentence. But the old crone also praises the blank sheet because it is the "material" out of which "art" is produced. Women's creativity, in other words, is prior to literacy: the sisterhood produces the blank sheets needed to accomplish writing.

Olive Schreiner, the great feminist theorist, explains what this implies about English culture when one of her heroines holds up a book and theorizes about literary history:

> When I hold these paper leaves between my fingers, far off across the countless ages I hear the sound of women beating out the fibres of hemp and flax to shape the first garment, and, above the roar of the wheels and spinnies in the factory, I hear the whirr of the world's first spinning wheel and the voice of the woman singing to herself as she sits beside it, and know that without the labor of those first women kneeling over the fibres and beating them swiftly out, and without the hum of those early spinning wheels, neither factory nor paper pulp would ever have come into existence. . . . This little book!—it has got its roots down, down, deep in the life of man on earth; it grows from there.[52]

If we take Schreiner's claim seriously, no woman is a blank page: every woman is author of the page and author of the page's author. The art of producing essentials—children, food, cloth—is woman's ultimate creativity. If it is taken as absence in the context of patriarchal culture, it is celebrated within the female community by the matrilineal traditions of oral storytelling. The veiled, brown, illiterate old woman who sits outside the city gates in Dinesen's tale therefore represents her grandmother and her grandmother's grandmother: "they and I have become one." Existing before man-made books, their stories let us "hear the voice of silence."

The blank page is created in Dinesen's story through the silent act of "sowing" the flax seed and "sewing" the linen, acts traditionally performed by the female community. This is the subversive voice of silence, and we can associate it with the silent sound of Philomela's shuttle. The process whereby "the seed is skillfully sown out by labor-hardened virginal hands" and the "delicate thread is spun, and the linen woven" is the secret of Dinesen's society of convent spin-sters. For the nuns who have raised the production of flax into art, then, the blank page is a tribute to what has been devalued as mere craft or service. The nuns refuse to relegate the domestic or the decorative to a category outside the realm of true creativity. At the same time, moreover, they sanctify their own creative efforts; for the germ of the story, the first seed of the flax, comes from the holy land of the daughter Achsah who sought and received a blessing—specifically, the blessing of springs of water. When the flax blooms, we are told, the valley becomes "the very color of the apron which the blessed virgin put on to go out and collect eggs within Saint Anne's poultry yard, the moment before the Archangel Gabriel in mighty wing-strokes lowered himself onto the threshold of the house, and while high, high up a dove, neck-feathers raised and wings vibrating, stood like a small clear silver star in the sky."

Members of this "blithe sisterhood" thus preserve the history of lesser lives in the blood-markings and glorify the blank page as a sacred space consecrated to female creativity, thereby pulling heaven down to earth. While the bloodstained sheets resemble the true icon of suffering divinity as seen on Veronica's veil, the virgin-blue flax blossoms remind us of Mary at the moment before the Annunciation—Mary waiting, about to become pregnant with divinity.[53] In her readiness for rapture, she represents the female community, and its blank page is therefore hers. The convent in Dinesen's story is a Carmelite order, the order which propagates a special devotion to our Lady; indeed, in the Middle Ages, Carmelite theologians were among the earliest defenders of the Immaculate Conception, the doctrine that Mary was conceived without original sin. But the Carmelites have also produced the greatest Christian mystics, most importantly Saint Theresa, who inspired Dorothea Brooke's, and George Eliot's, quest for a life of significant action. As the sanctity of Mary is hidden in the ordinary, so Theresa's mysticism was grounded in the everyday. The vows of poverty, chastity, and obedience taken by the Carmelite nuns are strenuous attempts to aid contemplation, to achieve Theresa's ordinary mysticism. Not martyrs who suffer death but prophets who suffer inspiration, the convent virgins spend much time in silence, seeking to duplicate Mary's receptivity to bearing and giving birth to the Incarnate Word.[54] Thus, the blank place, a female inner space, represents readiness for inspiration and creation, the self conceived and dedicated to its own potential divinity.

Many of the late-Victorian and twentieth-century women writers whom

I have mentioned were involved in the creation of a revisionary theology that allowed them to reappropriate and valorize metaphors of uniquely female creativity and primacy. I have space here only for a few examples. Florence Nightingale, in *Cassandra* (1852), pronounced her audacious belief that "the next Christ will perhaps be a female Christ."[55] Schreiner claimed by extension that God is female when she argued that "the desire to incarnate" in the true artist "is almost like the necessity of a woman to give birth to her child."[56] From the blessed Lady who carries the new Bible of blank pages in H. D.'s *Trilogy* to Gertrude Stein's liturgical drama in praise of *The Mother of Us All,* modernist texts by women appear to corroborate the contemporary French feminist Hélène Cixous's sentiment that the woman writer sanctifies herself when she gives birth to "an amniotic flow of words that reiterates the contractual rhythms of labor."[57] Margaret Anderson and Jane Heap's desire for a radically new kind of art is brilliantly illustrated by the *Little Review* volume that consisted of sixty-four blank pages.[58] The substitution of the female divinity for the male god, the womb for the penis, as the model of creativity was so pronounced by the turn of the century that it posed a real problem for such male modernists as T. S. Eliot, Lawrence, and Joyce. But of course, many women writers remained sensitive to the fact that such a mother-goddess myth was compensatory and that—unless freed from any biological imperative—it could entrap women in destructive stereotypes. To celebrate uniquely female powers of creativity without perpetuating destructive feminine socialization is the task confronted by writers as dissimilar as George Eliot, Rossetti, Schreiner, Wharton, H. D., and Mansfield, all of whom are involved in efforts to sanctify the female through symbols of female divinity, myths of female origin, metaphors of female creativity, and rituals of female power. "The Blank Page" is only one of many parables in an ongoing revisionary female theology.[59]

Since I have here persistently and perhaps perversely ignored history, I feel it is only fair to conclude by acknowledging that certain historical factors helped make this modulation in valuation possible. The shift in metaphors from the primacy of the pen to the primacy of the page is a late-nineteenth-century phenomenon. The Romantic movement in poetry, the suffrage movement in politics, the rise of anthropology with its interest in fertility gods and goddesses, the myth of mother right coming at a time when the infant mortality rate was significantly lowered and birth control became more widely available, and finally World War I—all of these need to be studied, for we are only just beginning to read the patterns and trace the figures in what all too recently has been viewed as nothing but the blank pages of women's cultural and literary history.

Denise Levertov expresses my own sense of excitement at engaging in such a task, even as she reminds us how attentive and patient we must be before the blank page to perceive genuinely new and sustaining scripts. Like Dinesen, moreover, Levertov seeks to consecrate her own repeated efforts to contribute to the blank pages of our future history. Recognizing that strenuous and risky readiness at the moment before conception is itself an art, a kind of balancing act, Levertov praises the discipline that allows the poet to stand firm on "one leg that aches" while upholding "the round table" of the "blank page." Such diligence receives its just reward when the round table of the blank page is transformed into living wood that sighs and sings like a tree in the wind. This attitude toward creativity substitutes for the artistic object an act or process. Furthermore, just as sexuality was previously identified with textuality, the text itself now becomes infused with potent sexual energy, or so Levertov claims in what we can now recognize as a decidedly female vision:

One at a time
books, when their hour is come
step out of the shelves.
Heavily step (once more, dusty, fingermarked,
but pristine!)
to give birth:

each poem's passion
ends in an Easter,
a new life.
The books of the dead
shake their leaves,
word-seeds fly and
lodge in the black earth.[60]

NOTES

I am indebted to Sandra M. Gilbert for her insights and encouragement on this paper.

[1]Ovid, *Metamorphoses,* trans. Rolfe Humphries (Bloomington: Indiana University Press, 1955), pp. 241–43.

[2]See Mary Daly, *Beyond God the Father: Toward a Philosophy of Women's Liberation* (Boston: Beacon Press, 1973), and Carol P. Christ and Judith Plaskow, eds., *Womanspirit Rising: A Feminist Reader in Religion* (New York: Harper & Row, 1979).

[3]Hopkins to Richard Watson Dixon, June 30, 1896, *The Correspondence of Gerard Manley Hopkins and Richard Watson Dixon,* ed. C. C. Abbott (London: Oxford University Press, 1935), p. 133. For a fuller discussion of the identification of

paternity and creativity, see Sandra M. Gilbert and Susan Gubar, *The Madwoman in the Attic: The Woman Writer and the Nineteenth-Century Literary Imagination* (New Haven, Conn.: Yale University Press, 1979), pp. 3–44.

[4]Margaret Atwood, untitled poem in the Circe/Mud sequence, *You Are Happy* (New York: Harper & Row, 1974), p. 61.

[5]See Simone de Beauvoir, *The Second Sex,* trans. H. M. Parshley (New York: Vintage Books, 1974).

[6]I am indebted for this view of Criseyde to Marcelle Thiebaux's "Foucault's Fantasia for Feminists: The Woman Reading," a paper delivered at the MMLA Convention, Indianapolis, November 8, 1979.

[7]The symbolic value of the "handkerchief/Spotted with strawberries" (3.3.434–45) is closely identified with Othello's fear that his "lust-stained" bedsheets must "with lust's blood be spotted." For a brilliant discussion of male sexual anxiety in *Othello,* see Stephen J. Greenblatt, "Improvisation and Power," in *Literature and Society: Selected Papers from the English Institute,* ed. Edward W. Said (Baltimore: Johns Hopkins University Press, 1980), pp. 57–99.

[8]George Eliot, *Middlemarch* (Boston: Houghton Mifflin, 1968), p. 166.

[9]Pound, quoted by H. D., *End To Torment: A Memoir of Ezra Pound,* ed. Norman H. Pearson and Michael King (New York: New Directions, 1979), p. 12.

[10]Henry James, *The Portrait of a Lady* (New York: W.W. Norton, 1978), pp. 238, 268. It is interesting to compare this view of the blank female text with the horror Margaret Laurence's heroine Morag feels at the dying, fat, and servile stepmother whose "face is as blank as a sheet of white paper upon which nothing will ever now be written" (*The Diviners* [Toronto, 1978], p. 250).

[11]Virginia Woolf, *To the Lighthouse* (New York: Harcourt Brace Jovanovich, 1955), p. 53.

[12]Joseph Conrad, *Victory* (Garden City, N.Y.: Anchor Books, 1959), p. 183.

[13]T. S. Eliot, *The Waste Land and Other Poems* (New York: Harcourt, Brace & World, 1955), sec. 2, I. 110; see also sec. 5, II. 378–90: "A woman drew her long black hair out tight/And fiddled whispered music on those strings." F. Scott Fitzgerald, *The Great Gatsby* (New York, 1953), p. 34; see also p. 119 where Jordan Baker is described as "a good illustration."

[14]Ishmael Reed, *Mumbo Jumbo* (New York: Avon Books, 1978), pp. 208–9.

[15]John Berryman, *Berryman's Sonnets* (New York: Farrar, Straus & Giroux, 1967), p. 114. Russell Baker recently compared women to books, bemoaning the fact that "it is common nowadays to find yourself confronting a woman no thicker than a slim volume of poetry while buying a book wider than a piano" ("Sunday Observer," *New York Times Magazine,* December 2, 1979, p. 28).

[16]See Roland Barthes, *The Pleasure of the Text,* trans. Richard Miller (New York: Hill & Wang, 1975), p. 32: "There are those who want a text (an art, a painting) without a shadow, without the 'dominant ideology'; but this is to want a text without fecundity, without productivity, a sterile text (see the myth of the Woman without a Shadow)." Barthes's next book, *A Lover's Discourse,* makes the connection explicit by moving directly from the eroticism of texts to the eroticism of bodies.

[17]Claude Lévi-Strauss, *Structural Anthropology,* trans. Claire Jacobson and Brooke Grundfest Schoepf (New York: Basic Books, 1963), p. 61.

[18]William H. Gass, *Fiction and the Figures of Life* (New York: Alfred A. Knopf, 1971), p. 93.

[19]David Lodge, *The Language of Fiction: Essays in Criticism and Verbal Analysis of the English Novel* (New York: Columbia University Press, 1967), p. 47.

[20]Pound's postscript to his translation of Remy de Gourmont's *Natural Philosophy of Love* is discussed and quoted by Lawrence S. Dembo in *Conceptions of Reality in Modern American Poetry* (Berkeley: University of California Press, 1966), p. 158.

[21]Gayatri Chakravorty Spivak, introduction to Jacques Derrida, *Of Grammatology* (Baltimore: Johns Hopkins University Press, 1976), pp. lxv–lxvi. See also Derrida's discussion of how "woman is (her own) writing" in *Spurs: Nietzsche's Styles/Eperons: Les Styles de Nietzsche* trans. Barbara Harlow (Chicago: University of Chicago Press, 1979), p. 57.

[22]Isak Dinesen, "The Blank Page," *Last Tales* (New York: Random House, 1957), pp. 99–105. Because of the frequent quotations and the brevity of the fable, I have omitted page numbers entirely. For useful criticism of this story, see Thomas R. Whissen, *Isak Dinesen's Aesthetics* (Port Washington, N.Y.: Associated Faculty Press, 1973), pp. 101–6; Robert Langbaum, *Isak Dinesen's Art: The Gayety of Vision* (Chicago: University of Chicago Press, 1975), p. 219; and Florence C. Lewis, "Isak Dinesen and Feminist Criticism," *North American Review* 264 (Spring 1979): 62–72.

[23]George Eliot, *Daniel Deronda* (Baltimore: Penguin Books, 1967), p. 91.

[24]Elinor Wylie (herself a beautiful woman) wrote a series of poems and novels about the "firing" of girls into porcelain artifacts. For a fuller discussion of Wylie's attraction to formal perfection, see Céleste Turner Wright, "Elinor Wylie: The Glass Chimaera and the Minotaur," *Women's Studies* 7 (1980): 159–70 (special issue on women poets, edited by Sandra M. Gilbert and Susan Gubar).

[25]Cynthia Griffin Wolff, *A Feast of Words: The Triumph of Edith Wharton* (New York and Oxford: Oxford University Press, 1977), p. 109; all further references to Wharton's *The House of Mirth,* ed. R. W. B. Lewis (New York: New York University Press, 1977), will be included in the text. Wharton's second provisional title, "The Year of the Rose," points up the ways in which the Jew Rosedale is a double for Lily, in part because his Semitism allows him to glimpse the sordid economic realities behind the veneer of culture, much as Wharton's feminism did for her. For a useful consideration of Wharton's debt to Eliot, see Constance Rooke, "Beauty in Distress: *Daniel Deronda* and *The House of Mirth,*" *Women and Literature* 4 (Fall 1976): 28–39.

[26]Diana Trilling, "*The House of Mirth* Revisited," in *Edith Wharton: A Collection of Critical Essays,* ed. Irving Howe (Englewood Cliffs, N.J.: Prentice-Hall, 1962), p. 109.

[27]Percy Lubbock, quoted in Millicent Bell, *Edith Wharton and Henry James: The Story of Their Friendship* (New York: George Braziller, 1965), p. 21.

[28]See Maxine Hong Kingston, *The Woman Warrior: Memoirs of a Girlhood among Ghosts* (New York: Vintage Books, 1977), pp. 41–42 and 62–63.

[29]Domestic artistry is repeatedly celebrated in Mansfield's stories, most especially in the figure of Mrs. Fairfield in "Prelude" (*The Short Stories of Katherine Mansfield,* ed. John Middleton Murry [New York: Alfred A. Knopf, 1976]), but also throughout the letters in which Mansfield writes about the culinary skills of a maid or the interior decorating she herself performs on a hotel room.

[30]For a photograph of Mierle Laderman Ukeles performing her *Washing, Tracks, Maintenance: Maintenance Art Activity III* (July 22, 1973), see Lucy R. Lippard, *From the Center: Feminist Essays on Women's Art* (New York: E. P. Dutton, 1976), p. 60; for her discussion of Carolee Schneemann, see p. 126.

[31]Arlene Raven and Deborah Marrow, "Eleanor Antin: What's Your Story?" *Chrysalis,* no. 8 (Summer 1979), pp. 43–51.

[32]See Judy Chicago, *Through the Flower: My Struggle as a Woman Artist* (New

York: Doubleday, 1975) and her book on the work, *The Dinner Party* (Garden City, N.Y.: Doubleday, 1979).

[33]Irigaray, quoted by Diana Adlam and Couze Venn in "Women's Exile: Interview with Luce Irigaray," *Ideology and Consciousness* (Summer 1978): 74.

[34]See *The Complete Poems of Christina Rossetti,* ed. R. W. Crump (Baton Rouge: University of Louisiana Press, 1979).

[35]See Deuteronomy 22:13–24. I am indebted to Stephen Booth for pointing out the relevance of this Biblical passage. The issue of blood and sacrifice is a complicated one in the Catholic tradition, as this quotation from Charles Williams illustrates: "There is also, of course, that other great natural bloodshed common to half the human race—menstruation. That was unclean. But it is not impossible that that is an image, naturally, of the great bloodshed on Calvary, and perhaps, supernaturally, in relation to it. Women share the victimization of the blood; it is why, being the sacrifice so, they cannot be the priests. They are mothers, and, in that special sense, victims; witnesses, in the body, to the suffering of the body, and the method of Redemption" (*The Forgiveness of Sins* [London: Bles, 1950], p. 138).

[36]Scheherazade is an important model of the female storyteller for Dinesen. See the conclusion of "The Deluge at Norderney," *Seven Gothic Tales* (New York: Vintage Books, 1972), p. 79, and Hannah Arendt's foreword, "Isak Dinesen, 1885–1962," to Dinesen's *Daguerreotypes and Other Essays* (Chicago: University of Chicago Press, 1979), p. xiv. See also Gilbert's poem "Scheherazade," *Poetry Northwest* 19 (Summer 1978): 43.

[37]On women's entrapment in erotic plots, see Elizabeth Hardwick, *Seduction and Betrayal: Women and Literature* (New York: Random House, 1974), pp. 175–208, and Joanna Russ, "What Can a Heroine Do? Or, Why Women Can't Write," in *Images of Women in Fiction: Feminist Perspectives,* ed. Susan Koppelman Cornillon (Bowling Green, Ohio: Bowling Green University Popular Press, 1972), pp. 3–20.

[38]H. D., *Trilogy* (New York: New Directions, 1973), p. 103.

[39]H. D., *Helen in Egypt* (New York: New Directions, 1961); all further references to this poem will be included in the text.

[40]Ovid, *Metamorphoses,* trans. Humphries, pp. 148–51. Significantly, once Procne reads Philomela's story, she kills her own son and cooks him up for Tereus, who is made to eat him. The sisters are transformed into birds, "And even so the red marks of the murder/Stayed on their breasts; the feathers were blood-colored."

[41]See May Swenson, "Cut," *Iconographs* (New York: Charles Scribner's Sons, 1970), p. 13, and Marge Piercy, "I Still Feel You," in *Psyche: The Feminine Poetic Consciousness,* ed. Barbara Segnitz and Carol Rainey (New York: Dell, 1973), pp. 187–88.

[42]Anne Sexton, "Hurry Up Please It's Time," *The Death Notebooks* (Boston: Houghton Mifflin, 1974), p. 62; "The Silence," *Book of Folly* (Boston: Houghton Mifflin, 1972), p. 32.

[43]See Joyce Kozloff, "Frida Kahlo," *Women's Studies* 7 (1978): 43–58.

[44]See Mary Elizabeth Coleridge, "The Other Side of a Mirror," *The World Split Open: Four Centuries of Women Poets in England and America, 1552–1950,* ed. Louise Bernikow (New York: Vintage Books, 1974), p. 137; Charlotte Brontë, *The Professor* (New York: E. P. Dutton, 1964), p. 195; and the discussion of Emily Dickinson in Gilbert and Gubar, *Madwoman in the Attic,* pp. 581–650.

[45]Margaret Drabble, *The Waterfall* (New York: Popular Library, 1977), pp. 114–15.

[46]Katherine Mansfield to Violet Schiff, October 1921, *The Letters of Katherine Mansfield,* ed. John Middleton Murry (1929; reprint ed., New York: Howard Fertig, 1975), pp. 405–6. It is significant in this regard that both Mansfield and H. D. can only imagine the reeducation and redemption of boys in terms of their learning to play with dolls.

[47]See Sylvia Plath, *Ariel* (New York: Harper & Row, 1965). Plath's paper doll collection can be seen in the Lilly Library at Indiana University.

[48]Adrienne Rich, "Waking in the Dark," *Adrienne Rich's Poetry,* ed. Barbara Charlesworth Gelpi and Albert Gelpi (New York: W. W. Norton, 1975), p. 61.

[49]Rich, "Women," in Segnitz and Rainey, *Psyche,* p. 152.

[50]Rich, "Power," *The Dream of a Common Language* (New York: W. W. Norton, 1978), p. 3.

[51]Rich, "Transcendental Etude," ibid., p. 77.

[52]Olive Schreiner, *From Man to Man* (Chicago: Academy Press, 1977), p. 409.

[53]I am indebted to Mary Jo Weaver for informing me that the image on Veronica's headcloth has been associated by the Gnostics with the woman cursed by blood in Matthew 9:20–22.

[54]See Thomas Merton, *Disputed Questions* (New York: Farrar, Straus & Giroux, 1960), pp. 222x and 227. For a feminist discussion of the usefulness of the figure of the Virgin Mary to Catholic women, see Elisabeth Schussler Fiorenza, "Feminist Spirituality, Christian Identity, and Catholic Vision," in Christ and Plaskow, *Womanspirit Rising,* pp. 138–39, and Drid Williams, "The Brides of Christ," in *Perceiving Women,* ed. Shirley Ardener (New York: Halsted Press, 1977), pp. 105–26. The most important feminist analysis of how the Virgin Mary is exalted for virtues men would like women to exhibit is Marina Warner, *Alone of All Her Sex: The Myth of the Virgin Mary* (New York: Alfred A. Knopf, 1976). While I agree that Mary has been used against women who cannot be virgin and mother, I am arguing here that women have reclaimed her image in positive ways.

[55]Florence Nightingale, *Cassandra* (Old Westbury, N.Y.: Feminist Press, 1979), p. 53.

[56]Schreiner, *From Man to Man,* p. 453.

[57]Hélène Cixous, quoted by Verena Andermatt, "Hélène Cixous and The Uncovery of a Feminine Language," *Women and Literature* 7 (Winter 1979): 42.

[58]See Margaret Anderson, *The Unknowable Gurdjieff* (London: Routledge & Kegan Paul, 1962), p. 75.

[59]Sandra M. Gilbert's two brilliant papers, "Potent Griselda: D. H. Lawrence's *Ladybird* and Literary Maternity" (unpublished) and "Soldier's Heart: Literary Men, Literary Women, and the Great War," *Signs* 8 (Spring 1983): 422–50, document the importance to women of rising anthropological theories of mother right and the significance of World War I to women writers.

[60]Denise Levertov, "Growth of a Poet," *The Freeing of the Dust* (New York: New Directions, 1975), pp. 83, 78–79. See also Susan Fromberg Schaeffer, "The Nature of Genres," *Granite Lady* (New York: Macmillan, 1974), p. 136.

The Thieves of Language

Women Poets and Revisionist Mythmaking

Alicia Ostriker

I

What would become of logocentrism, of the great philosophical systems, of world order in general if the rock upon which they founded their church were to crumble?

If it were to come out in a new day that the logocentric project had always been, undeniably, to found (fund) phallocentrism, to insure for masculine order a rationale equal to history itself?

Then all the stories would have to be told differently, the future would be incalculable, the historical forces would, will, change hands, bodies, another thinking, as yet not thinkable, will transform the functioning of all society.[1]

Hélène Cixous

Nudgers and shovers
In spite of ourselves,
Our kind multiplies:
We shall by morning
Inherit the earth.
Our foot's in the door.[2]

Sylvia Plath

A major theme in feminist theory on both sides of the Atlantic for the past decade has been the demand that women writers be, in Claudine Herrmann's phrase, *voleuses de langue,* thieves of language, female Prometheuses.[3] Though the language we speak and write has been an encoding of male privilege, what Adrienne Rich calls an "oppressor's language"[4] inadequate to describe or express women's experience, a "Law of the Father"[5] which transforms the daughter to "the invisible woman in the asylum corridor"[6] or "the silent woman" without access to authoritative expression,[7] we must also have it in our power to "seize speech" and make it say what we mean.

Women writers have always tried to steal the language. What several recent studies demonstrate poignantly is that throughout most of her history, the woman writer has had to state her self-definitions in code form, disguising passion as piety, rebellion as obedience.[8] Dickinson's "Tell all the Truth but tell it slant" speaks for writers who in every century have been inhibited both by economic dependence and by the knowledge that true *writer* signifies assertion while true *woman* signifies submission. Among poets, even more than novelists, the thefts have been filchings from the servants' quarters. When Elaine Marks surveys the *écriture féminine* movement in Paris, she observes that in their manifestos of desire "to destroy the male hegemony" over language, "the rage is all the more intense because the writers see themselves as prisoners of the discourse they despise. But is it possible," she asks, "to break out?"[9]

Does there exist, as a subterranean current below the surface structure of male-oriented language, a specifically female language, a "mother tongue"? This is a debated issue. A variety of theorists argue in favor, others argue against, while a number of empirical studies in America seem to confirm that insofar as speech is "feminine," its strength is limited to evoking subjective sensation and interpersonal responsiveness; it is not in other respects powerful.[10]

The question whether a female language, separate but equal to male language, either actually exists or can (or should) be created awaits further research into the past and further gynocentric writing in the present. My argument in this essay concerns the already very large body of poetry by American women, composed in the last twenty years, in which the project of defining a female self has been a major endeavor.[11] What distinguishes these poets, I propose, is not the shared, exclusive *langage des femmes* desired by some but a vigorous and various invasion of the sanctuaries of existing language, the treasuries where our meanings for "male" and "female" are themselves preserved. I have elsewhere examined the ways in which contemporary women poets employ traditional images for the female body—flower, water, earth—retaining the gender identification of these images but transforming their attributes so that flower means force instead of frailty, water means safety instead of death, and earth means creative imagination instead of passive generativeness.[12] Here I want to look at larger poetic structures and suggest the idea that revisionist mythmaking in women's poetry may offer us one significant means of redefining ourselves and consequently our culture.

At first thought, mythology seems an inhospitable terrain for a woman writer. There we find the conquering gods and heroes, the deities of pure thought and spirituality so superior to Mother Nature; there we find the sexually wicked Venus, Circe, Pandora, Helen, Medea, Eve, and the virtuously passive Iphigenia, Alcestis, Mary, Cinderella. It is thanks to myth we believe that woman must be either "angel" or "monster."[13]

Yet the need for myth of some sort may be ineradicable. Poets, at least, appear to think so. When Muriel Rukeyser in "The Poem as Mask" exclaimed "No more masks! No more mythologies,"[14] she was rejecting the traditional division of myth from a woman's subjectivity, rejecting her own earlier poem that portrays Orpheus and the bacchic women who slew him as separate from herself. "It was myself," she says, "split open, unable to speak, in exile from myself." To recognize this, however, is evidently to heal both the torn self and the torn god; the poem's final lines describe a resurrected Orpheus whose "fragments join in me with their own music." When Adrienne Rich in "Diving into the Wreck" carries with her a "book of myths . . . in which/our names do not appear" and declares that she seeks "the wreck and not the story of the wreck/the thing itself and not the myth," while enacting a watery descent that inverts the ascents and conquests of male heroism, she implies the necessity, for a woman, of distinguishing between myth and reality. Yet when Rich identifies with a "mermaid" and "merman" and says that "We are, I am, you are . . . the one who find our way/back to this scene," the androgynous being and the fluid pronouns imply that "the thing itself" is itself mythic.[15]

When Circe in Margaret Atwood's "Circe/Mud Poems" snarls at her lover, "It's the story that counts. No use telling me this isn't a story, or not the same story. . . . Don't evade, don't pretend you won't leave after all: you leave in the story and the story is ruthless," she too describes the depersonalizing effects of myths on persons, the way they replay themselves over and over and "the events run themselves through/almost without us." But at the point of stating this, the poet declares that there are "two islands" that "do not exclude each other" and that the second "has never happened," "is not finished," "is not frozen yet."[16] In all these cases the poet simultaneously deconstructs a prior "myth" or "story" and constructs a new one which includes, instead of excluding, herself.

Let me at this point therefore define the term "revisionist mythmaking" and sketch the background behind the work I will discuss. Whenever a poet employs a figure or story previously accepted and defined by a culture, the poet is using myth, and the potential is always present that the use will be revisionist: that is, the figure or tale will be appropriated for altered ends, the old vessel filled with new wine, initially satisfying the thirst of the individual poet but ultimately making cultural change possible. Historic and quasi-historic figures like Napoleon and Sappho are in this sense mythic, as are folktales, legends, and Scripture. Like the gods and goddesses of classical mythology, all such material has a double power. It exists or appears to exist objectively, in the public sphere, and consequently confers on the writer the sort of authority unavailable to someone who writes "merely" of the private self. Myth belongs to "high" culture and is handed "down" through the ages by religious, literary, and educational authority. At the same time, myth is quintessentially intimate material, the stuff of dream life, forbidden desire, inexplicable motivation—everything in the psyche that to rational consciousness is unreal, crazed, or abominable.

In the wave of poetic mythmaking that broke over England in the Romantic period, we hear two strains. One is public antirationalism, an insistence that there were more things in heaven and earth than were dreamt of by Newton and Locke. The other is an assurance that the poets had personally experienced forces within the self so overwhelming that they must be described as gods and goddesses, titans, demiurges, and demons. But Romantic revisionists do not simply take seriously what the Augustans took ornamentally. When Shelley invents for his defiant Prometheus an anima not present in any classical source, or when "knowledge enormous" of divine and human suffering makes a god and a poet of Keats's Apollo, who then dies into immortal life with a scream: that is mythic revisionism. (The same scream, by the way, tears through the young throat of Edna St. Vincent Millay, in a poem many women loved as girls and later learned to despise; "Renascence," too, is a poem about the genesis of a poet.)

Like the Romantics, the early moderns—Yeats, Pound, Eliot—turned to myth as a means of defying their culture's rationalism and materialism. But while the women poets I will speak of share a distrust for rationalism, they do not share the modernist nostalgia for a golden age of past culture, and their mythmaking grows at least as much from a subterranean tradition of female self-projection and self-exploration as from the system building of the Romantics and moderns.[17]

Since 1960 one can count over a dozen major works (poem-sequences, long poems, or whole books) of revisionist myth published by American women, and one cannot begin to count the individual poems in which familiar figures from male tradition emerge altered. These poems generically assume the high literary status that myth confers and that women writers have often been denied because they write "personally" or "confessionally." But in them the old stories are changed, changed utterly, by female knowledge of female experience, so that they can no longer stand as foundations of collective male fantasy. Instead, as I hope by a few brief examples to show, they are corrections; they are representations of what women find divine and demonic in themselves; they are retrieved images of what women have collectively and historically suffered; in some cases they are instructions for survival.

II

> *Women have had the power of* naming *stolen from us. . . . To exist humanly is to name the self, the world and God. . . . Words which, materially speaking, are identical with the old become new in a semantic context that arises from qualitatively new experience.*[18] MARY DALY

Since the core of revisionist mythmaking for women poets lies in the challenge to and correction of gender stereotypes embodied in myth, revisionism in its simplest form consists of hit-and-run attacks on familiar images and the social and literary conventions supporting them. Thus in the stroke of a phrase, Sylvia Plath's Lady Lazarus dismisses "Herr God, Herr Lucifer" as the two faces of a single authoritarian and domineering being for whom a woman's body is "your jewel . . . your valuable." Anne Sexton in "Snow White" disposes of centuries of reverence for the virgin "rolling her china-blue doll eyes. . . . Open to say/Good Day Mama/and shut for the thrust/of the unicorn." Jean Tepperman's "Witch" begins with the lines "They told me/I smile prettier with my mouth closed" and ends calling for a black dress, wild hair, and her broomstick. Of the passive Euridice who exists only as the tragic object of Orpheus's love, the poet Alta writes a motto for any woman poet:

> *all the male poets write of orpheus*
> *as if they look back & expect*
> *to find me walking patiently*
> *behind them. they claim i fell into hell.*
> *damn them, i say.*
> *i stand in my own pain*
> *& sing my own song.*

Another solution to the male creator–female muse convention is Erica Jong's "Arse Poetica," a role-reversing prose-poem that contrives at once to deflate centuries of male aesthetic pretentiousness and to assert the identity of female sexuality and female creativity:

> Once the penis has been introduced into the poem, the poet lets herself down until she is sitting on the muse with her legs outside him. He need not make any motions at all.[19]

With poems like these, one imagines the poets stepping out of the ring dusting their hands off. But revisionist poems do not necessarily confine themselves to defiance and reversal strategies.

A more central set of preoccupations concerns female-female relationships and the relation of the female to suppressed dimensions of her own identity. Kate Ellis's "Matrilineal Descent" uses the Demeter-Kore story as an aid in discovering how we may reconstitute lost families, becoming spiritual mothers and daughters for each other in time of need. Mothers, daughters, sisters must be recovered as parts "of the original woman we are"; after dreaming that a rivalrous younger sister is a daughter, and killing her in the dream, the poet movingly realizes that like Demeter she can "go down and get her/it is not too late." Sharon Barba's "A Cycle of Women" depicts women's history before and during patriarchy as "that dream world . . . that dark watery place" presided over by a goddess, which each individual woman must try to remember, although the knowledge is locked from her. "Each one is queen, mother, huntress" and must reconstruct the past "until she knows who she is":

> *Until she rises as though from the sea*
> *not on the half-shell this time*
> *nothing to laugh at*
> *and not as delicate as he[Botticelli] imagined her:*
> *a woman big-hipped, beautiful, and fierce.*[20]

Interlocked images of fertility and artistic creativity govern the poem-sequence "Eurydice" by Rachel DuPlessis. Here the heroine not only resents (like Alta's Euridice) the loss of herself to a husband whose powerful sex and art define her "like a great linked chain" but is herself the snake "whose deepest desire was to pierce herself." Withdrawing from her husband, far back into the moist, stony "fissure" and "cave" of herself, she becomes a self-generating plant and finally, amid an efflorescence of organic images, her own mother, giving birth to the girlchild who is herself—or, since the sequence can be read as an allegory of female creativity, her poem. The idea of giving birth, unaided, to the self is also the conclusion of Adrienne Rich's "The Mirror in Which Two Are Seen as One," and governs the "dry bulb" metaphor of "Necessities of Life."[21]

All such poems are, I believe, aspects of an attempt by women to retrieve, from the myth of the abstract father-god who creates the universe *ab nihilo*, the figure on which he was originally based, the female creatrix.[22] And this is a figure *not* divided (as she is in C. J. Jung's and Erich Neumann's versions of her) into Sky Goddess (asexual) and Earth Mother (sexual but brainless).[23] Female attributes of flesh and spirit that traditional culture sets asunder, female writers commonly reunite. "The Goddess" for Denise Levertov is a furious woman who seizes the poet where she lies asleep in "Lie Castle" and hurls her against the walls. Prostrate outside the castle "where her hand had thrown me," the poet tastes the mud of a forest, bites the seed in her mouth, and senses the passing of "her" without whom nothing "flowers, fruits, sleeps in season,/without whom nothing/speaks in its own tongue, but returns/lie for lie!" To identify an active, aggressive woman with Truth is to defy a very long tradition that identifies strong females with deception[24] and virtuous females, including muses, with gentle inactivity. In "Song for Ishtar," one of Levertov's most playful and most compact poems, a Babylonian goddess of both love and war evokes images for what is divine and mundane, spiritual and animal, delicate and violent in female sexuality and female art. Levertov declares that the moon, ancient figure of purity and chastity, is a sow who grunts in the poet's throat.

Her great shining shines through me
so the mud of my hollow gleams
and breaks in silver bubbles

She is a sow
And I a pig and a poet

When she opens her white
lips to devour me I bite back
and laughter rocks the moon

In the black of desire
we rock and grunt, grunt and
shine[25]

A muse imagined in one's own likeness, with whom one can fornicate with violence and laughter, implies the extraordinary possibility of a poetry of wholeness and joy, as against the poetry of the "age of anxiety" in which Levertov was writing. That a sacred joy can be found within the self; that it requires an embracing of one's sexuality; that access to it must be described as movement downward or inward, in gender-charged metaphors of water, earth, cave, seed, moon: such is the burden of these and many other poems by women. To Stevens's post-Nietzschean formula "God and the imagination are one,"[26] they would add a crucial third element: God and the imagination and *my body* are one.

At the opposite pole from the creatrix is the destroyer, a figure women's poetry has been inhibited from exploring in the past by the need to identify femininity with morality. When they traffic in the demonic, women poets have produced some of the most highly charged images in recent American poetry. One thinks immediately of Plath's "disquieting muses," the three ladies "with stitched bald heads" who assemble around the poet, precipitated by the girl-scout cheeriness of a mother who attempts to deny reality's darkness; or the clinging "Medusa" who is at once classic monster, jellyfish, and the poet's mother; or her image of herself as avenging Phoenix-fiend at the close of "Lady Lazarus"; or the depiction of demonic possession in "Elm." In Anne Sexton, demonic images associated with madness, guilt, and death proliferate with increasing intensity, from the witches in *To Bedlam and Part Way Back* to the set of "Angels" in *The Book of Folly* whom the poet acquaints with "slime . . . bedbugs . . . paralysis," to the staggering "death baby" who is the poet's alter ego in *The Death Notebooks.*[27]

Plath and Sexton are dramatic portraitists, in contemporary poetry, of what Joseph Conrad called "the horror . . . the horror." Like Conrad, they imply that the hypocrisies of civilized rationality are powerless to destroy what is destructive in the world and in ourselves; indeed, that "the horror" may well be the most devastating product of our demands for innocence and virtue. But what distinguishes their demonism from Conrad's, and from the standard personifications of "evil" throughout Western poetry, is the common characteristic of passivity. Wherever in these two poets we find images of compelling dread, there we also find images of muteness, blindness, paralysis, the condition of being manipulated.

Inactivity is also a motif in several poems written by women about classic female monsters. Of Medusa, a perennial figure in male poetry and iconography, Ann Stanford's sequence "Women of Perseus" and Rachel DuPlessis's "Medusa" both remind us of the key event in this female's life, though it goes unmentioned in either Bulfinch's or Edith Hamilton's *Mythology:* her rape by Poseidon. In Stanford's poem the trauma "imprisons" Medusa in a self-dividing anger and a will to revenge that she can never escape, though she yearns to. In DuPlessis's sequence the three Graeae—whose one eye Perseus steals—are conflated into one mother-figure for Medusa; her rapist and killer are conflated into one male; and she herself becomes a static boundary "stone" and regresses to an infantile ur-language.[28]

The Homeric earth-goddess and sorceress Circe, who turns Odysseus's fellow sailors to beasts and who throughout Western literature represents the evil magic of female sexuality, is transformed in Margaret Atwood's "Circe/Mud Poems" into an angry but also a quite powerless woman. Men turn themselves to animals; she has nothing to do with it. "Will you hurt me?" she asks Odysseus at his first armor-plated appearance. "If you do I will fear you,/If you don't I will despise you." Circe is "a desert island" or "a woman of mud" made for sexual exploitation, and her encounters with Odysseus are war games of rape, indifference, betrayal, which she can analyze caustically, mounting a shrewd critique of the heroic ethos:

Aren't you tired of killing
those whose deaths have been predicted
and who are therefore dead already?
Aren't you tired of wanting to live forever?
Aren't you tired of saying Onward?

But this is passive, not active, resistance and cannot alter Odysseus's intentions. In Atwood's "Siren Song" the figure whose name still means "fatal seductress" sings a libretto of confinement turned vicious, "a stupid song/but it works every time." What Atwood implies, as do other women who examine the blackness that has represented femaleness so often in our culture, is that the female power to do evil is a direct function of her powerlessness to do anything else.[29]

III

The short, passionate lyric has conventionally been thought appropriate for women poets if they insist on writing, while the longer, more philosophical epic belongs to the real (male) poet.[30]

SUSAN FRIEDMAN

If male poets write large, thoughtful poems while women poets write petite, emotional poems, the existence of book-length mythological poems by women on a literary landscape itself signifies trespass. Three such works are H. D.'s postwar masterpiece *Helen in Egypt,* Susan Griffin's extended prose-poem *Woman and Nature: The Roaring Inside Her,* and Anne Sexton's

Transformations. They revise, respectively, ancient Greek and Egyptian mythology, the myth of objective discourse derived from the Western concept of a God superior to Nature, and a set of fairy tales. All of them challenge not only our culture's concepts of gender but also its concepts of reality.[31]

The *donnée* of H. D.'s three-part *Helen in Egypt* is that Helen of Troy —our culture's archetypal woman-as-erotic-object—was actually a male-generated illusion, a "phantom," and that "the Greeks and Trojans alike fought for an illusion."[32] H. D.'s sources are a fifty-line fragment by Stesichorus of Sicily (ca. 640–555 B.C.) and Euripides' drama *Helen.* According to these texts (themselves revisionist ones), "the real Helen" was transported by the gods from Greece to Egypt, where she spent the duration of the Trojan War waiting chastely for her husband Menelaus. In H. D.'s version Menelaus is a trivial figure, and the poet makes clear that sexual chastity—or any conventional morality—is no more to be expected of an epic heroine than of an epic hero. The poet radically transforms these sources as well as the vast body of Greek and Egyptian mythology of which she was mistress, and which she believed composed "all myth, the one reality" in the same way that she believed all history was a "palimpsest," a reiterated layering of changeless patterns. A more significant issue than the heroine's virtue is her relation to "the iron band of war"—meaning not only the Trojan War but the two world wars H. D. had lived through. Still more significant is the fact that the revised heroine is not woman-as-object at all, is not seen from the outside, but is instead a quintessential woman-as-subject, engaged in what is not a single but a threefold quest.[33]

H. D.'s "real Helen" is a "Psyche/with half-dried wings" (sec. 166), a soul emerging from a chrysalis of ignorance and passivity. Spiritually her quest is to decipher symbols, beginning with the hieroglyphs on the temple of the Egyptian god Thoth-Amen, where we find her alone at the poem's opening. This Helen is an "adept," an initiate seeking knowledge of the gods. Psychologically, she is engaged in the recovery of her splintered selves, elements of her own character and past which, we gradually discover, because they are "hated of all Greece" (sec. 2), have been "forgotten" by herself. These two tasks are one task, because "she herself is the writing" (sec. 22). The goddess who manifests herself as Isis-Aphrodite-Thetis is at first a mother-goddess to Helen but ultimately an aspect of her own identity.

As avatar of Aphrodite, the heroine must reconcile herself with the "Helen of Troy" she has forgotten she ever was. That is, the spiritual seeker must accept the erotic woman within herself. These discoveries coalesce, again, with a third aspect of her quest: the reconstitution of a primal family, which among other things means that Helen must determine the meaning to herself of her Trojan and Greek lovers, the seductive Paris and the militant Achilles, and must choose (not be chosen by) a "final lover."

Achilles, the great protagonist of the *Iliad,* is H. D.'s paradigmatic patriarchal male as Helen is the paradigmatic female. Heroic, male-centered, immortality-seeking, Achilles ruthlessly leads a group of "elect" warriors dedicated to discipline and control, called (punningly) "The Command." To Achilles, woman is either sacrificial victim or sexual spoils. He has forgotten his boyhood love of the mother-goddess Thetis. Precisely for this reason, Thetis—that is, the repressed feminine principle within him—can cause him to fall in love with the figure of Helen pacing the Trojan ramparts, and, in a moment of carelessness over an ankle-greave, to receive the fatal wound from "Love's arrow" in his heel: "it was God's plan/to melt the icy fortress of the soul,/and free the man." Helen's first perception of him in Egypt is of a dim outline growing clearer, "as the new Mortal,/shedding his glory,/limped slowly across the sand" (secs. 9–10).

H. D.'s attitude toward conquest (including the conquest of Time) anticipates Atwood's "Aren't you tired of killing . . . ? Aren't you tired of wanting to live forever?" Her image of masculine defense against feeling as a hard armor that should be dissolved and melted, for the man's own sake, parallels Rich's question in "The Knight": "Who will unhorse this rider/and free him from between/the walls of iron, the emblems/crushing his chest with their weight?"[34] It is cognate as well with the fates meted out to the male protagonists at the conclusions of *Jane Eyre* and *Aurora Leigh.* Brontë's and Browning's heroes are blinded in "fires" of sexual, and punitive, import. H. D.'s "arrow" penetrating a masculine chink is explicitly and evocatively sexual.

But the dissolving of male invulnerability in *Helen in Egypt* is part of a larger pattern. Helen's Trojan lover, Paris, while a less violent, more sensuous and woman-centered figure than Achilles, is ultimately assigned the role of "son" rather than "father" in a mother-father-son romantic triangle. Moreover, late in the poem Helen hears within herself "an heroic voice, the voice of Helen of Sparta," one who glories in "the thunder of battle . . . and the arrows; O the beauty of arrows" and must ask herself, "Do I love War? Is this Helena?" (secs. 176–77). The unveiling of this element in Helen parallels the release of Achilles' capacity to love. Replicating in mortal form the pattern of Isis-Osiris, Aphrodite-Ares (fecundity-knowledge, beauty-war), they link equal and opposite forces, generating a child ("Euphorion," pleasure or joy, equivalent of the Egyptian Horus and the Greek Eros) who will unite the attributes of both.

For the driving intellectual impulse in *Helen in Egypt* is the synthesizing of opposites. Typhon and Osiris, killer and victim of Egyptian myth, were "not two but one . . . to the initiate" (sec. 27); the daughter of Helen's sister

Clytemnestra, and her own daughter Hermione, are identified as "one" sacrificial maiden (sec. 69); the Greek Zeus and the Egyptian Amen are "One," though manifested as "a series of multiple gods" (sec. 78). The same is true of some of the poem's key images or hieroglyphs: a beach of white "shells" and one of "skulls," the string of the lyre and the warrior's bowstring, the flaming brazier in the comforter's house and the flame of the burning Troy —these too are cognate, related forms, mutually dependent opposites. Eventually Helen intuits that Love and Death, Eros and Eris (strife), unlike the Eros and Thanatos posited by the aged Freud as eternally dual principles, "will merge in the final illumination" (sec. 271).

At the same time, the poem is primarily psychodrama, and, to a degree paralleled by very few poems in our literature, nonmimetic of the external material world beyond the psyche. That world is represented in it to a great extent by men in ships or at war, and the relation of such "realities" to Helen's identity is only one of the enigmas she is solving in the poem. Thus the fascinating, flickering alternation between prose and verse in *Helen in Egypt* is that of a single mind having an urgent dialogue with itself, probing, questioning—an extraordinarily large portion of the poem's text takes the form of questions—and persisting despite confusion ("What does he mean by that? . . . Helena? who is she?") in the effort of feminine self-definition: "I must fight for Helena" (sec. 37). "I am not, nor mean to be/The Daemon they made of me" (sec. 109). "I will encompass the infinite/in time, in the crystal/ in my thought here" (sec. 201). H. D. called the poem her "Cantos," and it is an implicit challenge to Ezra Pound's culturally encyclopedic *Cantos,* not only because it assails fascism and hero-worship, but also for its uncompromising inwardness, its rejection of all authority. For where Pound fills his poems with chunks of authorized, authoritative literature and history, history and literature are for *Helen in Egypt* never authoritative but always to-be-deciphered, tangential to, incorporated within, the feminine mind.

Helen in Egypt is first of all personal, one woman's quest epitomizing the struggle of Everywoman. Its interior life comes to include and transcend the external historical world represented and inhabited by males—but it does not reject that world. In Susan Griffin's *Woman and Nature: The Roaring Inside Her,* male and female are again represented as polar opposites, but from a different point of view and with a different set of conclusions.

"Matter" and "Separation," the long opening books of *Woman and Nature,* offer a pastiche-parody of the history of occidental patriarchal intellect. Griffin quotes and paraphrases hundreds of works, ranging from the clean abstractions of theology, metaphysics, physics, and mathematics, through the material facts of history, to such practical subjects as forestry, agriculture, animal husbandry, mining, and office management. The collective and anonymous "paternal voice" she creates is emotionless, toneless, authoritative. It pronounces "that matter is only a potential for form. . . . That the nature of woman is passive, that she is a vessel" with supposed objectivity.[35]

The attitude of this voice toward Nature ("matter") and toward Woman is the same. It conceptualizes both as essentially, ideally, and properly inferior, passive, intended for man's use; yet at the same time potentially dangerous, threatening, wild, and evil, requiring to be tamed by force. Extending in two directions, theoretical and practical, the analogy formulated by the anthropologist Sherry Ortner that "Woman is to Nature as Man is to Culture,"[36] Griffin on the one hand makes clear the connection between the myth (in the sense of metaphor) of active male God and passive female Nature, and the myth (in the sense of falsity) of rational objectivity in the life of the intellect and of civilization. On the other she composes a huge collage of the multiple ways in which male superiority, buttressed by its myths, destroys life.

To justify their exploitation and destruction, woman and nature must be seen both as morally evil and as metaphysically nonexistent. Thus of the "inordinate affections and passions" of Woman and the rich unpredictability of Nature, "it is decided that that which cannot be measured and reduced to number is not real" (p. 11). Scenes depicting depletion of nutrients in soil, courtship as a form of hunting, the extinction of species of beasts, the operation of clitoridectomy, the caging and drugging of a lioness, a woman muted by her husband's violence, the despoiling of forests, peasant women raped by invading soldiers, Raskolnikov's need to dispose of two female corpses, and the disposal of nuclear wastes become the logical extrapolation of such axioms. Though satiric, Griffin's portrait of the myth of rational objectivity is also playfully inventive with numerous sorts of male discourse, from logic to legalese, from Dantean mysticism to Einsteinian thought-experiment. At times it is also beautiful, as in the section called "Territory"; at times ironic, as in the section called "The Show Horse." Occasionally we hear whispers of the suppressed female/natural voice—confused, suffering, angry.

In the third book, "Passage," and the fourth, "Her Vision," this voice moves toward self-transformation. Through traditional female images of cave, water, earth, and seed, it gradually approaches images of light and flight. Altering from consciousness of "dreams" to knowledge of her body, her history, the body of the world; from passivity to rebellion, violence, dance, song; the "she" and "we" of this voice learn to accept "turbulence": "When the wind calls, will we go? Will this wind come inside us? Take from us? Can we give to the wind what is asked of us? Will we let go? . . . Can we sing back, this we ask, can we sing back, and not only sing, but in clear voices? Will this be, we ask, and will we keep on answering, keep on with our whole bodies? And do we know why we sing? Yes. Will we know why? Yes" (p. 222). Scenes from the first part of *Woman and Nature* reverse in the latter sections. Gynecologists become midwives. The lioness devours her captors. There is also a central asymmetry. Griffin portrays the relationships between mothers and daughters, midwives and birthing mothers; between women as friends, allies, and lovers; and between woman and earth as, in their ideal form, relationships of mirroring or interpenetration. Emotional closeness is derived from acknowledged likeness, not from the patriarchal relationship of dominance and submission, or from the dialectic between polarities envisioned by H. D. Consequently, in the last portion of *Woman and Nature,* the direct quotations are exclusively from women writers, and the male voice disappears from the book. At one point the "we" is a family of mourning elephants whose mother has been killed by a hunter and who vow to teach hatred and fear to their young: "And when we attack in their defense, they will watch and learn this too. From us, they will become fierce. And so a death like this death of our mother will not come easily to them. . . . And only if the young of our young or the young of their young never know this odor in their lifetime, . . . only then, when no trace is left of this memory in us, will we see what we can be without this fear, without this enemy, what we are" (p. 218). This pivotal passage offers a forceful metaphor for feminist separatism—man is simply too dangerous, too much a killer, for woman to do anything but fear, fight, and avoid him. The passage also, by virtue of imagining a time "when no trace is left of this memory in us," releases the author to conclude with a hymn of pleasure at once erotic and intellectual, a lesbian-feminist structural equivalent of the last movement of Beethoven's Ninth Symphony, the close of Blake's *Jerusalem,* Molly Bloom's soliloquy, or the Book of Revelation.[37]

Like *Helen in Egypt, Woman and Nature* is a book about process and psychic struggle. In a recent essay Griffin writes that her initial attempts to organize her "scientific" material logically or chronologically failed. She had to learn to structure "intuitively, putting pieces next to one another where the transition seemed wonderful." She also explains that "all the time I wrote the book, the patriarchal voice was in me, whispering to me . . . that I had no proof for any of my writing, that I was wildly in error."[38] Thus the gradual disclosure of the female voice in the book reproduces the process of its creation.

Unlike both *Helen in Egypt* and *Woman and Nature,* and unlike most revisionist mythmaking by women, Anne Sexton's *Transformations* is not structured around the idea of male and female as polar opposites and is consequently not gynocentric in the fashion of these books. Rather, it is a brilliant synthesis of public "story" and psychological revelation, revisionist both in its subversive readings of traditional plots, characters, and morals and in its portrait of a lady who exists beyond the plots, the female as creator.

Transformations consists of a prologue and sixteen tales from the Brothers Grimm, told in a wisecracking Americanese that simultaneously modernizes and desentimentalizes them. We have bits like "the dwarfs, those little hot dogs" ("Snow White"); "a wolf dressed in frills,/a kind of transvestite" ("Red Riding Hood"); or Sexton's Gretel who, "seeing her moment in history . . . turned the oven on to bake."[39] Under cover of entertainment, Sexton demolishes many of the social conventions, especially those connected with femininity, that fairy tales ostensibly endorse. She mocks virginity and beauty as values; the former makes one a fool ("Snow White, that dumb bunny"), the latter cruel ("pretty enough, but with hearts like blackjacks"). Love, in Sexton's versions, is a form of self-seeking. The happy ending of marriage is treated ironically as "a kind of coffin,/a kind of blue funk./Is it not?"

An important source of Sexton's effectiveness is her striking ability to decode stories we thought we knew, revealing meanings we should have guessed. Her "Rapunzel" is a tale of love between an older and a younger woman, ultimately doomed by heterosexual normality. Her "Rumplestiltskin" is about the naïveté and vulnerability of a dwarf manipulated by a calculating girl—or it is about the ability of the healthy ego to despise, suppress, and mutilate the libido. In "Hansel and Gretel," Sexton hints that the witch is a mother-goddess sacrificed by a female in alliance with the patriarchy.

Though Sexton is obviously indebted to psychoanalytic method in the retrieval of latent content, she is not limited by its dogmas. For example, psychoanalytical commentary on the "sleeping virgin" pattern in fairy tales interprets the theme as that of feminine pubescence.[40] Sexton in "Briar Rose (Sleeping Beauty)" takes this insight almost contemptuously for granted and organizes her version like a series of clues to quite another mystery. There is no mother in Sexton's version, only a father. The psychoanalytically sophisticated reader may speculate that the thirteenth fairy, "her fingers as long and thin as straws,/her eyes burnt by cigarettes,/her uterus an empty teacup" (p. 108) is a displaced mother figure, as evil stepmothers commonly are. The protective father who not only got rid of spinning wheels but "forced every male in the court/to scour his tongue with Bab-o" (p. 109) is apparently a possessive parent hoping to keep his young daughter sexually pure. But after the denouement, the hundred years' sleep, and the arrival of the Prince, Sexton presents Briar Rose as a lifelong insomniac, terrified of sleeping. For when she sleeps she dreams of a dinner table with "a faltering crone at my place,/her eyes burnt like cigarettes/as she eats betrayal like a slice of meat."

Why does the heroine identify with the crone? What betrayal? Only the last lines tell us just why the mother is not "in" Sexton's story. Waking from sleep Briar Rose cries, like a little girl, "Daddy! Daddy!" as she did when the Prince woke her—and what she sees is "not the prince at all,"

but my father,
drunkenly bent over my bed,
circling the abyss like a shark,
my father thick upon me
like some sleeping jellyfish.
(Pp. 111–12)

This is, of course, a version of the family romance that neither orthodox psychoanalysis nor our legal system is ready to accept,[41] but that countless women will recognize as painfully accurate.

In addition to the revivifying language and the revisionist interpretations of the stories, *Transformations* has another, framing element. The persona of the narrator-poet in the book's prologue is "a middle-aged witch, me" who talks like a den mother. Each of the ensuing tales has its own prologue, offering hints about the meaning of the story to come. The poet's personality alters with each prologue. In "Snow White" she is cynical, in "The White Snake," idealistic. Prior to "Rumplestiltskin" she announces that the dwarf is the suppressed "law of your members," out of Saint Paul's Epistles (p. 17), while in "One-Eye, Two-Eyes and Three-Eyes" she comments disapprovingly on the way parents with defective children "warm to their roles . . . with a positive fervor" where nature would sensibly let its malformed products die (pp. 59–60). In the prologue to "The Frog Prince" she addresses a "Mama Brundig" psychoanalyst, gaily declaiming:

My guilts are what
we catalogue.
I'll take a knife
and chop up frog.

But the gaiety plummets abruptly to horror: "Frog is my father's genitals./Frog is a malformed doorknob./Frog is a soft bag of green" (pp. 93–94).

Sexton as narrator is at times distant from the reader, at times intimate. She is unpredictably sensitive or brutal. What is important to notice here is that while the tales themselves are fixed—and Sexton stresses their ruthless changelessness, never letting us think that her "characters" act with free will or do anything but fill their slots in predetermined plots—the teller is mobile.

She emits an air of exhilarating mental and emotional liberty, precisely because she is distanced from the material she so penetratingly understands. Thus the full force of *Transformations* lies not only in its psychosocial reinterpretations of Grimm's tales, however brilliant, nor in the fact that it expressly attacks literary and social conventions regarding women. Philosophically, the axis *Transformations* turns on is Necessity (here seen as fixed and damaging psychosocial patterns) versus Freedom; the "middle-aged witch, me" represents the latter.

IV

What all these poems have in common is, first, that they treat existing texts as fence posts surrounding the terrain of mythic truth but by no means identical with it. In other words, they are enactments of feminist anti-authoritarianism opposed to the patriarchal praxis of reifying texts.

Second, most of these poems involve revaluations of social, political, and philosophical values, particularly those most enshrined in occidental literature, such as the glorification of conquest and the faith that the cosmos is—must be—hierarchically ordered with earth and body on the bottom and mind and spirit on the top.

Third, the work of these poets is conspicuously different from the modernist mythmaking of Yeats, Pound, Eliot, and Auden because it contains no trace of nostalgia, no faith that the past is a repository of truth, goodness, or desirable social organization. Prufrock may yearn to be Hamlet, but what woman would want to be Ophelia? While the myth of a golden age has exerted incalculable pressure in the shaping of Western literature and its attitude toward history, the revisionist woman poet does not care if the hills of Arcady are dead. Or rather, she does not believe they are dead. Far from representing history as a decline, or bemoaning disjunctions of past and present, her poems insist that past and present are, for better or worse, essentially the same. H. D.'s concept of the "palimpsest" seems to be the norm, along with a treatment of time that effectively flattens it so that the past is not then but now.

Fourth, revisionism correlates with formal experiment. This is important not only because new meanings must generate new forms—when we have a new form in art we can assume we have a new meaning—but because the verbal strategies these poets use draw attention to the discrepancies between traditional concepts and the conscious mental and emotional activity of female re-vision. As it accentuates its argument, in order to make clear that there *is* an argument, that an act of theft *is* occurring, feminist revisionism differs from Romantic revisionism, although in other respects it is similar.[42]

The gaudy and abrasive colloquialism of Alta, Atwood, Plath, and Sexton, for example, simultaneously modernizes what is ancient and reduces the verbal glow that we are trained to associate with mythic material. Even H. D., who takes her divinities entirely seriously, avoids the elevated or quasi-liturgical diction that, in the educated reader, triggers the self-surrendering exaltation relied on by the creators of such poems as *Four Quartets* or the *Cantos.* With women poets we look at, or into, but not up at, sacred things; we unlearn submission.

A variant of colloquial language is childish or infantile language, such as T. S. Eliot used in the nursery-rhyme echoes of "The Hollow Men" and at the close of *The Waste Land* to suggest a mix of regression and despair. In DuPlessis's "Medusa," passages of halting and sometimes punning baby talk become a way of revealing the power of sexual pain to infantilize, to thwart growth; the speaker's ultimate articulateness coincides with the growth of her avenging snakes. Regressive language also signals sexual trauma in Sexton. Another variant of the colloquial is the bawdy, a traditionally male linguistic preserve that women like Erica Jong have lately invaded.

The most significant large-scale technique in these poems is the use of multiple intertwined voices within highly composed extensive structures. In the three long works discussed here there is the alternating prose and verse of *Helen in Egypt,* with occasional interludes when one of Helen's lovers speaks, or she imagines him speaking; the male and female voices in *Woman and Nature,* along with the multitudinous direct quotations; and prologue and story in *Transformations.*[43] These balancings are crucially important to the texture and sense of the poems, just as the multiple voices of *The Waste Land,* the *Cantos,* or *Paterson* are. Insofar as the subject of the poem is always the "I" of the poet, her divided voices evoke divided selves: the rational and the passionate, the active and the suffering, the conscious life and the dream life, animus and anima, analyst and analysand. To read *Helen in Egypt* is uncannily like overhearing a communication between left brain and right brain.

In some ways, too, these poems challenge the validity of the "I," of any "I." Like the speaker of Adrienne Rich's "Diving into the Wreck," whose discovery of her submerged self is a discovery that she is a "we" for whom even the distinction between subject and object dissolves, the heroines we find in women's revisionist mythology are more often fluid than solid. But these are not books—or heroines—about which the authors are saying, as Pound tragically said of the *Cantos,* and his life, "I cannot make it cohere."[44] Although the divided self is probably the single issue women poets since 1960 most consistently struggle with, the most visionary of their works appear to be strengthened by acknowledging division and containing it, as H. D. says, "in my thought here."[45]

APPENDIX

The following are post-1960 myth-poems, listed alphabetically by author. Extended poems and poem-sequences are indicated by an asterisk (*). Readers of contemporary women's poetry will be able to supply other titles.

Alta. "euridice." *I Am Not a Practicing Angel.* Trumansburg, N.Y.: Crossing Press, 1975.

Atwood, Margaret. "Eventual Proteus," "Speeches for Dr. Frankenstein," "Siren Song," "Circe/Mud Poems."* *Selected Poems.* New York: Simon & Schuster, 1976.

Barba, Sharon. "A Cycle of Women." In *Rising Tides: Twentieth Century Women Poets,* ed. Laura Chester and Sharon Barba. New York: Simon & Schuster, 1973.

Broumas, Olga. "Twelve Aspects of God."* *Beginning with O.* New Haven, Conn.: Yale University Press, 1977.

Butcher, Grace. "Assignments." In *Rising Tides: Twentieth Century Women Poets,* ed. Laura Chester and Sharon Barba. New York: Simon & Schuster, 1973.

Clifton, Lucille. Kali poems.* *An Ordinary Woman.* New York: Random House, 1974.

H. D. *Helen in Egypt.** New York: New Directions, 1961.

———. *Hermetic Definition.** New York: New Directions, 1972.

Dienstfrey, Patricia. "Blood and the Iliad: The Paintings of Frida Kahlo." *Newspaper Stories.* Berkeley, Calif.: Kelsey St. Press, 1979.

Di Prima, Diane. *Loba.** Berkeley, Calif.: Wingbow Press, 1978.

DuPlessis, Rachel Blau. "Medusa,"* "Euridice."* *Wells.* New York: Montemora Foundation, 1980.

Ellis, Kate. "Matrilineal Descent." In *US 1: An Anthology,* ed. Rod Tulloss, David Keller, and Alicia Ostriker. Union City, N.J.: Wm. H. Wise, 1980.

Fenton, Elizabeth. "Under the Ladder to Heaven." In *No More Masks! An Anthology of Poems by Women,* ed. Florence Howe and Ellen Bass. Garden City, N.Y.: Doubleday, 1973.

Gilbert, Sandra. "Bas Relief: Bacchante." *Massachusetts Review* 18 (Winter 1976). "Daphne." In *Poetry Northwest* 18 (Summer 1977).

Giovanni, Nikki. "Ego Tripping." *The Women and the Men.* New York: William Morrow, 1975.

Glück, Louise. "Gretel in Darkness," "Jeanne d'Arc." *The House of Marshland.* New York: Ecco, 1975.

Grahn, Judy. "She Who."* *The Work of a Common Woman.* New York: St. Martin's Press, 1978.

Griffin, Susan. *Woman and Nature: The Roaring Inside Her.** New York: Harper & Row, 1978.

Hacker, Marilyn. "For Elektra," "The Muses," "Nimue to Merlin." *Presentation Piece.* New York: Viking Press, 1974.

Jong, Erica. "Arse Poetica." *Fruits and Vegetables.* New York: Holt, Rinehart & Winston, 1971.

———. "Back to Africa," "Alcestis on the Poetry Circuit." *Half-Lives.* New York: Holt, Rinehart & Winston, 1973.

Kizer, Carolyn. "The Dying Goddess." *Midnight Was My Cry.* Garden City, N.Y.: Doubleday, 1969.

Levertov, Denise. "The Goddess." *With Eyes at the Back of Our Heads.* New York: New Directions, 1959.

———. "The Jacob's Ladder," "The Well." *The Jacob's Ladder.* New York: New Directions, 1961.

———. "Song for Ishtar." *O Taste and See.* New York: New Directions, 1964.

———. "An Embroidery." *Relearning the Alphabet.* New York: New Directions, 1970).

Morgan, Robin. "The Network of the Imaginary Mother,"* "Voices from Six Tapestries."* *Lady of the Beasts.* New York: Random House, 1976.

Mueller, Lisel. "The Queen of Sheba Says Farewell," "Eros," " 'O Brave New World. . . .' " *Dependencies.* Chapel Hill: University of North Carolina Press, 1965.

———. "Letter from the End of the World." *The Private Life.* Baton Rouge: Louisiana State University Press, 1976.

Ostriker, Alicia. "Homecoming," "The Impulse of Singing," "Message from the Sleeper at Hell's Mouth."* *A Woman under the Surface.* Princeton, N.J.: Princeton University Press, 1982.

Owens, Rochelle. *The Joe 82 Creation Poems.** Los Angeles: Black Sparrow Press, 1974.

Piercy, Marge. "Icon," "Laying Down the Tower."* *To Be of Use.* Garden City, N.Y.: Doubleday, 1973.

Plath, Sylvia. "The Colossus," "Lorelei," "The Disquieting Muses," "Magi," "Two Sisters of Persephone," "Witch Burning," "Lady Lazarus," "Medusa," "Mary's Song," "Elm." *Collected Poems,* ed. Ted Hughes. New York: Harper & Row, 1981.

Rich, Adrienne. "The Knight," "Orion," "Planetarium," "I Dream I'm the Death of Orpheus." *Poems: Selected and New, 1950–1974.* New York: W. W. Norton, 1974.

Rukeyser, Muriel. "The Poem as Mask," "Myth," "Waiting for Icarus." *Collected Poems.* New York: McGraw-Hill, 1978.

Sarton, May. "At Lindos," "Orpheus," "The Birth of Venus," "The Muse as Medusa," "The Invocation to Kali." *Selected Poems.* New York: W. W. Norton, 1978.

Sexton, Anne. "Her Kind," "The Double Image." *To Bedlam and Part Way Back.* Boston: Houghton Mifflin, 1960.

———. *Transformations.** Boston: Houghton Mifflin, 1971.

———. "Angels of the Love Affair," "The Jesus Papers."* *The Book of Folly.* Boston: Houghton Mifflin, 1972.

———. "Gods," "The Death Baby," "Rats Live on No Evil Star," "The Furies," "Mary's Song," "Jesus Walking." *The Death Notebooks.* Boston: Houghton Mifflin, 1974.

Stanford, Ann. "Women of Perseus."* *In Mediterranean Air.* New York: Viking Press, 1977.

Tepperman, Jean. "Witch." In *No More Masks: An Anthology of Poems by Women,* ed. Florence Howe and Ellen Bass. Garden City, N.Y.: Doubleday, 1973.

Van Duyn, Mona. "Outlandish Agon," "Advice to a God," "Leda," "Leda Reconsidered." In *To See, To Take.* New York: Atheneum, 1970.

Wakoski, Diane. "The George Washington Poems."* *Trilogy.* Garden City, N.Y.: Doubleday, 1974.

NOTES

[1]Hélène Cixous, "Sorties," *La Jeune Née,* trans. Ann Liddle (Paris: Union Générale d'Editions, 1975), quoted by Elaine Marks in "Women and Literature in France,"

Signs 3 (Summer 1978): 832–42, esp. p. 841; appears also in Elaine Marks and Isabelle de Courtivron, eds., *New French Feminisms: An Anthology* (Amherst: University of Massachusetts Press, 1980), pp. 92–93.

[2]Sylvia Plath, "Mushrooms," *The Collected Poems,* ed. Ted Hughes (New York: Harper & Row, 1981), p. 139.

[3]Claudine Herrmann, *Les Voleuses de langue* (Paris: Des Femmes, 1976).

[4]Adrienne Rich, "The Burning of Paper Instead of Children," *Poems: Selected and New, 1950–1974* (New York: W. W. Norton, 1974), pp. 148–51, esp. p. 151.

[5]Jacques Lacan's term for the symbolic order of language is widely used by psychoanalytically oriented French feminists; see Jane Gallop, "Psychoanalysis in France," *Women and Literature* 7 (Winter 1979): 57–63.

[6]Robin Morgan, "The Invisible Woman," *Monster* (New York: Random House, 1972), p. 46.

[7]Marcia Landy, "The Silent Woman," in *The Authority of Experience: Essays in Feminist Criticism,* ed. Arlyn Diamond and Lee Edwards (Amherst: University of Massachusetts Press, 1977), pp. 16–27.

[8]See Suzanne Juhasz, *Naked and Fiery Forms: Modern American Poetry by Women* (New York: Harper & Row, 1976); Elaine Showalter, *A Literature of Their Own: British Women Novelists from Brontë to Lessing* (Princeton, N.J.: Princeton University Press, 1977); Ann Douglas, *The Feminization of American Culture* (New York: Alfred A. Knopf, 1977), which is, however, unsympathetic to the women writers discussed; Sandra M. Gilbert and Susan Gubar, *The Madwoman in the Attic: The Woman Writer and the Nineteenth-Century Imagination* (New Haven, Conn.: Yale University Press, 1979); Cheryl Walker, *The Nightingale's Burden: Women Poets in America, 1630–1900* (Bloomington: Indiana University Press, 1982). See also Florence Howe and Ellen Bass, eds., "Introduction," in *No More Masks! An Anthology of Poems by Women* (Garden City, N.Y.: Doubleday, 1973); Dolores Rosenblum, "Christina Rossetti: The Inward Pose," and Terence Diggory, "Armored Women, Naked Men: Dickinson, Whitman and Their Successors," in *Shakespeare's Sisters: Feminist Essays on Women Poets,* ed. Sandra M. Gilbert and Susan Gubar (Bloomington: Indiana University Press, 1979), pp. 82–98 and 135–50.

[9]Marks, "Women and Literature in France," p. 836.

[10]Robert Graves argues—without much evidence—in *The White Goddess* (New York: Creative Age Press, 1948) that a "magical" language honoring the Moon Goddess existed in prepatriarchal times, survived in the mystery cults, and was still taught "in the poetic colleges of Ireland and Wales, and in the witch covens of Western Europe" (p. x). Among French feminists, Herrmann claims that women use space and time, metaphor and metonymy differently than men, Cixous that women write with "mother's milk" or "the blood's language." Most interestingly, Luce Irigaray moves from *Speculum d'autre femme* (Paris: Editions de Minuit, 1974), which deconstructs Plato and Freud to demonstrate the history of systematic repression of woman as a concept in Western culture, to *Ce Sexe qui n'est pas un* (Paris: Editions de Minuit, 1977), which attempts to transpose the voices of Freud, Lacan, Derrida, and Lewis Carroll into a feminine language. Among Irigaray's techniques is the rejection of the "proper" name along with "property" and "propriety" in order to recover the self as "elle(s)," a plural being (see Carolyn G. Burke, "Irigaray Through the Looking Glass," *Feminist Studies* 7 [Summer 1981]: 288–306). This work parallels in many respects Susan Griffin's *Woman and Nature: The Roaring Inside Her* (New York: Harper & Row, 1978), discussed below. Julia Kristeva, on the other hand, argues that woman has no linguistic existence but a negative, pre-Oedipal one. For details of the debate, which in part centers on the question of whether feminists should use male abstractions, see

Elaine Marks and Carolyn G. Burke, "Report from Paris: Women's Writing and the Women's Movement," *Signs* (Summer 1978): 843–55. The most important American theoretical texts prophesying a woman's language are Mary Daly's *Beyond God the Father: Toward a Philosophy of Women's Liberation* (Boston: Beacon Press, 1973) and *Gyn/Ecology: The Metaethics of Radical Feminism* (Boston: Beacon Press, 1978). *Per contra,* see Robin Lakoff, *Language and Woman's Place* (New York: Harper & Row, 1975); Mary Hiatt, *The Way Women Write: Sex and Style in Contemporary Prose* (New York: Teacher's College Press, 1977); Barrie Thorne and Nancy Henley, eds., *Language and Sex: Difference and Dominance* (Rowley, Mass.: Newbury House, 1975); and the empirical studies referred to in Cheris Kramer, Barrie Thorne, and Nancy Henley, "Perspective on Language and Communication," *Signs* 3 (Spring 1978): 638–51.

[11]Here and in other essays on contemporary American women's poetry, I take 1960 as an approximate point of departure. Among the breakthrough works appearing between 1959 and 1965 are Mona Van Duyn, *Valentines to the Wide World* (Boston: Houghton Mifflin, 1959); H. D., *Helen in Egypt* (New York: New Directions, 1961); Anne Sexton, *To Bedlam and Part Way Back* (Boston: Houghton Mifflin, 1960) and *All My Pretty Ones* (Boston: Houghton Mifflin, 1962); Denise Levertov, *The Jacob's Ladder* (New York: New Directions, 1961) and *O Taste and See* (New York: New Directions, 1964); Diane Wakoski, *Coins and Coffins* (Garden City, N.Y.: Doubleday, 1962); Adrienne Rich, *Snapshots of a Daughter-in-Law* (New York: W. W. Norton, 1963); Carolyn Kizer, "Pro Femina," *Knock upon Silence* (Garden City, N.Y.: Doubleday, 1963); Sylvia Plath, *Ariel* (New York: Harper & Row, 1965). It needs to be stressed, however, that the women's movement in contemporary poetry is not confined to these and other well-known poets but includes hundreds of writers whose work appears in small-press and magazine publications.

[12]Alicia Ostriker, "Body Language: Imagery of the Body in Women's Poetry," in *The State of the Language,* ed. Leonard Michaels and Christopher Ricks (Berkeley: University of California Press, 1980), pp. 247–63, esp. pp. 256–60.

[13]The case against myth is exhaustively stated by Simone de Beauvoir in chap. 9, "Dreams, Fears, Idols," of *The Second Sex,* trans. H. M. Parshley (New York: Bantam Books, 1970), pp. 157–223. A discussion of the usefulness of some myths for women writers is Susan Gubar's "Mother, Maiden and the Marriage of Death: Women Writers and an Ancient Myth," *Women's Studies* 6 (1979): 301–15. Gubar argues that the figures of the Sphinx and the Mother-Goddess represent "secret wisdom," which women identify with "their point of view," and that they use the myth of Persephone and Demeter "to re-define, to re-affirm and to celebrate female consciousness itself" (p. 302). See also note 22 below.

[14]Muriel Rukeyser, "The Poem as Mask," *Collected Poems* (New York: McGraw-Hill, 1978), p. 435.

[15]Rich, "Diving into the Wreck," *Poems* (note 4 above), pp. 196–98, esp. p. 198.

[16]Margaret Atwood, "Circe/Mud Poems," *You Are Happy* (New York: Harper & Row, 1974), pp. 45–70, esp. pp. 68–69.

[17]Discussion of the ways in which American women poets have used myth to handle material dangerous for a feminine "I" appears in Emily Stipes Watts, *The Poetry of American Women from 1632 to 1945* (Austin: University of Texas Press, 1977).

[18]Daly, *Beyond God the Father,* p. 8.

[19]Sylvia Plath, "Lady Lazarus," *Collected Poems* (note 2 above); Anne Sexton, "Snow White," *Transformations* (Boston: Houghton Mifflin, 1971), p. 3; Jean Tepperman, "Witch," in Howe and Bass, *No More Masks!,* pp. 333–34; Alta, "euridice," *I*

Am Not a Practicing Angel (Trumansburg, N.Y.: Crossing Press, 1975); Erica Jong, "Arse Poetica," *Fruits and Vegetables* (New York: Holt, Rinehart & Winston, 1971), p. 27.

[20]Kate Ellis, "Matrilineal Descent," in *US 1: An Anthology,* ed. Rod Tulloss, David Keller, and Alicia Ostriker (Union City, N.J.: Wm. H. Wise, 1980), pp. 31–34; Sharon Barba, "A Cycle of Women," in *Rising Tides: Twentieth-Century American Women Poets,* ed. Laura Chester and Sharon Barba (New York: Simon & Schuster, 1973), pp. 356–57.

[21]Rachel Blau DePlessis, "Eurydice," *Wells* (New York: Montemora Foundation, 1980); Rich, "The Mirror in Which Two Are Seen as One," and "Necessities of Life," *Poems,* pp. 193–95, esp. pp. 195, 60–70.

[22]The feminist attempt to construct a redefined "Goddess" or "Great Goddess" is, of course, not confined to poetry or even to literature. See, in *Chrysalis,* no. 6 (1978), Gloria Z. Greenfield, Judith Antares, and Charlene Spretnak, "The Politics of Women's Spirituality" (pp. 9–15); and Linda Palumbo, Maurine Revnille, Charlene Spretnak, and Terry Wolverton, "Women's Survival Catalog: Spirituality," an excellent annotated listing of classic and recent texts, journals, and (a few) environmental artworks relating to "The Goddess" (pp. 77–99).

[23]See Erich Neumann, *The Great Mother: An Analysis of the Archetype,* trans. Ralph Manheim (Princeton, N.J.: Princeton University Press, 1963).

[24]Denise Levertov, "The Goddess," *With Eyes at the Back of Our Heads* (New York: New Directions, 1959), pp. 43–44. Levertov treats the association of women with falsity in "Hypocrite Women," which redefines feminine deception (and self-deception) as compliance with male demands for mothering and with the male pronouncement that "our cunts are ugly" (*O Taste and See,* p. 70).

[25]Levertov, "Song for Ishtar," *O Taste and See,* p. 3.

[26]Wallace Stevens, "Final Soliloquy of the Interior Paramour," *The Collected Poems of Wallace Stevens* (New York: Alfred A. Knopf, 1954), p. 524.

[27]Sylvia Plath, "The Disquieting Muses," "Medusa," "Lady Lazarus," "Elm," *Collected Poems,* pp. 74–76, 184, 244–46, 192; Sexton, "The Exorcists," *To Bedlam,* pp. 22–23, and "Angels of the Love Affair," *The Book of Folly* (Boston: Houghton Mifflin, 1972), pp. 57–62.

[28]Ann Stanford, "The Women of Perseus," *In Mediterranean Air* (New York: Viking Press, 1977), pp. 34–48; Du Plessis, "Medusa," *Wells.*

[29]Atwood, *You Are Happy,* pp. 51, 38–39.

[30]Susan Friedman, "Who Buried H. D.? A Poet, Her Critics, and Her Place in 'The Literary Tradition,'" *College English* 37 (March 1975): 807.

[31]I have selected these three works for both their excellence and their diversity —including their diverse perspectives on female sexuality, from which much else, ideologically and formally, follows. H. D.'s orientation is (in this book) heterosexual, Griffin's lesbian, Sexton's (in this book) asexual. I believe that these works illuminate, in a profound way, both the common ground and the differences among these three orientations toward women's sexuality, and I believe it is vital for feminist critics not to "prefer" one perspective to the others; we have only begun to learn what sexuality means to us and how various our options may be.

[32]H. D., *Helen in Egypt* (note 11 above), sec. 1. Future references to this poem will be included in the text.

[33]I am indebted to Susan Friedman, *Psyche Reborn: The Emergence of H. D.* (Bloomington: Indiana University Press, 1981), for her illuminating analysis of H. D.'s revisionist use of occult and mystical tradition in her quest for what she called "spirituality," and for her revisionist use of psychoanalytic doctrines and methods in her quest

for self-affirmation. As Friedman makes clear, the quests and methods are projected onto the Helen of *Helen in Egypt.* I am also indebted to Rachel Blau DuPlessis's "Romantic Thralldom in H. D.," *Contemporary Literature* 20 (Spring 1979): 178–203, for the discussion of H. D.–Helen's need to construct a "sufficient family" as an alternative to "romantic thralldom." Helen's successful quest for *(a)* knowledge of the gods, *(b)* integration of self, *(c)* a family consisting of parent figures, siblings, lover, and progeny, might be related to a revisionist scheme of superego, ego, libido, in terms of what is sought and necessary for human wholeness.

[34]Rich, "The Knight," *Poems,* pp. 43–44.

[35]Griffin, *Woman and Nature* (note 10 above). Future references to this work will be incorporated in the text.

[36]Sherry Ortner, "Is Female to Male as Nature Is to Culture?" in *Woman, Culture and Society,* ed. Michelle Zimbalist Rosaldo and Louise Lamphere (Stanford, Calif: Stanford University Press, 1974), pp. 67–88. Annette Kolodny's *The Lay of the Land: Metaphor as Experience and History in American Life and Letters* (Chapel Hill: University of North Carolina Press, 1978) pursues the metaphor of land as "virgin" or "mother" in American history and literature, with findings parallel to Griffin's. Mary Daly's *Gyn/Ecology* might provide a gloss on much of Griffin; Griffin and Daly review each other's books in *Chrysalis,* no. 7 (1979), pp. 109–12.

[37]Lest these comparisons appear outrageous, let me point out with respect to the most (apparently) outrageous of them that the ratio of "male" to "female" in the text of *Woman and Nature* is roughly equivalent to that between Old and New Testaments, with the "male" coming first. The "male" books of *Woman and Nature* cover a huge time span, are encyclopedic, multigenre, and polyvocal; they concern Conquest and Law but also contain Prophecy, like the Old Testament. Its "female" books cover a relatively brief time span, approach univocality, concern Salvation and Grace, and contain Fulfillment of Prophecy, like the New Testament. I do not suggest that Griffin intended the parallels; they are nonetheless visible and consonant with her over-all purpose of retrieving from patriarchal discourse a woman's language.

[38]Susan Griffin, "Thoughts on Writing: A Diary," in *The Writer on Her Work,* ed. Janet Sternburg (New York: W. W. Norton, 1980), pp. 112–13.

[39]Sexton, *Transformations* (19 above), pp. 6, 76, 104–5. Future references to this work will be incorporated in the text.

[40]See, e.g., Bruno Bettelheim, *The Uses of Enchantment: The Meaning and Importance of Fairy Tales* (New York: Alfred A. Knopf, 1976), pp. 225 ff. See Juhasz, *Naked and Fiery Forms* (note 8 above), pp. 118–32, for a discussion of "the psychoanalytic model" and Sexton's outgrowing of it.

[41]See Florence Rush, *The Best-Kept Secret: Sexual Abuse of Children* (Englewood Cliffs, N.J.: Prentice-Hall, 1980), esp. chap. 7, "The Freudian Cover-Up," which discusses Freud's conviction that incest is a female fantasy and the consequences of Freudian orthodoxy for incest victims today. See also Judith Lewis Herman (with Lisa Hirschman), *Father-Daughter Incest* (Cambridge, Mass.: Harvard University Press, 1981), esp. the appendix, "The Incest Statutes," by Leigh Bienen.

[42]For a discussion of formal experimentation and its aesthetic and political significance in women's prose, see Julia Penelope Stanley and Susan J. Wolfe [Robbins], "Toward a Feminist Aesthetic," *Chrysalis,* no. 6 (1978), pp. 57–71.

[43]Similar techniques appear in Diane Wakoski's "The George Washington Poems," *Trilogy* (Garden City, N.Y.: Doubleday, 1974), pp. 113–66; and Robin Morgan's "Network of the Imaginary Mother," *Lady of the Beasts* (New York: Random House, 1976), pp. 61–88. I cannot think of any major modern poem by a man in which the self is presented as split or plural while the total poetic structure remains

cohesive rather than fragmented. In the closest approximation, John Berryman's *Dream Songs* (New York: Farrar, Straus & Giroux, 1969), the "blackface" voice plays a distinctly minor role. *The Waste Land, Cantos,* and *Paterson* are, of course, classics of personal, social, *and* aesthetic fragmentation.

[44]Ezra Pound, *The Cantos of Ezra Pound* (New York: New Directions, 1970), p. 796.

[45]H. D., *Helen in Egypt,* p. 201.

Emphasis Added

Plots and Plausibilities in Women's Fiction

Nancy K. Miller

> *Nothing came down the street; nobody passed. A single leaf detached itself from the plane tree at the end of the street, and in that pause and suspension fell. Somehow it was like a signal falling, a signal pointing to a force in things which one had overlooked.*
>
> VIRGINIA WOOLF, *A Room of One's Own*[1]

If we take *La Princesse de Clèves* as the first text of women's fiction in France, then we may observe that French women's fiction has from its beginnings been *discredited.*[2] By this I mean literally and literarily denied credibility: "Mme de Clèves's confession to her husband," writes Bussy-Rabutin to his cousin Mme de Sévigné, "is extravagant, and can only happen [*se dire*] in a true story; but when one is inventing a story for its own sake [*à plaisir*] it is ridiculous to ascribe such extraordinary feelings to one's heroine. The author in so doing was more concerned about not resembling other novels than obeying common sense."[3] Without dwelling on the local fact that a similarly "singular" confession had appeared in Mme de Villedieu's *Les Désordres de l'amour* some three years before the publication of Mme de Lafayette's novel, and bracketing the more general fact that the novel as a genre has from its beginnings labored under charges of *invraisemblance,*[4] let us reread Bussy-Rabutin's complaint. In a true story, as in "true confessions," the avowal would be believable because in life, unlike art, anything can happen; hence the constraints of likeliness do not apply. In a made-up story, however, the confession offends because it violates our readerly expectations about fiction. In other words, art should not imitate life but *re*inscribe received ideas about the representation of life in art. To depart from the limits of common sense (tautologically, to be extravagant) is to risk exclusion from the canon.[5] Because —as Genette, glossing this same document in "Vraisemblance et motivation," puts it—"*extravagance is a privilege of the real,*"[6] to produce a work not like other novels, an original rather than a copy, means paradoxically that its literariness will be sniffed out: "The first adventure of the Coulommiers gardens is not plausible," Bussy-Rabutin observes later in his letter, "and reeks of fiction [*sent le roman*]."

Genette begins his essay with an analysis of contemporary reactions to *La Princesse de Clèves.* Reviewing the writings of seventeenth-century poeticians, Genette shows that *vraisemblance* and *bienséance,* "plausibility" and "propriety," are wedded to each other; and the precondition of plausibility is the stamp of approval affixed by public *opinion:* "Real or assumed, this 'opinion' is quite close to what today would be called an ideology, that is, a body of maxims and prejudices which constitute both a vision of the world and a system of values" (p. 73). What this statement means is that the critical reaction to any given text is hermeneutically bound to another and preexistent text: the *doxa* of socialities. Plausibility, then, is an effect of reading through a grid of concordance:

> What defines plausibility is the formal principle of respect for the norm, that is, the existence of a relation of implication between the particular conduct attributed to a given character, and a given, general, received and implicit maxim. . . . To understand the behavior of a character (for example), is to be able to refer it back to an approved maxim, and this reference is perceived as a demonstration of cause and effect. (Pp. 174–75)

If no maxim is available to account for a particular piece of behavior, that behavior is read as unmotivated and unconvincing. Mme de Clèves's confession makes no sense in the seventeenth-century sociolect because it is, Genette underlines, "*an action without a maxim*" (p. 75). A heroine without a maxim, like a rebel without a cause, is destined to be misunderstood. And she is.

To build a narrative around a character whose behavior is deliberately idiopathic, however, is not merely to create a puzzling fiction but to fly in the face of a certain ideology (of the text and its context), to violate a grammar of motives that describes while prescribing, in this instance, what wives, not to say women, should or should not do. The question one might then ask is whether this crucial barbarism is in any way connected to the gender of its author. If we were to uncover a feminine "tradition"—diachronic recurrences —of such ungrammaticalities, would we have the basis for a poetics of women's fiction? And what do I mean by women's fiction?

Working backward, I should say first that I do not mean what is designated in France these days as *écriture féminine,* which can be described roughly as a process or a practice by which the female *body,* with its peculiar drives and rhythms, inscribes itself as text.[7] "Feminine writing" is an important theoretical formulation; but it privileges a textuality of the avant-garde, a literary production of the late twentieth century, and it is therefore fundamentally a hope, if not a blueprint, for the future. In what is perhaps the best-known statement of contemporary French feminist thinking about women's writing, "The Laugh of the Medusa," Hélène Cixous states that, "with a few rare exceptions, there has not yet been any writing that inscribes femininity." On the contrary, what she finds historically in the texts of the "immense majority" of female writers is "workmanship [which is] in no way different from male writing, and which either obscures women or reproduces the classic representations of women (as sensitive—intuitive—dreamy, etc.)."[8] I think this assertion is both true and untrue. It is true if one is looking for a radical difference in women's writing and locates that difference in an insurgence of the body, in what Julia Kristeva has called the irruption of the semiotic.[9] And it is true again if difference is sought on the level of the sentence, or in what might be thought of as the biofeedback of the text. If, however, we situate difference in the insistence of a certain thematic structuration, in the form of content, then it is not true that women's writing has been in no way different from male writing. I consider the "demaximization" wrought by Mme de Lafayette to be one example of how difference can be read.

Before I proceed to other manifestations of difference, let me make a few general remarks about the status of women's literature—about its existence, in my view, as a viable corpus for critical inquiry. Whether one believes, as does Cixous, that there is "male writing," "marked writing . . . run by a libidinal and cultural—hence political, typically masculine economy,"[10] or that (great) literature has no sex because a "great mind must be androgynous," literary *history* remains a male preserve, a history of writing by men.[11] In England the history of the novel admits the names of Jane Austen, the Brontës, George Eliot, and Virginia Woolf. In France it includes Mme de Lafayette, although only for *La Princesse de Clèves* and always with the nagging insinuation that La Rochefoucauld had a hand in that. Mme de Staël, George Sand, and Colette figure in the national record, although mainly as the scandalous heroines of their times. Nevertheless, there have always been women writing. What is one to do with them? One can leave them where they are, like so many sleeping dogs, and mention them only in passing as epiphenomena in every period, despite the incontrovertible evidence that most were successful and even literarily influential in their day. One can continue, then, a politics of benign neglect that reads difference, not to say popularity, as inferiority. Or one can perform two simultaneous and compensatory gestures: the archaeological and rehabilitative act of discovering and recovering "lost" women writers and the reconstructive and reevaluative act of establishing a parallel literary tradition, as Elaine Showalter has done in *A Literature of Their Own* and Ellen Moers in *Literary Women.*[12] The advantage of these moves is that they make visible an otherwise invisible intertext: a reconstituted record of predecession and prefiguration, debts acknowledged and unacknowledged, anxieties and enthusiasms.

Elizabeth Janeway, by way of T. S. Eliot, has suggested another way of thinking about women's literature. She cites the evolution in Eliot's attitude toward that body of texts we know as American literature. At first he held, as many critics have about women's literature, that it does not exist: "There can only be one English literature. . . . There cannot be British or American literature." Later, however, he was to acknowledge "what has never, I think, been found before, two literatures in the same language."[13] That reformulation, as Janeway adapts it to delineate the continent of women's literature, is useful because it locates the problem of identity and difference not on the level of the sentence—not as a question of another language—but on the level of the text in all its complexities: a culturally bound and, I would even say, culturally overdetermined production. This new mapping of a parallel geography does not, of course, resolve the oxymoron of marginality: how is it that women, a statistical majority in our culture, perform as a "literary subculture"?[14] But it does provide a body of writing from which to begin to identify specificities in women's relation to writing and the specificities that derive from that relation. Because women are both of the culture and out of it (or under it), written by it and remaining a largely silent though literate majority, to look for *uniquely* "feminine" textual indexes that can be deciphered in "blind" readings is pointless. (Documentation on the critical reception of *Jane Eyre* and *Adam Bede,* for example, has shown how silly such pretensions can be.)[15] There are no infallible signs, no fail-safe technique by which to determine the gender of an author. But that is not the point of the *post*compensatory gesture that follows what I call the new literary history. At stake instead is a reading that *consciously* re-creates the object it describes, attentive always to a difference—what T. S. Eliot calls "strong local flavor"[16] not dependent on the discovery of an exclusive alterity.

The difficulty of the reading comes from the irreducibly complicated relationship women have historically had to the language of the dominant culture, a "flirtatious" relationship that Luce Irigaray has called mimetic:

> To play with mimesis is . . . for a woman to try to recover the place of her exploitation by language, without allowing herself to be simply reduced to it. It is to resubmit herself . . . to ideas—notably about her—elaborated in and through a masculine logic, but to "bring out" by an effect of playful repetition what was to remain hidden: the recovery of a possible operation of the feminine in language. It is also to unveil the fact that if women mime so well they are not simply reabsorbed in this function. *They also remain elsewhere. . . .*[17]

This "elsewhere"—which, needless to say, is not so easily pinpointed—is, she adds, an insistence of "matter" and "sexual pleasure" *(jouissance).* I prefer to think of the insistence Irigaray posits as a form of emphasis: an italicized version of what passes for the neutral or standard face. Spoken or written, italics are a modality of intensity and stress; a way of marking what has always already been said, of making a common text one's own. Italics are also a form of intonation, "the tunes," McConnell-Ginet writes, "to which we set the text of our talk." "Intonation," she continues, "serves to underscore the gender identification of the participants in certain contexts of communication," and because of differences in intonation, "women's tunes will be interpreted and evaluated from an androcentric perspective."[18] When I speak of italics, then, I mean the emphasis added by registering a certain quality of voice. And this expanded metaphor brings me back to my point of departure.

Genette codes the perception of plausibility in terms of silence:

> The relationship between a plausible narrative and the system of plausibility to which it subjects itself is . . . essentially mute: the conventions of genre function like a system of natural forces and constraints which the narrative obeys as if without noticing them, and *a fortiori* without naming them. (P. 76)

By fulfilling the "tacit contract between a work and its public" (p. 77) this silence both gives pleasure and signifies conformity with the dominant ideology. The text emancipated from this collusion, however, is also silent, in that it refuses to justify its infractions, the "motives and maxims of the actions" (p. 78). Here Genette cites the silence surrounding Julien Sorel's attempted murder of Mme de Rênal and the confession of Mme de Clèves. In the first instance, the ideologically complicitous text, the silence is a function of what

Genette calls "plausible narrative"; in the second it is a function of "arbitrary narrative" (p. 79). And the *sounds* of silence? They are heard in a third type of narrative, one with a motivated and *"artificial plausibility"* (p. 79): this literature, exemplified by the "endless chatting" of a Balzacian novel, we might call "other-directed," for here authorial commentary justifies its story to society by providing the missing maxims, or by inventing them. In the arbitrary narrative Genette sees a rejection of the ideology of a certain plausibility—an ideology, let us say, of accountability. This "inner-directed" posture would proclaim instead "that rugged individuality which makes for the unpredictability of great actions—and great works" (p. 77).

Two remarks are in order here. Arbitrariness can be taken as an ideology in itself, that is, as the irreducible freedom and originality of the author (Bussy-Rabutin's complaint, *en somme*). But more specifically, the refusal of the demands of one economy may mask the inscription of another. This inscription may seem silent, or unarticulated in/as *authorial commentary (discours),* without being absent. (It may simply be inaudible to the dominant mode of reception.) In *La Princesse de Clèves,* for example, "extravagance" is in fact accounted for, I would argue, both by maxims and by a decipherable effect of italicization. The maxims I refer to are not direct commentary; and it is true, as Genette writes, that "nothing is more foreign to the style [of the novel] than sententious epiphrasis: as if the actions were always either beyond or beneath all commentary" (p. 78). It is also true that within the narrative the characters do comment on the actions; and although Genette does not "count" such comments as "chatting," I would suggest that they constitute an internally motivating discourse: an artificial plausibility *en abyme.* This intratext is maternal discourse; and its *performance* through the "extraordinary feelings" of Mme de Clèves is an instance of italicization. The confession, to state the obvious, makes perfect sense in terms of the idiolect spoken by Mme de Chartres: "Be brave and strong, my daughter; withdraw from the court, force your husband to take you away; do not fear the most brutal and difficult measures; however awful they may seem at first, in the end they will be milder in their effects than the misery of a love affair" (p. 68).[19] Moreover, the confession *qua* confession is set up by *reference* to a "real-life" precedent and is presented by the prince himself as a model of desirable behavior: "Sincerity is so important to me that I think that if my mistress, and even my wife, confessed to me that she was attracted by another . . . I would cast off the role of lover or husband to advise and sympathize with her" (p. 76). Seen from this perspective the behavior of the princess is both *motivated* within the narration and supplied with a pre-text: the conditions of *imitation.*

But the confession, which I may already have overemphasized, is not an isolated extravagance in the novel. It is a link in the chain of events that lead to Mme de Clèves's decision not to marry Nemours, even though in *this* instance, the maxims of the sociolect might support, even expect, the marriage. As Bussy-Rabutin again observes: "And if, against all appearances and custom, this combat between love and virtue were to last in her heart until the death of her husband, then she would be delighted to be able to bring love and virtue together by marrying a man of quality, the finest and the most handsome gentleman of his time." Mme de Lafayette clearly rejects this delightful denouement. Now, Stendhal has speculated that if Mme de Clèves had lived a long life she would have regretted her decision and would have wanted to live like Mme de Lafayette.[20] We shall never know, of course, but his comment raises an interesting question: why did Mme de Lafayette keep Mme de Clèves from living in fiction the life she herself had led? The answer to that question would be an essay in itself, but let us tackle the question here from another angle: what do Mme de Clèves's "renunciation" and, before that, her confession tell us about the relation of women writers to fiction, to the heroines of their fiction? Should the heroine's so-called "refusal of love" be read as a defeat and an end to passion—a "suicide," or "the delirium of a *précieuse*"?[21] Or is it, rather, a *bypassing* of the dialectics of desire, and, in that sense, a peculiarly feminine "act of victory"?[22] To understand the refusal as a victory and as, I believe, a rewriting of eroticism (an emphasis placed "elsewhere"—as Irigaray and, curiously, Woolf say), from which we might generalize about the economy of representation regulating the heroine and her authors, let us shift critical gear for a while.

Claudine Herrmann describes the princess as a heroine "written in a language of dream, dreamt by Mme de Lafayette."[23] What is the language of that dream, and what is the dream of that language? In the essay called "The Relation of the Poet to Daydreaming" (1908), Freud wonders how that "strange being, the poet, comes by his material."[24] He goes on to answer his question by considering the processes at work in children's play and then moves to daydreams and fantasies in adults. When he begins to describe the characteristics of this mode of creativity, he makes a blanket generalization about its impulses that should immediately make clear the usefulness of his essay for our purposes: "Unsatisfied wishes are the driving power behind phantasies; every separate phantasy contains the fulfillment of a wish, and improves upon unsatisfactory reality" (p. 47). What then is the nature of these wishes and, more to our point, does the sex of the dreamer affect the shaping of the daydream's text? Here, as might be expected, Freud does not disappoint:

> The impelling wishes vary according to the sex, character and circumstances of the creator; they may easily be divided,

> however, into two principal groups. Either they are ambitious wishes, serving to exalt the person creating them, or they are erotic. In young women erotic wishes dominate the phantasies *almost exclusively,* for their ambition is *generally comprised* in their erotic longings; in young men egoistic and ambitious wishes assert themselves plainly enough alongside their erotic desires. (Pp. 47–48; emphasis added)

Here we see that the either/or antinomy, ambitious/erotic, is immediately collapsed to make coexistence possible in masculine fantasies: "In the greater number of ambitious daydreams . . . we can discover a woman in some corner, for whom the dreamer performs all his heroic deeds and at whose feet all his triumphs are to be laid" (p. 48).

But is this observation reversible? If, to make the logical extrapolation, romance dominates the female daydream and constitutes its primary heroineism, is there a *place* in which the ambitious wish of a young woman asserts itself? Has she an egoistic desire to be discovered "in some corner"? Freud elides the issue—while leaving the door open (for us) by his modifiers, "almost exclusively" and "generally comprised"—presumably because he is on his way to establishing the relationship between daydreaming and literary creation. The pertinence of difference there is moot, of course, because he conjures up only a male creator: not the great poet, however, but "the less pretentious writers of romances, novels and stories, who are read all the same by the widest circles of men and women" (p. 50). Freud then proceeds to identify the key "marked characteristic" of these fictions: "They all have a hero who is the centre of interest, for whom the author tries to win our sympathy by every possible means, and whom he places under the protection of a special providence" (p. 50). The hero in this literature is continually exposed to danger, but we follow his perilous adventures with a sense of security, because we know that at each turn he will triumph. According to Freud, the basis for this armchair security, for our tranquil contemplation, is the hero's own conviction of invincibility, best rendered by the expression "Nothing can happen to me!" And Freud comments, "It seems to me . . . that this significant mark of invulnerability very clearly betrays—His Majesty the Ego, the hero of *all daydreams* and *all novels*" (p. 51; emphasis added). Now, if the plots of male fiction chart the daydreams of an ego that would be invulnerable, what do the plots of female fiction reveal? Among French women writers, it would seem at first blush to be the obverse negative of "nothing can happen to me." The phrase that characterizes the heroine's posture might well be a variant of Murphy's law: If anything can go wrong, it will. And the reader's sense of security, itself dependent on the heroine's, comes from feeling, not that the heroine will triumph in some *conventionally* positive way, but that she will transcend the perils of plot with a self-exalting dignity. Here national constraints on the imagination, or what in this essay Freud calls "racial psychology," do seem to matter: the second-chance rerouting of disaster typical of Jane Austen's fiction, for example, is exceedingly rare in France. To the extent that we can speak of a triumph of Her Majesty the Ego in France, it lies in being beyond vulnerability, indeed beyond it all. On the whole, French women writers prefer what Peter Brooks has described as "the melodramatic imagination," a dreamlike and metaphorical drama of the "moral occult."[25] There are recurrent melodramatic plots about women unhappy in love because men are men and women are women. As I said earlier, however, the suffering seems to have its own rewards in the economy of the female unconscious. The heroine proves to be better than her victimizers; and perhaps this ultimate superiority, which is to be read in the choice to go beyond love, beyond "erotic longings," is the figure that the "ambitious wishes" of women writers (dreamers) takes.

In the economy of Freud's plot, as we all know, fantasy scenarios are generated by consciously repressed content; and so he naturally assumes a motive for the "concealment" of "ambitious wishes": "the overweening self-regard" that a young man "acquires in the indulgent atmosphere surrounding his childhood" must be suppressed "so that he may find his proper place in a society that is full of other persons making similar claims" (p. 48)—hence the daydreams in which the hero conquers all to occupy victoriously center stage. The content that a young woman represses comes out in erotic daydreams because "a well-brought-up woman is, indeed, credited with only a minimum of erotic desire" (p. 48). Indeed. Now, there is a class of novels by women that "maximizes" that minimum, a type of fiction that George Eliot attacks as "Silly Novels by Lady Novelists": "The heroine is usually an heiress . . . with perhaps a vicious baronet, an amiable duke, and an irresistible younger son of a marquis as lovers in the foreground, a clergyman and a poet sighing for her in the middle distance, and a crowd of undefined adorers dimly indicated beyond."[26] After sketching out the variations of plot that punctuate the heroine's " 'starring' expedition through life" (p. 302), Eliot comments on the security with which we await the inevitably happy end:

> Before matters arrive at this desirable issue our feelings are tried by seeing the noble, lovely and gifted heroine pass through many *mauvais moments,* but we have the satisfaction of knowing that her sorrows are wept into embroidered pocket-handkerchiefs . . . and that whatever vicissitudes she may undergo . . . she comes out of them all with a complex-

> ion more blooming and locks more redundant than ever. (P. 303)

The plots of these "silly novels" bring grist to Freud's mill—that is, the grist I bring to his mill—in an almost uncanny way; and they would seem to undermine the argument I am on the verge of elaborating. But as Eliot says:

> Happily, we are not dependent on argument to prove that Fiction is a department of literature in which women can, after their kind, fully equal men. A cluster of great names, both living and dead, rush to our memories in evidence that women can produce novels not only fine, but among the very finest;—novels too, that have a precious speciality, lying quite apart from masculine aptitudes and experience. (P. 324)

(Let me work through her essay to my own.) What Eliot is attacking here is not only the relationship of certain women writers to literature but the critical reception given women's fiction. We might also say that she is attacking, the better to separate herself from, those women writers whose language is structured exactly like the unconscious that Freud has assigned to them, those writers (and their heroines) whose ambitious wishes are contained *entirely* in their erotic longings. And she is attacking these novelists, the better to defend, *not* those women who write *like* men (for she posits a "precious specialty" to women's production), but those women who write in their own way, "after their kind," and implicitly about something else. Silly novels are that popular artifact which has always been and still is known as "women's literature"—a term, I should add, applied to such fiction by those who do not read it.[27]

Women writers then, in contrast to lady novelists, are writers whose texts would be "among the finest" (to stay with Eliot's terminology) and for whom the "ambitious wish" (to stay with Freud's) manifests itself as fantasy within another economy. In this economy, egoistic desires would assert themselves paratactically alongside erotic ones. The repressed content, I think, would be, not erotic impulses, but an impulse to power: a fantasy of power that would revise the social grammar in which women are never defined as subjects; a fantasy of power that disdains a sexual exchange in which women can participate only as objects of circulation. The daydreams or fictions of women writers would then, like those of men, say, "Nothing can happen to me!" But the modalities of that invulnerability would be marked in an essentially different way. I am talking, of course, about the power of the weak. The inscription of this power is not always easy to decipher, because, as has been noted, "the most essential form of accommodation for the weak is to conceal what power they do have."[28] Moreover, to pick up a lost thread, when these modalities of difference are perceived, they are generally called implausibilities. They are not perceived, or are misperceived, because the scripting of this fantasy does not bring the aesthetic "forepleasure" Freud says fantasy scenarios inevitably bring: pleasure bound to recognition and *identification* (p. 54), the "agrément" Genette assigns to plausible narrative. (Perhaps we shall not have a poetics of women's literature until we have more weak readers.)

In *Les Voleuses de langue,* Claudine Herrmann takes up what I call the politics of dreams, or the ideology of daydreaming, in *La Princesse de Clèves:*

> A daydream is perpetuated when it loses all chance of coming true, when the woman dreaming [*la rêveuse*] cannot make it pass into reality. If women did not generally experience the love they desire as a repeated impossibility, they would dream about it less. They would dream of other, perhaps more interesting things. Nevertheless, written in a language of dream, dreamt by Mme de Lafayette, the Princesse de Clèves never dreams . . . for she knows that *love as she imagines it* is not realizable. What is realizable is a counterfeit she does not want. Her education permits her to glimpse this fact: men and women exchange feelings that are not equivalent. . . . Woman's "daydreaming" is a function of a world in which nothing comes true on her terms.[29]

"Men and women exchange feelings that are not equivalent." Mme de Clèves's brief experience of the court confirms the principle of difference at the heart of her mother's maxims. Mme de Clèves's rejection of Nemours on his terms, however, derives its necessity not only from the logic of maternal discourse (Nemours's love, like his name, is negative and plural: *ne/amours*) but also from the demands of Mme de Lafayette's dream. In this dream nothing can happen to the heroine, because she understands that the power and pleasure of the weak derive from circumventing the laws of contingency and circulation. She withdraws then and confesses, not merely to resist possession, as her mother would have wished, but to improve on it: to *rescript* possession.

The plausibility of this novel lies in the structuration of its fantasy. For if, to continue spinning out Herrmann's metaphor, the heroine does not dream, she does daydream. And perhaps the most significant confession in the novel is neither the first (to her husband, that she is vulnerable to desire) nor the third (to Nemours, that she desires him) but the second, which is silent and entirely telling: I refer, of course, to her nocturnal *rêverie* at Coulommiers. Although all three confessions prefigure by their extravagance the heroine's retreat from the eyes of the world, it is this dreamlike event that is least ambiguous in underlining the erotic valence of the ambitious scenario.

At Coulommiers, her country retreat, Mme de Clèves sits one warm evening, secretly observed by Nemours, winding ribbons of his colors around an India cane. (I take her surreptitious acquisition of his cane to be the counterpart of his theft of her miniature, in this crisscrossing of desires by metonymy.) As Michel Butor observes in his seductive reading of this scene, "the mind of the princess is operating at this moment in a zone obscure to herself; it is as if she is knotting the ribbons around the cane in a dream, and her dream becomes clear little by little; the one she is thinking of begins to take on a face, and she goes to look for it."[30] Thus, having finished her handiwork, she places herself in front of a painting, a historical tableau of members of the court that she has had transported to her retreat, a painting including a likeness of Nemours: "She sat down and began to look at this portrait with an intensity and dreaminess [*rêverie*] that only passion can inspire" (p. 155). And Butor comments, "One hardly needs a diploma in psychoanalysis to detect and appreciate the symbolism of this whole scene."[31] Indeed, it is quite clear that the princess is seen here in a moment of solitary pleasure, in a daydream of "fetichistic sublimation." This autoeroticism would seem to be the only sexual performance she can afford in an economy regulated by dispossession.[32]

Her retreat to Coulommiers, though, must be thought of not as a flight from sexuality but as a movement *into* it. As Sylvère Lotringer has observed, Mme de Clèves leaves the court not to flee passion but to preserve it.[33] To preserve it, however, on her own terms. Unlike Nemours—who is not content to possess the object of his desire in representation (the purloined portrait) and who pleads silently after this scene, "Only look at me the way I saw you look at my portrait tonight; how could you look so gently at my portrait and then so cruelly fly from my presence?" (p. 157)—the princess chooses "the duke of the portrait, not the man who seeks to step out of the frame."[34] Here she differs from Austen's heroine Elizabeth Bennet, who stands gazing before her lover's portrait and feels "a more gentle sensation towards the original than she had ever felt in the height of their acquaintance."[35] Elizabeth can accept the hand of the man who steps out of the frame; the princess cannot. For if, in the world of *Pride and Prejudice,* "between the picture's eyes and Elizabeth's hangs what will be given shape when the marriage of the lovers is formalized" (Brownstein), in the world of the court the princess's response to Nemours must remain specular. Her desire cannot be framed by marriage—*à l'anglaise.* If, however, as I believe, the withdrawal to Coulommiers is homologous to the *final* withdrawal, then there is no reason to imagine that at a remove from the world—or rather, in the company of the world contained by representation in painting—the princess does not continue to experience her "erotic longings." But the fulfillment of the wish is to be realized in the daydream itself.

The daydream, then, is both the stuff of fairy tales ("Someday my prince will come") and their rewriting ("Someday my prince will come, but we will not live happily ever after"). The princess refuses to marry the duke, however, not because she does not want to live happily ever after, but because she does. And by choosing not to act on that desire but to preserve it in and as fantasy, she both performs maternal discourse and italicizes it as repossession. Her choice is therefore not the simple reinscription of the seventeenth-century convention of female renunciation, dependent on the logic of either/or, but the sign of both-and, concretized by her final dual residence: in the convent *and* at home. "Perverted convention," as Peggy Kamuf names it, writing of another literary fetichist (Saint-Preux in Julie's closet): "The scene of optimal pleasure is within the prohibition which forms the walls of the house. Just on this side of the transgressive act, the fetichist's pleasure . . . is still in the closet."[36] This form of possession by metonymy both acknowledges the law and short-circuits it. Nobody, least of all the Duc de Nemours, believes in her renunciation (just as her husband never fully believed her confession):

> Do you think that your resolutions can hold against a man who adores you and who is fortunate enough to attract you? It is more difficult than you think, Madame, to resist the attractions of love. You have done it *by an austere virtue which has almost no example;* but that virtue is no longer opposed to your feelings and I hope that you will follow them despite yourself. (Pp. 174–75; emphasis added)

Mme de Clèves will not be deterred by sheer difficulty, by mere plausibility, by Nemours's *maxims.* She knows herself to be without a text. "No woman but you in the world," she has been told earlier in the novel, "would confide everything she knows in her husband" (p. 116). "The singularity of such a confession," the narrator comments after the *fait accompli,* "for which she could find no example, made her see all the danger of it" (p. 125). The danger of singularity precisely is sociolinguistic: the attempt to *communicate* in a language, an idiolect, that would nonetheless break with the coded rules of communication. An impossibility, as Jakobson has seen: "Private property, in the domain of language, does not exist: everything is socialized. The verbal exchange, like every form of human relation, requires at least two interlocutors; an idiolect, in the final analysis, therefore can only be a *slightly perverse fiction.*"[37] Thus in the end Mme de Clèves herself becomes both the impossibility of an example for others "in life" and its possibility in fiction.

"Her life," the last line of the novel tells us, which "was rather short, left inimitable examples of virtue" (p. 180). The last word in French is the challenge to reiteration—*inimitables,* the mark of the writer's ambitious wish.

I hope it is understood that I am not suggesting we read a heroine as the clone of her author—a reductionist strategy that has passed for literary criticism on women's writing from the beginning. Rather, I am arguing that the peculiar shape of a heroine's destiny in novels by women, the implausible twists of plot so common in these novels, is a form of insistence about the relation of women to writing: a comment on the stakes of difference within the theoretical indifference of literature itself.

Woolf begins her essay on Eliot in the *Common Reader* by saying, "To read George Eliot attentively is to become aware how little one knows about her." But then, a few pages later, she comments:

> For long she preferred not to think of herself at all. Then, when the first flush of creative energy was exhausted and self-confidence had come to her, she wrote more and more from the personal standpoint, but she did so without the unhesitating abandonment of the young. *Her self-consciousness is always marked when her heroines say what she herself would have said. . . .* The disconcerting and stimulating fact remained that she was compelled by the very power of her genius to step forth in person upon the quiet bucolic scene.[38]

What interests me here is the "marking" Woolf identifies, an underlining of what she later describes as Eliot's heroines' "demand for something—they scarcely know what—for something that is perhaps incompatible with the facts of human existence."[39] This demand of the heroine for something else is in part what I mean by "italicization": the extravagant wish for a *story* that would turn out differently.

In the fourth chapter of book 5 of *The Mill on the Floss* Maggie Tulliver, talking with Philip Wakem in the "Red Deeps," returns a novel he has lent her:

> "Take back your *Corinne,*" said Maggie. . . . "You were right in telling me she would do me no good, but you were wrong in thinking I should wish to be like her."
>
> "Wouldn't you really like to be a tenth muse, then, Maggie?" . . .
>
> "Not at all," said Maggie laughing. "The muses were

> uncomfortable goddesses, I think—obliged always to carry rolls and musical instruments about with them. . . ."
>
> "You agree with me in not liking Corinne, then?"
>
> "I didn't finish the book," said Maggie. "As soon as I came to the blond-haired young lady reading in the park, I shut it up and determined to read no further. I foresaw that that light-complexioned girl would win away all the love from Corinne and make her miserable. I'm determined to read no more books where the blond-haired women carry away all the happiness. I should begin to have a prejudice against them. If you could give me some story, now, where the dark woman triumphs, it would restore the balance. I want to avenge Rebecca, and Flora MacIvor, and Minna, and all the rest of the dark unhappy ones. . . ."
>
> "Well, perhaps you will avenge the dark women in your own person and carry away all the love from your cousin Lucy. She is sure to have some handsome young man of St. Ogg's at her feet now, and you have only to shine upon him —your fair little cousin will be quite quenched in your beams."
>
> "Philip, that is not pretty of you, to apply my nonsense to anything real," said Maggie looking hurt.[40]

Maggie's literary instincts are correct. True to the laws of genre, Corinne—despite, that is, because of, her genius and exceptionality—is made miserable and the blond Lucile, her half sister, carries the day, although she is deprived of a perfectly happy end. But whatever Eliot's, or Maggie's, "prejudices" against the destinies of Scott's heroines, Maggie no more than Corinne avenges the dark woman in her own person. Even though, as Philip predicts, Maggie's inner radiance momentarily quenches her fair-haired cousin, Lucy, "reality"—that is to say, Eliot's novel—proves to be as hard on dark-haired women as literature is. What is important in this deliberate intertextuality, which has not gone unnoted,[41] is that both heroines revolt against the text of a certain "happily ever after." As Madelyn Gutwirth observes in her book on Mme de Staël, Corinne prefers "her genius to the . . . bonds of marriage, but that is not to say she thereby renounces happiness. On the contrary, it is her wish to be happy, that is to be herself *and* to love, that kills her."[42] Maggie Tulliver, too, would be herself and love, but the price for *that* unscriptable wish proves again to be the deferral of conventional erotic longings, what Maggie calls "earthly happiness." Almost two hundred years after the challenge to the maxim wrought by the blond (as it turns out) Princesse de Clèves,

George Eliot, through the scenario of definitive postponement, "imitates" Mme de Lafayette.

The last two books of *The Mill on the Floss* are called, respectively, "The Great Temptation" and "The Final Rescue." As the plot moves toward closure, the chapter headings of these books—"First Impressions," "Illustrating the Laws of Attraction," "Borne Along by the Tide," "Waking," "St. Ogg's Passes Judgment," "The Last Conflict"—further emphasize the sexual struggle at the heart of the novel. For, as Philip had anticipated, Maggie dazzles blond Lucy's fiancé, Stephen Guest, in "First Impressions," but then, surely what Philip had not dreamt of, the pair is swept away. Maggie, previously unawakened by *her* fiancé, Wakem, awakens both to her desire and to what she calls her duty, only to fulfill both by drowning, attaining at last that "wondrous happiness that is one with pain" (p. 545). Though I do great violence to the scope of Eliot's narrative by carving a novel out of a novel, the last two books taken together as they chart the culmination of a heroine's erotic destiny have a plot of their own—a plot, moreover, with elective affinities to the conclusion of *La Princesse de Clèves,* and to the conclusion of my argument.

Like Mme de Clèves after her husband's death, Maggie knows herself to be technically free to marry her lover but feels bound, though not for the same reasons, to another script. And Stephen Guest, who like Nemours does not believe in "mere resolution" (p. 499), finds Maggie's refusal to follow her passions "unnatural" and "horrible": "If you loved me as I love you, we should throw everything else to the winds for the sake of belonging to each other" (p. 470). Maggie does love him, just as the princess loves the duke, passionately; and she is tempted: part of her longs to be transported by the exquisite currents of desire. But her awakening, like that of the princess, though again not for the same reasons, is double. She falls asleep on the boat ride down the river. When she awakens and disentangles her mind "from the confused web of dreams" (p. 494), like Mme de Clèves after her own brush with death, Maggie pulls away from the man who has briefly but deeply tempted her. She will not build her happiness on the unhappiness of others:

> It is not the force that ought to rule us—this that we feel for each other; it would rend me away from all that my past life has made dear and holy to me. I can't set out on a fresh life and forget that; I must go back to it, and cling to it, else I shall feel as if there were nothing firm beneath my feet. (P. 502)

What is the content of this sacred past? Earlier, before the waking on the river, when Maggie was tempted only by the "fantasy" of a "life filled with all luxuries, with daily incense of adoration near and distant, and with all possibilities of culture at her command," the narrator had commented on the pull of that erotic scenario:

> But there were things in her stronger than vanity—passion, and affection, and long deep memories of early discipline and effort, of early claims on her love and pity; and the stream of vanity was soon swept along and mingled imperceptibly with that wider current which was at its highest force today. . . . (P. 457)

Maggie's renunciation of Stephen Guest, then, is not so simple as I have made it out to be, for the text of these "early claims," this archaic wish, has a power both erotic and ambitious in its own right. That "wider current" is, of course, the broken bond with her brother. And the epigraph to the novel, "In their death they were not divided," is the telos toward which the novel tends; for it is also the last line of the novel, the epitaph on the tombstone of the brother and sister who drown in each other's arms.

Maggie, obeying what Stephen called her "perverted notion of right," her passion for a "mere idea" (p. 538), drowns finally in an implausible flood. Maggie, no more than Mme de Clèves, could be *persuaded* (to invoke Jane Austen's last novel); for neither regarded a second chance as an alternative to be embraced. Maggie's return home sans husband is not understood by the community. And the narrator explains that "public opinion in these cases is always of the feminine gender—not the world, but the world's wife" (pp. 512–13). Despite the phrase, Eliot does not locate the inadequacy of received social ideas in gender per se; her attack on the notion of a "master-key that will fit all cases" is in fact directed at the "men of maxims": "The mysterious complexity of our life is not to be embraced by maxims . . ." (p. 521). This commentary seeks to justify Maggie's choice, her turning away from the maxim, and thus inscribes an internal "artificial plausibility": the text within the text, as we saw that function in *La Princesse de Clèves.* The commentary constitutes another *reading,* a reading by "reference," as Eliot puts it, to the "special circumstances that mark the individual lot" (p. 521). Like Mme de Clèves, Maggie has been given extraordinary feelings, and those feelings en*gender* another and extravagant narrative logic.

There is a feminist criticism today that laments Eliot's ultimate refusal to satisfy her heroine's longing for that "something . . . incompatible with the facts of human existence":

> Sadly, and it is a radical criticism of George Eliot, she does not commit herself fully to the energies and aspirations she

> lets loose in these women. Does she not cheat them, and cheat us, ultimately, in allowing them so little? Does she not excite our interest through the breadth and the challenge of the implications of her fiction, and then deftly dam up and fence round the momentum she has so powerfully created? She diagnoses so brilliantly "the common yearning of womanhood," and then cures it, sometimes drastically, as if it were indeed a disease.[43]

It is as though these critics, somewhat like Stendhal disbelieving the conviction of Mme de Clèves, would have Maggie live George Eliot's life. The point is, it seems to me, that the plots of women's literature are not about "life" and solutions in any therapeutic sense, nor should they be. They are about the plots of literature itself, about the constraints the maxim places on rendering a female life in fiction. Mme de Lafayette quietly, George Eliot less silently, both italicize by the demaximization of their heroines' texts the difficulty of curing plot of life, and life of certain plots.[44]

Lynn Sukenick, in her essay "On Women and Fiction," describes the uncomfortable posture of all women writers in our culture, within and without the text: what I would call a posture of imposture. And she says of the role of gender in relation to the literary project: "Like the minority writer, the female writer exists within an inescapable condition of identity which distances her from the mainstream of the culture and forces her either to stress her separation from the masculine literary tradition or to pursue her resemblance to it." Were she to forget her double bind, the "phallic critics" (as Mary Ellman describes them) would remind her that she is dreaming: "Lady novelists," Hugh Kenner wrote not so long ago, "have always claimed the privilege of transcending *mere plausibilities.* It's up to men to arrange such things. . . . Your bag is sensitivity, which means knowing what to put into this year's novels" (emphasis added).[45] And a recent reviewer of a woman's novel in a popular magazine complains:

> Like most feminist novels [this one] represents a triumph of sensibility over plot. Why a strong, credible narrative line that leads to a satisfactory resolution of conflicts should visit these stories so infrequently, I do not know. Because the ability to tell a good story is unrelated to gender, I sometimes suspect that the authors of these novels are simply indifferent to the rigors of narrative.[46]

The second gentleman is slightly more generous than the first. He at least thinks women capable of telling a good—that is, credible—story. The fault lies in their *in*difference. I would not have descended to the evidence of the middlebrow mainstream if it did not, with curious persistence, echo the objections of Bussy-Rabutin.

The attack on female plots and plausibilities assumes that women writers cannot or will not obey the rules of fiction. It also assumes that the truth devolving from *veri*similitude is male. For sensibility, sensitivity, "extravagance"—so many code words for feminine in our culture that the attack is in fact tautological—are taken to be not merely inferior modalities of production but deviations from some obvious truth. The blind spot here is both political (or philosophical) and literary. It does not see, nor does it want to, that the fictions of desire behind the desiderata of fiction are masculine and not universal constructs. It does not see that the maxims that pass for the truth of human experience, and the encoding of that experience in literature, are organizations, when they are not fantasies, of the dominant culture. To read women's literature is to see and hear repeatedly a chafing against the "unsatisfactory reality" contained in the maxim. Everywhere in *The Mill on the Floss* one can read a protest against the division of labor that grants men the world and women love. Saying no to Philip Wakem and then to Stephen Guest, Maggie refuses the hospitality of the happy end: "But I begin to think there can never come much happiness to me from loving; I have always had so much pain mingled with it. I wish I could make myself a world outside it, as men do" (p. 430). But as in so much women's fiction a world outside love proves to be out of the world altogether. The protest against that topographical imperative is more or less muted from novel to novel. Still, the emphasis is always there to be read, and it points to another text. To continue to deny the credibility of women's literature is to adopt the posture of the philosopher of phallogocentrism's "credulous man who, in support of his testimony, offers truth and his phallus as his own proper credentials."[47] Those credentials are more than suspect.

NOTES

[1]Although what is being pointed to ultimately is an "elsewhere" under the sign of an androgyny I resist, I respond here to the implicit invitation to look again. The quotation should be replaced both in its original context and within Carolyn Heilbrun's concluding argument in *Toward a Recognition of Androgyny* (New York: Alfred A. Knopf, 1973), pp. 167–72, which is where I (re)found it.

[2]If one must have a less arbitrary origin—and why not?—the properly inaugural fiction would be Hélisenne de Crenne's *Les Angoysses douloureuses qui procèdent d'amours* (1538). But *La Princesse de Clèves* has this critical advantage: it also marks the beginning of the modern French novel.

[3]Bussy-Rabutin's oft-cited remarks on the novel are most easily found in Maurice Laugaa's excellent volume of critical responses, *Lectures de Mme de Lafayette* (Paris:

Armand Colin, 1971), pp. 18–19. The translation is mine, as are all other translations from the French in my essay, unless otherwise indicated.

[4]On the function and status of the confession in Mme de Villedieu's novel and on the problems of predecession, see Micheline Cuénin's introduction to her critical edition of *Les Désordres de l'amour* (Geneva: Droz, 1970). The best account of the attack on the novel remains Georges May's *Le Dilemme du roman au XVIIIe siècle* (New Haven, Conn.: Yale University Press, 1963), esp. his first chapter.

[5]I allude here (speciously) to the first definition of "extravagant" in *Le Petit Robert* (Paris: Société du Nouveau Littré, 1967), p. 668: "S'est dit de textes non incorporés dans les recueils canoniques"—"Used to refer to texts not included in the canon."

[6]I refer here, as I indicate below, to Gérard Genette's "Vraisemblance et motivation," included in his *Figures II* (Paris: Editions du Seuil, 1969), p. 74. In my translation-adaptation of Genette's analysis I have chosen to render *vraisemblance* by "plausibility," a term with a richer semantic field of connotations than "verisimilitude." Page references to Genette's essay are hereafter given in the text.

[7]For an overview of the current discussion about women's writing in France, see Elaine Marks's fine piece "Women and Literature in France," *Signs* 3 (Summer 1978): 832–42.

[8]Cixous, "The Laugh of the Medusa," trans. Keith Cohen and Paula Cohen, *Signs* 1 (Summer 1976): 878.

[9]For a recent statement of her position on a possible specificity to women's writing, see "Questions à Julia Kristeva," *Revue des sciences humaines* 168 (1977): 495–501.

[10]Cixous, "Laugh of the Medusa," p. 879.

[11]The opposition between these positions is more rhetorical than actual, as Woolf's gloss on Coleridge in *A Room of One's Own* shows. See esp. chap. 6.

[12]Elaine Showalter, *A Literature of Their Own: British Women Novelists from Brontë to Lessing* (Princeton, N.J.: Princeton Univ. Press, 1977), and Ellen Moers, *Literary Women: The Great Writers* (Garden City, N.Y.: Doubleday, 1976). I understate the stakes of recognizing and responding to an apparently passive indifference. As Edward Said has written in another context: "Any philosophy or critical theory exists and is maintained in order not merely *to be there, passively around everyone and everything,* but in order to be taught and diffused, to be absorbed decisively into the institutions of society or to be instrumental in maintaining or changing or perhaps upsetting these institutions and that society" ("The Problem of Textuality," *Critical Inquiry* 4 [Summer 1978]: 682).

[13]T. S. Eliot, quoted by Elizabeth Janeway in her insightful essay on women's writing in postwar America, "Women's Literature," *Harvard Guide to Contemporary American Writing,* ed. Daniel Hoffman (Cambridge, Mass.: Harvard University Press, 1979), p. 344.

[14]See in particular Showalter's first chapter, "The Female Tradition," pp. 3–36.

[15]See Showalter's chapter "The Double Critical Standard and the Feminine Novel," pp. 73–99.

[16]Eliot, quoted in Janeway, "Women's Literature," p. 344.

[17]Luce Irigaray, *Ce Sexe qui n'en est pas un* (Paris: Editions de Minuit, 1977), p. 74.

[18]Sally McConnell-Ginet, "Intonation in a Man's World," *Signs* 3 (Spring 1978): 542.

[19]My translations from *La Princesse de Clèves* are deliberately literal; page references to the French are from the readily available Garnier-Flammarion edition (Paris,

1966) and are incorporated within the text. The published English translation (New York: Penguin Books, 1978) is, I think, rather poor.

[20]Stendhal, "Du Courage des femmes," *De L'Amour* (Paris: Editions de Cluny, 1938), chap. 29, p. 111.

[21]Serge Doubrovsky, "*La Princesse de Clèves:* Une Interprétation existentielle," *La Table ronde,* no. 138 (1959), p. 48. Jean Rousset, *Forme et signification* (Paris: Corti, 1962), p. 25.

[22]A. Kibédi Varga, "Romans d'amour, romans de femme à l'époque classique," *Revue des sciences humaines* 168 (1977): 524. Jules Brody, in "*La Princesse de Clèves* and the Myth of Courtly Love," *University of Toronto Quarterly* 38 (January 1969): 105–35, esp. pp. 131–34, and Domna C. Stanton, in "The Ideal of *Repos* in Seventeenth-Century French Literature," *L'Esprit créateur* 15 (Spring–Summer 1975): 79–104, esp. pp. 95–96, 99, 101–2, also interpret the princess's final refusal of Nemours (and her renunciation) as heroic and self-preserving actions within a certain seventeenth-century discourse.

[23]Claudine Herrmann, *Les Voleuses de langue* (Paris: Des Femmes, 1976), p. 77.

[24]Sigmund Freud, *On Creativity and the Unconscious,* trans. I. F. Grant Duff (New York: Harper & Brothers, 1958), p. 44. Subsequent references to this edition are given in the text.

[25]Peter Brooks, *The Melodramatic Imagination: Balzac, Henry James, Melodrama, and the Mode of Excess* (New Haven, Conn.: Yale University Press, 1976), p. 20.

[26]*The Essays of George Eliot,* ed. Thomas Pinney (London: Routledge & Kegan Paul, 1963), pp. 301–2. Hereafter page references to this edition are included in the text.

[27]On the content of popular women's literature and its relationship to high culture, see Lillian Robinson's "On Reading Trash," *Sex, Class, and Culture* (Bloomington: Indiana University Press, 1978), pp. 200–22.

[28]Barbara Bellow Watson, "On Power and the Literary Text," *Signs* 1 (Fall 1975): 113. Watson suggests that we look instead for "expressive symbolic structures."

[29]Herrmann, *Les Voleuses de langue,* pp. 77–79.

[30]Michel Butor, "Sur *La Princesse de Clèves,*" *Répertoire* (Paris: Editions de Minuit, 1960), pp. 76–77.

[31]Ibid., p. 76.

[32]David Grossvogel, *Limits of the Novel* (Ithaca, N.Y.: Cornell University Press, 1971), p. 134. In Doubrovsky's terms, love in this universe means "being dispossessed of oneself and bound to the incoercible spontaneity of another" ("Une Interprétation existentielle," p. 47).

[33]Sylvère Lotringer, "La Structuration romanesque," *Critique,* 26 (1970): 517.

[34]Ibid., p. 519.

[35]The importance of this scene from Austen is underscored by Rachel Mayer Brownstein in *Becoming a Heroine* (New York: Viking Press, 1982), pp. 129–31.

[36]Peggy Kamuf, "Inside *Julie's* Closet," *Romanic Review* 69 (November 1978): 303–4.

[37]Roman Jakobson, *Essais de linguistique générale* (Paris: Editions de Minuit, 1963), p. 33; quoted by Sylvère Lotringer, "Vice de Forme," *Critique* 27 (1971): 203; italics mine.

[38]Virginia Woolf, *The Common Reader* (New York: Harcourt, Brace & World, 1953), pp. 166, 173; emphasis added.

[39]Ibid., p. 175.

[40]George Eliot, *The Mill on the Floss* (New York: New American Library, 1965),

pp. 348–49. Subsequent references to the novel are to this edition and are given in the text.

[41]See, e.g., Moers, *Literary Women,* p. 174.

[42]Madelyn Gutwirth, *Madame de Staël, Novelist: The Emergence of the Artist as Woman* (Urbana: University of Illinois Press, 1978), p. 255.

[43]Jenni Calder, e.g., in *Women and Marriage in Victorian Fiction* (New York: Oxford University Press, 1976), p. 158.

[44]I echo here, with some distortion, the terms of Peter Brooks's analysis of the relations between "plot" and "life" in his illuminating essay "Freud's Master-plot," *Yale French Studies,* no. 55–56 (1977), pp. 280–300, esp. p. 298.

[45]Lynn Sukenick's essay is quoted from *The Authority of Experience: Essays in Feminist Criticism,* ed. Arlyn Diamond and Lee R. Edwards (Amherst: University of Massachusetts Press, 1977), p. 28; Hugh Kenner's observation is quoted in the same essay, p. 30. Mary Ellman's term is taken from *Thinking about Women* (New York: Harcourt, Brace & World, 1968), pp. 28–54.

[46]Peter Prescott, in *Newsweek,* October 16, 1978, p. 112.

[47]Jacques Derrida, "Becoming Woman," trans. Barbara Harlow, *Semiotext(e)* 3 (1978): 133.

Writing the Body

Toward an Understanding of l'Écriture féminine

Ann Rosalind Jones

France is today the scene of feminisms. The Mouvement de libération des femmes (MLF) grows every year, but so do the factions within it: feminist journals carry on bitter debates, a group of women writers boycotts a feminist publishing house, French women at conferences in the United States contradict each other's positions at top volume (Monique Wittig to Hélène Cixous: "Ceci est un scandale!"). But in the realm of theory, the French share a deep critique of the modes through which the West has claimed to discern evidence —or reality—and a suspicion concerning efforts to change the position of women that fail to address the forces in the body, in the unconscious, in the basic structures of culture that are invisible to the empirical eye. Briefly, French feminists in general believe that Western thought has been based on a systematic repression of women's experience. Thus their assertion of a bedrock female nature makes sense as a point from which to deconstruct language, philosophy, psychoanalysis, the social practices, and the direction of patriarchal culture as we live in and resist it.

This position, the turn to *féminité* as a challenge to male-centered thinking, has stirred up curiosity and set off resonances among American feminists, who are increasingly open to theory, to philosophical, psychoanalytic, and Marxist critiques of masculinist ways of seeing the world. (Speakers at recent U.S. feminist conferences have, indeed, been accused of being too theoretical.) And it seems to me that it is precisely through theory that some of the positions of the French feminists need to be questioned—as they have been in France since the beginnings of the MLF. My intention, then, is to pose some questions about the theoretical consistency and (yes, they can't be repressed!) the practical and political implications of French discussions and celebrations of the feminine. For if one posits that female subjectivity is derived from women's physiology and bodily instincts as they affect sexual experience and the unconscious, both theoretical and practical problems can and do arise.

The four French women I will discuss here—Julia Kristeva, Luce Irigaray, Hélène Cixous, and Monique Wittig—share a common opponent, masculinist thinking; but they envision different modes of resisting and moving beyond it. Their common ground is an analysis of Western culture as fundamentally oppressive, as phallogocentric. "I am the unified, self-controlled center of the universe," man (white, European, and ruling-class) has claimed. "The rest of the world, which I define as the Other, has meaning only in relation to me, as man/father, possessor of the phallus."[1] This claim to centrality has been supported not only by religion and philosophy but also by language. To speak and especially to write from such a position is to appropriate the world, to dominate it through verbal mastery. Symbolic discourse (language, in various contexts) is another means through which man objectifies the world, reduces it to his terms, speaks in place of everything and everyone else—including women.

How, then, are the institutions and signifying practices (speech, writing, images, myths, and rituals) of such a culture to be resisted? These French women agree that resistance does take place in the form of *jouissance,* that is, in the direct reexperience of the physical pleasures of infancy and of later sexuality, repressed but not obliterated by the Law of the Father.[2] Kristeva stops here; but Irigaray and Cixous go on to emphasize that women, historically limited to being sexual objects for men (virgins or prostitutes, wives or mothers), have been prevented from expressing their sexuality in itself or for themselves. If they can do this, and if they can speak about it in the new languages it calls for, they will establish a point of view (a site of *différence*) from which phallogocentric concepts and controls can be seen through and taken apart, not only in theory but also in practice. Like Cixous, Wittig has produced a number of *textes féminins,* but she insists that the theory and practice of *féminité* must be focused on women among themselves, rather than on their divergence from men or from men's views of them. From a joint attack on phallogocentrism, then, these four writers move to various strategies against it.

Julia Kristeva, a founding member of the semiotic-Marxist journal *Tel Quel,* and the author of several books on avant-garde writers, language, and philosophy, finds in psychoanalysis the concept of the bodily drives that survive cultural pressures toward sublimation and surface in what she calls "semiotic discourse": the gestural, rhythmic, prereferential language of such writers as Joyce, Mallarmé, and Artaud.[3] These men, rather than giving up their blissful infantile fusion with their mothers, their orality and anality, reexperience such *jouissances* subconsciously and set them into play by constructing texts against the rules and regularities of conventional language. How do women fit into this scheme of semiotic liberation? Indirectly, as mothers, because they are the first love objects from which the child is typically separated and turned away in the course of his initiation into society. In fact, Kristeva sees semiotic discourse as an incestuous challenge to the symbolic order, asserting as it does the writer's return to the pleasures of his preverbal identification with his mother and his refusal to identify with his father and the logic of paternal discourse. Women, for Kristeva, also speak and write as "hysterics," as outsiders to male-dominated discourse, for two reasons: the predominance in them of drives related to anality and childbirth, and their marginal position vis-à-vis masculine culture. Their semiotic style is likely to involve repetitive, spasmodic separations from the dominating discourse, which, more often, they are forced to imitate.[4]

Kristeva doubts, however, whether women should aim to work out alternative discourses. She sees certain liberatory potentials in their marginal position, which is (admirably) unlikely to produce a fixed, authority-claiming subject/speaker or language: "In social, sexual and symbolic experiences, being a woman has always provided a means to another end, to becoming something else: a subject-in-the-making, a subject on trial." Rather than formulating a new discourse, women should persist in challenging the discourses that stand: "If women have a role to play . . . it is only in assuming a *negative* function: reject everything finite, definite, structured, loaded with meaning, in the existing state of society. Such an attitude places women on the side of the explosion of social codes: with revolutionary movements."[5] In fact, "woman" to Kristeva represents not so much a sex as an attitude, any resistance to conventional culture and language; men, too, have access to the *jouissance* that opposes phallogocentrism:

> A feminist practice can only be . . . at odds with what already exists so that we may say "that's not it" and "that's still not it." By "woman" I mean that which cannot be represented, what is not said, what remains above and beyond nomenclatures and ideologies. There are certain "men" who are familiar with this phenomenon.

For Luce Irigaray, on the contrary, women have a specificity that distinguishes them sharply from men. A psychoanalyst and former member of l'École freudienne at the University of Paris (Vincennes), she was fired from her teaching position in the fall of 1974, three weeks after the publication of her study of the phallocentric bias in Freud. *Speculum de l'autre femme* is this study, a profound and wittily sarcastic demonstration of the ways in which Plato and Freud define woman: as irrational and invisible, as imperfect (castrated) man. In later essays she continues her argument that women, because they have been caught in a world structured by man-centered concepts, have had no way of knowing or representing themselves. But she offers as the starting point for a female self-consciousness the facts of women's bodies and women's sexual pleasure, precisely because they have been so absent or so misrepresented in male discourse. Women, she says, experience a diffuse sexuality arising, for example, from the "two lips" of the vulva, and a multiplicity of libidinal energies that cannot be expressed or understood within the identity-claiming assumptions of phallocentric discourse ("I am a unified, coherent being, and what is significant in the world reflects my male image").[7] Irigaray argues further that female sexuality explains women's problematic relationship to (masculine) logic and language:

> *Woman has sex organs just about everywhere.* She experiences pleasure almost everywhere. . . . The geography of her pleasure is much more diversified, more multiple in its differences, more complex, more subtle, than is imagined—in an imaginary [system] centered a bit too much on one and the same.
>
> "She" is infinitely other in herself. That is undoubtedly the reason she is called temperamental, incomprehensible, perturbed, capricious—not to mention her language in which "she" goes off in all directions and in which "he" is unable to discern the coherence of any meaning. Contradictory words seem a little crazy to the logic of reason, and inaudible for him who listens with ready-made grids, a code prepared in advance. In her statements—at least when she dares to speak out—woman retouches herself constantly.[8]

Irigaray concedes that women's discovery of their autoeroticism will not, by itself, arrive automatically or enable them to transform the existing order: "For a woman to arrive at the point where she can enjoy her pleasure as a woman, a long detour by the analysis of the various systems that oppress her is certainly necessary."[9] Irigaray herself writes essays using Marxist categories to analyze men's use and exchange of women, and in others she uses female physiology as a source of critical metaphors and counterconcepts (against physics, pornography, Nietzsche's misogyny, myth),[10] rather than literally. Yet her focus on the physical bases for the difference between male and physical sexuality remains the same: women must recognize and assert their *jouissance* if they are to subvert phallocentric oppression at its deepest levels.

Since 1975, when she founded women's studies at Vincennes, Hélène Cixous has been a spokeswoman for the group Psychanalyse et politique and a prolific writer of texts for their publishing house, Des Femmes. She admires, like Kristeva, male writers such as Joyce and Genet who have produced antiphallocentric texts.[11] But she is convinced that women's unconscious is totally different from men's, and that it is their psychosexual specificity that will empower women to overthrow masculinist ideologies and to create new female discourses. Of her own writing she says, "Je suis là où ça parle" ("I am there where it/id/the female unconscious speaks").[12] She has produced a series of analyses of women's suffering under the laws of male sexuality (the first-person narrative *Angst,* the play *Portrait de Dora,* the libretto for the opera *Le Nom d'Oedipe*) and a growing collection of demonstrations of what id-liberated female discourses might be: *La, Ananké,* and *Illa.* In her recent *Vivre l'orange* (1979), she celebrates the Brazilian writer Clarice Lispector for what she sees as a peculiarly female attentiveness to objects, the ability to perceive and represent them in a nurturing rather than dominating way. She believes that this empathetic attentiveness, and the literary modes to which it gives rise, arise from libidinal rather than sociocultural sources: the "typically feminine gesture, not culturally but libidinally, [is] to produce in order to bring about life, pleasure, not in order to accumulate."[13]

Cixous criticizes psychoanalysis for its "thesis of a 'natural' anatomical determination of sexual difference-opposition," focusing on physical drives rather than body parts for her definition of male-female contrasts: "It is at the level of sexual pleasure in my opinion that the difference makes itself most clearly apparent in as far as woman's libidinal economy is neither identifiable by a man nor referrable to the masculine economy."[14] In her manifesto for *l'écriture féminine,* "The Laugh of the Medusa" (1975), her comparisons and lyricism suggest that she admires in women a sexuality that is remarkably constant and almost mystically superior to the phallic single-mindedness it transcends:

> Though masculine sexuality gravitates around the penis, engendering that centralized body (in political anatomy) under the dictatorship of its parts, woman does not bring about the same regionalization which serves the couple head/genitals and which is inscribed only within boundaries. Her libido is cosmic, just as her unconscious is worldwide.

She goes on immediately, in terms close to Irigaray's, to link women's diffuse sexuality to women's language—written language, in this case:

> Her writing can only keep going, without ever inscribing or discerning contours. . . . She lets the other language speak —the language of 1,000 tongues which knows neither enclosure nor death. . . . Her language does not contain, it carries; it does not hold back, it makes possible.

The passage ends with her invocation of other bodily drives (*pulsions* in the French) in a continuum with women's self-expression.

> Oral drive, anal drive, vocal drive—all these drives are our strengths, and among them is the gestation drive—just like the desire to write: a desire to live self from within, a desire for the swollen belly, for language, for blood.[15]

In her theoretical and imaginative writing alike (*La Jeune Née,* 1975, typically combines the two) Cixous insists on the primacy of multiple, specifically female libidinal impulses in women's unconscious and in the writing of the liberatory female discourses of the future.

What Kristeva, Irigaray, and Cixous do in common, then, is to oppose women's bodily experience (or, in Kristeva's case, women's bodily effect as mothers) to the phallic-symbolic patterns embedded in Western thought. Although Kristeva does not privilege women as the only possessors of prephallocentric discourse, Irigaray and Cixous go further: if women are to discover and express who they are, to bring to the surface what masculine history has repressed in them, they must begin with their sexuality. And their sexuality begins with their bodies, with their genital and libidinal difference from men.

For various reasons, this is a powerful argument. We have seen versions of it in the radical feminism of the United States, too. In the French context, it offers an island of hope in the void left by the deconstruction of humanism, which has been revealed as an ideologically suspect invention by men. If men are responsible for the reigning binary system of meaning—identity/other, man/nature, reason/chaos, man/woman—women, relegated to the negative and passive pole of this hierarchy, are not implicated in the creation of its myths. (Certainly, they are no longer impressed by them!) And the immediacy with which the body, the id, *jouissance,* are supposedly experienced promises a clarity of perception and a vitality that can bring down mountains of phallocentric delusion. Finally, to the extent that the female body is seen as a direct source of female writing, a powerful alternative discourse seems possible: to write from the body is to re-create the world.

But *féminité* and *écriture féminine* are problematic as well as powerful concepts. They have been criticized as idealist and essentialist, bound up in the very system they claim to undermine; they have been attacked as theoretically fuzzy and as fatal to constructive political action.[16] I think all these objections are worth making. What's more, they must be made if American women are to sift out and use the positive elements in French thinking about *féminité.*

First off, the basic theoretical question: Can the body be a source of self-knowledge? Does female sexuality exist prior to or in spite of social experience? Do women in fact experience their bodies purely or essentially, outside the damaging acculturation so sharply analyzed by women in France and elsewhere? The answer is no, even in terms of the psychoanalytic theory on which many elements in the concept of *féminité* depend. Feminists rereading Freud and Jaques Lacan and feminists doing new research on the construction of sexuality all agree that sexuality is not an innate quality in women or in men; it is developed through the individual's encounters with the nuclear family and with the symbolic systems set into motion by the mother-father pair as the parents themselves carry out socially imposed roles toward the child. Freud, Juliet Mitchell has shown, describes the process through which girls in our society shift their first love for their mothers to a compensatory love for their fathers and develop a sense of their own anatomy as less valued socially than that of boys.[17] Nancy Chodorow has documented and theorized the difficulty of this shift and used it to account for the complex affective needs of girls and women.[18] To the analysis of the process through which sexual identity is formed Lacan adds the role of the father as bearer of language and culture; he identifies the symbolic value attributed to the phallus as the basis for contrasts and contrasting values that the child incorporates as she attempts to make sense of and fit herself into the phallocentric world. So if early gender identity comes into being in response to patriarchal structures—as, for example, Chodorow, Lacan, and Dorothy Dinnerstein argue[19]—and if even the unconscious is sexed in accordance with the nuclear family, then there seems to be no essential stratum of sexuality unsaturated with social arrangements and symbolic systems. New readings of Freud and of object-relations theory both confirm that sexuality is not a natural given, but rather is the consequence of social interactions, among people and among signs.

Theoretical work and practical evidence strongly suggest that sexual identity ("I am a woman, I experience my body as sexual in this way") never takes shape in isolation or in a simply physical context. The child becomes male or female in response to the females and males she encounters in her family and to the male and female images she constructs according to her experience—especially her loss of direct access to either parent.[20] The desires of the child and of the adult who grows out of the child finally result not from the isolated erotic sensitivities of the child's body; these sensitivities are interpreted through the meanings the child attaches to her body through early experience in a sexed world. To take from psychoanalysis the concepts of drive and libido without talking about what happens later to the child's systems of self-perception is to drop out the deepest level at which phallocentric society asserts its power: the sexed family as it imprints itself on the child's sense of herself as a sexed being.

Psychoanalytic theory is not feminist dogma, and feminists have also analyzed the sexist ideologies that confront women past the age of childhood in the family. Not surprisingly, these ideologies make their way into many women's day-to-day experience of their bodies, even in situations that we have designed to be free of male domination. For instance, liberatory practices such as masturbation, lesbianism, and woman-centered medicine coexist with thoroughly phallocentric habits of thought and feeling; they are not liberatory simply because they aspire to be. Some women discover, for example, that their masturbation is accompanied by puzzlingly unenlightened fantasies; contrary to the claims of *féminité,* women's autoeroticism, at least in these decades, is shot through with images from a phallicly dominated world. Similarly, many lesbians recognize their need to resist roles of domination and submission that bear a grim, even parodic resemblance to heterosexual relationships. Women giving birth may wonder whether the optimistic, even heroic terminology of natural childbirth is not related to the suspect ideal of "taking it like a man." Even in the self-help clinics set up to spare women the sexist bias of the male gynecological establishment, a phallocentric *magasin des images* may prevail. A counselor at such a clinic, showing a friend of mine her cervix for the first time in a mirror, made a remark (unintentionally, that's the point) that struck us both as far less liberating than it was intended to be: "Big, isn't it? Doesn't it look powerful? As good as a penis any day." All in all, at this point in history, most of us perceive our bodies through a jumpy, contradictory mesh of hoary sexual symbolization and political counterresponse. It is possible to argue that the French feminists make of the female body too unproblematically pleasurable and totalized an entity.

Certainly, women's physiology has important meanings for women in various cultures, and it is essential for us to express those meanings rather than to submit to male definitions—that is, appropriations—of our sexuality. But the female body hardly seems the best site to launch an attack on the forces that have alienated us from what our sexuality might become. For if we argue for an innate, precultural femininity, where does that position (though in *content* it obviously diverges from masculinist dogma) leave us in relation to earlier theories about women's "nature"? I myself feel highly flattered by Cixous's praise for the nurturant perceptions of women, but when she speaks of a drive toward gestation, I begin to hear echoes of the coercive glorification of motherhood that has plagued women for centuries. If we define female subjectivity through universal biological/libidinal givens, what happens to the project of changing the world in feminist directions? Further, is women's sexuality so monolithic that a notion of a shared, typical femininity does justice to it? What about variations in class, in race, and in culture among women? What about changes over time in *one* woman's sexuality (with men, with women, by herself)? How can one libidinal voice—or the two vulval lips so startlingly presented by Irigaray—speak for all women?

The psychoanalytic critique of *féminité* as a concept that overlooks important psychosocial realities is not the only critique that can be brought against positions like Irigaray's and Cixous's. Other French women have made a strong, materialist attack on what they call *néo-féminité,* objecting to it as an ideal bound up through symmetrical opposition in the very ideological system feminists want to destroy. (*Questions féministes,* the journal founded in 1977 with Simone de Beauvoir as titular editor, is a central source for this kind of thinking in France.) Materialist feminists such as Christine Delphy and Colette Guillaumin are suspicious of the logic through which *féminité* defines men as phallic—solipsistic, aggressive, excessively rational—and then praises women, who, by nature of their contrasting sexuality, are other-oriented, empathetic, multi-imaginative. Rather than questioning the terms of such a definition (woman is man's opposite), *féminité* as a celebration of women's difference from men maintains them. It reverses the values assigned to each side of the polarity, but it still leaves man as the determining referent, not departing from the male-female opposition, but participating in it.

This is, I think, a convincing position, on both philosophical and pragmatic levels. What we need to do is to move outside that male-centered, binary logic altogether. We need to ask not how Woman is different from Man (though the question of how women differ from what men *think* they are is important). We need to know how women have come to be who they are through history, which is the history of their oppression by men and male-designed institutions. Only through an analysis of the power relationships between men and women, and practices based on that analysis, will we put an end to our oppression—and only then will we discover what women are or can be. More strategically, we need to know whether the assertion of a shared female nature made by *féminité* can help us in feminist action toward a variety of goals: the possibility of working, or working in marginal or newly defined ways, or of not working in the public world at all; the freedom for a diversity of sexual practices; the right to motherhood, childlessness, or some as yet untheorized participation in reproduction; the affirmation of historically conditioned female values (nurturance, communal rather than individualistic ambitions, insistence on improving the quality of private life), *and* the exploration of new ones. If we concentrate our energies on opposing a counterview of Woman to the view held by men in the past and the present, what happens to our ability to support the multiplicity of women and the various life possibilities they are fighting for in the future?

In a critique of *féminité* as praise of women's difference from men, the name of Monique Wittig must be mentioned. Active in the early seventies in the Féministes révolutionnaires and a contributor from the beginning to *Questions féministes,* Wittig has written four quite different books, which are nonetheless related through her focus on women among themselves: the schoolgirls of *L'Opoponax,* the tribal sisterhood of *Les Guérillères,* the passionate couple of *Le Corps lesbien,* the users of the postphallocentric vocabulary laid out in *Brouillon pour un dictionnaire des amantes.* Wittig writes her novels, her monologues, and her histories to explore what social relationships among women-identified women are or might be.[21] She rewrites traditional culture in mocking takeovers: one entry in *Brouillon pour un dictionnaire* is "Ainsi parlait Frederika, conte pour enfants" ("Thus Spake Frederika, children's story"), surely one of the least reverent allusions to Friedrich Nietzsche to come out of French critiques of culture. She also invents new settings, such as the ceremonies and festivals of *Les Guérillères* and *Le Corps lesbien,* and new modes, such as the feminized epic of *Les Guérillères* and the lyric dialogue of *Le Corps lesbien,* to represent what a female/female life—separatist but not isolationist—might be.

As Wittig's talks at recent conferences in the United States show, she is suspicious both of the oppositional thinking that defines woman in terms of man and of the mythical-idealist strain in certain formulations of *féminité.*[22] In her argument for a more politically centered understanding of women at the Second Sex Conference in New York (September 1979), she used a Marxist vocabulary which may be more familiar to U.S. feminists than the philosophical and psychoanalytic frameworks in which Irigaray and Cixous work:

> It remains . . . for us to define our oppression in materialist terms, to say that women are a class, which is to say that the category "woman," as well as "man," is a political and economic category, not an eternal one. . . . Our first task . . . is thoroughly to dissociate "women" (the class within which we fight) and "woman," the myth. For "woman" does not exist for us; it is only an imaginary formation, while "women" is the product of a social relationship.[23]

Colette Guillaumin, arguing along similar lines in *Questions féministes,* points out that the psychic characteristics praised by advocates of *féminité* have in fact been determined by the familial and economic roles imposed on women by men. There is nothing liberatory, she insists, in women's claiming as virtues qualities that men have always found convenient. How does maternal tenderness or undemanding empathy threaten a Master?[24] The liberating stance is, rather, the determination to analyze and put an end to the patriarchal structures that have produced those qualities without reference to the needs of women.

I have another political objection to the concept of *féminité* as a bundle of Everywoman's psychosexual characteristics: it flattens out the lived differences among women. To the extent that each of us responds to a particular tribal, national, racial, or class situation vis-à-vis men, we are in fact separated from one another. As the painful and counterproductive splits along class and racial lines in the American women's movement have shown, we need to understand and respect the diversity in our concrete social situations. A monolithic vision of shared female sexuality, rather than defeating phallocentrism as doctrine and practice, is more likely to blind us to our varied and immediate needs and to the specific struggles we must coordinate in order to meet them. What is the meaning of "two lips" to heterosexual women who want men to recognize their clitoral pleasure—or to African or Middle Eastern women who, as a result of pharaonic clitoridectomies, have neither lips nor clitoris through which to *jouir*? Does a celebration of the Maternal versus the Patriarchal make the same kind of sense, or any sense, to white, middle-class women who are fighting to maintain the right to abortion, to black and Third World women resisting enforced sterilization, to women in subsistence-farming economies where the livelihood of the family depends on the work of every child who is born and survives? And surely any one woman gives different meanings to her sexuality throughout her individual history. Freedom from sexual expectations and activity may well be what girls in the Western world most need because they are typically sexualized all too soon by media, advertising, peer pressures, and child pornography; women of various ages undergo radical changes in sexual identity and response as they enter relationships with men, with women, or choose celibacy and friendship as alternatives. And it is hard to see how the situations of old women, consigned to sexual inactivity because of their age or, if they are widowed, to unpaid work in others' families or to isolated poverty, can be understood or changed through a concept of *jouissance.* I wonder again whether one libidinal voice, however nonphallocentrically defined, can speak to the economic and cultural problems of all women.

Hence, I would argue that we need the theoretical depth and polemical energy of *féminité* as an alternative idea. But a historically responsive and powerful unity among women will come from our ongoing, shared practice, our experience in and against the material world. As a lens and a partial strategy, *féminité* and *écriture féminine* are vital. Certainly, women need to shake off the mistaken and contemptuous attitudes toward their sexuality that permeate Western (and other) cultures and languages at their deepest levels, and working out self-representations that challenge phallocentric discourses is an important part of that ideological struggle. Women have already begun to transform not only the subject matter but also the ways of producing meaning in poetry, fiction, film, and the visual arts. (Indeed, feminist research suggests that the French may have been too hasty in their claim that women are only now beginning to challenge the symbolic order.) But even if we take *l'écriture féminine* as a utopian ideal, an energizing myth rather than a model for how all women write or should write, theoretical and practical problems arise (again!) from an ideal defined in this way. Can the body be the source of a new discourse? Is it possible, assuming an unmediated and *jouissant* (or, more likely, a positively reconstructed) sense of one's body, to move from that state of unconscious excitation directly to a written female text?

Madeleine Gagnon says yes, in *La Venue à l'écriture,* written with Cixous in 1977. Her view is that women, free from the self-limiting economy of male libido ("I will come once and once only, through one organ alone; once it's up and over, that's it, so I must beware, save up, avoid premature overflow"), have a greater spontaneity and abundance in body and language both:

> We have never been the masters of others or of ourselves. We don't have to confront ourselves in order to free ourselves. We don't have to keep watch on ourselves, or to set up some other erected self in order to understand ourselves. All we have to do is let the body flow, from the inside; all we have to do is erase . . . whatever may hinder or harm the new forms of writing; we retain whatever fits, whatever suits us. Whereas man confronts himself constantly. He pits himself against and stumbles over his erected self.[25]

But psychoanalytic theory and social experience both suggest that the leap from body to language is especially difficult for women.[26] Lacanian theory holds that a girl's introduction into language (the symbolic order represented by the father and built on phallic/nonphallic oppositions) is complex, because she cannot identify directly with the positive poles of that order. And in many preliterate and postliterate cultures, taboos against female speech are enforced: injunctions to silence, mockery of women's chatter or "women's books" abound. The turn-taking in early consciousness-raising groups in the United

States was meant precisely to overcome the verbal hesitancy induced in women by a society in which men have had the first and the last word. Moreover, for women with jobs, husbands or lovers, children, activist political commitments, finding the time and justification to write at all presents an enormous practical and ideological problem.[27] We are more likely to write, and to read each other's writing, if we begin by working against the concrete difficulties and the prejudices surrounding women's writing than if we simplify and idealize the process by locating writing as a spontaneous outpouring from the body.

Calls for a verbal return to nature seem especially surprising coming from women who are otherwise (and rightly!) suspicious of language as penetrated by phallocentric dogma. True, conventional narrative techniques, as well as grammar and syntax, imply the unified viewpoint and mastery of outer reality that men have claimed for themselves. But literary modes and language itself cannot be the only targets for transformation; the *context* for women's discourses needs to be thought through and broadened out. A woman may experience *jouissance* in a private relationship to her own body, but she writes for others. Who writes? Who reads? Who makes women's texts available to women? What do women want to read about other women's experience? To take a stance as a woman poet or novelist is to enter into a role crisscrossed with questions of authority, of audience, of the modes of publication and distribution. I believe that we are more indebted to the "body" of earlier women writers and to feminist publishers and booksellers than to any woman writer's libidinal body flow. The novelist Christiane Rochefort sums up with amusing directness the conflicting public forces and voices that create the dilemma of the French woman who wants to write:

> Well. So here you are now, sitting at your writing table, alone, not allowing anybody anymore to interfere. Are you free?
>
> First, after this long quest, you are swimming in a terrible soup of values—for, to be safe, you had to refuse the so-called female values, which are not female but a social scheme, and to identify with male values, which are not male but an appropriation by men—or an attribution to men—of all human values, mixed up with the anti-values of domination-violence-oppression and the like. In this mixture, where is your real identity?
>
> Second, you are supposed to write in certain forms, preferably: I mean you feel that in certain forms you are not too much seen as a usurper. Novels. Minor poetry, in which

> case you will be stigmatized in French by the name of "poetesse": not everybody can afford it. . . .
>
> You are supposed, too, to write *about* certain things: house, children, love. Until recently there was in France a so-called *littérature féminine.*
>
> Maybe you don't want to write *about,* but to write, period. And of course, you don't want to obey this social order. So, you tend to react against it. It is not easy to be genuine.[28]

Whatever the difficulties, women are inventing new kinds of writing. But as Irigaray's erudition and plays with the speaking voice show (as do Cixous's mischievous puns and citations of languages from Greek through German to Portuguese, and Wittig's fantastic neologisms and revision of conventional genres), they are doing so deliberately, on a level of feminist theory and literary self-consciousness that goes far beyond the body and the unconscious. That is also how they need to be read. It takes a thoroughgoing familiarity with *male* figureheads of Western culture to recognize the intertextual games played by all these writers; their work shows that a resistance to culture is always built, at first, of bits and pieces of that culture, however they are disassembled, criticized, and transcended. Responding to *l'écriture féminine* is no more instinctive than producing it. Women's writing will be more accessible to writers and readers alike if we recognize it as a conscious response to socioliterary realities, rather than accept it as an overflow of one woman's unmediated communication with her body. Eventually, certainly, the practice of women writers will transform what we can see and understand in a literary text; but even a woman setting out to write about her body will do so against and through her socioliterary mothers, midwives, and sisters. We need to recognize, too, that there is nothing universal about French versions of *écriture féminine.* The speaking, singing, story-telling, and writing of women in cultures besides that of the Ile de France need to be looked at and understood in their social context if we are to fill in an adequate and genuinely empowering picture of women's creativity.

But I risk, after all this, overstating the case against *féminité* and *écriture féminine,* and that would mean a real loss. American feminists can appropriate two important elements, at least, from the French position: the critique of phallocentrism in all the material and ideological forms it has taken, and the call for new representations of women's consciousness. It is not enough to uncover old heroines or to imagine new ones. Like the French, we need to examine the words, the syntax, the genres, the archaic and elitist attitudes toward language and representation that have limited women's self-knowledge and expression during the long centuries of patriarchy. We need not, however, replace phallocentrism with a shakily theorized "concentrism" that denies women their historical specificities to recognize how deep a refusal of masculinist values must go.[29] If we remember that what women really share is an oppression on all levels, although it affects us each in different ways—if we can translate *féminité* into a concerted attack not only on language, but also directly upon the sociosexual arrangements that keep us from our own potentials and from each other—then we are on our way to becoming "les jeunes nées" envisioned by French feminisms at their best.

NOTES

[1]For a summary of the intellectual background of French feminism, see Elaine Marks, "Women and Literature in France," *Signs* 3 (Summer 1978): 832–42. Phallogocentrism at work is powerfully analyzed by Shoshana Felman in her study of the characters and critics of a short story by Balzac, "Women and Madness: The Critical Phallacy," *Diacritics* 5 (Winter 1975): 2–10.

[2]*Jouissance* is a word rich in connotations. "Pleasure" is the simplest translation. The noun comes from the verb *jouir,* meaning to enjoy, to revel in without fear of the cost; also, to have an orgasm. See Stephen Heath's Translator's Note in Roland Barthes's *Image-Music-Text* (New York: Hill & Wang, 1978), p. 9. A note to Introduction 3 in *New French Feminisms: An Anthology,* ed. Elaine Marks and Isabelle de Courtivron (Amherst: University of Massachusetts Press, 1980), explains feminist connotations of *jouissance* as follows:

> This pleasure, when attributed to a woman, is considered to be of a different order from the pleasure that is represented within the male libidinal economy often described in terms of the capitalist gain and profit motive. Women's jouissance carries with it the notion of fluidity, diffusion, duration. It is a kind of potlatch in the world of orgasms, a giving, expending, dispensing of pleasure without concern about ends or closure. (P. 36, n. 8)

The Law of the Father is Lacan's formulation for language as the medium through which human beings are placed in culture, a medium represented and enforced by the figure of the father in the family. See Anika Lemaire, *Jacques Lacan,* trans. David Macey (London: Routledge & Kegan Paul, 1977), esp. pt. 7, "The Role of the Oedipus in Accession to the Symbolic."

[3]Julia Kristeva's books include *Semiotike: Recherches pour une semanalyse* (Paris: Tel Quel, 1969); *Le Texte du roman* (The Hague: Mouton, 1970); *Des Chinoises* (Paris: Des Femmes, 1974); *La Révolution du langage poétique* (Paris: Editions du Seuil, 1974); *Polylogue* (Paris: Editions du Seuil, 1977); and *Pouvoirs de l'horreur: essai sur l'abjection* (Paris: Editions du Seuil, 1980). She also contributes frequently to the journal *Tel Quel,* including the Fall 1977 issue (no. 74) on women and women's writing. For her criticism of certain notions of *féminité,* see her interview with Françoise van Rossum-Guyon, "Féminité et écriture: en réponse à deux questions sur *Polylogue,*" *Revue des sciences humaines* 168 (December 1977): 495–501.

[4]Kristeva, "Le Sujet en procès," in *Polylogue,* p. 77. See, in the same volume, her discussion of maternity as an experience that breaks down the categories of masculinist

thought, in "Maternité selon Giovanni Bellini," pp. 409–38. She expands her argument about the meanings of maternity for women's creativity in "Un Nouveau Type d'intellectuel: le dissident" and "Héréthique de l'amour," *Tel Quel,* no. 74 (Fall 1977), pp. 3–8, 30–49. For an explanation of her theory of the semiotic and of Irigaray's concepts of *l'écriture féminine,* see Josette Féral, "Antigone, or the Irony of the Tribe," *Diacritics* 8 (Fall 1978): 2–14.

[5]"Oscillation du 'pouvoir' au 'refus,' " interview by Xavière Gauthier in *Tel Quel,* no. 58 (Summer 1974), trans. in Marks and Courtivron, *New French Feminisms,* pp. 166–67. This collection of translated excerpts from French feminist writers is likely to be very useful to English-language readers.

[6]Kristeva, "La Femme, ce n'est jamais ça," interview in *Tel Quel,* no. 59 (Fall 1974), trans. in *New French Feminisms,* pp. 134–38. Kristeva has written mainly about male writers, but see her comments on some typically feminine themes in a dozen recent French women writers in "Oscillation," *Tel Quel,* no. 58 (Summer 1974), pp. 100–2. She comments on certain elements of women's style in her interview with van Rossum-Guyon (see note 3 above), although she derives them from social rather than libidinal sources.

[7]Luce Irigaray, an interview, "Women's Exile," in *Ideology and Consciousness,* no. 1 (1977), pp. 62–67, trans. and intro. Diana Adlam and Couze Venn.

[8]Irigaray, "Ce Sexe qui n'en est pas un," *Ce Sexe qui n'en est pas un* (Paris: Editions de Minuit, 1977), trans. in *New French Feminisms,* p. 103. Irigaray's books since *Ce Sexe* are *Et l'une ne bouge sans l'autre* (Paris: Editions de Minuit, 1979) and *Amante marine* (Paris: Editions de Minuit, 1980). Her first book was a clinical study, *Le Langage des déments* (The Hague: Mouton, 1973).

[9]*New French Feminisms,* p. 105.

[10]Irigaray discusses the historical position of women in Marxist terms in "Le Marché aux femmes," in *Ce Sexe.* Her responses to Nietzsche are in *Amante marine.*

[11]Hélène Cixous's studies of male writers include her doctoral thesis, *L'Exil de Joyce ou l'art du remplacement* (Paris: Grasset, 1968); *Prénoms de personne (sur Hoffman, Kleist, Poe, Joyce)* (Paris: Editions du Seuil, 1974); and introductions to James Joyce and Lewis Carroll for Aubier. Since 1975, all her books have been published by Des Femmes.

[12]Cixous, "Entretien avec Françoise van Rossum-Guyon," *Revue des sciences humaines* 168 (December 1977): 488. "Ça parle" is a Lacanian formula, but elsewhere (in her fiction/essay *Partie* [Paris: Des Femmes, 1976], for example) she mocks what she sees as the Father/phallus obsession of recent psychoanalysis.

[13]Cixous, "Entretien," p. 487; and *Vivre l'orange* [includes an English version by Cixous with Ann Liddle and Sarah Cornell] (Paris: Des Femmes, 1980), pp. 9, 105–7.

[14]Cixous, "Sorties," *La Jeune Née* (Paris: Union Générale d'Editions, 1975), trans. in *New French Feminisms,* p. 98.

[15]*New French Feminisms,* pp. 259–60.

[16]The opening manifesto of *Questions féministes* is a long and persuasive critique of *néo-féminité,* translated in *New French Feminisms* as "Variations on Common Themes," pp. 212–30. See also the appraisal by Beverly Brown and Parveen Adama, "The Feminine Body and Feminist Politics," *m/f* 3 (1979): 33–37.

[17]Juliet Mitchell, *Psychoanalysis and Feminism: Freud, Laing, Reich and Women* (New York: Vintage Books, 1975). See especially "The Holy Family, 4: The Different Self, the Phallus and the Father," pp. 382–98.

[18]Nancy Chodorow, *The Reproduction of Mothering: Psychoanalysis and the Sociology of Gender* (Berkeley: University of California Press, 1978).

[19]Dorothy Dinnerstein, *The Mermaid and the Minotaur: Sexual Arrangements and Human Malaise* (New York: Harper & Row, 1977).

[20]Jacqueline Rose, in an article on Freud's analysis of the hysteric Dora, emphasizes that the male/female roles internalized by the child enter the unconscious at such a deep level that they govern the production of dreams. Dora, who desires a woman, represents herself as a man—a striking example of the socialized image of desire. " 'Dora'—Fragment of an Analysis," *m/f* (1979): 5–21.

[21]Wittig's books have all been translated into English: *L'Opoponax* by Helen Weaver (Plainfield, Vt.: Daughter's Press Reprint, 1976); *Les Guérillères* by David Le Vay (New York: Avon Books, 1973); *The Lesbian Body* by David Le Vay (New York: Avon Books, 1976); *Lesbian Peoples: Material for a Dictionary* (with substantial revisions) by Wittig and Sande Zeig (New York: Avon Books, 1979).

[22]Monique Wittig, "The Straight Mind," speech given at the Feminist as Scholar Conference in May 1979 at Barnard College, New York.

[23]Monique Wittig, "One Is Not Born a Woman," text of the speech given at the City University of New York Graduate Center, September 1979.

[24]Colette Guillaumin, "Question de différence," *Questions féministes* 6 (September 1979): 3–21. Guillaumin points out that the claim to "difference" comes from other oppressed groups as well (Third World and U.S. blacks, for example) who have not yet succeeded in putting their desire for political self-determination into effect. To assert their difference against the ruling class strengthens their group solidarity, but at the expense of an analysis of the political sources of that difference.

[25]Madeleine Gagnon, "Corps I," *New French Feminisms,* p. 180. See Chantal Chawaf for a similar statement, in "La Chair linguistique," *New French Feminisms,* pp. 177–78.

[26]Cora Kaplan combines psychoanalytic and anthropological accounts of women's hesitations to speak, in "Language and Gender," *Papers on Patriarchy* (Brighton, England: Women's Publishing Collective, 1976). Similarly, Sandra M. Gilbert and Susan Gubar demonstrate how socially derived ambivalence toward the role of writer has acted upon women's writing in English, in *The Madwoman in the Attic: The Woman Writer and the Nineteenth-Century Literary Imagination* (New Haven, Conn.: Yale University Press, 1979).

[27]See Tillie Olsen's *Silences* (New York: Delacorte Press, 1979) for a discussion of the practical demands and self-doubts that have hindered women's writing, esp. "The Writer-Woman: One out of Twelve," pp. 177–258.

[28]Christiane Rochefort, "Are Women Writers Still Monsters?" a speech given at the University of Wisconsin, Madison, February 1975; translated in *New French Feminisms,* pp. 185–86.

[29]"Concentrism" is Elaine Showalter's term, used in a speech, "Feminist Literary Theory and Other Impossibilities," given at the Smith College Conference on Feminist Literary Criticism, Northampton, Mass., October 25, 1980.

Bibliography

I. Feminist Critical Theory, English and American

Abel, Elizabeth, ed. *Writing and Sexual Difference.* Chicago: University of Chicago Press, 1982.

Beck, Evelyn Torton, and Julia A. Sherman, eds. *The Prism of Sex: Essays in the Sociology of Knowledge.* Madison: University of Wisconsin Press, 1979.

Booth, Wayne. "Freedom of Interpretation: Bakhtin and the Challenge of Feminist Criticism." *Critical Inquiry* 9 (Fall 1982): 45–76.

Brown, Cheryl L., and Karen Olsen, eds. *Feminist Criticism: Essays on Theory, Poetry, and Prose.* Metuchen, N.J.: Scarecrow Press, 1978.

Cunningham, Stuart. "Some Problems of Feminist Literary Criticism." *Journal of Women's Studies in Literature* 1 (1979): 159–78.

Diamond, Arlyn, and Lee R. Edwards, eds. *The Authority of Experience: Essays in Feminist Criticism.* Amherst: University of Massachusetts Press, 1977.

Donovan, Josephine, ed. *Feminist Literary Criticism: Explorations in Theory.* Lexington: University Press of Kentucky, 1975.

Edwards, Lee R. "The Labors of Psyche: Toward a Theory of Female Heroism." *Critical Inquiry* 6 (Fall 1979): 33–49.

Eisenstein, Hester. *Contemporary Feminist Thought.* Boston: G. K. Hall, 1983. An intellectual history.

Eisenstein, Hester, and Alice Jardine, eds. *The Future of Difference: The Scholar and the Feminist.* Boston: G. K. Hall, 1980.

Ellman, Mary. *Thinking About Women.* New York: Harcourt, Brace & World, 1968.

Farwell, Marilyn R. "Feminist Criticism and the Concept of the Poetic Persona." *Bucknell Review* 24 (Spring 1978): 139–56.

Feminist Issues in Literary Scholarship. Special issue. *Tulsa Studies in Women's Literature* 3 (Fall 1984).

Frye, Marilyn. *The Politics of Reality: Essays in Feminist Theory.* Trumansburg, N.Y.: Crossing Press, 1983.

Gilbert, Sandra M. "Patriarchal Poetics and the Woman Reader: Reflections on Milton's Bogey." *PMLA* 93 (May 1978): 368–82.

Heilbrun, Carolyn G. *Toward a Recognition of Androgyny.* New York: Harper & Row, 1973.

———. *Reinventing Womanhood.* New York: W. W. Norton, 1979.

Heilbrun, Carolyn G., and Catharine R. Stimpson. "Theories of Feminist Criticism: A Dialogue." In Donovan, *Feminist Literary Criticism,* pp. 61–73.

Jacobus, Mary. "Is There a Woman in This Text?" *New Literary History* 14 (Fall 1982): 117–41.

Kahn, Coppélia, and Gayle Greene, eds. *Making a Difference: Feminist Literary Criticism.* New York and London: Methuen, 1985.

Annette Kolodny. "Some Notes on Defining a 'Feminist Literary Criticism.' " *Critical Inquiry* 2 (Fall 1975): 75-92.

———. "The Feminist as Literary Critic." Critical Response. *Critical Inquiry* 3 (Summer 1976): 822–32.

———. "Literary Criticism." Review Essay. *Signs* 2 (Winter 1976): 404–21.

Leger, Susan. "The Lure of Symmetry: or, The Strange Impossibility of Feminist Criticism." *Massachusetts Review* 24 (Summer 1983): 330–36.

Lipking, Lawrence. "Aristotle's Sister." *Critical Inquiry* 10 (Fall 1983): 61–81.

McConnell-Ginet, Sally, Ruth Borker, and Nelly Furman, eds. *Women and Language in Literature and Society.* New York: Praeger, 1980.

Millett, Kate. *Sexual Politics.* Garden City, N.Y. Doubleday, 1970.

Mora, Gabriela, and Karen S. Van Hooft, eds. *Theory and Practice of Feminist Literary Criticism.* Ypsilanti, Mich.: Bilingual Press/Editorial Bilingue, 1982.

Pratt, Annis. "The New Feminist Criticisms." In *Beyond Intellectual Sexism: A New Woman, a New Reality,* ed. Joan I. Roberts, pp. 175–95. New York: David McKay, 1976.

Radway, Janice. "Women Read the Romance: The Interaction of Text and Context." *Feminist Studies* 9 (Spring 1983): 53–78.

The Rhetoric of Feminist Writing. Special issue. *Denver Quarterly* 18 (Winter 1984).

Showalter, Elaine. "Literary Criticism." Review Essay. *Signs* 1 (Winter 1975): 435–60.

———. "Critical Cross-Dressing: Male Feminists and the Woman of the Year." *Raritan* 3 (October 1983): 130–49.

———. "Women's Time, Women's Space: Writing the History of Feminist Criticism." *Tulsa Studies in Women's Literature* 3 (Fall 1984): 29–43.

Spacks, Patricia Meyer "The Difference It Makes." In *A Feminist Perspective in the Academy,* ed. Elizabeth Langland and Walter Gove, pp. 7–24. Chicago: University of Chicago Press, 1981.

Stanley, Julia Penelope, and Susan J. Wolfe (Robbins). "Towards a Feminist Aesthetic." *Chrysalis,* no. 6 (1978), pp. 57–71.

Stimpson, Catharine R. "Feminism and Feminist Criticism." *Massachusetts Review* 24 (Summer 1983): 272–88.

Watson, Barbara Bellow. "On Power and the Literary Text." *Signs* 1 (Fall 1975): 111–18.

Woman: An Issue. Special issue. *Massachusetts Review* 13 (Winter–Spring 1972).

Woman: The Arts 2. Special issue. *Massachusetts Review* 23 (Summer 1983).

Woolf, Virginia. *A Room of One's Own.* 1928. Reprint. New York: Harcourt Brace Jovanovich, 1981.

II. Women's Writing, American and English

Abel, Elizabeth. "[E]Merging Identities: The Dynamics of Female Friendship in Contemporary Fiction by Women." *Signs* 6 (Spring 1981): 413–35. See also Judith Kegan Gardiner's response, "The [US]es of [I]dentity," pp. 436–42.

Abel, Elizabeth, Marianne Hirsch, and Elizabeth Langland, eds. *The Voyage In: Fictions of Female Development.* Hanover, N.H.: University Press of New England, 1983. On the female *Bildungsroman.*

Baym, Nina. *Woman's Fiction: A Guide to Novels by and about Women in America, 1820–1870.* Ithaca, N.Y.: Cornell University Press, 1978.

Christ, Carol P. *Diving Deep and Surfacing: Women Writers on Spiritual Quest.* Boston: Beacon Press, 1980.

DeKoven, Marianne. *A Different Language: Gertrude Stein's Experimental Writing.* Madison: University of Wisconsin Press, 1983. Applies French feminist theory to Stein.

Delany, Sheila. *Writing Women: Women Writers and Women in Literature, Medieval to Modern.* New York: Schocken Books, 1984. A Marxist-feminist view.

Donovan, Josephine. *New England Local Color Literature: A Women's Tradition.* New York: Frederick Ungar, 1983.

Douglas (Wood), Ann. "The 'Scribbling Women' and Fanny Fern: Why Women Wrote." *American Quarterly* 23 (Spring 1971): 3–24.

———. "The Literature of Impoverishment: The Women Local Colorists in America 1865–1914." *Women's Studies* 1 (1972): 3–45.

———. *The Feminization of American Culture.* New York: Alfred A. Knopf, 1978.

The Female Novelist in Twentieth-Century Britain. Special issue. *Studies in the Literary Imagination* 11 (Fall 1978).

Gilbert, Sandra M., and Susan Gubar. *The Madwoman in the Attic: The Woman Writer and the Nineteenth-Century Literary Imagination.* New Haven, Conn.: Yale University Press, 1979.

Gubar, Susan. "Mother, Maiden, and the Marriage of Death: Women Writers and an Ancient Myth." *Women's Studies* 6 (1979): 301–15.

Hanscombe, Gillian E. *The Art of Life: Dorothy Richardson and the Development of Feminist Consciousness.* Athens: Ohio University Press, 1982.

Jacobus, Mary, ed. *Women Writing and Writing About Women.* New York: Barnes & Noble Imports, 1979.

Janeway, Elizabeth. "Women's Literature." In *The Harvard Guide to Contemporary American Writing,* ed. Daniel Hoffman, pp. 342–95. Cambridge, Mass.: Harvard University Press, 1979.

Jelinek, Estelle C., ed. *Women's Autobiography: Essays in Criticism.* Bloomington: Indiana University Press, 1980.

Kaplan, Sydney Janet. *Feminist Consciousness in the Modern British Novel.* Urbana: University of Illinois Press, 1975.

Kelley, Mary. *Private Woman, Public Stage: Literary Domesticity in Nineteenth-Century America.* New York: Oxford University Press, 1984.

Little, Judith. *Comedy and the Woman Writer: Woolf, Spark, and Feminism.* Lincoln: University of Nebraska Press, 1983.

Marcus, Jane, ed. *New Feminist Essays on Virginia Woolf.* Lincoln: University of Nebraska Press, 1981.

Moers, Ellen. *Literary Women: The Great Writers.* Garden City, N.Y.: Doubleday, 1976.

Olsen, Tillie. *Silences.* New York: Delacorte Press, 1979.

Poovey, Mary. *The Proper Lady and the Woman Writer: Ideology as Style in the Works of Mary Wollstonecraft, Mary Shelley, and Jane Austen.* Chicago: University of Chicago Press, 1984.

Pratt, Annis. "Aunt Jennifer's Tigers: Notes Toward a Preliterary History of Women's Archetypes." *Feminist Studies* 4 (February 1978): 163–94.

———. *Archetypal Patterns in Women's Fiction.* Bloomington: Indiana University Press, 1981.

Rich, Adrienne. *On Lies, Secrets, and Silence: Selected Prose 1966–1978.* New York: W. W. Norton, 1979.

Rigney, Barbara H. *Madness and Sexual Politics in the Feminist Novel: Studies in Brontë, Woolf, Lessing, and Atwood.* Madison: University of Wisconsin Press, 1978.

Russ, Joanna. *How to Suppress Women's Writing.* Austin: University of Texas Press, 1983.

Showalter, Elaine. *A Literature of Their Own: British Women Novelists from Brontë to Lessing.* Princeton, N.J.: Princeton University Press, 1977.

———., ed. *These Modern Women: Autobiographical Essays from the Twenties.* Old Westbury, N.Y.: Feminist Press, 1978.

Snitow, Ann Barr. "The Front Line: Notes on Sex in Novels by Women, 1969–1979." *Signs* 5 (Summer 1980): 702–18.

Spacks, Patricia Meyer. *The Female Imagination.* New York: Alfred A. Knopf, 1975.

Squier, Susan Merrill. *Women Writers and the City: Essays in Feminist Literary Criticism.* Knoxville: University of Tennessee Press, 1984.

Sternburg, Janet. *The Writer on Her Work.* New York: W. W. Norton, 1980.

Todd, Janet M., ed. *Gender and Literary Voice.* New York: Holmes & Meier, 1980.

———. *Women Writers Talking.* New York: Holmes & Meier, 1983.

Wandor, Michelene, ed. *On Gender and Writing.* Boston and London: Routledge & Kegan Paul, 1983.

III. Women's Poetry and Poetics

Bowles, Gloria, ed. *Women's Poetry.* Special issue. *Women's Studies* 5 (1977).

Carruthers, Mary. "Imagining Women: Notes Toward a Feminist Poetic." *Massachusetts Review* 20 (Summer 1979): 281–307.

Diehl, Joanne Feit. " 'Come Slowly—Eden': An Exploration of Women Poets and Their Muse." *Signs* 3 (Spring 1978): 572–87. See also "Comments" by Lillian Faderman and Louise Bernikow. *Signs* 4 (Fall 1978): 188–95.

Friedman, Susan Stanford. *Psyche Reborn: The Emergence of H. D.* Bloomington: Indiana University Press, 1981.

Gilbert, Sandra M. "From *Patria* to *Matria:* Elizabeth Barrett Browning's Risorgimento." *PMLA* 99 (March 1984): 194–211.

Gilbert, Sandra M., and Susan Gubar, eds. *Shakespeare's Sisters: Feminist Essays on Women Poets.* Bloomington: Indiana University Press, 1979.

Homans, Margaret. *Women Writers and Poetic Identity: Dorothy Wordsworth, Emily Brontë, and Emily Dickinson.* Princeton, N.J.: Princeton University Press, 1980.

Howe, Florence, and Ellen Bass, eds. *No More Masks! An Anthology of Poems by Women.* Garden City, N.Y.: Anchor Books, 1973.

Juhasz, Suzanne. *Naked and Fiery Forms: Modern American Poetry by Women.* New York: Harper & Row, 1976.

———. "The Critic as Feminist: Reflections on Women's Poetry, Feminism, and the Art of Criticism." *Women's Studies* 5 (1977): 113–27.

———, ed. *Feminist Critics Read Emily Dickinson.* Bloomington: Indiana University Press, 1983.

Martin, Wendy. *An American Triptych: Anne Bradstreet, Emily Dickinson, and Adrienne Rich.* Chapel Hill: University of North Carolina Press, 1984.

Montefiore, Janet. "Feminist Identity and the Poetic Tradition." *Feminist Review,* no. 13 (Spring 1983), pp. 69–84.

Ostriker, Alicia. "Body Language: Imagery of the Body in Women's Poetry." In *The State of the Language,* ed. Leonard Michaels and Christopher Ricks, pp. 247–63. Berkeley: University of California Press, 1980.

———. *Writing Like a Woman.* Ann Arbor: University of Michigan Press, 1983. Essays on modern woman poets.

Sadoff, Dianne F. "Mythopoeia, the Moon, and Contemporary Women's Poetry." *Massachusetts Review* 19 (Spring 1978): 93–110.

Walker, Cheryl. *The Nightingale's Burden: Women Poets and American Culture Before 1900.* Bloomington: Indiana University Press, 1982.

Watts, Emily Stipes. *The Poetry of American Women from 1632 to 1945.* Austin: University of Texas Press, 1977.

IV. Black Feminist Criticism

Bell, Roseann P., et al. *Sturdy Black Bridges: Visions of Black Women in Literature.* Garden City, N.Y.: Anchor Books, 1979.

Blackburn, Regina. "In Search of the Black Female Self: African-American Women's Autobiographies and Ethnicity." In *Women's Autobiography: Essays in Criticism,* ed. Estelle C. Jelinek, pp. 133–48. Bloomington: Indiana University Press, 1980.

Christian, Barbara. *Black Women Novelists: The Development of a Tradition, 1892–1976.* Westport, Conn.: Greenwood Press, 1980.

Evans, Mari, ed. *Black Women Writers, 1950–1980: A Critical Evaluation.* New York: Anchor Press, 1984.

Hull, Gloria T. "Afro-American Women Poets: A Bio-Critical Survey." In *Shakespeare's Sisters: Feminist Essays on Women Poets,* ed. Sandra M. Gilbert and Susan Gubar, pp. 165–82. Bloomington: Indiana University Press, 1979.

Hull, Gloria T., Patricia Bell Scott, and Barbara Smith. *But Some of Us Are Brave: Black Women's Studies.* Old Westbury, N.Y.: Feminist Press, 1982.

Lorde, Audre. "Poetry Is Not a Luxury." In *The Future of Difference: The Scholar and the Feminist,* ed. Hester Eisenstein and Alice Jardine, pp. 125–27. Boston: G. K. Hall, 1980.

Smith, Barbara, ed. *Home Girls: A Black Feminist Anthology.* New York: Watertown, Mass.: Persephone Press, 1983.

Stetson, Erlene. *Black Sister: Poetry by Black American Women, 1764–1980.* Bloomington: Indiana University Press 1981.

———. "Black Women In and Out of Print." In *Women in Print I: Opportunities for Women's Studies Research in Language and Literature,* ed. Ellen Messer-Davidow and Joan E. Hartman, pp. 87–107. New York: Modern Language Association, 1982.

Tate, Claudia, ed. *Black Women Writers at Work.* New York: Crossroad/ Continuum, 1983.

Walker, Alice. *In Search of Our Mothers' Gardens: Womanist Prose.* New York: Harcourt Brace Jovanovich, 1983.

Washington, Mary Helen. "Introduction: In Pursuit of Our Own History." *Midnight Birds: Stories of Contemporary Black Women Writers.* Garden City, N.Y.: Anchor Books, 1980.

———. "New Lives and New Letters: Black Women Writers at the End of the Seventies." *College English* 43 (January 1981): 1–11.

V. Lesbian Feminist Criticism

Carruthers, Mary. "The Re-Vision of the Muse: Adrienne Rich, Audre Lord, Judy Grahn, Olga Broumas." *Hudson Review* 36 (Summer 1983): 293–322.

Cook, Blanche Weisen. " 'Women Alone Stir My Imagination': Lesbianism and the Cultural Tradition." *Signs* 4 (Summer 1979): 718–39.

Cruikshank, Margaret, ed. *Lesbian Studies.* Old Westbury, N.Y.: Feminist Press, 1982.

Faderman, Lillian. *Surpassing the Love of Men: Romantic Friendship and Love Between Women from the Renaissance to the Present.* New York: William Morrow, 1981.

Lesbian History. Special issue. *Frontiers* 4 (Fall 1979). Essays by Judith Schwartz and Josephine Donovan.

The Lesbian Issue. Special issue. *Signs* 9 (Summer 1984). Essays by Sharon O'Brien, Martha Vicinus, Esther Newton, Bonnie Zimmerman, and Jean Kennard.

Marks, Elaine. "Lesbian Intertexuality." In *Homosexualities and French Liter-*

ature: Cultural Contexts, Critical Texts, ed. George Stambolian and Elaine Marks, pp. 353–77. Ithaca, N.Y.: Cornell University Press, 1979.

McDaniel, Judith. "Lesbians and Literature." *Sinister Wisdom* 1 (1976): 20–23.

Rich, Adrienne. *On Lies, Secrets, and Silence: Selected Prose 1966–1978.* New York: W. W. Norton, 1979.

Stimpson, Catharine R. "Zero Degree Deviancy: The Lesbian Novel in English." *Critical Inquiry* 8 (Winter 1981): 363–80.

Wittig, Monique. "Paradigm." In Stambolian and Marks, *Homosexualities and French Literature,* pp. 114–21.

———. "The Straight Mind." *Feminist Issues* 1(1980): 103–12.

Zimmerman, Bonnie. "Exiting from Patriarchy:. The Lesbian Novel of Development." In *The Voyage In: Fictions of Female Development,* ed. Elizabeth Abel, Marianne Hirsch, and Elizabeth Langland, pp. 244–57. Hanover, N.H.: University Press of New England, 1983.

VI. Gender, Genre, and Representation

Allen, Mary. *The Necessary Blankness: Women in Major American Fiction of the Sixties.* Urbana: University of Illinois Press, 1976.

Armstrong, Nancy. "The Rise of Feminine Authority in the Novel." *Novel* 15 (Winter 1982): 127–45.

Auerbach, Nina. *Communities of Women: An Idea in Fiction.* Cambridge, Mass.: Harvard University Press, 1978.

———. *Woman and the Demon: The Life of a Victorian Myth.* Cambridge, Mass.: Harvard University Press, 1982.

Backscheider, Paula. "Woman's Influence." *Studies in the Novel* 11 (Spring 1979): 3–22.

Bamber, Linda. *Comic Women, Tragic Men: A Study of Gender and Genre in Shakespeare.* Palo Alto, Calif.: Stanford University Press, 1981.

Basch, Françoise. *Relative Creatures: Victorian Women in Society and the Novel.* New York: Schocken Books, 1974.

Boumelha, Penny. *Thomas Hardy and Women: Sexual Ideology and Narrative Form.* New York: Barnes & Noble Imports, 1982.

Bradbrook, Muriel C. *Women and Literature: Seventeen Seventy-Nine to Nineteen Eighty-Two.* New York: Barnes & Noble Imports, 1982.

Brickman, Richard, Susan MacDonald, and Myra Stark. *Corrupt Relations: Dickens, Thackeray, Trollope, Collins, and the Victorian Sexual System.* New York: Columbia University Press, 1982.

Brownstein, Rachel Mayer *Becoming a Heroine: Reading About Women in Novels.* New York: Viking Press, 1982.

Calder, Jenni. *Women and Marriage in Victorian Fiction.* New York: Oxford University Press, 1976.

Cornillon, Susan Koppelman, ed. *Images of Women in Fiction: Feminist Perspectives.* Bowling Green, Ohio: Bowling Green University Popular Press, 1972.

Davidson, Cathy N., and E. M. Broner, eds. *The Lost Tradition: Mothers and Daughters in Literature.* New York: Frederick Ungar, 1980.

Doody, Margaret Anne. "Deserts, Ruins and Troubled Waters: Female Dreams in Fiction and the Development of the Gothic Novel." *Genre* 10 (Winter 1977): 529–72.

Edwards, Lee R. *Psyche as Hero: Female Heroism and Fictional Form.* Middletown, Conn.: Wesleyan University Press, 1984.

Fetterley, Judith. *The Resisting Reader: A Feminist Approach to American Fiction.* Bloomington: Indiana University Press, 1978.

Fleenor, Juliann, ed. *The Female Gothic.* Montreal: Eden Press, 1983.

Fleischmann, Fritz, ed. *American Novelists Revisited: Essays in Feminist Criticism.* Boston: G. K. Hall, 1982.

Ferguson, Mary Anne. *Images of Women in Literature.* Boston: Houghton Mifflin, 1977.

Gilbert, Sandra M. "Costumes of the Mind: Transvestism in Modern Literature." *Critical Inquiry* 7 (Winter 1980): 391–417.

Goode, John. "Woman and the Literary Text." In *The Rights and Wrongs of Women,* ed. Juliet Mitchell and Ann Oakley, pp. 217–55. Harmondsworth, Middlesex: Penguin Books, 1976.

Heilbrun, Carolyn G., and Margaret Higonnet, eds. *The Representation of Women in Fiction.* Baltimore: Johns Hopkins University Press, 1982.

Homans, Margaret. " 'Her Very Own Howl': The Ambiguities of Representation in Recent Women's Fiction." *Signs* 9 (Winter 1983): 186–205.

Huf, Linda. *A Portrait of the Artist as a Young Woman: The Writer as Heroine in American Literature.* New York: Frederick Ungar, 1983.

Hunt, Linda. "Books About Women's Lives: The New Best Sellers." *Radical America* 14 (September–October 1980): 45–52.

Kahn, Coppélia. *Man's Estate: Masculine Identity in Shakespeare.* Berkeley: University of California Press, 1981.

Kennard, Jean E. *Victims of Convention.* Hamden, Conn.: Archon Books, 1978.

Lenz, Carolyn R., Gayle Green, and Carol Thomas Neely. *The Woman's Part: Feminist Criticism of Shakespeare.* Urbana: University of Illinois Press, 1980.

Martin, Wendy. "Seduced and Abandoned in the New World: The Images of Women in American Fiction." In *Woman in Sexist Society,* ed. Vivian Gornick and Barbara K. Moran, pp. 329–46. New York: New American Library, 1972.

Miller, Beth, ed. *Women in Hispanic Literature: Icons and Fallen Idols.* Berkeley: University of California Press, 1983.

Miller, Nancy K. *The Heroine's Text: Readings in the French and English Novel, 1722–1782.* New York: Columbia University Press, 1980.

Mitchell, Sally. *The Fallen Angel: Chastity, Class and Women's Reading, 1835–1880.* Bowling Green, Ohio: Bowling Green University Popular Press, 1981.

Newton, Judith Lowder. *Women, Power, and Subversion: Social Strategies in British Fiction, 1778–1860.* Athens: University of Georgia Press, 1981.

Perry, Ruth. *Women, Letters, and the Novel,* New York: AMS Press, 1980.

Pratt, Annis. "Women and Nature in Modern Fiction." *Contemporary Literature* 13 (Fall 1972): 476–90.

Rabine, Leslie. *Reading the Romantic Heroine: Text, History, Ideology.* Ann Arbor: University of Michigan Press, 1984.

Rowe, Karen. "Feminism and Fairy Tales." *Women's Studies* 6 (1979): 237–57.

Showalter, Elaine. "The Unmanning of the Mayor of Casterbridge." In *Critical Approaches to Thomas Hardy,* ed. Dale Kramer, pp. 99–115. New York and London: Macmillan, 1980.

Springer, Marlene, ed. *What Manner of Woman: Essays on English and American Life and Literature.* New York: New York University Press, 1977.

Stewart, Grace. *A New Mythos: The Novel of the Artist as Heroine, 1877–1977.* 2nd ed. Montreal: Eden Press, 1981.

Stubbs, Patricia. *Women and Fiction: Feminism and the Novel, Eighteen-Eighty to Nineteen Twenty.* New York: Barnes & Noble Imports, 1979.

Todd, Janet M. *Women's Friendship in Literature.* New York: Columbia University Press, 1980.

———, ed. *Men by Women.* New York: Holmes & Meier, 1981.

VII. French Feminist Critical Theory

Andersen, Margret. "La Jouissance, principe d'écriture." *L'Esprit Créateur* 19 (Summer 1979): 3–12.

Beauvoir, Simone de. *The Second Sex.* Trans. and ed. H. M. Parshley. 1953. Reprint. New York: Vintage Books, 1974.

Cherchez la Femme. Special issue. *Diacritics* 12 (Summer 1982).

Cixous, Hélène. "The Laugh of the Medusa." Trans. Keith Cohen and Paula Cohen. *Signs* 1 (Summer 1976): 875–93. In French, in *L'Arc* 61 (1975): 39–54.

———. *La Venue à l'écriture.* Paris: Union Générale d'Editions, 1977.

———. "Rethinking Difference: An Interview." In *Homosexualities and French Literature: Cultural Contexts, Critical Texts,* ed. George Stambolian and Elaine Marks, pp. 70–86. Ithaca, N.Y.: Cornell University Press, 1979.

———. "Castration or Decapitation." Trans. Annette Kuhn. *Signs* 7 (Fall 1981): 41–55. See also Introduction by Annette Kuhn, pp. 36–40.

Cixous, Hélène, and Catherine Clément. *La Jeune Née.* Paris: Union Générale d'Editions, 1975.

Felman, Shoshana. "Women and Madness: The Critical Phallacy." *Diacritics* 5 (Winter 1975): 2–10.

———. "Rereading Femininity." *Yale French Studies,* no. 62 (1981), pp. 19–44.

Feminist Readings: French Texts, American Contexts. Special issue. *Yale French Studies,* no. 62 (1981).

Les Femmes s'entêtent. Special issue. *Les Temps modernes* 29 (April–May 1974).

Féral, Josette. "China, Women, and the Symbolic: Interview with Julia Kristeva." Trans. Penny Kritzman. *Sub-stance,* no. 13 (1976), pp. 9–18.

Forrester, Viviane. "Féminin pluriel." *Tel Quel,* no. 74 (1977), pp. 68–77.

French Feminist Theory. Special issue. *Signs* 7 (Fall 1981). Includes essays by Kristeva, Cixous, Irigaray, Faure.

Furman, Nelly. "Textual Feminism." In *Women and Language in Literature and Society,* ed. Sally McConnell-Ginet, Ruth Borker, and Nelly Furman, pp. 45–54. New York: Praeger, 1980.

Houdebine, Anne-Marie. "Les Femmes et la langue." *Tel Quel,* no. 74 (1977), pp. 84–95.

Irigaray, Luce. *Speculum de l'autre femme.* Paris: Editions de Minuit, 1974.

———. *Ce Sexe qui n'en est pas un.* Paris: Editions de Minuit, 1977.

———. "And the One Doesn't Stir Without the Other." *Signs* 7 (Fall 1981): 60–67. See also Introduction by Hélène Wenzel, pp. 56–59.

Jardine, Alice. "Theories of the Feminine: Kristeva." *enclitic* 4 (1980): 5–16.

———. "Gynesis." *Diacritics* 12 (Spring 1982): 54–65.

Kristeva, Julia. "La Femme, ce n'est jamais ça." *Tel Quel,* no. 57–58 (1974), pp. 19–25.

———. *About Chinese Women.* Trans. Anita Barrows. New York: Urizen Books, 1977.

———. "Féminité et écriture: en réponse à deux questions sur *Polylogue.*" *Revue des sciences humaines* 168 (December 1977): 495–501.

———. "Women's Time." *Signs* 7 (Fall 1981): 13–35. See also Introduction by Alice Jardine, pp. 5–12.

———. *Desire in Language: A Semiotic Approach to Literature and Art.* Trans. Léon S. Roudiez, Alice Jardine, and Thomas Gora. New York: Columbia University Press, 1982.

———. *Powers of Horror: An Essay on Abjection.* Trans. Léon S. Roudiez. New York: Columbia University Press, 1982.

Makward, Christiane. "La Critique féministe: éléments d'une problématique." *Revue des sciences humaines* 168 (December 1977): 619–24.

———. "To Be or Not to Be . . . A Feminist Speaker." In *The Future of Difference: The Scholar and the Feminist,* ed. Hester Eisenstein and Alice Jardine, pp. 95–105. Boston: G. K. Hall, 1980.

Marks, Elaine. "Women and Literature in France." Review Essay. *Signs* 3 (Summer 1978): 832–42.

Marks, Elaine, and Isabelle de Courtivron, eds. *New French Feminisms: An Anthology.* Amherst: University of Massachusetts Press, 1980.

Miller, Nancy K. "D'une solitude à l'autre: vers un intertexte féminin." *French Review* 54 (May 1981): 797–803.

Mythes et représentations de la femme. Special issue. *Romantisme* 13–14 (1976).

Recherches féminines. Special issue. *Tel Quel,* no. 74 (Winter 1977).

Richman, Michèle. "Sex and Signs: The Language of French Feminist Criticism." *Language and Style* 13 (Fall 1980): 62–80.

Spivak, Gayatri Chakravorty. "French Feminism in an International Frame." *Yale French Studies,* no. 62 (1981), pp. 154–84.

Textual Politics. Special issue. *Diacritics* 5 (Winter 1975).

VIII. French Women Writers and *l'Écriture féminine*

Andermatt, Verena. "Writing the Letter: The Lower-case of hélène cixous." *Visible Language* 12 (1978): 305–18.

———. "Hélène Cixous and the Uncovery of a Feminine Language." *Women and Literature* 7 (Winter 1979): 38–48.

Brée, Germaine. *Women Writers in France: Variations on a Theme.* New Brunswick, N.J.: Rutgers University Press, 1973.

———. "French Women Writers: A Problematic Perspective." In *Beyond Intellectual Sexism: A New Woman, a New Reality,* ed. Joan I. Roberts, pp. 196–209. New York: David McKay, 1976.

Burke, Carolyn G. "Report from Paris: Women's Writing and the Women's Movement." *Signs* 3 (Summer 1978): 843–55.

Collins, Marie, and Sylvie Weil-Sayre, eds. *Les Femmes en France.* New York: Charles Scribner's Sons, 1974.

Contemporary Women Writers in France. Special issue. *L'Esprit Créateur* 19 (Summer 1979).

Crowder, Diane Griffin. "Amazons and Mothers? Monique Wittig, Hélène Cixous, and Theories of Women's Writing." *Contemporary Literature* 24 (Summer 1983): 117–44.

Didier, Béatrice. "Femme/identité/écriture: à propos de *L'Histoire de ma vie* de George Sand." *Revue des sciences humaines* 168 (1977): 561–76.

———. *L'écriture-femme.* Paris: Presses Universitaires de France, 1981.

Duras, Marguerite, and Xavière Gauthier. *Les Parleuses.* Paris: Editions de Minuit, 1974.

Ecriture, féminité, féminisme. Special issue. *Revue des sciences humaines* 168 (December 1977).

L'Ecriture féminine. Special issue. *Contemporary Literature* 24 (Summer 1983).

Eisenger, Erica M., and Mari McCarty, eds. *Colette: The Woman, the Writer.* University Park: Pennsylvania State University Press, 1981.

Fauchery, Pierre. *La Destinée féminine dans le roman européen du dix-huitième siècle, 1713–1807: Essai de gynécomythie romanesque.* Paris: Armand Colin, 1972.

Gauthier, Xavière. *Surréalisme et sexualité.* Paris: Nouvelle Revue Française, 1971.

Gelfand, Elissa D., and Virginia Thorndike Hules. *French Feminist Criticism: Women, Language, and Literature.* New York: Garland, 1984.

Groult, Benoîte. *Le Féminisme au masculin.* Paris: Denoël/Gonthier, 1977.

Gutwirth, Madelyn. *Madame de Staël, Novelist: The Emergence of the Artist As Woman.* Urbana: University of Illinois Press, 1978.

Herrmann, Claudine. *Les Voleuses de langue.* Paris: Des Femmes, 1976.

Kamuf, Peggy. "Writing Like a Woman." In *Women and Language in Literature and Society,* ed. Sally McConnell-Ginet, Ruth Borker, and Nelly Furman, pp. 284–99. New York: Praeger, 1980.

Larnac, Jean. *Histoire de la littérature féminine en France.* Paris: Editions Kra, 1929.

Mercier, Michel. *Le Roman féminin.* Paris: Presses Universitaires de France, 1976.

Miller, Nancy K. "Women's Autobiography in France: For a Dialectics of Identification." In McConnell-Ginet, Borker, and Furman, *Women and Language in Literature and Society,* pp. 258–73.

Rabine, Leslie. "George Sand and the Myth of Femininity." *Women and Literature* 4 (Fall 1976): 2–17.

———. "Feminist Writers in French Romanticism." *Studies in Romanticism* 16 (Fall 1977): 491–507.

Resch, Yannick. *Corps féminin, corps textuel: essai sur le personnage féminin dans l'oeuvre de Colette.* Paris: Klincksieck, 1973.

Wenzel, Hélène V. "The Text as Body/Politics: An Appreciation of Monique Wittig's Writings in Context." *Feminist Studies* 7 (Summer 1981): 264–87.

IX. Psychoanalysis and Feminist Theory

Bernheimer, Charles, and Claire Kahane, eds. *In Dora's Case: Freud—Hysteria—Feminism*. New York: Columbia University Press, 1985.

Clément, Catherine, and Luce Irigaray. "La Femme, son sexe, et le langage." *Nouvelle Critique* 82 (March 1975): 36–39.

Felman, Shoshana. "Women and Madness: The Critical Phallacy." *Diacritics* 5 (Winter 1975): 2–10.

———. "Rereading Femininity." *Yale French Studies,* no. 62 (1981), pp. 19–44.

Gallop, Jane. "The Ghost of Lacan, the Trace of Language." *Diacritics* 5 (Winter 1975): 18–24.

———. "The Seduction of an Analogy." *Diacritics* 9 (Spring 1979): 46–51.

———. "Psychoanalysis in France." In *The Future of Difference: The Scholar and the Feminist,* ed. Hester Eisenstein and Alice Jardine, pp. 114–22. Boston: G. K. Hall, 1980.

———. "Sade, Mothers, and Other Women." *enclitic* 4 (1980): 60–69.

———. "Snatches of Conversation." In *Women and Language in Literature and Society,* ed. Sally McConnell-Ginet, Ruth Borker, and Nelly Furman, pp. 274–83. New York: Praeger, 1980.

———. *The Daughter's Seduction: Feminism and Psychoanalysis.* Ithaca, N.Y.: Cornell University Press, 1982.

Gardiner, Judith Kegan. "Psychoanalytic Criticism and the Female Reader." *Literature and Psychology* 26, no. 3 (1976): 100–107.

Gearhart, Suzanne. "The Scene of Psychoanalysis: The Unanswered Questions of *Dora.*" *Diacritics* 9 (Spring 1979): 114–26.

Gilligan, Carol. *In a Different Voice: Psychological Theory and Women's Development.* Cambridge, Mass.: Harvard University Press, 1982.

Griffin, Susan. *Woman and Nature: The Roaring Inside Her.* New York: Harper & Row, 1978.

Heilbrun, Carolyn G. "Androgyny and the Psychology of Sex Differences." In Eisenstein and Jardine, *The Future of Difference,* pp. 258–66.

Kofman, Sarah. "Ex: The Woman's Enigma." *enclitic* 4 (1980): 17–28.

———. "The Narcissistic Woman: Freud and Girard." *Diacritics* 10 (Fall 1980): 36–45.

Lacan, Jacques. *Le Séminaire XX: Encore.* Paris: Editions du Seuil, 1975.

Miller, Jean Baker. *Toward a New Psychology of Women.* Boston: Beacon Press, 1976.

———, ed. *Psychoanalysis and Women.* Baltimore: Penguin Books, 1973.

Mitchell, Juliet. *Psychoanalysis and Feminism: Freud, Reich, Laing, and Women.* New York: Pantheon Books, 1974. Reprint. New York: Vintage Books, 1975.

Mitchell, Juliet, and Jacqueline Rose, eds. *Feminine Sexuality: Jacques Lacan and the École Freudienne.* New York: W. W. Norton, 1982.

Moi, Toril. "Representations of Patriarchy: Sexuality and Epistemology in Freud's Dora." *Feminist Review* 9 (October 1981): 60–74.

Ramas, Maria. "Freud's Dora, Dora's Hysteria: The Negation of a Woman's Rebellion." *Feminist Studies* 6 (Fall 1980): 472–510.

Schor, Naomi. "Female Paranoia: The Case for Psychoanalytic Feminist Criticism." *Yale French Studies,* no. 62 (1981), pp. 204–19.

Strouse, Jean, ed. *Women and Analysis: Dialogues on Psychoanalytic Views of Femininity.* New York: Grossman, 1974.

X. Maternity as Metaphor and Experience

Auerbach, Nina. "Artists and Mothers: A False Alliance." *Women and Literature* 9 (Spring 1978): 3–5.

Burke, Carolyn G. "Rethinking the Maternal." In *The Future of Difference: The Woman and the Scholar,* ed. Hester Eisenstein and Alice Jardine, pp. 107–13. Boston: G. K. Hall, 1980.

Castle, Terry. "ab'ring Bards: Birth *Topoi* and English Poetics 1660–1820." *Journal of English and Germanic Philology* 78 (April 1979): 193–208.

Chodorow, Nancy. *The Reproduction of Mothering: Psychoanalysis and the Sociology of Gender.* Berkeley: University of California Press, 1978.

———. "Gender, Relation, and Difference in Psychoanalytic Perspective." In Eisenstein and Jardine, *The Future of Difference,* pp. 3–19.

Chodorow, Nancy, et al. "On *The Reproduction of Mothering:* A Methodological Debate." *Signs* 6 (Spring 1981): 482–514.

Dash, Irene. "The Literature of Birth and Abortion." *Regionalism and the Female Imagination* 3 (Spring 1977): 8–13.

DuPlessis, Rachel Blau. "Washing Blood." *Feminist Studies* 4 (June 1978): 1–12.

Flax, Jane. "The Conflict Between Nurturance and Autonomy in Mother-Daughter Relationships and Within Feminism." *Feminist Studies* 4 (June 1978): 171–91.

———. "Mother-Daughter Relationships: Psychodynamics, Politics, and Philosophy." In Eisenstein and Jardine, *The Future of Difference,* pp. 20–40.

Friday, Nancy. *My Mother, Myself: The Daughter's Search for Identity.* New York: Delacorte Press, 1977.

Gardiner, Judith Kegan. "A Wake for Mother: The Maternal Deathbed in Women's Fiction." *Feminist Studies* 4 (June 1978): 146–65.

Gubar, Susan. "The Birth of the Artist as Heroine." In *The Representation of Women in Fiction,* ed. Carolyn G. Heilbrun and Margaret Hignonnet, pp. 19–59. Baltimore: Johns Hopkins University Press, 1982.

Jong, Erica. "Creativity vs. Generativity: The Unexamined Lie." *New Republic* January 13, 1979, pp. 27–30.

MacPike, Loralee. "The Social Values of Childbirth in the Nineteenth-Century Novel." *International Journal of Women's Studies* 3 (1980): 117–30.

Perry, Ruth, and Martine Watson Brownley, eds. *Mothering the Mind: Twelve Studies of Writers and Their Silent Partners.* London and New York: Holmes & Meier, 1983.

Poston, Carol H. "Childbirth in Literature." *Feminist Studies* 4 (June 1978): 18–31.

Rich, Adrienne. *Of Woman Born: Motherhood as Experience and Institution.* New York: W. W. Norton, 1976.

Walker, Alice. *In Search of Our Mother's Gardens: Womanist Prose.* New York: Harcourt Brace Jovanovich, 1983.

XI. Women and Language

Berryman, Cynthia L., and Virginia A. Eman. *Communication, Language, and Sex.* Rowley, Mass.: Newbury House, 1980.

Butturff, Douglass, and Edmund Epstein, eds. *Women's Language and Style.* Studies in Contemporary Language, vol. 1. Published with the assistance of the English Department, University of Akron. Akron, Ohio, 1978.

Furman, Nelly. "The Study of Women and Language: Comment on Vol. 3, No. 3." *Signs* 4 (Fall 1978): 182–85.

Lakoff, Robin. *Language and Woman's Place.* New York: Harper & Row, 1975.

McConnell-Ginet, Sally. "Our Father Tongue: Essays in Linguistic Politics." *Diacritics* 5 (Winter 1975): 44–50.

———. "Intonation in a Man's World." *Signs* 3 (Spring 1978): 541–59.

———. "Difference and Language: A Linguist's Perspective." In *The Future of Difference: The Woman and the Scholar,* ed. Hester Eisenstein and Alice Jardine, pp. 157–66. Boston: G. K. Hall, 1980.

———. "Linguistics and the Feminist Challenge." In *Women and Language in Literature and Society,* ed. Sally McConnell-Ginet, Ruth Borker, and Nelly Furman, pp. 3–25. New York: Praeger, 1980.

Michaels, Leonard, and Christopher Ricks, eds. *The State of the Language.* Berkeley: University of California Press, 1980.

Orasanu, Judith, Leonore Adler, and Mariam K. Slater, eds. *Language, Sex, and Gender.* New York: New York Academy of Sciences, 1979.

Thorne, Barrie, and Nancy Henley. *Language and Sex: Difference and Dominance.* Rowley, Mass.: Newbury House, 1975.

Thorne, Barrie, Cheris Kramer, and Nancy Henley, eds. *Language, Gender, and Society.* Rowley, Mass.: Newbury House, 1983.

XII. Marxist-Feminist Theory and Marxist Aesthetics

Barrett, Michèle. *Women's Oppression Today: Problems in Marxist Feminist Analysis.* New York: Schocken Books, 1981.

Berger, John. *Ways of Seeing.* New York: Viking Press, 1972.

Brunt, Rosalind, and Caroline Rowan. *Feminism, Culture and Politics.* London: Lawrence & Wishart, 1982.

Delphy, Christine, and Danièle Léger. "Debate on Capitalism, Patriarchy, and the Women's Struggle." *Feminist Issues* 1 (1980): 41–50.

Eagleton, Terry. *Criticism and Ideology: A Study in Marxist Literary Theory.* New York: Schocken Books, 1978.

———. *The Rape of Clarissa: Writing, Sexuality, and Class Struggle in Richardson.* Minneapolis: University of Minnesota Press, 1982.

Eisenstein, Zillah R., ed. *Capitalist Patriarchy and the Case for Socialist Feminism.* New York: Monthly Review Press, 1979.

Kuhn, Annette, and Annmarie Wolpe, eds. *Feminism and Materialism: Women and Modes of Production.* Boston and London: Routledge & Kegan Paul, 1978.

MacKinnon, Catharine A. "Feminism, Marxism, Method, and the State." *Signs* 7 (Spring 1982): 515–44.

Marxist-Feminist Literature Collective. "Women's Writing." *Ideology and Consciousness* 3 (Spring 1978): 27–48.

Mitchell, Juliet. *Woman's Estate.* New York: Pantheon Books, 1971.

———. *Women : The Longest Revolution.* New York: Pantheon Books, 1984.

O'Brien, Mary. "Feminist Theory and Dialectical Logic." *Signs 7* (Fall 1981): 144–57.

Robinson, Lillain S. *Sex, Class, and Culture.* Bloomingotn: Indidana University Press, 1978.

Robinson, Lillian S., and Lise Vogel. "Modernism and History." In *Images of Women in Fiction,* ed. Susan Koppelman Cornillion, pp. 278–307. Bowling Green, Ohio: Bowling Green University Popular Press, 1972.

Vogel, Lise. *Marxism and the Oppression of Women: Toward a Unitary Theory.* New Brunswick, N.J.: Rutgers University Press, 1984.

XIII. Teaching, Curriculum, and Research

Greer, Germaine. "The Tulsa Center for the Study of Women's Literature: What We Are Doing and Why We Are Doing It." *Tulsa Studies in Women's Literature* 1 (Spring 1982): 5–26.

Hoffmann, Leonore, and Deborah Rosenfelt, eds. *Teaching Women's Literature from a Regional Perspective.* New York: Modern Language Association, 1982.

Howe, Florence. "Those We Still Don't Read." *College English* 43 (January 1981): 11–16.

Messer-Davidow, Ellen, and Joan E. Hartman, eds. *Women in Print I: Opportunities for Women's Studies Research in Language and Literature.* New York: Modern Language Association, 1982.

———. *Women in Print II: Opportunities for Women's Studies Publication in Language and Literature.* New York: Modern Language Association, 1982.

XIV. Bibliographies of Feminist Criticism

Backscheider, Paula, and Felicity A. Nussbaum. *An Annotated Bibliography of Twentieth-Century Critical Studies of Women and Literature, 1660–1800.* New York: Garland, 1977.

Batchelder, Eleanor. *Plays by Women: A Bibliography.* New York: Womanbooks, 1977.

Bibliography of Literature in English by and about Women. Annual supplement to Women and Literature Collective, *Women and Literature: An Annotated Bibliography.* 1975–.

Daims, Diva, and Janet Grimes. *Towards a Feminist Tradition: An Annotated Bibliography of Novels in English by Women, 1891–1920.* New York: Garland, 1982.

Damon, Gene, Jan Watson, and Robin Jordan. *The Lesbian in Literature: A Bibliography.* 2nd ed. Reno, Nev.: Naiad Press, 1975.

Fairbanks, Carol. *More Women in Literature: Criticism of the Seventies.* Metuchen, N.J.: Scarecrow Press, 1979.

Fries, Maureen, and Anne M. Daunis. *A Bibliography of Writings by and about Women Authors, British and American, 1957–1969.* Charleston: Women's Caucus for the Modern Languages, 1971.

Hageman, Elizabeth H. "Images of Women in Renaissance Literature: A Selected Bibliography of Scholarship." *Women's Studies Newsletter* 5 (Spring 1977): 15–17.

Lewis, Linda K. "Women in Literature: A Selected Bibliography." *Bulletin of Bibliography* 35 (July–September 1978): 116–22, 131.

Myers, Carol Fairbanks. *Women in Literature: Criticism of the Seventies.* Metuchen, N.J.: Scarecrow Press, 1976.

Pomeroy, Sarah B. "Selected Bibliography on Women in Antiquity." *Arethusa* 6 (Spring 1973): 125–57.

Register, Cheri. "American Feminist Literary Criticism: A Bibliographical Introduction." In *Feminist Literary Criticism: Explorations in Theory,* ed. Josephine Donovan, pp. 1–27. Lexington: University Press of Kentucky, 1975.

Rossum-Guyon, Françoise van. "Sélection bibliographique." *Revue des sciences humaines* 168 (December 1977): 625–32.

Schibanoff, Susan. "Images of Women in Medieval Literature: A Selected Bibliography." *Women's Studies Newsletter* 4 (Fall 1976): 10–11.

Schwartz, Narda Lacey. *Articles on Women Writers, 1960–1975: A Bibliography.* Santa Barbara, Calif.: ABC-Clio Press, 1977.

White, Barbara Anne. *American Women Writers: An Annotated Bibliography of Criticism.* New York: Garland, 1977.

Women and Literature Collective. *Women and Literature: An Annotated Bibliography of Women Writers.* 3rd rev. ed. Cambridge, Mass.: Women and Literature Collective, 1976.

XV. Current Journals Publishing Feminist Criticism

camera obscura: A Journal of Feminism and Film Theory
P.O. Box 25899
Los Angeles, Calif. 90025

Conditions
P.O. Box 56
Van Brent Station
Brooklyn, N.Y. 11215

Connexions: A Women's Quarterly of News, Analysis, and Interviews Translated from the International Feminist Press
4228 Telegraph Avenue
Oakland, Calif. 94609

Critical Inquiry
Wieboldt Hall 202
University of Chicago
1050 E. 59th Street
Chicago, Ill. 60637

Diacritics
278 Goldwin Smith
Cornell University
Ithaca, N.Y. 14853

enclitic
200 Folwell Hall
9 Pleasant Street East
University of Minnesota
Minneapolis, Minn. 55455

Feminist Issues
A Publication of the Feminist Forum, Berkeley, Calif.
Subscriptions: Transaction, Inc., Department 8200
Rutgers, the State University
New Brunswick, N.J. 08903

Feminist Review
11 Carleton Gardens
Brecknock Road
London N19 5AQ

Feminist Studies
c/o Women's Studies Program
University of Maryland
College Park, Md. 20742

Frontiers: A Journal of Women's Studies
c/o Women's Studies
University of Colorado
Boulder, Colo. 80309

Hecate
P.O. Box 99
St. Lucia
Queensland 4067
Australia

Helicon Nine: The Journal of Women's Arts and Letters
P.O. Box 22412
Kansas City, Mo. 64113

Heresies: A Feminist Publication on Art and Politics
P.O. Box 766
Canal Street Station
New York, N.Y. 10013

International Journal of Women's Studies
4626 Saint Catherine Street West
Montreal, Quebec
Canada H3Z 1S3

Journal of Women's Studies in Literature
245 Victoria Avenue
Suite 12
Montreal, Quebec
Canada H3Z 2M6

Legacy
Department of English
Bartlett Hall
University of Massachusetts
Amherst, Mass. 01003

m/f: A Feminist Journal
22 Chepstow Crescent
London W11
England

Massachusetts Review
Memorial Hall
University of Massachusetts
Amherst, Mass. 01003

Nouvelles Questions féministes
34, passage du Ponceau
75002 Paris
France

Quest
Human Kinetics Pub. Inc.
P.O. Box 5076
Champaign, Ill. 61820

Questions féministes
Editions tierce
1, rue des Fossés-St.-Jacques
75005 Paris
France

RFR/DRF: A Canadian Journal for Feminist Scholarship
(Resources for Feminist Research-/Documentation sur la recherche féministe)
Ontario Institute for Studies in Education
252 Bloor Street West
Toronto
Canada M5S 1V6

Sage: A Scholarly Journal on Black Women
P.O. Box 42741
Atlanta, Ga. 30311-0741

Signs: Journal of Women in Culture and Society
Serra House, Stanford University,
Stanford, Calif. 94305.
(University of Chicago Press,
5801 Ellis Avenue
Chicago, Ill. 60637)

Sinister Wisdom: A Journal of Lesbian/Feminist Experience
P.O. Box 1023
Rockland, Maine 04841

Sojourner: The New England Women's Journal of News, Opinions, and the Arts
143 Albany Street
Cambridge, Mass. 02139

Trouble and Strife
30 Brudenell Avenue
Leeds 6
England

Tulsa Studies in Women's Literature
600 South College
Tulsa, Okla. 74104

Turn of the Century Women
Department of English
Wilson Hall
University of Virginia
Charlottesville, Va. 22903

Woman's Art Journal
7008 Sherwood Drive
Knoxville, Tenn. 37919

Women's Diaries: A Quarterly Newsletter
P.O. Box 18
Pound Ridge, N.Y. 10576

Women's Review of Books
Wellesley College Center for Research on Women
Wellesley, Mass. 02181

Women's Studies International Forum
Pergamon Press, Inc.
Journals Division
Maxwell House,
Fairview Park
Elmsford, N.Y. 10523

Women's Studies
Department of English
Queens College
City University of New York
Flushing, N.Y. 11367

NOTE: There are dozens of other journals specializing in women or related subjects. Many are ephemeral, and the addresses change frequently. The following sources may be useful in identifying others or obtaining more current data:

Fulton, Len, and Ellen Ferber, eds. *The International Directory of Little Magazines and Small Presses.* Paradise, Calif.: Dustbooks, annual (19 vols. to 1983). Subject index.

Mackesy, Eileen, and Karen Mateyek, eds. *MLA Directory of Periodicals: A Guide to Journals and Series in Languages and Literatures.* New York: Modern Language Association, biannual. Subject index.

Ulrich's International Periodicals Directory. 22nd ed. New York and London: R. R. Bowker, 1983. Subject index.

Notes on the Contributors

Nina Baym is Professor of English and Director of the School of Humanities at the University of Illinois at Urbana-Champaign. She is the author of *The Shape of Hawthorne's Career* (1976); *Woman's Fiction: A Guide to Novels By and About Women in America, 1820–1870* (1979); and *Novels, Readers, and Reviewers: Response to Fiction in Antebellum America* (1984).

Rosalind Coward lectures in visual communications at Goldsmiths College, London. Her books include *Language and Materialism* (1977), with John Ellis; *Patriarchal Precedents* (1984); and *Female Desire* (1984).

Rachel Blau DuPlessis is Associate Professor of English at Temple University. She is the author of a book of poems, *Wells* (1980), and of *Writing Beyond the Ending: Narrative Strategies of Twentieth-Century Women Writers* (forthcoming 1985).

Sandra M. Gilbert will be Professor of English at Princeton University in fall 1985. With Susan Gubar, she has written *The Madwoman in the Attic* (1979), and edited *Shakespeare's Sisters: Feminist Essays on Women Poets* (1979) and *The Norton Anthology of Literature by Women: The Tradition in English* (1985). She is also a poet whose most recent book is *Emily's Bread* (1984).

Susan Gubar is Professor of English at Indiana University. With Sandra Gilbert, she has written *The Madwoman in the Attic* and edited *The Norton Anthology of Literature by Woman* and *Shakespeare's Sisters: Feminist Essays on Women's Poetry*. She is also the author of numerous essays on eighteenth-century literature, science fiction, and contemporary women's writing.

Ann Rosalind Jones is Assistant Professor of Comparative Literature at Smith College. She has published articles on theories of the novel and French feminist criticism. She is currently working on a book on Renaissance women poets.

Annette Kolodny is Professor of Literature at Renssalaer Polytechnic Institute. Her books include *The Lay of the Land: Metaphor as Experience and History in American Life and Letters* (1975), and *The Land Before Her: Fantasy and Experience of the American Frontiers, 1630–1860* (1984). She is the author of many articles on feminist criticism and American literature.

Deborah E. McDowell is Assistant Professor of English at Colby College, Waterville, Maine, where she teaches American, Afro-American, and women's literature. She is currently at work on a booklength study of black women novelists.

Nancy K. Miller is Associate Professor of Women's Studies and Director of the Women's Studies Program at Barnard College. She is the author of *The Heroine's Text: Readings in the French and English Novel 1722–1782* (1980) and numerous essays on feminist criticism. She is currently working on a book on female authorship in France.

Alicia Ostriker, a poet and critic, is Professor of English at Rutgers University. She is the author of five books of poetry, most recently *A Woman Under the Surface* (1982); and a book of essays, *Writing Like a Woman* (1983). She is currently working on a study of the American women's poetry movement since 1960.

Lillian S. Robinson is NEH Visiting Professor at Albright College, and is an affiliated scholar at the Stanford University Center for Research on Women. She is the author of *Sex, Class, and Culture* (1978), and of two forthcoming books, *Monstrous Regiment: The Lady Knight in Sixteenth Century Epic* (Garland) and *Feminst Scholarship: Kindling in the Groves of Academe* (Illinois; co-authored with Ellen DuBois, Gail Kelly, Elizabeth Kennedy, and Carolyn Korsmeyer.

Elaine Showalter is Professor of English at Princeton University. She is the author of *A Literature of Their Own: Women Writers from Brontë to Lessing* (1977) and *The Female Malady: Women, Madness, and Culture,* forthcoming from Pantheon in 1985. She has edited *Women's Liberation and Literature* (1971) and *These Modern Women: Autobiographies of American Women in the 1920s* (1979). She is currently working on a literary history of American women writers.

Barbara Smith is a writer and activist who has been involved in black feminist organizing since 1973. She was a founding member of the Combahee River

Collective, a black feminist organization in Boston (1974–80), and cofounder of Kitchen Table: Women of Color Press. She has coedited *Conditions Five: The Black Women's Issue* (1979) and *All the Women Are White, All the Blacks Are Men, But Some of Us Are Brave: Black Women's Studies* (1982), and edited *Home Girls: A Black Feminist Anthology* (1983). She is currently working on a book of her own short fiction.

Jane P. Tompkins is Visiting Professor of English at the Graduate Center of the City University of New York. Her forthcoming book, *Sensational Designs: The Cultural Work of American Fiction*, deals with the politics of literary reputations, canon-formation, and the relationship of popular texts to their literary milieu.

Bonnie Zimmerman is Associate Professor of Women's Studies at San Diego State University. She has published essays on George Eliot and on lesbian literature, critical theory, and pedagogy.